Clancy Hayes - The Swinging Minstrel

Clancy in action with Bob Scobey's band, mid 1950s
(Courtesy of Stanford University Libraries Archive / SFTJF)

Clancy Hayes - The Swinging Minstrel
(a Biography and Discography)

Chris Reid
with Hal Smith

and contributions from Thomas 'Spats' Langham,
Melissa Phillippe, Frank Selman, and others

Hardinge Simpole

Hardinge Simpole
An imprint of Zeticula Ltd
Unit 13,
44-46 Morningside Road,
Edinburgh, EH10 4BF
Scotland

http://www.hardingesimpole.co.uk

First published in 2025

Text © Chris Reid 2025
Cover photograph © Julia Carroll 2025

ISBN 978-1-84382-236-3 hardback
ISBN 978-1-84382-237-0 paperback

All rights reserved. No reproduction, copy or transmission of this publication may be made without prior written permission.

Dedication

This book is dedicated to all jazz musicians who have given their audiences the gift of the joy that only music can bring.

I also dedicate the book to Robert and Katherine Reid who have given me the gift of William, Emily, Joseph and Matilda and the joy that only grandchildren can bring. More than that.

Contents

Dedication — v
Illustrations — ix
Contributors — xvii
Acknowledgements — xix
Introduction — xxvii

1	Arrival Of The Seventh Son	1
	Family Photos	17
2	The Radio Years Part One 1928-1938	23
3	The Radio Years Part Two 1939 -1950	52
	Photographs	64
4	The Call Of Jazz	68
5	The Scobey Years Part One 1950-1952	98
6	The Scobey Years Part Two: San Francisco and Chicago 1953-1959	118
7	The Scobey Split: He's A Good Man (But 1,850 Miles From Home) 1960-1961	141
8	(Back Home Again In) San Francisco 1961-1962	152
9	Golden Years 1963-1969	167
10	Melancholy (Clancy's Illness 1969-1972)	197
11	Clancy's Legacy	225
12	An Appreciation of Clancy Hayes' Singing *By Hal Smith*	243
13	Clancy Hayes in the Rhythm Section *By Hal Smith*	247
14	Clancy's Banjos	251
15	The Songs Of Clancy Hayes: Winners and Compositions.	258
16	The Scobey and Clancy Recordings — An Overview	283
17	Clancy's Albums (And Four Rare Songs From The Satchel)	288

18	A Jazz Journey: Encountering Clancy Hayes	297
	By Frank Selman	
19	My Uncle Clancy	299
	By Melissa Phillippe	
Afterword		301

Transcriptions   *304*
Notes   *344*
Reference Sources   *351*

Gallery   353

Discography   367
    Clancy Hayes: Commercially Issued Vocal Recordings   372
    Clancy Hayes: The Private Vocal Recordings   394
    Song Title Index   418

Index   424

Illustrations

Clancy in action with Bob Scobey's band, mid 1950s	ii
Hal Smith	ix
Clancy the radio star, late 1930s	xxvi
Sam Linschooten finds treasure	xxix
Master Clarence Hayes	4
Young Clancy	6
Elks' Charity Carnival, advertisement 1924	10
Boy 16 on Check Charge, newspaper article	11
Ann and Clancy	13
Marriage Licence	14
Ann and Clancy	15
Clancy, Ann and Bill circa 1933	16
Clancy's parents: William Kelly Hayes and Clara May Hayes	17
Della, Clancy, Ashton, Wallace and Mrs Clara May Hayes	18
The youngest musical Hayes brothers	19
Proud fathers, Clancy and Ashton	20
Ann and Clancy	21
Ann and Clancy	22
Clancy and Charlie Marshall	25
Clancy Hayes' NBC Schedule 1930	26
Script page 1: Aunt Jemima radio show	27
Script page 3: Aunt Jemima radio show	28
Fan mail from 'A Devoted Blonde'	29
The Boswell Sisters ... and their review	30
Los Angeles Ostrich Farm, July 1930	31
Mahlon Merrick Orchestra, Palace Hotel, San Francisco, November 1931, poster	32
Letter from Albers Bros. Milling Company	33
Dance at Del Rio Woods, June 1932, advertisement	34
Clancy on the radio	35
Fan mail from 'Three Girls from Seattle', page 1	36

Fan mail from 'Three Girls from Seattle', page 2	37
Clancy Hayes behind the moustache, unknown location	38
Letter from Ambassador Hotel, Los Angeles	39
Cheque from bandleader Bob Beale, September 1934	40
Clancy and Marjorie Beattie	41
Clancy Hayes publicity photo circa 1930	43
Letter from Hank Mingie	44
Thank you letter from San Francisco Chronicle	45
Fan mail from Dorothy Wickman	46
Fan mail from Misses Lena and Louise Lerza	48
Clancy and John Wolfe	50
Clancy and John Wolfe	52
NBC Identification card, 1941	54
Armed Forces Volunteer Card	55
Sonia Shaw, Clancy, Archie Persby	56
Burt Bales at the piano	56
Clancy with unknown Hawaiian band	57
Mother's Cookies	58
Clancy with orchestra	58
Bill, Ann and Clancy c.1946	64
Bill Hayes	65
Ann and Clancy	66
Clancy, c. 1946	67
Big Bear session late 1930s	71
Jazz at the Dawn Club	74
Tickets for Ernie Lewis and Lu Watters at the Dawn Club 1941	74
Lu Watters' Yerba Buena Jazz Band, Dawn Club San Francisco c.1940	76
Bob Scobey, Lu Watters, Ellis Horne	76
Lu Watters' YBJB, Dawn Club: Bob Scobey, Lu Watters, Clancy Hayes, Turk Murphy, Ellis Horne, c.1942	77
Jazz Man 78: Maple Leaf Rag, label	78
Jazz Man 78: Black And White Rag, label	79
Jazz Man 78: Fidgety Feet, label	80
Lu Watters' YBJB Newspaper advertisement, 30 October 1942	81
Wartime Yerba Buena Jazz Band, 1942	82

Ellis Horne, Bunk Johnson	83
Hot Jazz Society Newsletter, 1942	85
Hambone Kelly's advertising poster	86
Vogue 78: My Little Bimbo, label	87
Down Home 78: Auntie Skinner's Chicken Dinners (sic), label	88
Mercury 78: Waiting For The Robert E. Lee, label	89
The Zanzibar advertisement for the Frisco Jazz Band	91
Pacific 78: A Huggin' And A Chalkin', label	92
Ace 78: She's A Good Girl, label	95
Melody Club advertisement	96
Victor's and Roxie's, advertisement	99
Possibly a version of the House Band at Club Hangover	100
Alexander's Jazz Band	101
Jazz Man 78: Some Of These Days, label	102
Jazz Man 78: St. Louis Blues, label	103
Bayside Jazz Society ticket, Sunday 5 November 1950	103
Victor's and Roxie's Advertisement	104
Alexander's Jazz Band at Victor's and Roxie's early 1950s:	104
Ragtime records 78: Beale Street Mama, label	105
Dixieland Jubilee 78: Coney Island Washboard, label	106
Alexander's Jazz Band 1951 at Alexander's	107
Clancy in reflection	108
Jenny Lind Hall, Telegraph Ave. Oakland, 2009	109
Jenny Lind Hall, Main Hall	109
Bob Scobey's Frisco Band 1951	110
Bob Scobey's Frisco Band 1951	111
Test pressing 45: Chicago, label	113
Bob Scobey, Wally Rose, Jack Buck	114
Bob Scobey's band at the Rancho Grande, Lafayette, 1953	119
Clancy Hayes at the Rancho Grande, advertisement	120
Down Beat's Award telegram	121
Bill Napier, Bob Scobey, Clancy Hayes	122
Letter from Mari Ladowski	124
The Frisco Jazz Band at the Tin Angel, poster	126
Bob Scobey's Frisco Band, advertisement, September 1955	130
Bob Scobey's Frisco Band, Las Vegas 1956	131

Letter from J Walter Thompson Co.	132
Clancy Hayes, Bob Scobey, Brian Shanley - Sinton Hotel, Cincinnati	135
Members of the Bob Scobey band at George Hulme's gig	136
Floyd Bean and Clancy Hayes	137
Lizzie Miles, Bob Scobey, Professor Hayakawa with fans	137
Bob Scobey's Band c. 1957	138
Bob Scobey at the Cafe Continental, advertisement	141
Clancy's Chicago home: 6200 North Kenmore (2023)	143
Clancy with his Vegaphone Deluxe six-string banjo, 1960	145
Nappy Trottier's Band with Clancy Hayes advertisement	148
Kenkel's Dixieland Band, Dayton OH advertisement	149
Clancy Hayes with his Dixiecrats 1960	151
Clancy Hayes at Earthquake McGoon's advertisement	153
Letter from Andy Bartha	154
Earthquake McGoon's: Clancy Hayes is Back, advertisement	156
Kenny Ball at Bourbon Street, Chicago IL advertisement	157
Ragtime 45 Midnight in Moscow, label	158
Letter from New Orleans Jazz Club, August 16, 1962	159
Letter from New Orleans Jazz Club, August 21, 1962	160
Letter from New Orleans Jazz Club, September 11, 1962	161
Letter to "my darlings"	165
Earthquake McGoon's, advertisements	166
Docs of Dixieland Concert, 20 April 1963, advertisement	169
The Dayton Scene, album cover	170
Oh By Jingo! Delmark album cover	172
Clancy at Earthquake McGoon's	173
Letter from Dick Gibson	175
The World's Greatest Jazz Band 1968	178
Clancy seems to be recalling sweeping up from his radio days	180
Clancy Hayes – the well dressed man	181
Happy Birthday!	183
Jazz in the Troc, album cover	184
Jack Wood's Oceania, Fort Lauderdale FL, advertisement	186
Blues Alley, Washington WA, advertisement	187
Tommy Gwaltney, Pee Wee Russell, Clancy	187

Dixieland Monterey, advertisement	189
Pops Foster, Clancy Hayes and two gas heaters!	190
Proceedings of the Blue Angel Jazz Club, album cover	193
Clancy at the Blue Angel Jazz Club, probably 1968	194
Letter from Jack Gurtler	199
Greetings telegram, May 31, 1970	202
Letter from George Zack, page 1	203
Letter from the Garlinghouses, 1970	204
Letter from Billie and Don Leach	205
Letter from Earl Watkins	206
Letter from Peanuts and Louise Hucko	207
Band photos - Clancy Hayes Day, 1971. Dick Oxtot, Ray Skjelbred, Bob Mielke, Bob Neighbor, Bob Helm	208
Clancy Hayes Day poster	209
Clancy, brother Ashton and Bill Hayes	210
Faces in the crowd: Phil Howe and Fred Higuera	210
Proclamation of 'Clancy Hayes Day', 1970	211
Clancy Hayes Day at Earthquake McGoon's, ticket	213
McGoon's Club Tent Card	213
Resolution from the California State Assembly	214
Letter on behalf of Ronald Reagan	215
Request to Ray Skjelbred	217
Letter from Ed Watson, page 1	218
Letter from Ed Watson, page 2	219
Clancy's tape log for Bill Bacin, page 1	220
Clancy's tape log for Bill Bacin, page 2	221
A tribute to Clancy Hayes, four LP gift set cover	224
Barrel House Nightingale, 3 April 1960, poster	226
Stereoscopic Society Annual Report	228
Notes on tape box recording at the Ethiopian Baptist Church	231
Letter of thanks to the Hayes Family	232
Letter from Lizzie Miles to Ann Hayes page 1	233
Letter from Lizzie Miles to Ann Hayes page 2	234
A Cadillac 60 Special	236
Clancy with Dick Lammi	245
Clancy in action, 1958.	246

Clancy drumming, a study in concentration	249
Clancy circa mid 1950s	250
Jamming at the Big Bear c. 1939	252
Yerba Buena Jazz Band at the Dawn Club, early 1940s.	253
The Bacon Peerless, from The Semantics of Popular Song	254
The Restored Instrument	255
Clancy with The Vegaphone Deluxe, 1960	256
The Weymann with resonator, Blues Alley, Steve Jordan, Clancy, Pee Wee Russell circa 1968	257
Jazz in the Troc, album cover	261
Ace In The Hole, label	263
Silver Dollar, label	264
Frisco Jazz Band advertisement	265
Sheet music for Huggin' And A Chalkin'	266
Clancy with camera and companion	268
Yerba Buena Jazz Band at the Dawn Club	269
78 George Washington label	272
Ten To One It's Tennessee. UK 78 rpm release	273
Otto's New Auto, handwritten lyrics	275
Weddin' Day, sheet music	276
Bob Scobey's Frisco Band 1955	281
Bob Scobey, August 1953	284
Scobey and Clancy, mid 1950s, location unknown	285
Clancy Hayes and His Washboard Five, album cover	289
Clancy Hayes and His Washboard Five, record label	290
Mr Hayes Goes to Washington, album cover	294
Three unknown lads but possibly Wallace, Clancy and Ashton?	353
Clancy and John Wolfe c.1930	354
Clancy and a young admirer	354
The great Bob Scobey	355
Clancy waiting for a haircut?	356
Tex Hayes	357
Another cowboy outfit	358
Wally Rose, for once not obscured by a piano	359
Jack Buck, a wonderful musician	360
The final chorus	360

A clear view of Dick Lammi, with Bob Helm on clarinet	361
Bob Scobey's Frisco Band c.1958	361
Rehearsal Time; Bob Scobey's Frisco Band, late 1957	362
Clancy, Ann and Wallace Hayes	362
On the bandstand	363
Clancy and Ann at home - 702 46th Street, San Francisco	364
American Federation of Radio Artists Hon. Withdrawal Card	365
American Federation of Musicians Life Member Card	365
New Orleans Jazz Club Honorary Life Membership Card	366
Coon-Sanders Original Nighthawks Club Hon. Member Card	366
Clint Baker receives the collection from Frank Selman	368

Hal Smith
(author's collection)

Contributors

Hal Smith is a drummer and bandleader based in Searcy, Arkansas. He became a fan of traditional jazz after hearing the Firehouse Five Plus Two at Disneyland in 1962. He met and heard almost all of the San Francisco Jazz pioneers — including Clancy Hayes — and has played with many of them over the years.

Currently he leads the El Dorado Jazz Band, Mortonia Seven and the San Francisco Jazz all stars. He is on the faculty of the New Orleans Trad Jazz Camp and is the Band Advisor for the Bix Beiderbecke Jazz Festival.

Hal was one of the editors of the 'lost' Danny Alguire biography 'Dust Bowl To Dixieland' and is a contributing writer for The Syncopated Times.

Spats Langham was born in 1971 and grew up in Buxton, Derbyshire, England. In a career spanning nearly forty years he has earned the status of elder statesman for traditional jazz, playing with Acker Bilk, The Temperance Seven, Pasadena Roof Orchestra, Marty Grosz, Jeff Barnhart, Sammy Rimington and a host of others, as well as leading his own bands for two decades.

Spats' much-loved blend of music and entertainment is constantly in demand for appearances in jazz clubs, festivals and recording sessions across Britain, Europe and the USA. Like Clancy he has a remarkable knowledge of rare songs and is renowned for his exceptional performances on banjo, guitar and vocals.

Rev. Dr. Melissa Phillippe is the great-niece of Clancy Hayes. She is a singer-songwriter with eight albums of original inspirational music in release. In addition to her work in the music field, she is also a spiritual counsellor and teacher.

Together with her wife, Z Egloff, Melissa runs an on-line and traveling non-profit, OhMyGod Life! You can find their music, books, cartoons, and videos at www.OhMyGodLife.com

Frank Selman, another Dutch 'Frisco' fan and collector, born in 1943 in Amsterdam, currently living in France, came across the Frisco Jazz of Watters, Scobey and Clancy vocals in 1958 as the GTJ records became available in The Netherlands. A chance meeting with Hal Smith in New Orleans in 1991 resulted in some serious educational listening to our beloved Frisco music at his home, together with his advice to visit the Trad Festivals in California, resulting in a lifelong passion for Traditional Jazz and 30 visits to the San Diego Traditional Jazz Festival. Selman was an importer of Afghan handicrafts.

Acknowledgements

One of the joys of writing this book was my contact with so many informed, helpful and supportive people. I am grateful to all those who provided help, information, text, images, comments, ideas and more besides; thanks go to each and every one of you. The project also had a real bonus in bringing me into contact with Clancy's great-niece Melissa Phillippe and step granddaughter Julia Carroll. As you can imagine it was a real pleasure to connect with relatives.

I would not have completed the biography without the help and support of three people in particular; Hal Smith and Trevor and Anne Bannister. Hal looked at a very rough first draft and suggested significant edits and improvements to the layout and style. He also added a lot of valuable additional detailed information and text based on his thorough knowledge of the Great Jazz Revival; his musical knowledge of course goes far wider.

As a lifelong musician who had met Clancy and played with many of the musicians who knew and recorded with him (including Bob Helm, George Probert, Wally Rose, Bob Mielke, Art Hodes and many more) Hal's input was invaluable. His two chapters and recollections of attending the second Clancy Hayes Day event add an additional dimension to Clancy's story.

As you may know Hal Smith trained as a journalist and has written countless articles for jazz periodicals and magazines, currently he contributes regularly to the Syncopated Times — a truly superb monthly jazz magazine. Hal is of course still very active performing and recording.[1]

A heavily revised and tidied version was then passed to Anne and Trevor Bannister for proof reading. However, Trevor and Anne offered advice on further redrafting and re-wrote large sections of the text which transformed a rather mechanical prose into the readable version now in your hands. It is difficult to explain how invaluable their input into the process was; and how supportive they have been.

Trevor Bannister developed an 'ear' for all forms of jazz as a teenager in the 1960s. He also discovered a well-stocked selection of jazz literature in his local library, fuelling a lifelong quest to find out more about this wonderful music and the lives of the people who created it. Only slowly did the penny drop: that many of these larger-than-life characters with their links to the 'exotic' melting pots of New Orleans, Chicago, Kansas City and Harlem were not only still active, but playing as well as ever; an evident truth when he sat as an awe struck member of the audience for a performance by Duke Ellington and His Famous Orchestra at the Odeon, Hammersmith in 1964.

Trevor Bannister introduced jazz to the classroom in his career as a primary school teacher. This led, in 1984, to the Michael Garrick Travelling Jazz Faculty joining forces with a choir of two hundred children from five schools, to perform 'All God's Children', composed by Michael Garrick to depict the story of rhythm.

Trevor kept up his association with Garrick and they collaborated in the writing and publication of Garrick's autobiography, 'Dusk Fire: Jazz in English Hands' published in 2010. His wife Anne kept the project on track, fulfilling the multiple roles of proof-reader, copy editor and sales manager.

Following his retirement, Trevor became involved in promoting jazz concerts in his home town of Reading and in assisting discographer Derek Coller with the organisation of the International Association of Jazz Record Collectors' (IAJRC) annual 'Get Together', bringing together like-minded enthusiasts from all over the UK as well as from the USA, Ireland and Austria. He also published a second book; 'It Won't Sound the Same: Great Jazz Never Does', the autobiography of Scottish saxophonist Jim Philip.

When Trevor Bannister was once asked "What is jazz all about?" he answered, 'It's the joy spring of life and you meet some wonderful people in the wake of its flow.' How true.

The last line of defence on the editing front was none other than lifelong jazz fan, discographer and author Derek Coller. Derek discovered jazz in his early teens and edited his first jazz magazine whilst overseas with the Army in 1944. He published The Discophile, a bi-monthly discographical magazine, for ten years and has written biographies of Jess Stacy and Dick Cary. In 2023 he published the biography of Big Joe Turner. Derek's interest and activities include his generous sharing of an amazing knowledge of jazz and, as already mentioned, bringing jazz fans together through the IAJRC. In addition to helping with editing support, Derek provided information, suggestions and extracts from books and articles which added important points of detail. His excellent *The Second Line: Chicago Jazz*, written with his close friend Bert Whyatt was a valuable source of information. Thank you, Derek.

Dave Radlauer kindly proof-read Hal's chapters along with Chapter 11 to ensure this Anglo-American effort didn't contain any grammatical errors due to possible slight misalignment in the two languages! (There is further reference to Dave's involvement below.)

As to the research for the book there are three people to whom I owe very special thanks. A two-day trawl of the Clancy Hayes collection at Stanford University was carried out by my good friends Alexandra and Robert Hardy of Streatham, South London. It was my great fortune that they were due to visit a relative in Palo Alto in July 2022 and offered to 'look in' at Stanford University. (Both were familiar with Stanford, having previously visited to meet a relative who studied there.)

Originally scheduling a single afternoon visit, the two brimming boxes which they were handed and their diligent approach to the task necessitated a second visit. I am indebted to Alexandra and Robert for their assistance and their incredibly well-presented research (both have academic backgrounds which shone through).

To obtain print quality copies of certain documents and photos I had the help of Melissa Phillippe, granddaughter of Clancy's brother Ashton. I'd first contacted Melissa in 2009 when she helped me to locate Clancy's resting place in Santa Rosa which enabled me to pay my respects during a visit to California. I contacted Melissa again in 2022 to seek help in better understanding the Hayes' family history. The friendship we developed led to her kind offer to visit Stanford and retrieve documents and photos I needed (based on the information and images Alexandra and Robert had provided) for print quality copying.

During her visit Melissa found other photos including the delightful one of Clancy aged 8. One of the busiest and most energetic people I have ever known, Melissa gave constant encouragement and support in addition to her Palo Alto excursion. It is a real pleasure to have made friends with a member of Clancy's family to whom he was 'Uncle Clancy'; her recollections in Chapter 19 are a delight. Clancy's collection includes a thank-you note sent by Melissa, then aged 8, to Clancy's wife Ann.

Another family connection came via John Gill who met Julia Carroll, Clancy's step-granddaughter at a gig in June 2024. Julia requested *Broken Promises* to which John commented 'that's a Clancy Hayes song': the response came back — 'he was my step-grandfather'! Julia and partner Dom Adinolfi provided several publicity photographs taken in 1960 plus other photographs of Bill Hayes, Clancy and several cards from Clancy's wallet. Again John's chance encounter with Julia and my correspondence with her and Dom was another of the unexpected joys.

Special thanks must go to Nathan Coy, Librarian at Stanford, who was my point of contact throughout both this book, and as you will read in the appendix, during the two years researching for the discography. It was Nathan who facilitated the visits mentioned above, arranging for Clancy's collection to be available and for material to be sent for copying.

There are two others who deserve special mention. I need to once again thank Dave Radlauer who first sowed the seed of this biography. In congratulating me on the discography he compared it to the single beautiful leg of a table; the other legs and oak top would be a biography; such an allegory was hard to ignore. It was Dave who made the 1998 radio programme on Clancy's life and career which included the interviews with Daphne June King and Pete Clute - an incredible resource which I have drawn upon heavily. A multi-award winning radio host and nowadays also a writer and lecturer, his Jazz Rhythm website is a magnificent achievement with information, stories and music on dozens of Bay Area artists as well as many musicians from other jazz and entertainment spheres. His interviews with Bill Bardin and Bob Helm were also a source of some wonderful background information. I urge you to take a look/listen to the Jazz Rhythm website (and support it if you can).

Special thanks are also due to musician Russ Whitman. His account in Chapter 11 of Clancy's 1961 visit to the Whitman home, and recording with Russ and his friends, gives a first-hand insight into Clancy's good nature and willingness to make music at any opportunity. I am very grateful for his permission to share his fond memories of the occasion.

John Gill, a lifelong musician and long-time member of Turk Murphy's Jazz Band and leader of several of his own exceptional outfits, was also very helpful and supportive. His tribute to Clancy in Chapter 11 and assistance in identifying and explaining Clancy's banjos is greatly appreciated, as was his putting me into contact with Julia Carroll. This is also a good opportunity to thank both John and Hal for the many superb albums and CDs they have recorded; continuing the tradition of San Francisco Jazz and other superb styles of jazz and American music. Thank you both and I can only concur with Trevor Bannister's 'joyous' description in the text above.

It was a real bonus and pleasure when British musician and bandleader 'Spats' Langham generously agreed to write something for the book. I am sure you will agree that his insight and knowledge provide something very special in our understanding of what Clancy's music, and that of the Great Jazz Revival, did for musicians and music this side of the pond. Along with Hal Smith and John Gill, it is so valuable to have the input of musicians who clearly possess a love of jazz equal to that of Clancy's; and they are today's torch bearers.

Before getting to the list of the many other people who have been so helpful, I need to mention Frank Selman who was kind enough to write something for the book. A member of the Bob Scobey Society –Holland and close friend of Sam Linschooten, Frank spent over 30 years (from the mid-1980s to 2020) attending jazz festivals in the USA to enjoy and support the music he loves. When things got a bit difficult in writing for the book, an upbeat and energising Facetime conversation or email (with the sign off 'Frisco Forever') would do the trick. Frank's friendship and knowledge of jazz has been an enormous help as were his images from the Clancy Hayes collection, obtained before he returned it to Clint Baker and the SFTJF in the USA. Frank also took the photo of Clancy's Kenmore apartment block, Chicago during a 2024 visit.

Thanks also go to the following people who have assisted, some unknowingly, along the way:
Steve Pistorius
Ray Skjelbred
Charlie Crump
Nigel Carr
Clint Baker, Margaret Moos Peck and everyone involved in the San Francisco Traditional Jazz Foundation
Rachael Stoeltje, Director, Indiana University Library Moving Image Archive
David Kunian, Curator, New Orleans Jazz Museum
Nina Bozak, Curator of Rare Books, The Historic New Orleans Collection
Lori Schexnayder, Research Services, Tulane University Special Collections
Charlene Bonette, State Library of Louisiana
Susan Lynn, Editor and Publisher of the Iola Register
Ray Nolting, Editor of the Parsons Sun
Ruthie Hauge, Photo Director, The Capital Times
Sofia Adinolfi
Mike Barrett
Danny Collins
Linda Colvill
Linda and Richard Courtney
Mick Dickens
Paul Dickerson
Lars Edegran
John Hill
Duncan Larkin
Tim Maloney
Mary and Richard Moore
Graham Parry
Randall Phillippe
Pim Van Nieuwkerk
Carolynne and John Wales

Last but not least thanks go to Jan Reid for tolerating the many happy hours I spent locked away immersed in the joy of researching, writing and listening.

Gallery 1

Bayside Jazz Society concert 1951 Left to Right: Bob Helm,
Clancy Hayes, Turk Murphy, Bob Hoskins.
(Courtesy Hal Smith)

Alexander's Jazz Band at Alexander's (formerly Hambone Kelly's)
1951. Left to Right: George Probert, Squire Girsback, Jack Buck,
Bob Scobey, Fred Higuera (hidden), Clancy Hayes, Wally Rose.
(Courtesy Hal Smith)

Lu Watters' YBJB, Dawn Club Left to right: Bob Scobey, Lu Watters, Clancy Hayes, Turk Murphy, Ellis Horne. c.1942
(Courtesy Stanford University Libraries Archive / SFTJF)

Bob Scobey's Frisco Band at San Quentin, December 1955: Left to Right Jesse 'Tiny' Crump, Clancy Hayes, Hal McCormick, Bob Scobey, Fred Higuera, Bill Napier, Jack Buck.
(Courtesy Hal Smith)

Bayside Jazz Society concert 1951 Left to Right: Bob Helm, Don Kinch, Bob Hoskins, Turk Murphy, Bill Dart. Taken at same session seen on p. xxv
(Courtesy Hal Smith)

Lu Watters' Yerba Buena Jazz Band at Hambone Kelly's 1949 Left to Right: Charlie Sonnanstine, Lu Watters, Bob Helm, Bill Dart, Dick Lammi, Pat Patton, Clancy Hayes
(Courtesy Hal Smith)

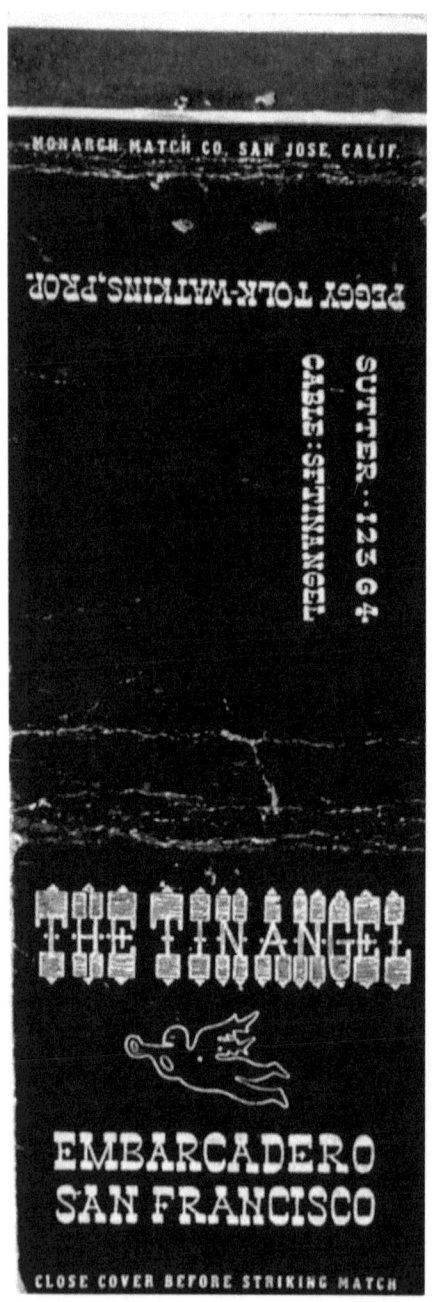

Match-books from The Tin Angel and Earthquake McGoon's
(Courtesy Hal Smith)

At Victor's and Roxie's early 1950s. Burt Bales. Fred Higuera and Clancy Hayes in the background.
(Courtesy Hal Smith)

Bob Helm and Bill Dart
(Courtesy Hal Smith)

Dick Lammi
(Courtesy Hal Smith)

Fred Higuera
(Courtesy Hal Smith)

Darnell Howard in San Francisco
(Courtesy Hal Smith)

A young Jack Buck
(Courtesy Stanford University Libraries / SFTJF)

Introduction

I hope this book will help you to capture the infectious spirit of Clancy Hayes' colourful life and wonderful music. He was a born entertainer. From his earliest days, growing up in the small Kansas town of Iola, his exploits, along with those of his parents and four musical older brothers were faithfully reported in local newspapers. Family happenings, travels, visits, social events and performances by the 'Hayes Clan' found their way into print.

Clancy enjoyed two lengthy and overlapping careers working in radio (1928-1950) and as a jazz artist (1938-1970). The story of his career is drawn from his collection of personal papers, newspaper and magazine articles, photographs and private tapes held in the San Francisco Traditional Jazz Foundation Collection at Stanford University Library. Recordings from YouTube and the Standard Hour broadcasts held by the Old-Time Radio catalogue were also an invaluable source of music and information. His broadcasting career involved many roles from solo artist and session musician to Musical Director at KGO, San Francisco in 1945. His famous radio characters included Pancake Boy, the Voice Of The South, Tune Termite, Jack of All Tunes and as he put it himself, 'I also swept up'.

Clancy's jazz years are best known through three career phases. First came his association with Lu Watters and the Yerba Buena Jazz Band in the pioneering days of the Great Jazz Revival. 'San Francisco Jazz' originated around 1938 and developed alongside the revival of New Orleans jazz. Secondly, Clancy was featured vocalist with Bob Scobey's Frisco Band throughout the 1950s. During these times he added song composition to his accomplishments, most famously *Huggin' And A Chalkin'* which made the Billboard top sellers chart in 1947.

Finally, Clancy spent the last decade of his performing years as a 'single' entertainer with a base at Turk Murphy and Pete Clute's Earthquake McGoon's in San Francisco. He also appeared regularly as a guest with various bands at numerous concerts and on records.

Clancy the radio star, late 1930s
(Courtesy of Stanford University Libraries Archive / SFTJF)

Fittingly, he was a member of the Greats of Jazz, led by Yank Lawson and Bob Haggart. This outfit went on to become the World's Greatest Jazz Band; an immodest title perhaps, but faithful to the musicians involved.

After almost fifty years in music Clancy's legacy is an eternal gift for everyone.

Clancy Hayes amassed a significant collection of memorabilia during his life. He kept fan mail, letters from musicians, contracts, and even some of his own jottings on hotel notepaper. Importantly, he also made and kept many private music tapes. That his collection has remained intact is a remarkable story in its own right.

Clancy's beloved wife Anne guarded the collection until her death in 1976 when it passed to their only son, Bill. On his death in 1989, it found its way to Clancy's friend Peter Clute. Hearing of Pete's death in 2001, Sam Linschooten, a fan of Revivalist Jazz and a member of The Bob Scobey Society — Holland, corresponded with Pete Clute's widow Carol and arranged for the collection to be shipped overseas to his home at Apeldoorn. The exact contents were unknown, but of course Sam was hoping to discover 'Frisco Treasure' in the form of music. In this respect he was disappointed. At some stage Clancy's considerable collection of private tapes had gone elsewhere. Nevertheless, despite this absence, the photographs, letters, press articles, contracts and other documents were definitely treasure. Sam copied and distributed many of the photographs and letters but soon realised that the collection needed to be preserved properly.

In 2008 Frank Selman, another Dutch 'Frisco' fan and collector, personally took the Hayes collection to musician Clint Baker, then acting as archivist for the San Francisco Traditional Jazz Foundation in the Bay Area. Eventually the SFTJF's sizeable collection went to be housed amongst the vast holdings of the Stanford University Library. At any stage of these transfers, the collection could have been damaged, discarded or lost. That it eventually arrived safely at Stanford is testimony to the care it received in each stage of its journey. Fortuitously, Clancy's tape collection also wound up at Stanford.

The availability of so much material not only eased the task of putting Clancy's story together but made it a thoroughly enjoyable experience. How lucky we are to be able to share the joy of his great legacy and that of the other musicians who came together in the late 1930s to spark the Great Jazz Revival.

New Orleans pianist Steve Pistorius, who has sung many of the numbers made famous by Clancy Hayes, made this interesting affirmation of the qualities needed to play jazz:

> When you play a certain type of music the first thing is that you have to love it — that's the first ingredient. Secondly, you have to have a little bit of talent and then you have to develop that talent. But the first thing is you have to love it. [1]

Clancy Hayes was a man of many talents. Above all, he loved music and he loved entertaining. He was not overly concerned with prosaic words, rather his words needed to be sung or sometimes delivered in entertaining rhyme, as part of a radio show. It would be very satisfying to me if this book encourages you to explore his rich musical legacy for yourself as well as the music of the associated musicians who played - and still play - traditional jazz. Thankfully in this modern age there are many ways to listen to Clancy's music, including the following options:

San Francisco Traditional Jazz Foundation Charles Huggins Project at Stanford University
Dave Radlauer's Jazz Rhythm website
YouTube — 'Clancy Hayes Jazz' channel and others
Music Streaming Services such as Spotify, Apple and others which include many Bob Scobey, Lu Watters and Clancy recordings in their playlists.

The music lives.

Regrettably, but unsurprisingly, writing this book fifty-two years after Clancy's death meant that it was difficult to obtain first-hand information from musicians who actually played with 'the minstrel'. I am therefore especially grateful to Russ Whitman for his wonderful account of recording with Clancy; to Hal Smith for his recollections of playing at the second Clancy Hayes Day fundraiser in 1971 and to Dave Radlauer — award-winning radio host, lecturer and proprietor of the Jazz Rhythm website. His 1998 radio series on Clancy's jazz career included priceless interviews with Pete Clute and Clancy's songwriting partner of the early 1950s, Daphne June King.

Sam Linschooten finds treasure
(Courtesy Sam Linschooten, photographer unknown)

A note about the images in this book. Many come from Clancy's own collection as copies made by Stanford University Digital Imaging Service. In addition there are downloaded images from the San Francisco Traditional Jazz Charles Huggins Project on the Stanford University website and images sent directly to me by Sam Linschooten and Frank Selman. Hal Smith, Julia Carroll and Dominic Adinolfi also provided a number of excellent images.

Every effort has been made to identify the source of images not from Clancy's collection and these are identified where possible. Most album and record photographs were taken by my friend Graham Parry - a talented photographer and photographic club judge.

Unless otherwise stated, all opinions expressed are my own and to the best of my capabilities the facts presented are as accurate as possible.

1

Arrival Of The Seventh Son

Clarence Leonard Hayes was born on Saturday 14 November 1908 in the small Kansas town of Caney, close to the Oklahoma border. His arrival raised the population to 3,597. Clarence was the youngest child born to William Kelly Hayes (1861-1943) and Clara May Hayes (1864-1956). Album sleeve notes refer to Clancy being a seventh son giving him the folklore allure of good fortune and special gifts — including the ability to cure. Although Clancy was the seventh child, the fact that he had an elder sister spoils the true qualification which requires a line of seven male children. Nevertheless, it looked good within the text and for sure he was gifted — as were his siblings.

Within a year of Clancy's birth, the Hayes family moved fifty miles north to the town of Iola which over the previous decade had been a boom town based on the discovery of a copious supply of natural gas. Between 1890 and 1910 the Iola population grew from 1,700 to an all-time peak of 9,000. The gas resource was such that it was offered free to encourage industries to relocate. Several zinc ore smelting works from southeastern Kansas were quick to take up the offer. One town close to Iola is named simply Gas. As Iola's economy grew, brickworks and ironworks were established and the Kansas Southern Electric Railroad Company's new railway helped the rapidly expanding population get around. Other improvements to infrastructure included a piped water supply, sewerage system and a paved main street. The town was ready for the arrival of the Hayes clan.

A rapidly expanding and wealthy town was just the place for railway ticket agent William Kelly Hayes. Business and pleasure trips to other towns and cities were in demand and Mr W. K. Hayes had spotted the opportunity.

Iola appeared to be an idyllic hometown but inevitably it had real life issues during the boom years. 'Jim Crow' laws did not exist in

Kansas, neither was there segregation, but racism and prejudice existed meaning African-Americans and foreigners found difficulty finding good jobs and law enforcement was sometimes biased. Another issue for the town was the bars and saloons — referred to as 'Joints'. This is surprising as Kansas was a 'dry state'. An attempt by one Charles Melvin on 9 July 1905 to enforce this status by dynamiting any building accommodating a 'Joint' was only partly successful. Three saloons, the Eagle, Red Light and Blue Front were destroyed but faulty fuses in others saved the day. [1]

Clancy spent his formative years in Iola with four musical brothers (Glenn, born 1895; Phil, 1897; Ashton, 1900 and Wallace,1905). His two eldest siblings — Martha, born 1886 and Dean, born 1890 — had fled the nest prior to Clancy's somewhat belated arrival. Clancy said, 'it just seemed like I grew up in a band.' It is likely their musical talent stemmed from the paternal line; William Kelly was a regular and celebrated participant in theatrical and musical events. Also, if a stereotypical conclusion may be forgiven, William's father may have had a role to play. 'Jno' H. Hayes was a Welsh speaking native of the 'land of song'. The story of his migration to the USA remains to be discovered but his marriage to Catharine Helman of Pennsylvania started, or continued, a musical dynasty.

The Hayes brothers regularly performed at social gatherings around Iola and when their kid brother was old enough, he joined the band. At the American Legion Dance at the Masonic Hall in Iola on 20 December 1920 'they danced to excellent music which was furnished by the Hayes Brothers'. Pillars of the local community, family events such as social gatherings, visitors and travels were regularly featured in the social column of the *Iola Register* and the *Parsons Sun*. This insight into life in small town America in the early decades of the 20th century shows the closeness of communities in the pre-electronic era. Life revolved around gatherings in homes and public halls and of course any dance required live music. Community events and the attendees, plus invariably upbeat descriptions of the proceedings, were staple items for the social columns. It was a gathering at the Hayes' residence that captured the promise of a certain young Iolan:

The Iola Register of 10 May 1916 reported:

> Only one member of the Golden Link Club was absent yesterday afternoon when Mrs Hayes entertained at her home 422 South Colborn Street. The program was unusually good. It began with roll call to which each of the members responded with a current event. Then Mrs J. F. Varner took charge of the history lesson which was an account of the political and religious institutions of Ancient Greece. Mrs W.W. Peck read a paper on the countries south of the United States telling some particularly interesting things about South America and Mrs I.E. Steele read a pretty story — 'The Prize that Mother Won'. As usual a bit of poetry completed the program and this time there were two poems. The first 'Watching Yourself Go By' was read by Mrs F.M. Broadus and the second 'The Little Old Home Town' was read by Mrs E.S. Davis. Mrs Hayes is a most delightful hostess and the members of the club feel especially well repaid for the afternoon spent with her. During the social part of the afternoon she was assisted by her daughter, Mrs W.W. Peck, in serving luncheon, and her seven year old son, Master Clarence Hayes sang several times. There are few children so young as Master Hayes who sing so well and his contribution to the afternoon's entertainment was very pleasing.

This was possibly Clancy's first review, but more would be published within a short time. Following is another mention of Clancy which indicates that his career as an entertainer was already underway:

> Master Clarence Hayes, the talented young son of Mr and Mrs W.K. Hayes will favor the public of Iola with one of his remarkable pleasing solos in this year's American Legion Minstrel Show. Young Mr Hayes has a really big voice which is full of quality and this solo will be a treat to all local lovers of good music [2]

Master Clarence Hayes
(Courtesy of Stanford University Libraries Archive / SFTJF)

So, it was clear that the boy singer had a good voice. His next step was learning to play an instrument. Perhaps unwisely, Clancy chose the drum set — a relatively new instrument. An article in the *Indianapolis Star* from 1914 stated 'it was great to watch a trap drummer; one would think he kept a junk store and had gone crazy'. Traps — short for con*trap*tion — allowed a drummer to play bass drum, snare and cymbals; one person could do the work of three.

Clancy's drumming suffered an abrupt interruption earned the day he broke a leg, necessitating a temporary change of instrument. Banjo and guitar soon replaced the traps. There are two versions of how Clancy took up the banjo. Version one is that a brother gave him a Model N Little Wonder Vega after his accident. The more colourful story is that a neighbour's daughter took pity on him sitting on the front porch with his broken leg resting on a chair and loaned him a ukulele. Perhaps both are true. In any case, Clancy was soon proficient on the stringed instruments. He was back in the Hayes brothers' band as well as entertaining his pals.

Phil Hayes' obituary from the *Iola Register* of 10 August 1945 made reference to the brothers' musical activities in the 1920s: 'He and his guitar will particularly be remembered by those who knew the musically talented Hayes brothers during their High School days.'

Musically gifted Phil and Ashton swapped their music books for profit and loss accounts; both became qualified accountants. Brother Wallace chose to study pharmacy and Glenn also studied accountancy before going into the oil business. All five brothers were musical but perhaps it was enough to have just one professional musician in a family.

The *Indianapolis Star* of 6 September 1959 had Clancy recalling: 'I was 12 years old and I was lionized, who knows a 12 year old kid who could play all the popular tunes of the day. I remember I was a big hit at Boy Scout camp that year.' As a youngster Clancy also enjoyed visiting The Green Lantern — a popular hangout in Parsons frequented by 'gay young blades'. Our enterprising youngster also jerked soda there.

Young Clancy
(Courtesy of Stanford University Libraries Archive / SFTJF)

On Saturday 28 October 1922, Clancy was back in drumming action at Miss Lola Smiley's house where she held a Hallowe'en masquerade which was 'a most delightful affair'.

'The hours from 8-10 pm were made merry with Hallowe'en games. There was bobbing for apples and gumdrops, the stately Virginia reel and several contest games in which prizes were awarded to Wilson Stroup, Charles Scott and Hazel Cline. An orchestra with Hazel Cline, piano, and Clarence Hayes at the drums furnished music.' [3]

It was also in 1922 that thirteen-year-old Clancy formed his first band, the topically named King Tut Tooters. Clancy told the story to radio host Bill Dyer in a 1965 interview: [4]

> I started playing drums when I was about seven and when I was twelve, I learned to play the banjo and I had a little kid band in Southeastern Kansas, a little town named Iola. To give you an idea about when it started my original name for the band — having to get in on the free publicity and a topical name — we were called the King Tut Tooters. At the time all the girls were wearing King Tut print dresses, King Tut hairdos and so on.

The Tooters — described in the local press as a 'boy band' — went on to toot at dances, cafes and social gatherings throughout 1923 including:

> 12 June: Iola Country Club School Year Closing Party: *The King Tut Tooters, an orchestra of young boys, furnished excellent music.'*

> 26 June: The Tooters serenaded diners at the Kansas Grain Dealers Association Banquet.

> 17 July: Crystal Lake Pavilion Dance where the inaugural event took place on a newly laid wooden dance floor set beside a swimming pool at Carlyle, but things came to a sticky end. Having laid and varnished the floor, a perfectionist manager decided it needed a second coat that didn't have time to dry. Dancers found their feet covered by 'gummy materials'. The Tooters played again at a gum-free event three days later.

Clancy picks up the story, again from the 1965 Bill Dyer interview:

> **CH**: Soon after that we changed our name to the Harmony Aces and we played for school dances, the local tea room and whatever else we could scrounge around. In the summer we always had very good work. I recall one summer we had some boys down from Lawrence, Kansas who were going to University and we were working five nights a week all summer. And that's pretty good when you are booking yourself.
>
> **BD**: How old were you?
>
> **CH**: I was thirteen.
>
> **BD**: An enterprising young capitalist?
>
> **CH**: I was just interested in music, I loved to play and I loved to study it. I think it's a very fascinating vocation; I just like to play.

With Clancy's busy schedule, and his vocational calling, it was probably inevitable that he would drop out of school. His principal warned him, 'you're leading people straight to hell with that jazz band of yours'. But he never believed that line for one minute. More supportive was his music teacher Mr Roberts; Clancy acknowledged him as being a great help in developing his musical ability.

On 23 October 1923, between 9 and 9.45 pm, Clancy made his first radio broadcast with the Klinginsmith's Radio Trio, playing popular dance numbers from the Hotel Kelley Studio, K.F.I.D. Arbuckle Garage on South Washington, Iola. The trio comprised J.T. Klinginsmith, violin, Porter Thomas, piano and Clancy on banjo.

As for the Harmony Aces, the name change was noted in the *Iola Register* of 25 October 1923:

> The Harmony Aces, formerly known as the King Tut Tooters, played last night at a dance at Westphalia. The dance was in connection with a general community social gathering sponsored by the ladies of the local Catholic Church and was a big affair; about 65 couples were on the floor.

Clancy was billed as a 'star' in a future-gazing programme titled Follies of 1943 which was part of the Iola Elks' Lodge three-day charity event running from 25-27 October 1923. The review of the show in the *Iola Register* was headlined, 'A Crowd Was There' and stated:

> The Follies anticipate and form a review of all that will be new and unique in vodeville and musical comedy in 1943. With its bevy of Iola's most attractive young singers and dancers forming the ballet, supporting such well known and popular stars as Clarence Hayes, Lyndith Geery, Jennie Davis, Porter Thomas and others too numerous to mention, the revue goes over with a bang and the SRO sign was in evidence at each performance. [5]

The format was repeated in 1924 and, as this extract from a very detailed advertisement shows, Clancy was obviously enjoying life with his 'Bountiful Bevy of Beauties'. The ad. also promises 'a diamond ring will be given away ABSOLUTELY FREE to the most popular girl attending the carnival'. Strangely, there is no information on the judging process!

The *Iola Register* of 25 February 1924 noted that: 'Kenneth Smith, Porter Thomas, Clair Dawson, Clarence Hayes and Ellis McKinley — members of the Harmony Aces Orchestra will leave on the 5.48 this evening for Greenley where they will play for a dance tonight.'

Clancy was still with the band in December 1924 when the *Iola Register* carried the following:

> The Harmony Aces, a group of Iola boys who constituted a snappy little jazz orchestra here last year have come together again during the vacation and are going to play for a dance tonight at the M.W.A. hall. The members who will be here tonight are: Porter Thomas, piano; Clarence Hayes, banjo; Kenneth Smith, saxophone; and Ellis McKinley, drums.

Everybody Is Cordially Invited to Attend
THE THIRD ANNUAL

Elks' Charity Carnival

Elks' Club Rooms   Third Floor Northrup Bldg.
Seven O'clock Thursday, Friday, Saturday Evenings.

All-Star Bill—Including the Following Headliners:
Mr. Floyd Kelley presents Miss Catherine Cannon's Latest Revusical Comedy

"FOLLIES OF 1944"

Featuring Mr. Clarence Hayes—Supported by a Bountiful Bevy of Beauties.

Abe—**Kohlenbrenner & Thompson**—Tub
Klever Karnival Komedians

Frank McCarthy, assisted by "Elmer, the Duck Boy" presents
"THE LIVE DUCK POND"
"Ring 'em and carry 'em away."

That Smashing Melodramatic Sensation
"THE AUCTION BLOC"
With an All-Star Cast—Including Jack Griffin, Roy Fry and Louis Schlanger.

Horace—**Miller & Pendarvis**—Doc
"Those Clever Extractors"

GEORGE L. WILLIAMS, The Kandy Kid.

Prof. Annual Carnival Scott's Symphonic Jazz Band
"Pharoahs of Syncopation"
Assisted by
30————BEAUTIES————30
In the Dance Palace.

Dulica, Brune and Keitzman offer for your approval
"THE DOLL HOUSE"

Gene—**COOK & SIFERS**—Sam
in an original
HORSE SHOE JUGGLING ACT

Neal, Hughes & Carter present for your approval
That Pathetic Drama of Life in the Early Sixties—
"The Old Corner Grocery"
By the Author of "Way Out East"

Reeves & Brownfield in "Sweet Cider Time"

Ray—**Enfield & O'Flaherty**—Eddie
In a quaint little skit all their own.

Geery and Young Present Their Justly Famous
"CHAMBER of HORRORS"
"Nothing Like It Either Side of Coney Island."

A Score of Other Equally Good Attractions.

A DIAMOND RING will be given away ABSOLUTELY FREE to the most popular girl attending the carnival.
GENERAL ADMISSION   —   TEN CENTS

Elks' Charity Carnival, advertisement 1924
(The Iola Register, 29 Octobern 1924)

The Harmony Aces would go on to play in Iola and surrounding towns into the mid-1930s. However, Clancy most likely left the band in 1925 and toured with several different groups in the Midwest and Southwest for a couple of years. On 13 July 1925 he made his first recording as a member of the Kansas City based Coon-Sanders Original Nighthawks Orchestra on *I'm Gonna Charleston Back To Charleston*. Unfortunately there is no information on how long he was with the band. [6]

THURSDAY.

Boy 16 on Check Charge.

Clarence Hayes, 16 years old, was taken before Justice of the Peace J. L. Corkwell this morning on a charge of drawing checks upon a bank in which he had no funds. He admitted doing so, and asked permission to communicate with his father, who lives in Iola, saying his father had promised to come down and straighten things out as soon as he knew how much money it would take. Clarence put out two checks for a total of $4.50. They were drawn against an Iola bank and cashed by a local cafe. The costs were $10.50, making a total of $15. Clarence was sent back to jail to be kept there until the $15 was paid, otherwise to be taken to Erie for trial in district court.

Boy 16 on Check Charge, newspaper article
(Chanute Weekly Tribune 18 September 1925)

Young Clancy's travels in 1925 found him in the small town of Chanute where the hungry teenager learned a valuable life lesson. Fifteen-(he was almost sixteen)year-old Clarence Hayes had cashed cheques in a café for a total value of $4.50, but there was one problem.

Thankfully, W. K. Hayes made the 20-mile trip from Iola in good time and our teenager's expensive café experience was something he never repeated; but forevermore he delivered *Waiting For The Evening Mail* with remarkable feeling.

In the mid-1920s Clancy worked the midwestern 'Medicine Show' circuit and also had a stint with Prof. and Mrs Hall's Dancing School. The Halls toured small towns, giving lessons in the afternoon and sponsoring dances at night. Clancy said, 'Professor Hall claimed he was the only man ever to blow a high C on a trumpet on top of Pikes Peak, Colorado and he had newspaper clippings to prove it.' Some years earlier Professor and Mrs Hall had premises in Parsons, Kansas and according to the *Parsons Times* (22 Feb.1919) theirs was, 'a reputable dancing academy that caters only to the best'.

April 1926 found Clancy in Arizona with Ham Crawford's Louisiana Blue Devils which included ace musicians Wingy Manone and Jack Teagarden. The Ham Crawford outfit was well-established and toured throughout the United States. However, it seems band relationships weren't as harmonious as the music. Clancy explained that things went awry in Phoenix when Wingy got into a fight with the leader, leaving the band and Clancy stranded. Doubtlessly, Clancy was pondering where better musical situations might be found.

California Here I Come

By 1926 several members of the Hayes family had taken a foothold in California: brothers Ashton and Wallace and their parents were now settled in Santa Rosa. Realising the 'Territory Band' and touring lifestyle was not for him, Clancy decided to head west and join the family.

Perhaps with his principal's words still echoing in his ears, or unsettled by the Crawford-Manone bout, Clancy momentarily decided to try another path to fortune. His one and only venture outside of entertainment and music occurred in late 1926 or early 1927 when he temporarily pumped gas until securing a job in the world of finance as a bank teller. But for a man who just loved to play, inevitably music put a permanent end to the concept of a 'day job'. Whilst the other musical Hayes brothers chose to keep their talent a hobby, Clancy simply had to entertain and so sought a new challenge. But his brief banking career did have one life-changing bonus — meeting another young bank employee, Anna Marie Stuhlmacher. On 17 June 1928 Miss Stuhlmacher became Mrs Anna Hayes. The marriage was destined to last a lifetime.

Ann and Clancy
(Courtesy of Stanford University Libraries Archive / SFTJF)

This Certifies that Clarence Leonard Hayes and Anna Marie Stuhlmacher were united by me in

Holy Matrimony

on Sunday the seventeenth day of June A. D. One Thousand Nine Hundred and 28 at Trinity Church in Oakland according to the rites of the Protestant Episcopal Church and in accordance with the Laws of the State of California

Dated Sunday this seventeenth day of June A. D. 1928

Lloyd B. Thomas,
Rector, Trinity Parish

Marriage Licence
(Courtesy of Stanford University Libraries Archive / SFTJF)

Ann and Clancy
(Courtesy of Stanford University Libraries Archive / SFTJF)

Clancy, Ann and Bill circa 1933
(Courtesy Julia Carroll and Dom Adinolfi)

Family Photos

Clancy's parents: William Kelly Hayes and Clara May Hayes
(Courtesy Sam Linschooten / SFTJF)

Della, Clancy, Ashton, Wallace and Mrs Clara May Hayes
(Courtesy Stanford University Libraries Archive / SFTJF)

The youngest musical Hayes brothers: Ashton, Wallace and Clarence, Ash's house, 1930, Santa Rosa, California
(Courtesy Stanford University Libraries Archive / SFTJF)

Proud fathers, Clancy and Ashton
(Courtesy Stanford University Libraries Archive / SFTJF)

Ann and Clancy
(Courtesy Sam Linschooten / SFTJF)

Ann and Clancy
(Courtesy Stanford University Libraries Archive / SFTJF)

2

The Radio Years Part One 1928-38

The mid to late 1920s was a busy and exciting period in the rapidly expanding world of radio, bringing news and entertainment to the masses - or at least those wealthy enough to have a radio set. The U.S. Census of 1930 sought the following 'home data': Is your home owned or rented? What is the value if owned or monthly rental? Does your family own a farm? Do you have a radio set? In the Western states alone, 44% of families possessed a radio while the average across the USA was 40%.

With his innate desire to entertain, in 1928 Clancy put down his cashier's stamp and joined NBC station KGO in San Francisco as a staff musician. NBC had established a national network with key stations and affiliated chain stations. Programmes were relayed over telephone wires for regional broadcasting by the affiliates so that local programmes such as The Vagabonds, broadcast from the Palace Hotel, San Francisco were heard across the USA.

Regrettably no recordings of the early radio programmes detailed in this chapter have come to light — with the exception of the 1934 broadcasts by the Bob Beale-Herb Taylor Orchestra, again from the Palace Hotel. The details of Clancy's radio career are gleaned from newspaper articles, magazines, letters and documents in his personal papers which include two radio scripts. Most shows lasted fifteen minutes and were broadcast locally. Special shows and broadcasts varied between thirty minutes and an hour and were often networked 'Coast to Coast'. As an antidote to the depression years, entertainment programmes were generally light-hearted and upbeat to lift the gloom — and put people in a mood to buy the sponsor's product!

It didn't take long for Clancy to escape the relative obscurity of the NBC staff orchestra. As usual with Mr Hayes, a colourful story accompanies his move from orchestra guitarist to featured artist on stations KGO and KPO.

Clarence Hayes was holidaying with a party of friends near Russian River in California in the fall of 1928. He had taken his guitar along and each member of the party participated in the entertainment. When his turn came the talent level went up somewhat and he sang several numbers accompanying himself on guitar. Sitting in different company, but within earshot, was Howard Milholland, manager of radio station KGO Oakland. He liked Hayes' voice and, thinking it would appeal to his radio audience, sought out Clancy and induced him to step out of the orchestra and try the air. And so began a radio career that would span the next twenty years. First and foremost Clancy was a vocalist of real quality (with some 'jazz-it' according to one fan) but his other roles would include actor, reporter, newsreader, comedian, impersonator, writer, orchestra director and as already noted he 'also swept up'.

Clancy's first programme in January 1929 was as a vocalist in the New Big Show, an hour-long variety programme where he featured as The Voice Of The South — a name that would stick with him on and off for many years. Two other Specials with an emcee introducing a series of musical variety acts were held during the year. Clancy was also a regular in the Cotton Blossom Minstrels, directed by Charlie Marshall, which recreated the format of the mid-19th century minstrel shows with the traditional characters of Interlocutor, Tambo, Bones and End Men. Broadcast from 10-11 pm across the NBC network, Clancy was a member of the Southern Quartet as well as a featured solo artist on guitar and vocal.

By the end of 1929, Clancy's role as a featured vocalist was secure. From the autumn he sang with Walter Beban's Orchestra (sometimes billed as the Cigar Band) in a series of half-hour shows. Programme listings occasionally detailed the vocal numbers; on 29 December Clancy delivered *Song of the Islands* and *Black and Blue*.

Some other listings detailed the full programme. The 9.30 pm half-hour show the following evening featured — *Louisiana Bo-Bo / The Web of Love / Breakaway / I'm Only Making Believe / Climbing the Stairs Into Your Heart / Every Now and Then / Share Your Lips With Me*

/ *Cherie* and *I'm Referrin' Just To Her and Me*. Few of these songs will be familiar to most present-day listeners but they demonstrate just how much music was available, and needed, to feed the programmes for the new radio age. Other Walter Beban broadcast rarities included *I Lift Up My Finger and I Say Tweet Tweet / I Don't Want Your Kisses / I Actually Am In Love / Go To Bed / Close Fit Blues* and *Where Are You, Dream Girl?*

1930 saw Clancy featured in many programmes including the Pacific Vagabonds, Brownbilt Footlites, Musical Musketeers, the Jolly Time Review, Aces of Harmony, Camel Pleasure Hour and Women's Magazine of the Air.

Clancy and Charlie Marshall
(Courtesy Sam Linschooten / SFTJF)

This picture of Clancy with Charlie Marshall was probably taken shortly after 1928 when both joined NBC. Marshall was an NBC staff artist specialising in hillbilly music, leading the Hillbillies and Marshall's Mavericks.

NAME   CLARENCE HAYES

You have been tentatively cast on programs for the week beginning **Feb. 22**   **1930**.

Vagabonds–11 PM	Sun. 22
re–9:30 PM	
Pac. Vagabonds–1 PM	Tues. 24
re–11 AM	
Vagabonds–3:45 PM	Thurs. 26
re–2 PM	
Brown Bilt–8:15 PM	Fri. 27
re–7 PM	
NBC Matinee–2 PM	Sat. 28
re–1:30 PM	

The above does not constitute a guarantee or agreement of employment, and is only for the purpose of advising you of a tentative program for the week, which we may cancel or alter at will, without notice or obligation.

NATIONAL BROADCASTING CO., INC.

By

Clancy Hayes' NBC Schedule 1930
(Courtesy Stanford University Libraries Archive / SFTJF)

```
ANNOUNCEMENTS AND DESCRIPTIONS
     THE AUNT JEMIMA BOY
    WEDNESDAY, APRIL 30, 1930.
7.45 to 8.00 A.M.
ANNOUNCER: You will now be entertained by the Aunt Jemima Boy.
ROOSTER CROW.
ALARM CLOCK.
YAWN.
OPENING SONG.
Mornin', folks. How is you all dis nice, bright, sunshiny mornin?
It sho am a joy to get up dese mornins. Eh? No, ah didn't get all
mah sleep last night. You see it was dis way: Bud Judson an his
gal, and me and mah gal went on a moonlight picnic last night in
Bud's car. Yes, sah, and it was a real picnic with real eats.
When we got to de shores of de lake de gals said dey had a surprise
for us. And it sho was a surprise. Dey each had a fryin pan and a
                                     flour.
package of Aunt Jemima's Pancake. And did dose gals know how to
cook pancakes? Um, um! Well, Bud and I got to racin, and we was
a-runnin neck-and-neck, but we jest had to quit, 'cause if we didn't
                                              we
there would a-bin none left for de gals. After was through eatin
dose delicious, golden browns Bud's gal sang us a couple o'songs.
While ah's waitin for mah stack ah'll sing one of 'em for you. SHAW!
   Down Among The Sugar Cane
                                                        de
Bud's gal was tellin us about takin her little sister to the circus
last week. Her name am Nanny. Ah means de sister's name am Nanny.
Dey calls her Nanny 'cause it am easy to get her goat. Well, when
day came out o'de side show Nanny kicked 'cause she hadn't seen de
"Also." Bud's gal got sore and said, "Dere aint no Also in dat
shaw. "Yes dere am," said Nanny. What makes you all tink dere's
```

A transcription of this script is on pages 304/5

Script page 1: Aunt Jemima radio show.
(Courtesy Stanford University Libraries Archive / SFTJF)

Clancy was anonymous in his first starring role; the identity of 'Aunt Jemima's Pancake Boy' was not disclosed. The breakfast time programme was upbeat and fun with the emphasis on selling pancakes whilst serving up topical news and songs to reward listeners for tuning in. The show opened with a song *I See By The Papers* with the verse changed daily to reflect the news, with comments on the humour, pathos, drama and human interest in the day's stories. The ingenuity of the format is all the more impressive bearing in mind it went on air at 7.45 am. The part script (page 2 is missing) from Clancy's personal papers gives an insight into the show.

```
                    FROM THE CLANCY HAYES
                    COLLECTION
                         3
                                    offered
said: "Yes, mother, ah sho was good, a man xxxxxxx me a big
plate full of money xxxxxxxxxxxxxxxxxxx!an ah said 'no,
thank you.' "  SHAW!

Well, Dad, ah tinks you had better xx wipe off your chops and
tear yoself away from dose light, flaky, golden browns, or
you'll be late for work. Jes hand me de paper over here an
ah'll give it de once-over, and see what's goin on.
SONG......I SEE BY THE PAPERS.
Well, folks, now dat Tillie is at liberty to go to work
cookin me a couple o'stacks of dose luscious Aunt Jemima hot
cakes ah'll get busy with these two sets of white ivories of
mine a-masticatin of 'em
CLOSING SONG.
```

Script page 3: Aunt Jemima radio show.
(Courtesy Stanford University Libraries Archive / SFTJF))

There must have been something special in twenty-one-year-old Clancy's radio voice; some of the fan mail was bordering on the salacious as this excerpt from a 1930 fan letter shows:

> Just a line to say 'hello' to my sweet daddy. Last Saturday night darling you sang so sweet, when you sang *My Dream Man* and *Scissors to Grind*. Daddy you were so sweet. Honey Boy, I guess you want to cut one of my curls.

This morning sweetheart (Wed.) you made me so happy when you sang *Dapper Dan*. It was sure cute just like my daddy. I love it. It was the first time I had ever heard it. Daddy you were a little love too this morning with your little guitar. Daddy, an' how! you can play like nobody else can Sugar Daddy when you talk and sing I get so excited……...

The letter continues (and hots up) for a further five pages. As I do not want this book restricted to the adult section I'll leave it there, you've got the idea.

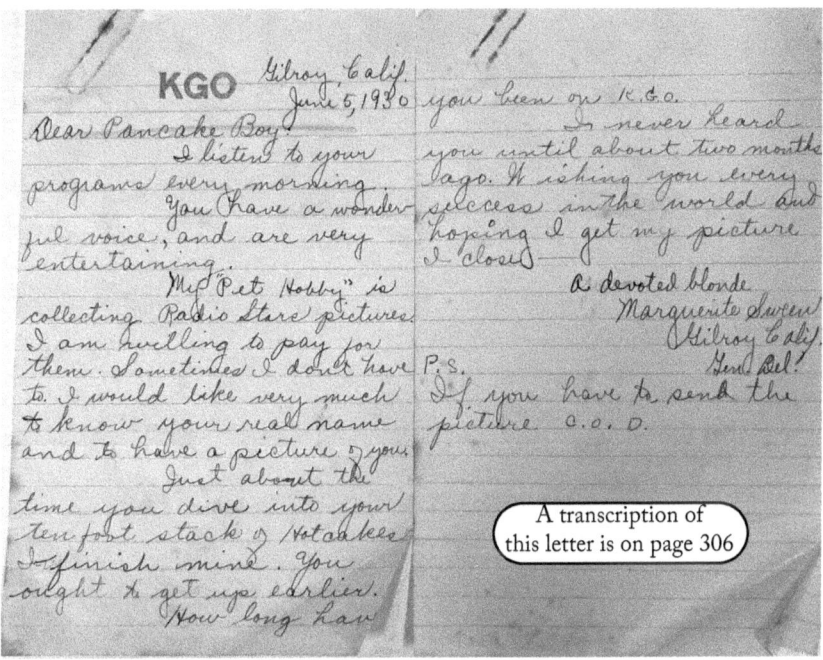

Fan mail from 'A Devoted Blonde'
(Courtesy Stanford University Libraries Archive / SFTJF)

In late 1930 Clancy was featured with Mart Grauenhorst's Orchestra in the Jolly Time Review; in the 17 December show he sang *It Seems To Be Spring* from the film *Let's Go Native* starring Jack Oakie and Janette McDonald. The lyrics are wonderful as is the melody and it was one of the songs Clancy sang on a private tape for his friend Squirrel Ashcraft in 1958.[1]

The Pacific Vagabonds show on 9 December 1930 included the Boswell Sisters who obviously hit it off with young Clarence.

The Boswell Sisters ... and their review
(Courtesy Stanford University Libraries Archive / SFTJF)

As busy as he was, thankfully he and Ann found time for a little recreation enjoying Los Angeles and exploring alternative forms of transport.

Los Angeles Ostrich Farm, July 1930
(Courtesy Stanford University Libraries Archive / SFTJF)

1931 saw Clancy continue with the Pacific Vagabonds, Brownbilt Footlights and Jolly Time Review as well as joining another crop of shows including Radio Ramblings — again teaming up with Mart Grauenhorst's Orchestra.

This invitation for the opening night of the winter social season on 14 November 1931 shows Clancy as a featured vocalist with Mahlon Merrick, NBC's Musical Director and Maestro of the Palace Hotel Vagabonds. Adjacent to the Palace Hotel on Market Street is Annie Street, an alley where a night club was to become part of revivalist jazz history. The Vagabonds became the Palace Hotel house band broadcasting 6 nights a week.

All entertainment shows needed commercial sponsors, and Albers Bros. were keen to make sure their excellent products were fully understood:

Mahlon Merrick Orchestra. Palace Hotel,
San Francisco, November 1931, poster
(Courtesy Stanford University Libraries Archive / SFTJF)

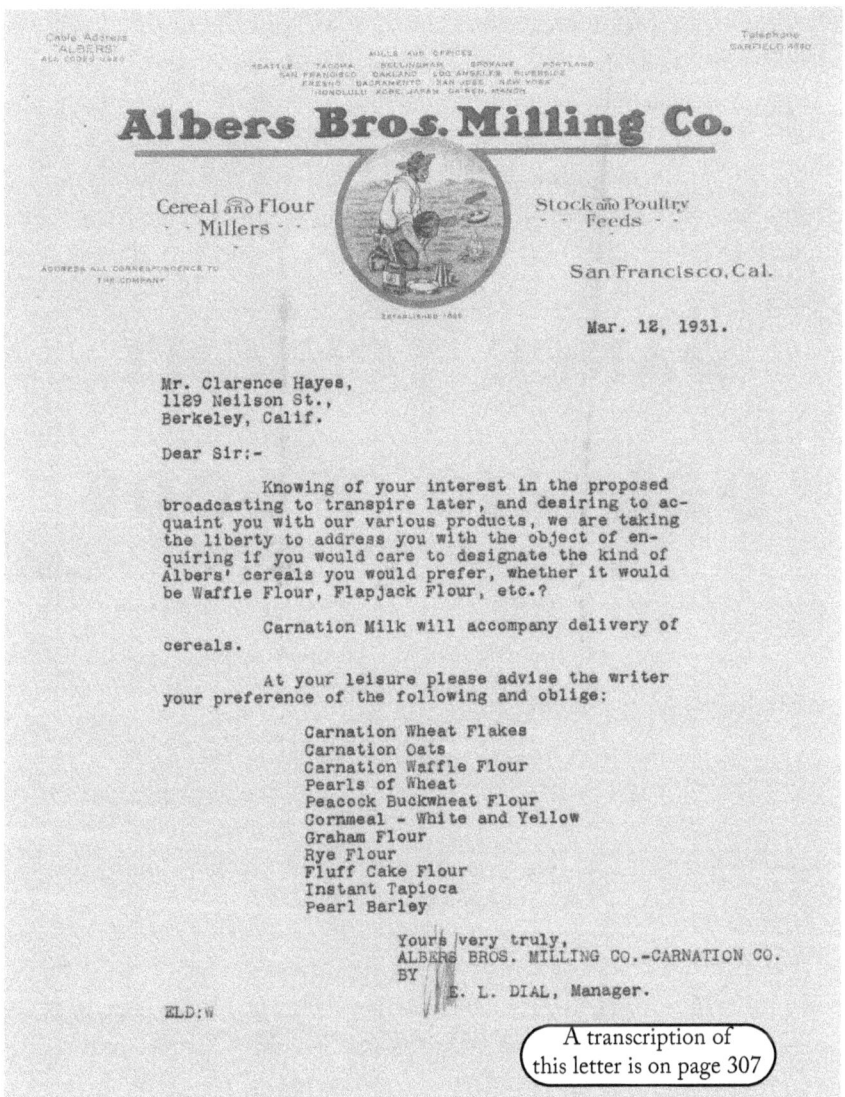

Letter from Albers Bros. Milling Company
(Courtesy Stanford University Libraries Archive / SFTJF)

In 1932 Clancy sang on The Buccaneers and had his own 15-minute show billed simply as Entertainment: Clarence Hayes. He also featured as a 'tenor' in a regular late night half hour broadcast Rhythm Vendors with orchestra direction by Walter Beban. The 31

October broadcast featured vocals on *Cabin in the Cotton / We Just Couldn't Say Goodbye* and *Let's Have a Party*. As a radio personality, Clancy was also able to pick up private gigs such as his emcee role for a series of summer dances at the Del Rio Woods entertainment centre in Sonoma Valley. Whether he had any say as to his billing in this ad. of 4 June 1932 is doubtful. Hopefully single males were allowed to join in the fun to partner the extra ladies, but at what cost?

Dance at Del Rio Woods, June 1932, advertisement
(Santa Rosa Republican, 4 June 1932)

The Buccaneers programme was broadcast on station KGO from 3-4 pm, while musical extracts were also played in the evening. The perceptive admirers from Seattle (pages 36 and 37) spot two things in Clancy's singing that would be remarked on throughout his career - his sense of time and his ability to 'jazz-it'. Sadly, as yet (we live in hope) there is nothing available from this period to corroborate the opinion of this fan, although Clancy would of course show his 'jazz-it' in later years. Whether he obliged with *When Yuba Plays The Rhumba On The Tuba* or *Is I In Love, Is I?* remains a mystery.

By 1933 Clancy was appearing in three regular programmes, Rhythm Vendors, Powderpuff Review and The Melodians with Walter Beban's Orchestra. Guest appearances continued on other shows including Spotlight, Women's Magazine of the Air, and Radio City. He was working hard but despite the success of his radio career, or perhaps because of it, in the latter part of the year Clancy took a break from broadcasting.

Clancy on the radio
(Courtesy Stanford University Libraries Archive / SFTJF)

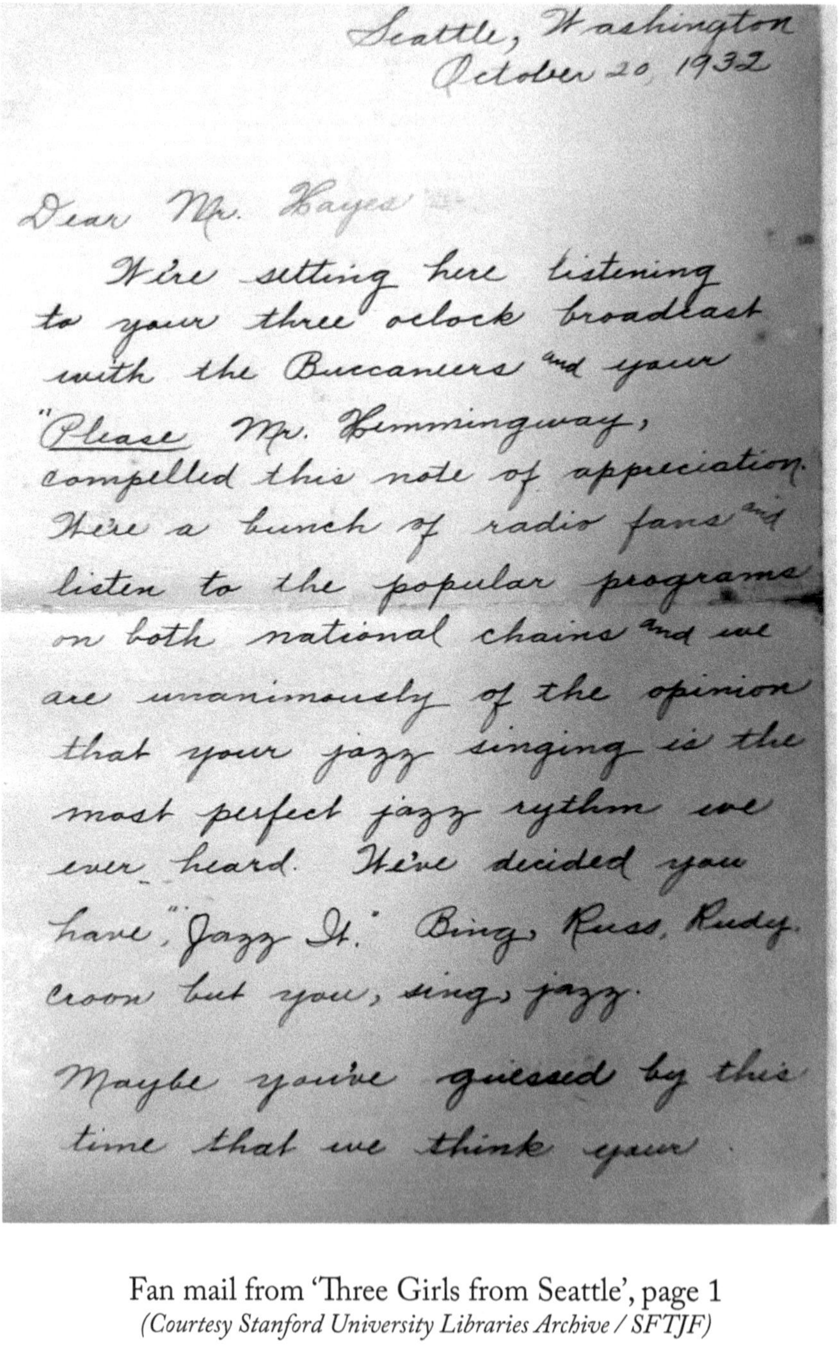

> Seattle, Washington
> October 20, 1932
>
> Dear Mr. Hayes
>
> We're setting here listening to your three o'clock broadcast with the Buccaneers and your "Please Mr. Hemmingway," compelled this note of appreciation. We're a bunch of radio fans and listen to the popular programs on both national chains and we are unanimously of the opinion that your jazz singing is the most perfect jazz rythm we ever heard. We've decided you have "Jazz It." Bing, Russ, Rudy, croon but you, sing, jazz.
>
> Maybe you've guessed by this time that we think your

Fan mail from 'Three Girls from Seattle', page 1
(Courtesy Stanford University Libraries Archive / SFTJF)

> "Good." Well you're exactly right. Will you sing, "When Uba Plays the Rumba On the Tuba," and, "Is I In Love I Is." sometime please.
>
> Thanks for the pleasure received,
>
> Sincerely Yours.
> Three Girls in Seattle.
>
> P.S. We're having fits over your "Goofus."
>
> M. A.

(A transcription of this letter is on page 308)

Fan mail from 'Three Girls from Seattle', page 2
(Courtesy Stanford University Libraries Archive / SFTJF)

In early October he travelled to Los Angeles to sing with Sid Lippman's Orchestra at the luxurious Cocoanut Grove nightclub within the Ambassador Hotel. This opulent and exclusive venue attracted the wealthy and showbiz celebrities who enjoyed its 'no cameras' policy (presumably the policy was dropped on the five occasions it hosted the Academy Awards Ceremony). The décor was based on exotic styles from across the world and included palm trees with mechanical monkeys complete with glowing amber eyes. Performing in such surroundings would have been an education for the now 25-year-old Clancy who had perhaps wanted a change of work and scenery, but his Los Angeles stay was not overly long. Whether this picture is from the Grove is uncertain, but if it was, it may have been a factor in Clancy's decision to swing northwards back to San Francisco and his radio career.

Clancy Hayes behind the moustache, unknown location
(Courtesy Frank Selman / SFTJF)

By July 1934 Clancy had returned to NBC to star in a daily 15-minute show where he was billed as the Morning Chanticleer. Presumably this kept evenings free so in August he was back at the Palace Hotel singing and broadcasting with the Bob Beale-Herb Taylor Orchestra. Clancy brought his Cocoanut Grove experience along and his excellent vocals in these band appearances were very much of the period, but it appears he hadn't completely given up on LA.

B. L. FRANK
MANAGER

PRIVATE OFFICE

THE AMBASSADOR
LOS ANGELES

October 26, 1934

Mr. Clarence Hayes,
2355 Bay Street,
San Francisco, Calif.

Dear Clarence:

I am in receipt of your letter of October 8th and must apologize for this tardy reply. However, during the past month I have been devoting practically all of my time to the liquor questions coming before the voters on November 6th and have neglected all other work. I realize that your letter required a prompt reply but so much work was needed to be done to defeat these proposed Local Option Laws that I felt it necessary to devote all possible time to it. If we are not successful in our efforts we may not need any band, as you can well realize.

Now regarding your band. It is impossible to consider it now, Clarence, as I am under contract for many months to come so could not use them in the Grove. So far as being interested in placing them outside the Grove, I just could not undertake this as running the Ambassador is about all I can manage. No doubt your band is all that you say it is but it is just impossible to consider it at this time.

With my kindest regards to you, I am

Sincerely yours,

Ben

BLF:H

(A transcription of this letter is on page 309)

Letter from Ambassador Hotel, Los Angeles.
(Courtesy Stanford University Libraries Archive / SFTJF)

The above letter may throw more light on Clancy's departure from Los Angeles — and perhaps a desire to return there in a different capacity. Later in this book there is debate about whether Clancy was attempting to form a band in the period 1946-48. This letter could influence the 'yes' camp for here we have evidence that in 1934

39

Clarence appears to be attempting to do exactly that. Sadly we don't have Clancy's letter of 8 October. However, Mr Frank's reply makes it clear he needed a prompt response to his offer to supply a band for the Ambassador Hotel — or another establishment if that was a possibility. In any case, it shows that in his mid-twenties Clancy was keen to operate a band, although a legal eye would possibly see reasonable doubt in the words 'your band'. Either way, wouldn't it be great to know how Clancy had sold the offer: 'No doubt your band is all that you say it is ...' As it turned out, Clancy's future lay in San Francisco for the next 24 years.

Marjorie Beattie sang duets with Clancy in the Palace Hotel broadcasts. Thankfully songs from the broadcasts including *Sweetie Pie / You're A Builder Upper / Dames** and *How's About Tomorrow Night** (*duets with Marjorie Beattie) survive.[2] These are the earliest available examples of Clancy's singing and the performances are wonderful; he deserved every cent of what appears to be a well-paid engagement.

Cheque from bandleader Bob Beale, September 1934
(Courtesy Stanford University Libraries Archive / SFTJF)

Clancy and Marjorie Beattie
(Courtesy Stanford University Libraries Archive / SFTJF)

During his life, Clancy's voice was given many descriptions. His first radio moniker 'The Voice of the South' could of course be challenged but I suppose the distance of about ten miles from Caney to the Oklahoma state line, plus artistic licence by the radio company, would make any challenge seem churlish. Certainly it was Clancy's spoken, as well as his singing voice, that seemed to make a big hit with his audience. Other names such as Pancake Boy were less flattering, but in fairness, the name came from the product and any discomfort Clancy had with the name was no doubt soothed by the free samples and fan mail. Names or descriptions didn't seem to put off Clancy's female fans, and there were lots of them. Whilst they were drawn by the charm of Clancy's voice through the radio loudspeaker, at least one fan was not disappointed when she saw young Clarence in the flesh as this undated letter from Phyllis Lee shows:

> Dear Mr Hayes,
> Probably you are bored by fan mail but I couldn't resist writing after visiting the studios.
> I've heard you sing over the radio often and have enjoyed it — and when I saw you the other day, I am happy to say I wasn't a bit disappointed.
> You see, I hesitated about visiting KPO for fear of being disillusioned.
> Before I close, would it be asking too much if you would send me a picture of yourself?
> I'd like to have something to take back with me to Santa Cruz, (I'm visiting here).
> Sincerely, Phyllis Lee

Sometimes fan mail would provide a reminder of Clancy's Kansas roots.

Hank Mingie's letter no doubt brought back happy memories:

Clancy Hayes publicity photo circa 1930
(Courtesy Frank Selman / SFTJF)

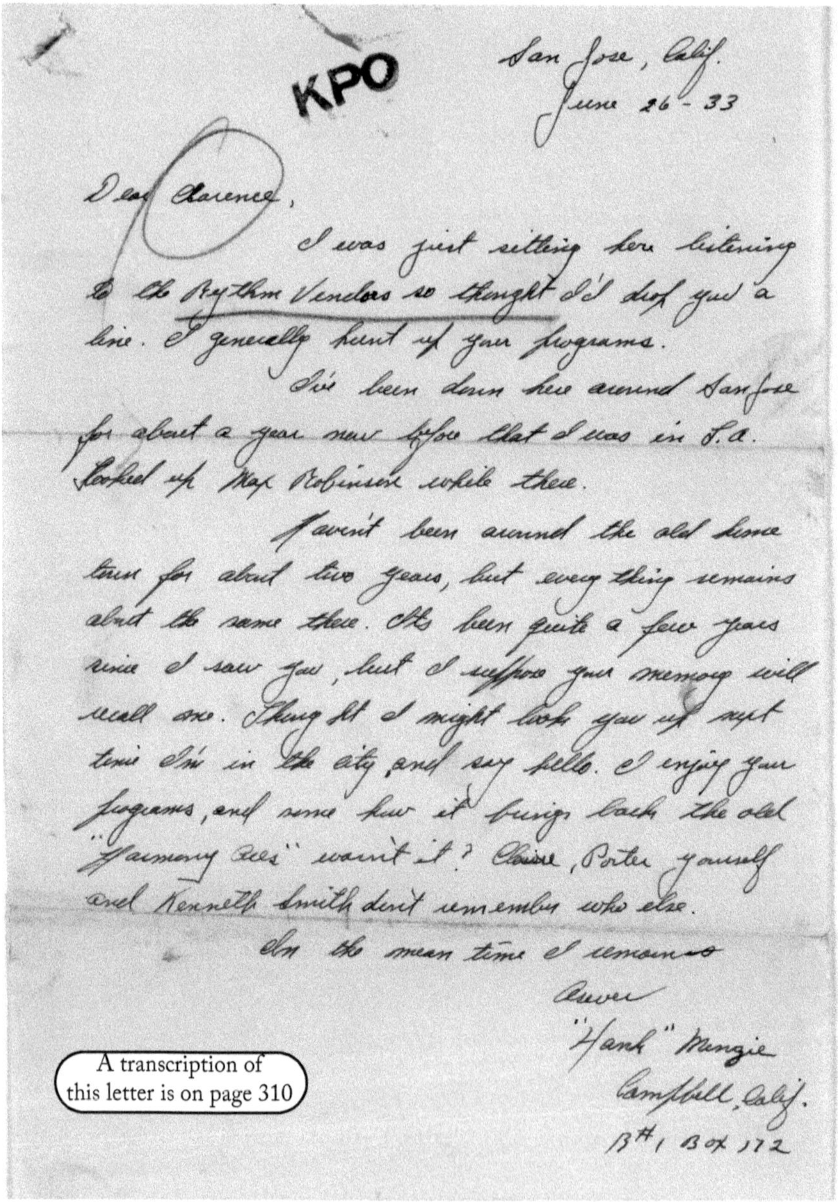

KPO

San Jose, Calif.
June 26 - 33

Dear Clarence,

I was just sitting here listening to the Rythm Vendors so thought I'd drop you a line. I generally hunt up your programs.

I've been down here around San Jose for about a year now before that I was in L.A. Looked up Max Robinson while there.

Haven't been around the old home town for about two years, but every thing remains about the same there. Its been quite a few years since I saw you, but I suppose your memory will recall me. Thought I might look you up next time I'm in the city and say hello. I enjoy your programs, and some how it brings back the old "Harmony Aces" wasn't it? Claire, Porter yourself and Kenneth Smith don't remember who else.

In the mean time I remain

Answer

"Hank" Mingie
Campbell, Calif.
R#1 Box 172

A transcription of this letter is on page 310

Letter from Hank Mingie
(Courtesy Stanford University Libraries Archive / SFTJF)

Letters from appreciative and satisfied sponsors were a real bonus. This letter also makes the point about the diversity of Clancy's material!

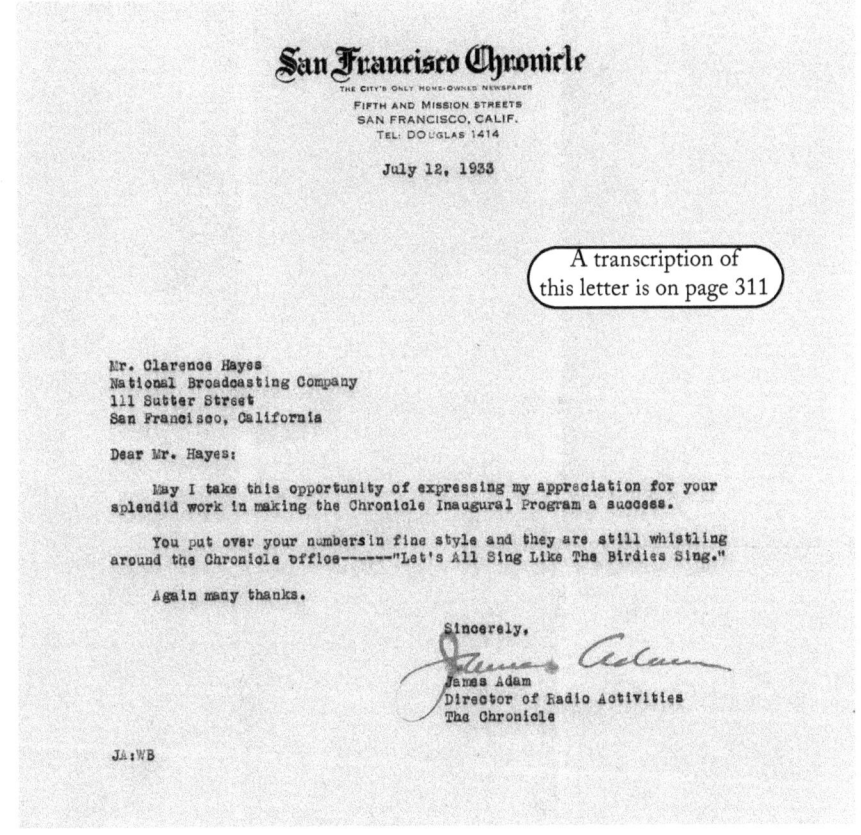

Thank you letter from San Francisco Chronicle
(Courtesy Stanford University Libraries Archive / SFTJF)

This fan letter starts with a slightly negative tone but all is well when one reads on. Miss Wickman is only 16 years old and ninety years later, Dorothy Wickman could not have been more wrong about the fate of her letter!

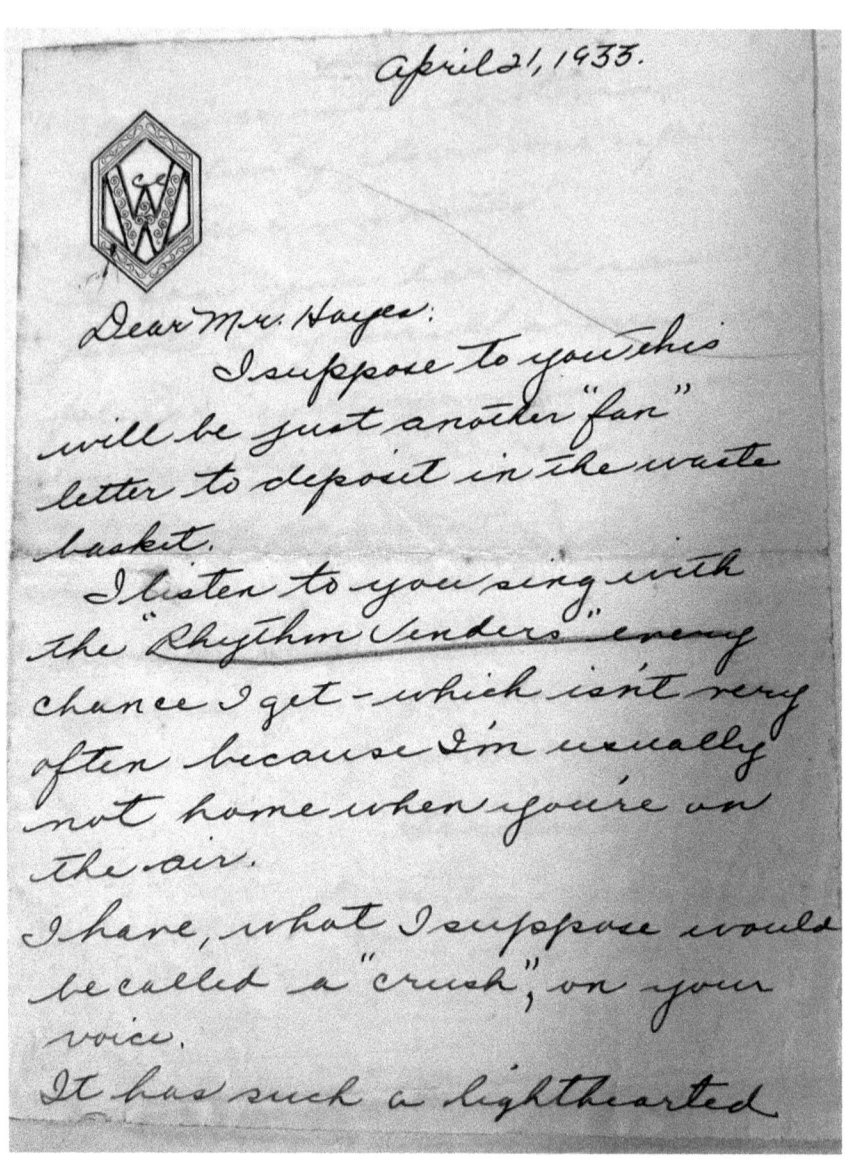

Fan mail
(Courtesy Stanford University Libraries Archive / SFTJF)

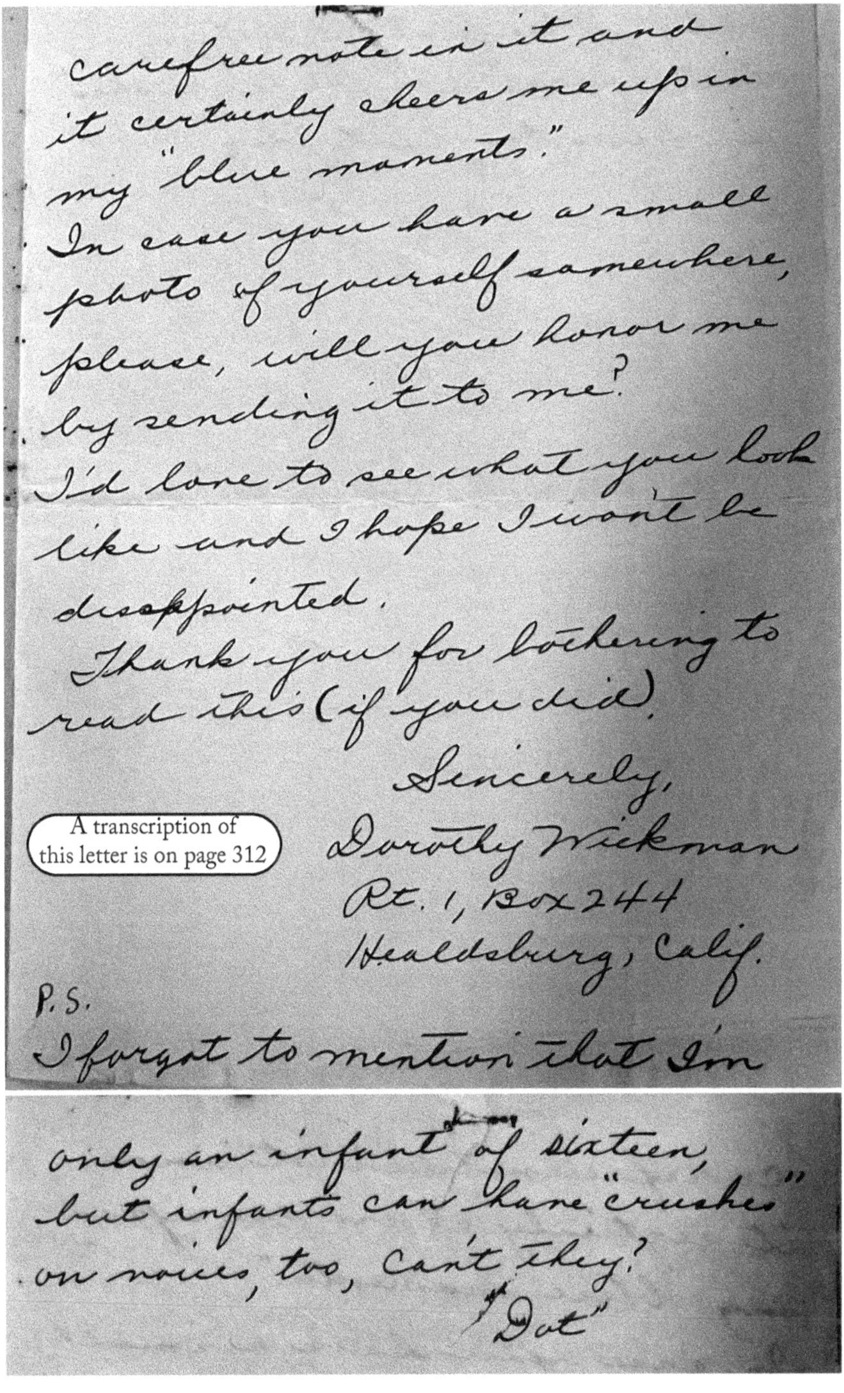

carefree note in it and it certainly cheers me up in my "blue moments."
In case you have a small photo of yourself somewhere, please, will you honor me by sending it to me? I'd love to see what you look like and I hope I won't be disappointed.
Thank you for bothering to read this (if you did).

Sincerely,
Dorothy Wickman
Rt. 1, Box 244
Healdsburg, Calif.

P.S. I forgot to mention that I'm only an infant of sixteen, but infants can have "crushes" on voices, too, can't they?

"Dot"

Here's another early letter from a couple of smitten misses:

(A transcription of this letter is on page 313)

Lodi, California

July 15, 1931

Mr. Clarence Hayes
Radio Station K.G.O.
Oakland, California

Dear Mr. Hayes:

My sister and I have been listening to your singing for quite some time. We never fail to tune in when the "Vagabonds" are on the air. We were certainly surprised to hear you sing with Jesse Stafford and his orchestra several months ago.

Mr. Hayes, do you appear on any other program besides with Mahlon Merrick and the "Vagabonds?" Another question, you play some instrument, do you not? We enjoy your singing so very much--maybe because it's such a different type of singing. "The Hour of Parting" is, at present, the number we would like to hear you repeat. Could you state a definite day when you could do this number for us? Maybe this is asking too much--how we hope it isn't!

One more favor, and that is, do you send out photographs of yourself to fans? We would appreciate it very much if you would send us any picture of yourself.

Two sincere admirers,

Misses Lena & Louise Lerza

Box 546

Lodi, California

Fan mail
(Courtesy Stanford University Libraries Archive / SFTJF)

The Hayes story takes on something of a mystery in 1935-36 as there is no specific reference to Clancy on any of the NBC shows, nor any other articles about him performing. Details of family gatherings in Santa Rosa were reported in the local press but nothing else. On 7 March 1936 Clancy appeared at the Santa Rosa Elks' Temple Dance as master of ceremonies, supporting brother Ashton.

The apparent radio silence was broken in May 1936 when the Hayes' name reappears together with John Wolfe in Jingle-Town Gazette airing over the NBC Pacific Coast Network. The 15-minute afternoon 'air newspaper' programme was set to a syncopated background and along with the news came harmonized singing. The broadcast on 7 August included *I'm Hatin' This Waiting Around / Tumbling Tumbleweeds / Carolina Moon* and *Moonrise on the Lowlands*. The show was highly successful and ran for the next two years.

In June 1936 Clancy and John Wolfe started another show called Songs and Patter — an early morning (7.45-8.00 am) weekday slot providing news and entertainment. First broadcast at the end of June, it ran for the remainder of the year with a name change towards the end simply to John Wolfe and Clarence Hayes. John Wolfe had originally been a businessman but apparently in 1932, when calling on a girlfriend, he found a guy named Ned Tollinger who had the same idea. Rather than *hit it out*, the two men *hit it off*. Somehow during the evening, they discovered they could sing harmony. Hearing their voices, the girl suggested the boys go 'into radio' — and they did. The partnership ended a couple of years later and in 1936 Mr Wolfe discovered his new partner.

In addition to these two regular shows, Clancy continued to appear as a guest in other broadcasts and specials. The get-up in this picture relates to a 1936 programme on station KFI which featured Clancy on banjo and vocal as one of the 'Sailors with Saylors' along with John Wolfe.

Clancy and John Wolfe
(Courtesy Stanford University Libraries Archive / SFTJF)

On 12 August Clancy appeared on the Women's Radio Review and on 28 August in Bughouse Rhythm in which he is credited with delivering the world premiere of the song *Hector The Garbage Collector*. Sadly there is no trace of Clancy's rendition, but *Hecto*r didn't disappear, resurfacing a couple of years later and providing a big hit for Jerry Colonna. In December Clancy was featured in a new NBC-Red network show Care Free Carnival, a late-night half-hour programme aimed at 'fading away the cares of the day'.

Clancy continued with Jingle-Town Gazette in 1937 and in August featured in a new regular 15-minute show String Along. Another of the specials included a performance on the Old Ranger Show on 26 October which previewed the dedication of the Mount Whitney-Death Valley Highway, linking the highest and lowest points in the USA. November saw a series of 15-minute morning broadcasts sponsored by Oxo billed simply as Clarence Hayes, for by now the audience knew exactly what to expect. The Oxo shows continued into 1938 along with Jingle-Town Gazette. In addition Clancy did some straight reporting. On 5 February he and Saunders King joined Jack Meakin's transcontinental broadcast about 'seeing eye' dogs.

Despite Clancy's busy radio schedule, by the mid to late 1930s something was stirring in the Bay Area that captured his interest and talent. Whilst his association with the airwaves would continue for the whole of the next decade, a parallel career in Jazz was about to begin.

3

The Radio Years Part Two 1939 -1950

This chapter concentrates on the high spots of the second period of Clancy's radio career from 1939 through to 1950 when he would leave the airwaves to concentrate on a full-time jazz career. The transition was eased as throughout these years Clancy led a double life with both radio work and involving himself in the Great San Francisco Jazz Revival. He also turned his hand to composing songs and jingles as well as taking on several other musical assignments. Clancy's extra-curricular activities are covered in Chapter 4.

Clancy and John Wolfe
(Courtesy Stanford University Libraries Archive / SFTJF)

Clancy's radio shows in 1939 continued with the Jingle Town Gazette and in May came a new NBC Blue networked programme covering 24 states — Dancing with Clancy. The half-hour broadcast went out between 11-11.30 pm on most stations and ran through the summer, closing in September. As always, radio was focused on advertising income. *Variety* magazine published the advertising revenue of the major networks and the June 1939 edition carried an article on a return by advertisers to sign up 'name bands' to promote their products following an unexplained lull. That summer, twenty-five regular radio programmes featuring nationally known bands were scheduled, including Paul Whiteman (*Chesterfield*), Tommy Dorsey (*Raleigh*), Artie Shaw (*Old Gold*) and Benny Goodman (*Camel*) —these sponsors were all cigarette brands. The networks also had their own orchestra, and Clancy spent the summer of 1939 encouraging people to dance.

After temporarily putting away his 'dancing shoes', Clancy embarked upon a new programme that aired over NBC for two years — with occasional reruns into the mid-1940s. The Tune Termites show was remarkable as it was presented in rhyme — a format borrowed from the minstrel shows of the previous century. Equally remarkable, the show was made by just two people: Clancy and pianist Glen Hurlburt (Musical Director at NBC in 1937; on the Glen Hurlburt and his Music programmes he performed tangos and rumbas — his specialty).

The weekly Tune Termites shows, averaging 10-15 minutes in length, were first broadcast on 22 October from NBC's station KGO in San Francisco to stations in Arizona, Nevada, Washington State, British Columbia and other cities in California. Thankfully, a few sketches from the Tune Termites, as well as songs and dialogue, were preserved in his private tape collection. Each track includes introductory rhyming patter by the termite characters Tommy and Tilford (both voiced by Clancy), followed by his vocal. A few of the songs that still exist are *I Can't Remember To Forget / I Want To Live* and *Ziz-Zizzy-Zum-Zum*.[1] The first series ended on 24 December 1940. Such was the appeal of the show that Clancy made personal appearances at the 1940 San Francisco World's Fair billed as a Tune Termite and on 14 May, when he visited the KSRA radio station in Santa Rosa the press headline read: '*Tune Termite here to visit folks*'. A second series followed in April, 1941, continuing for the rest of the year.

NBC Identification card, 1941
(Courtesy Stanford University Libraries Archive / SFTJF)

Also in April, Dancing with Clancy recommenced airing late at night throughout the year. Yet another weekly programme, Clancy and his Orchestra launched in the same month and broadcast from 6 to 6:30 pm to western and midwestern states for the remainder of 1941. Sadly, to date no surviving broadcasts or newspaper reviews have come to light. Dancing with Clancy was referenced in an advertisement for the Lu Watters' Orchestra playing at Redwood City on 9 August 1941, with Mr Hayes as an added attraction.

The audience's familiarity had seen his billing change from Clarence Hayes to Clancy Hayes and finally, simply Clancy. And so in 1942, in his sixteenth year at NBC, a 15-minute programme entitled Clancy Calling aired on weekdays from October to December. He also featured as vocalist on other NBC programmes including the Bonnie Walker and Phil Bovero shows. In his parallel jazz activities Clancy was heard on station KYA's broadcasts of Lu Watters' Yerba Buena Jazz Band from the Dawn Club in San Francisco. While there is no trace of the NBC programmes from this era, there are some wonderful recordings of the Dawn Club broadcasts. Jazz fans would sit at the ready with home recording equipment to capture the exciting new music coming through their radios from 11–11:30 pm on Friday nights.[2]

In 1943, a twice-weekly show entitled Clancy's Music premiered along with other 10-15 minute programmes simply called Clancy Hayes or Songs by Clancy Hayes. In addition, 'Clancy and his Dixieland Band' were appearing in the Stage Door Canteen Show for servicemen at the refurbished Native Sons Hall on Mason Street, San Francisco. The rehearsal, running from 2-11 pm on 28 April, was open to the public as a 'package party'; the required package being a food parcel (or a one-dollar contribution). This was the only chance for civilians to see the show apart from a single 'angels' table which could be bought for an evening. The event provides a sad reminder that there was of course a war going on and entertainers were keen to donate their services in support of U.S. Armed Forces personnel. Stars on hand for the San Francisco opening event included Eddie Cantor, Yehudi Menuhin, Kay Kyser and Boris Karloff. Music was provided by Phil Sapiro, Glen Hurlburt, Dude Martin and Clancy's Dixieland Band.[3] Less successful was a performance at an unnamed jazz club a few days earlier when it was reported that, 'Clancy Hayes and his so called Down Home Jazz turned out to be a bit too homey for the local jazz hounds'. The unflattering report explained that the Dixielanders exited backstage, gig over.[4] If you don't succeed the first time…

Armed Forces Volunteer Card
(Courtesy Julia Carroll and Dom Adinolfi)

Left to Right: Sonia Shaw, Clancy, Archie Persby,
Burt Bales at the piano
(Courtesy Frank Selman / SFTJF)

In 1944 the weekly Remember Hour starred Clancy as emcee and vocalist. The programme suited his musical tastes very well. The 11 June broadcast featured Clancy and Sonia Shaw singing songs from 1927-28 with Phil Bovero's Orchestra. Other shows offered more up to date numbers, such as the 17 September broadcast when Clancy sang *East Of The Sun* and *Alone Together*. (Governor Ronald Reagan, fondly recalled Remember Hour when he sent a good will message to Clancy in 1970. This letter is reproduced on page 256). Other 1944 broadcasts included Clancy's Music aired in January and February and the Tune Termite shows were broadcast weekly on California and Washington stations during March and April.

Clancy with unknown Hawaiian band
(Courtesy Stanford University Libraries Archive / SFTJF)

Tight budgets based on advertising income, and possibly personnel shortages due to the war, meant that in some shows Clancy played all parts; he had a remarkable ability to switch dialogue and seamlessly break into song. In the 1945 KGO weekly Bob Sheridan shows, sponsored by Mother's Cakes and Cookies, he played three roles supported by piano accompaniment on the vocals. The characters comprised the eponymous eccentric Englishman with a wonderfully exaggerated 'upper class' accent, a cartoon comedy voice and a superb vocalist. Despite the show being light-hearted and comical — almost zany — things change dramatically whenever Clancy sings; it is spellbinding. We are fortunate that one of the 15-minute shows has survived.[5] An example of the zany dialogue is at the end of this chapter.

Clancy's career advanced further in 1945 when he became the Musical Director at KGO. Luckily, an episode of Swinging on the Golden Gate, a weekly programme featuring The Clancy Hayes Orchestra, is preserved. The show is upbeat, entertaining and contains excellent music — particularly *My Dearest Darling*, *Martha* and *Lucky To Be Me*, which were sung by Clancy with the orchestra. Another song, *It's Never Too Late to Pray*, was performed by the entire cast. [6]

Mother's Cookies
(Newspaper advertisement)

Clancy with orchestra, Phil Bovero is holding the clarinet
(Courtesy of Frank Selman / SFTJF)

The Clancy Hayes Orchestra and Bob Sheridan broadcasts continued into the spring of 1946 but thereafter Clancy's prominence on the NBC network significantly diminished. However, just before his radio silence, Clancy directed the orchestra on the Jack Webb Comedy Show (a pre-Dragnet outing) standing in for regular host Phil Bovero. In the 17 April broadcast titled Slim Slade, Western Bandleader, Clancy was introduced as follows, '*That spiritual singer Clancy Hayes will conduct his usual contest with the Orchestra.*' He wins the contest and also delivers a good vocal on *My Baby Just Cares For Me*.[7]

It is likely that Clancy's absence from the airwaves was due to his greater involvement in jazz bands, making records and composing songs and radio jingles. His 1946 composition *Huggin' And A Chalkin'* became a big hit, reaching #23 on the Billboard top 100 and no doubt he was keen to have another hit song. There is also a theory, examined in the next chapter, that he may also have been working on forming his own jazz band. Private tapes certainly seem to suggest this as a strong possibility. In February 1947 Clancy made a guest appearance at the opening of the Stanroy Music Centre on Fourth Street in Santa Rosa: '*In Person — Clancy Hayes — composer of Huggin' And A Chalkin' and NBC radio star*'. The store had Clancy's record for sale which he would be happy to autograph. I am sorry to say I have never come across a signed copy of this Pacific 78.

The only specific radio mention of Clancy in 1947 is as part of an NBC special Power Premier, which was broadcast coast to coast on Monday 1 December and then throughout the week to mark the launch of KGO's new 50,000-watt transmitter. Such was the auspicious nature of the event that California Governor Earl Warren flicked the switch at 9.50 am. Immediately, the original 7,500-watt unit (installed in January 1924) was retired. The new transmitter promised to provide better sound quality, less interference and greater coverage. Power Premier featured Clancy as one of three vocalists accompanied by Phil Bovero's Orchestra; the show also included greetings from Bing Crosby.

In 1947 there was unwelcome press coverage resulting from a suit brought against Clancy by his former NBC partner, John Wolfe. Wolfe contested that he was the co-composer of *Huggin' And A Chalkin'* and was seeking $50,000 in damages, plus future royalties. Wolfe claimed to have written the song with Clancy in the spring of 1945 and that it was he who had suggested doing a song about a fat girl. Whether this was a genuine suit, or a magnificent piece of promotion is not known.

However, as the saying goes, *'there is no such thing as bad publicity'*. Headline writers had a ball with variations on the theme of *'Wolfe takes a bite out of the fat girl'*. Although the lawsuit was reported across the USA, there is no mention of the outcome. If the lawsuit had been heard in court, the defendant could have produced his 1942 private acetate — virtually the same song — in his defence.

Clancy returned to radio prominence in 1948, featured on an excellent series of broadcasts sponsored by the Standard Oil Company of California. The shows had made their debut in 1928, with one series devoted to popular music and a second to classical. Originally conceived as programmes for children, the commercial-free broadcasts attracted listeners of all ages and were eventually carried by affiliate stations throughout the west.

Each show incorporated music from around the world to illustrate culture, history and geography. Clancy was engaged to appear in six programmes in the role of Jack of All Tunes, co-starring with Jack Cahill as Matt the Mapmaker. These episodes were based on an imaginary tour around the United States using various forms of transport. The first programme included songs about the legendary railroad engineer Casey Jones; other shows covered travel by foot, donkey, wagon train and boat.

In 1949 and 1950, Clancy's appearances on a further series of Standard Oil broadcasts revolved around the theme of famous Americans and American cities. Individual shows focused on the music of New York, Hollywood, Chicago, New Orleans and others. Once again Jack and Matt anchored the programme with Jack delivering one or more vocals on nine of the shows. Musical Director Carmen Dragon was responsible for providing most of the excellent music and John Grover was narrator. Each programme is informative and entertaining, with a wide variety of musical styles. Songs featuring Clancy's vocals include *At Pierrot's Door / Kentucky Babe / Ta Ra Ra Boom De Ay / Chicago / Laura / Some Enchanted Evening / The Yodel Blues / Baby, It's Cold Outside* and *Dixie*.[8]

One particularly noteworthy programme, simply titled Music Map of America, focuses on New Orleans. No doubt Clancy got a real thrill admitting that he was both the announcer *and* a fan in this show. Leading the demonstration of New Orleans music is Louis Armstrong and his band. In a private tape recording of the music for the programme, Clancy fluffs the introduction; caught off guard by an unscripted question as to what 'cats' (the musical variety) are? In response, he explains they are the ones who *'make the jump joint'*. His trademark aplomb shone through, making a joke at his own expense and then introducing the musicians who play a set to define New Orleans jazz. Armstrong's regular clarinettist Barney Bigard, bassist Arvell Shaw and drummer Sid Catlett did not appear on the broadcast. Lyle Johnson is credited with the clarinet work and the bassist and drummer remain 'unknown'. Clancy recalled later that he played guitar on some numbers, though the instrument is difficult to hear. Still, to be in the studio with such musicians must have been a real treat.

Although a total of nine tunes were recorded, the broadcast (#19 in the series) only contained five tracks. At the beginning of the programme, Jack and Matt arrive in New Orleans during Carnival season. They hear a band playing *Waiting For The Robert E. Lee*. Jack begins to sing and Matt, full of excitement, joins in too! While walking through the city they encounter a Juba dance and a helpful local (Mr Banjo) explains the dance to them. With their new acquaintance they move on to the French Market. As they walk, Mr Banjo tells them about the history of the city including slavery and drainage problems. 'Many of the streets were built with open canals running down the middle of the boulevard', he explains.

Next, they encounter a carnival parade. As they follow the parade, they are given advice on which New Orleans cuisine to try (crawfish, gumbo, jambalaya). When they reach Basin Street, Jack and Matt enter a club where Louis and His All Stars are playing *Up A Lazy River*. Jack introduces Matt to Louis, Jack Teagarden and Earl Fatha Hines and persuades them to play *Do You Know What It Means To Miss New Orleans / Back O' Town Blues* and *Struttin' With Some Barbecue*. The programme fades out with the band playing *Boogie Woogie on St. Louis Blues*. Other (non-Louis) music in the early part of the show includes *African American Symphony / Juba Dance / Dark Dancers Of The Mardi Gras* and *Dance In Place Congo*. [9]

Clancy Hayes was certainly a man of many parts. Towards the end of his NBC career he appeared in a comedic role — on the Candy Matson Show. In an episode titled Valley Of The Moon, he portrays 'Jess' a shady bartender working on a ranch. Clancy's character voice could pass for that of a young John Wayne (though on radio it is not possible to tell whether he could also mimic Wayne's famous way of walking).

Clancy never spoke about the end of his career as a radio performer. There are several factors that may have led to his departure from the airwaves. Tape recording allowed radio stations to pre-record programmes rather than dealing with the expense of live broadcasts and employing staff musicians. Changing public tastes and the advent of television as the primary source of entertainment may have affected revenue? Or perhaps, at the age of 42, Clancy just wanted to play and sing jazz instead of spending his days in the studio. Whatever the reason, the Standard Oil programmes were Clancy's last major radio appearance and his time would now be focused on other creative activities.

Mother's Cakes and Cookies Dialogue

To give an idea of the stark contrast between the zany dialogue and wonderful singing, here is an excerpt from the programme: The nonsense dialogue — all voiced by Clancy - ran as follows:

> **Bob Sheridan**: Here we go, Mothers. And now Mother's Cakes and Cookies bring you music for mothers with Bob Sheridan singing the songs mothers love (piano arpeggio). That's right, mothers, it's Tuesday afternoon and this is Bob Sheridan dusting the cookie crumbs off the old piano while the little green men clamber around inside the mailbag to see what we've got in the way of songs and letters for today.
>
> Here comes one of them now running over here with a card all the way up from Seaside. Yes, it's from young Mr Bobby Wetzel to ask, 'Please could I sing a song for his mum'. You just bet I will. The one he chose for her is the same one that's a very special favourite with Mrs. Betty Keeler up there in Sebastopol. (There follows a superb vocal on *If I Didn't Care*).

Bob Sheridan: Ah hah Mothers, it's that little man with the lavender moustache speaking shyly at us from 'round the end of the piano. When we ask him what he wants he just raises his lavender eyebrows and cries out… (bugle call played on the piano).

Cartoon comedy voice advertisement: If you enjoy the good things in life, you'll really go for Mother's vanity cream sandwiches. Yep, they got real eye appeal as well as appetite appeal, delicate designs and that golden brown goodness. Look for Mother's delicious vanity cream sandwiches at your grocers today.

Bob Sheridan: Having said which the little bashful man disappears behind the piano once more and right about here I am going to drop in next door in Daly City and help Mrs Audrey Cove serenade her mother, Mrs Kerr. We have a song especially in her honour. Here for Mrs Kerr from Audrey is *I'll Close My Eyes*.

Clancy delivers the song in real style and the preceding nonsense is immediately forgotten. The programme continues in similar style and Clancy sings *I Love You Truly*, but this time his delivery has some comical interjections, including singing in the corny announcer voice.

Photographs

Bill, Ann and Clancy c.1946
(Courtesy Stanford University Libraries Archive / SFTJF)

Bill Hayes
(Courtesy Julia Carroll and Dom Adinolfi)

Ann and Clancy
(Courtesy Stanford University Libraries Archive / SFTJF)

Clancy, c. 1946
(Courtesy Stanford University Libraries Archive / SFTJF)

4

The Call Of Jazz

The story of the musicians who launched the 'Great Jazz Revival' in the 1940s has been told many times. While the major driving force was the music itself, a collateral benefit for the musicians was the lure of escaping the nightly grind of playing arranged Swing and dance music in touring and hotel bands. Swing had dominated popular music from the early 1930s and orchestras such as Artie Shaw, Glenn Miller and Benny Goodman influenced what the public wanted, and expected, to hear. Black bands, such as those of Duke Ellington and Count Basie, played sophisticated, arranged music far removed from the jazz of the 1920s and early 1930s. Virtually no-one played in the original jazz style; commercially the music was to all intents and purposes dead. Even in its birthplace the music was almost silent. Lu Watters recalled in a 1976 interview with Rusty Stiers and others, that when he visited New Orleans in 1932 with Carol Lofner's Orchestra, no commercial New Orleans jazz bands were playing - only casual gigs existed.[1]

Apart from the potential musical frustration of Swing, travelling bands had to suffer long journeys in ill-equipped buses, second rate hotels and dangers which detracted from the potential fun in playing music professionally. As an example, Minneapolis band leader Red Sievers and five band members were killed returning home from a one-night gig in Iowa on the morning of 16 October 1941. Homeward bound from Marshaltown — 500 miles away — they were sideswiped in fog by a cattle truck.

Equally tedious, if less dangerous, was life for the musicians playing in the many 'Taxi Dances' or 'Dime Jigs' (also known as 'Dime Grinds'). These activities were immortalised in Rodgers and Hart's 1930 song *Ten Cents A Dance*. Musicians at dancing joints played one-minute versions of popular tunes to maximise the flow of tickets. While these engagements may have been musically unsatisfying, at least it was regular employment during the Great Depression.

Dime Jigs are an interesting part of American cultural history and, unsurprisingly, opinion was divided on their merits. *'The dance hall situation in Oakland is worse than any other large city,'* wrote Reverend Charles A. Wells of the 23rd Ave. Baptist Church in early June 1930. The dime dances were seen as a sordid relic of the past when there was little law to govern the relationships of men in the lawless West. On the plus side, they of course provided work for the hostesses, musicians and the floor man and they were popular with the patrons — most of the time. In June 1930 dancer Clara Hanks, aka Clara Nelson, of the Oakland Taxi Dance Hall, was seemingly on more than 'Charleston' terms with an industrialist, and relieved him of cheques worth $17,521.[2]

But not all Taxi dance sessions were lowbrow. On 16 October 1931 a group of enterprising female students at Stanford University Pi Beta Phi sorority held a 'Depression Dance' offering dances to 'Jazz Music' at ten cents. It was their effort to combat the lack of dates being offered due to the low economic status of the male students. There is no mention of the timings of the dances but let's hope the jazz tunes lasted a little longer than sixty seconds!

After studying Taxi Dances for several years, Paul Cressey, sociologist at the University of Chicago, concluded that Taxi Dances served a legitimate need. Equally it was clear that some were fields for commerce in sex, a hideaway for runaway girls and a haven for fugitives from justice. The girls were required to dance with anyone presenting a ticket; proceeds being theoretically split evenly with the hall operator. Although he denounced Taxi dance halls, Mr Cressey believed that, if allowed under proper regulation, they were an alternative to even less wholesome associations. He felt that if proprietors co-operated with social agencies to provide supervision, dance halls could fill an honest human need in the lives of lonely men. As the song says, *'Hear that floor man yelling move your feet'*. The task for the musicians was to provide non-stop music; individuals left the stand for short breaks but to quote another song, *'the band played on'*. Provided the dance hall used Union musicians they were paid reasonably, but the tedium in condensing the hits of the day into an endless stream of one-minute tunes required an antidote.

To relieve the monotony of playing arranged Swing music and sixty-second tunes, a small group of Bay Area musicians got together to play jazz from the classics era. After-hours they assembled at the Big Bear Roadhouse in Redwood Canyon, seventeen miles from Oakland. Here they played the music of King Oliver, Jelly Roll Morton and Louis Armstrong's hot bands along with more obscure original jazz numbers unearthed by the record and sheet music hunters in their midst. Pete Clute, musician, writer and club owner explained to Dave Radlauer in a 1998 interview: [3]:

> They used to go up to a place called the Big Bear which was in the Oakland Hills, and they'd go up there and just practice. Both [Lu] Watters and Turk [Murphy] were tired of playing in bands that were just jam sessions so they attempted to put together a band that would have more than one strain — that would have two, three and sometimes even four strains and they would woodshed 'em and learn to play them up at the Big Bear Tavern. Clancy would come up there; the sessions would start late in the night and Clancy would come up after his radio shows and they'd have a jam session but a more organized one and usually with the same people all the time. That's where Wally (Rose) started out with the Watters band and Clancy was there, and Turk.

Clancy had got to know the local musicians with jazz interests through his many contacts via the radio station. Pete Clute explained 'Clancy loved, and had an affinity for, the music of the South and that fitted right in with what Watters and Turk were trying to do'. Having him on board had another benefit, Clute continued, 'Clancy was the one that brought some notoriety to Watters and the band; he was a radio personality and it was good to have him with the band. It opened-up doors.'

Big Bear session late 1930s: Left to right: Wally Rose, Clancy, Turk Murphy, Lu Watters, Bill Dart, Bob Scobey, Ellis Horne
(Courtesy Stanford University Libraries Archive / SFTJF)

The Big Bear was a colourful place. The remote location gave it a special atmosphere that the musicians no doubt enjoyed as they were able to play through the night after arriving in the early hours from their paying jobs. However, the Big Bear also attracted *less* artistically minded patrons. It was reported that on a cold evening in late January 1938 a young lady and three male youths intent on 'whooping it up' entered the Big Bear. With a touch of old wild-west charm, the Christy twins, twenty-five and Jack Remers, twenty-one, had thoughtfully brought along plenty of their own bottled beer. When bartender Manuel Smith pointed out that beer could actually be purchased from the bar the youths poured their beer on the bar and demanded whisky. Mr Smith's polite refusal was met with a well-aimed bottle flying through the air and making a direct hit on the unfortunate barman. With further wild-west flavour, four cow-punchers seated in the tap room leapt into action and a general fight broke out. Also enjoying a quiet drink, up to that moment at least, was Roy Linderman, a special officer employed by the Tom King Detective Agency. To calm matters, Mr Linderman shot one of the three young men in the arm. When the sawdust had settled the young lady in the dudes' company, a Miss Dimny Long, gave a different version of events explaining that 'when they quietly and peacefully entered the bar they had been attacked'. [4]

Disappointingly, the story has no mention of hot jazz music nor is there any indication that this event was the muse for Lu Watters' *Big Bear Stomp*. Undaunted by such distractions, the Big Bear remained the musicians' after-hours venue of choice; and so began the nucleus of the Great Jazz Revival.

Other musicians who braved the Big Bear included Burt Bales, Paul Lingle, Bob Scobey, Bob Helm, Gordon Edwards, Bill Dart, Don Noakes and Dick Lammi. Lu Watters was a brilliant musician who played and arranged for five years with Carol Lofner's Orchestra. Such was his talent he had also arranged for Bing Crosby. Watters emerged as the key individual to lead the Great Jazz Revival in San Francisco.

In 1938 Watters secured a gig at Sweet's Ballroom in Oakland to provide a twelve-piece house band; Sweet's also featured big name visiting bands including Duke Ellington, Count Basie and Louis Armstrong. Although brothers William and Eugene Sweet expected their house band to play popular tunes of the day and dance tempos, they may have been only partially satisfied by Watters' orchestra. Lu could not resist including jazz tunes in the repertoire and confessed to slipping two jazz tunes into each set of six numbers. For the jazz tunes an eight-piece two trumpet formation was used, cunningly disguised by using the full band in the final chorus to keep the Sweet brothers happy. The Lu Watters' Sweet's Ballroom Orchestra included Bob Scobey, Turk Murphy, Bob Helm, Henry Abrahamson, Bus Greene and Clancy.[5] Despite the brothers' reservations, the patrons liked — and danced to — the jazz numbers. Tunes like *Copenhagen* and *Shake That Thing* were unknown to most of the crowd, but they got the message. In a 1993 interview [6] reed player Bob Helm recalled that the brothers were always asking Lu to tone it down to avoid the dancers getting overexcited, urging him to play more waltzes and 'moonbeam tunes' towards the end of the evening. However the band was successful, the ballroom was full and for the time being things were looking rosy.

Musical differences did not end the band's run at Sweet's Ballroom; unfortunately they fell foul to a combination of over-exuberance and a live microphone at a rehearsal. Bob Helm explained, 'We were engaging in all kinds of fantasies, as we thought we were talking privately — some alluded to them [the Sweet brothers]'. Unfortunately, the live microphone relayed everything straight to the office, the conversation was not private at all. 'The Sweet brothers took offence,' Helm continued. 'We didn't work there long after that. It wasn't because the band wasn't a success; we were a little too wild, I guess.' Thankfully, band member Henry Abrahamson managed to capture the brilliance of the orchestra with his home recording machine at an afternoon rehearsal.[7]

The Sweet's Ballroom exit provided the impetus for Lu Watters to break away from a twelve-piece orchestra and fulfill his wish to move to a smaller, King Oliver style jazz band. Lu also wanted to move away from tunes of the day and have more freedom in the choice of music. He thus turned down a lucrative offer to put his orchestra into the Palace Hotel on Market Street. Ironically, he ended up playing in a club in the alley beside the Palace. Bob Helm recalled;

> Lu decided he didn't want to continue with a big band. It was too confining to play the same way, the same tunes in the same manner and as a consequence everybody would suffer from the usual boredom that comes from playing stock arrangements and even very good specials nightly. He recruited some old friends and that was the start of the Yerba Buena band which started about 1938 after the end of the Sweet's Ballroom Band.

Bob Helm also stated that for the first Yerba Buena Jazz Band rehearsal Lu's 'old friends' included himself on reeds, Paul Lingle, piano; Squire Girsback, bass and Bill Dart, drums.

Jazz at the Dawn Club
(Courtesy Stanford University Libraries Archive / SFTJF)

Tickets for Ernie Lewis and Lu Watters at the Dawn Club 1941
(Courtesy Stanford University Libraries Archive / SFTJF)

One of the problems facing the newly formed band was audience unfamiliarity with the older material in their repertoire. A small group of jazz fans had formed the Hot Jazz Society of San Francisco and its members knew the music well, but not the general public. Now playing at the Dawn Club on Annie Street, San Francisco the band's popularity grew and a more general crowd came along. Bob Helm:

We didn't have much of a problem when we played for the jazz society because its members were mostly people who were acquainted with the music and the tunes; but when we started the full-time date at the Dawn Club a lot of the people enjoyed the music but didn't know what tunes to ask for. So as a result they were left with the band on the bandstand trying to answer questions — 'What was that tune you guys played last Tuesday evening?' So we devised a method of sort of dealing with this; we went to a programme of music like a string quartet and salon groups used. We passed out a programme at the door of the five sets we would play in the evening. Turk or Harry Mordecai* also had a flash card stand and instead of putting up 'Foxtrot', 'Waltz' or 'Two Step' they would be flashing the name of the tune. It helped so much that some people requested it and when the band moved to Hambone Kelly's we used the mirror back of the front bar for the repertoire of the whole band library, so that made a big difference too...

[* Bob Helm may have been mistaken, as Harry Mordecai didn't play with the band until 1946]

Clancy's involvement with the music and musicians of the 1940s Great Jazz Revival — and in particular the Yerba Buena Jazz Band — was restricted by his full-time radio work. As such, he was an occasional rather than permanent member of what was now Lu Watters' Yerba Buena Jazz Band. However, importantly he was present for the YBJB's historic first recording session for Jazz Man records on 19 December 1941. These records would spread the seeds of a Jazz Revival around the globe. As Pete Clute noted previously, Clancy's participation was an added attraction because of his radio fame. In the early days, the other musicians in the YBJB were largely unknown outside of the small circle of jazz fans. When the Lu Watters' Orchestra played at Redwood City's Recreational Center in the summer of 1941, the billing highlighted their two widely known vocalists, 'Patsy Parker (a throaty blues singer who has sung with Harry James, Ted Weems and George Olsen) and Clarence Hayes (NBC baritone heard daily over stations KGO and KPO)'.

Lu Watters' Yerba Buena Jazz Band, Dawn Club San Francisco c.1940. Left to Right: Bill Dart, Wally Rose, Turk Murphy, Bob Scobey, Lu Watters, Ellis Horne.
(Courtesy Stanford University Libraries Archive / SFTJF)

One of the stranger aspects of Clancy's involvement with the band is that their first and second recording sessions for Jazz Man records in 1941 and 1942 contained no vocals, despite the fact that Clancy always sang when the band performed live. The mystery is solved by Cary Ginell in his superb book *Hot Jazz for Sale* [8] telling the story of Hollywood's Jazz Man record shop (1940-84) and its six colourful owners. Founder Dave Stuart was a purist of early jazz and didn't want any vocals on the first issues of his Jazz Man label formed specifically to record the band. His no vocal decree was reinforced by the fact that he was also not a fan of the Hayes voice. So strong were Mr Stuart's convictions about jazz, he flatly refused to sell Swing records despite the obvious impact on the bottom line.

Lu had adopted a King Oliver style line up but added an extra banjo for good measure and a tuba replaced the string bass. The musicians on the historic 19 December 1941 recordings were Lu Watters, Leader and cornet; Bob Scobey, trumpet; Turk Murphy, trombone; Ellis Horne, clarinet; Wally Rose, piano; Russ Bennett and Clancy Hayes, banjos; Dick Lammi, tuba; Bill Dart, drums.

Lu Watters' Yerba Buena Jazz Band at the Dawn Club c.1941
Left to Right: Wally Rose, Turk Murphy, Bob Scobey, Lu Watters, Clancy Hayes, Dick Lammi, Ellis Horne, Bill Dart.
(Courtesy Hal Smith)

Having made their first recordings just twelve days after the attack on Pearl Harbor, the young men of the Yerba Buena Jazz Band were soon caught up in the Second World War. Lu and several others joined the Navy. Those not on active service, or enlisted bandsmen like Turk Murphy who was stationed in the Bay Area, participated in a wartime version of the band. The YBJB's announcer, Hal McIntyre, captured six performances on acetate from a KYA Dawn Club airshot in August 1942. The band on that occasion was fronted by trumpeter Benny Strickler. This version of the band included only one trumpet, but both Bob Helm and Ellis Horne played clarinet. Trombonist Bill Bardin, pianist Burt Bales, banjoist Russ Bennett and Clancy Hayes (reverting to drums) completed the group. Clancy stayed with the wartime YBJB throughout 1942.

Jazz Man 78: Maple Leaf Rag, label
(Author's Collection)

Jazz Man 78: Black And White Rag, label
(Author's Collection)

On 11th April 1943, recently rediscovered legendary New Orleans trumpeter Bunk Johnson arrived in San Francisco to headline a forthcoming concert organized by historian Rudi Blesh. 'This Is Jazz', at the Geary Theater, would also feature Kid Ory, trombone; Mutt Carey, trumpet; Wade Whaley, clarinet; Buster Wilson, piano; Frank Pasley, guitar; Ed Garland, bass and Everett Walsh, drums. In addition, pianist Bertha Gonsoulin (a San Francisco resident who had been tutored by Jelly Roll Morton and had played with King Oliver) was added to the programme.

Jazz Man 78: Fidgety Feet
(Author's Collection)

The concert, sponsored by the San Francisco Museum of Modern Art, took place on the afternoon of 9 May. Clancy was narrator and gave a brief history of jazz emphasising the point that Paul Whiteman's designation as 'King of Jazz' was strictly a commercial gimmick, intimating that true jazz was about to be witnessed. Clancy turned in his usual professional job, although he confessed that he felt 'starry-eyed and open-mouthed' in the company of such legendary jazzmen. The concert opened with Pat Patton's Jazz Band playing from the theatre pit and the group also played during the intermission when the audience called for Clancy to sing *Ace In The Hole;* he was happy to oblige.

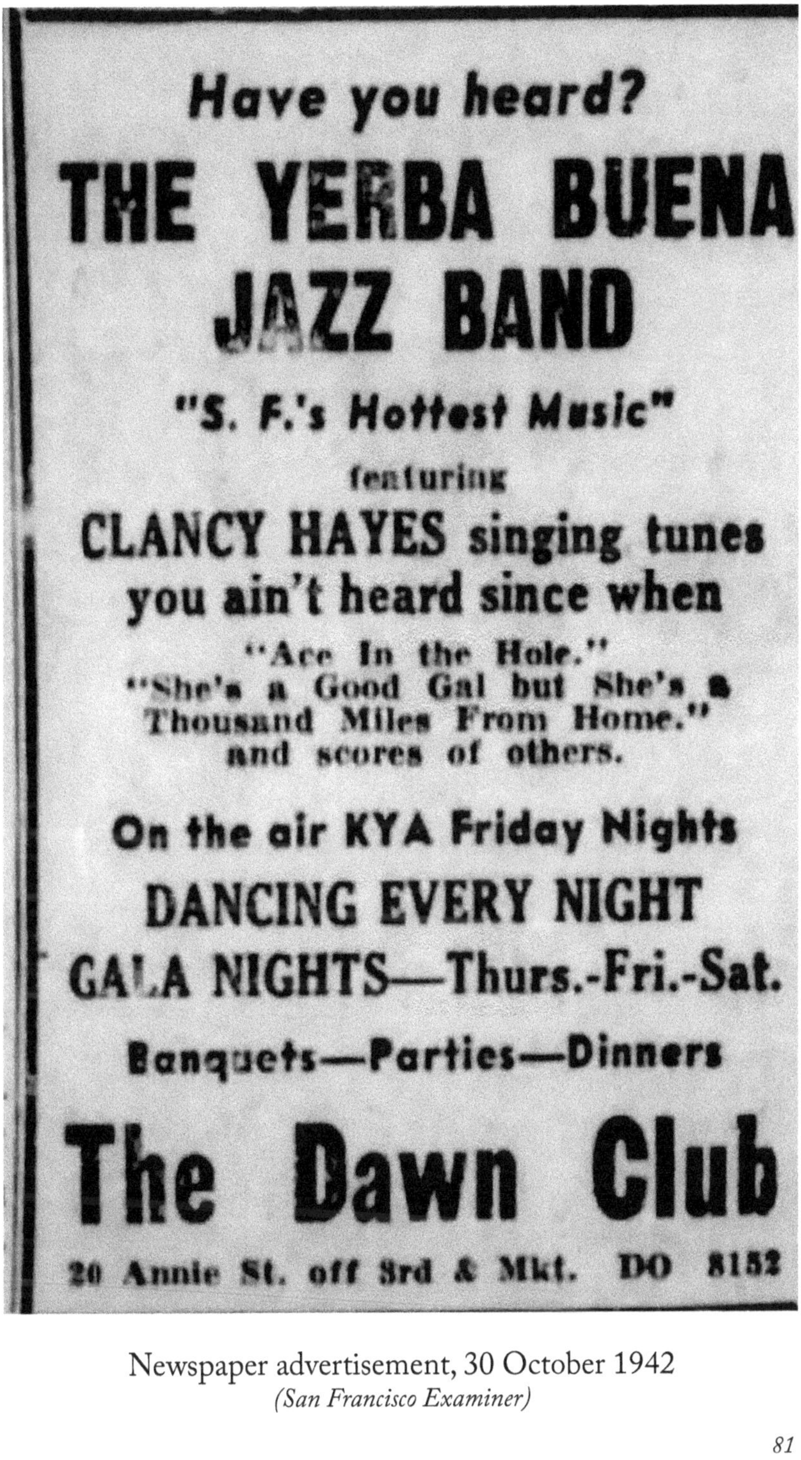

Have you heard?

THE YERBA BUENA JAZZ BAND

"S. F.'s Hottest Music"

featuring

CLANCY HAYES singing tunes you ain't heard since when

"Ace In the Hole."
"She's a Good Gal but She's a Thousand Miles From Home."
and scores of others.

On the air KYA Friday Nights

DANCING EVERY NIGHT
GALA NIGHTS—Thurs.-Fri.-Sat.

Banquets—Parties—Dinners

The Dawn Club

20 Annie St. off 3rd & Mkt.   DO 8152

Newspaper advertisement, 30 October 1942
(San Francisco Examiner)

Wartime Yerba Buena Jazz Band, 1942
Left to Right: Burt Bales, Bill Coonley, Clancy Hayes,
Ellis Horne, Bob Helm, Russ Bennett, Al Zohn, Bill Bardin.
(Courtesy Stanford University Libraries Archive / SFTJF)

Rudi Blesh addressed the lucky patrons and expressed genuine excitement for the great New Orleans musicians on stage. He gave a brief outline of how to identify a *real* jazz performance and cautioned the audience that jazz would be lost as *the* original American art form 'unless you listeners demand it'.

Rudolph Pickett Blesh supported Jazz as a writer, radio presenter, concert promoter and record label owner (Circle records) throughout his life. His 1947 weekly This is Jazz radio series ran from January to October and did much to promote New Orleans and revivalist jazz music. Lu Watters' Yerba Buena Jazz Band (without Clancy) featured in programme number 28, recorded in San Francisco on 18 August.[9]

Bunk Johnson spent a considerable amount of time in San Francisco during visits in 1943 and 1944. One of his regular engagements was a series of concerts, sponsored by the Hot Jazz Society of San Francisco, at CIO Hall (Congress of Industrial Organizations). Union leader Harry Bridges was responsible for providing a performance space for Bunk's band — one of the few venues in the Bay Area where a racially mixed band could perform. Meeting and working with a true jazz original was a pleasure and an education for the young musicians of the wartime Yerba Buena Jazz Band, including Ellis Horne, Bill Bardin and Burt Bales. As well as the thrill of playing with a first-generation jazzman, Bunk knew several New Orleans 'head tunes'.

Ellis Horne, Bunk Johnson
(Courtesy Stanford University Libraries Archive / SFTJF)

All went well for Bunk and the wartime Yerba Buena Jazz Band for over six months until, unbelievably, Musicians' Union Local 6 stepped in to stop the show. Band member Bill Bardin recalled: 'When the Union found out this was happening, they put their collective foot down. They had a rule that racially mixed bands couldn't be. You couldn't have white players and black players in the same band. Everybody was in the whites' only Local 6 Union; there was a black union, but they were separate.' To continue the Sunday concerts the Saunders King band was brought in but without success. 'It didn't work out; Bunk didn't like them and they didn't like Bunk.' [10]

In December 1943 Bunk Johnson played a concert at the Geary Theatre, San Francisco supported by members of the wartime Yerba Buena Jazz Band. The concert went well and Dave Rosenbaum, a co-founder of the Hot Jazz Society and record collector, decided to record Bunk with the band. The sessions took place over several weeks in the spring of 1944 but were plagued by Bunk's failure to show up and his sometimes casual attitude when he did. However, at one Bunk date, Sister Lottie Peavey (who sang with the Emmanuel Church of God in Christ) was in attendance and scheduled to record. Clancy was drumming for the band at this session and explained 'Sister Peavey put Bunk on his mettle. He (Bunk) was very contrite as only he could be, and he really played. Everything we made that day was good.' With wartime in full flow the original record masters were not processed and lay untouched for nine years. Thankfully Good Time Jazz acquired them and issued eight sides in 1953. Apart from playing drums, Clancy at last got to sing on record with the Yerba Buena Jazz Band on two excellent tracks — *Ace In The Hole* and *2.19 Blues*, albeit their release was somewhat delayed.

Clancy's absence from the YBJB activities later in 1944 and the following years was likely due to his busy radio schedule and the fact that in 1945 he was promoted to Musical Director at KGO San Francisco. At this time he was also focused on song writing and was no doubt a very busy man.

In 1946, with the musicians back from Army service, Lu Watters reorganized the Yerba Buena Jazz Band which made a triumphant return to the Dawn Club in April. However, Clancy Hayes was not part of the post-war outfit, nor was he involved when the YBJB relocated to Hambone Kelly's in El Cerrito in June 1947. It was not until mid-1948, when Bob Scobey and Turk Murphy departed as full-time members, that Clancy once again linked with the band as a featured performer.

At last, in 1949/50 Clancy was finally heard vocalising with the band on record singing *Oh By Jingo!*, *My Little Bimbo* and others, which were recorded during the day at Hambone Kelly's. Lu Watters independently released these sides, as well as several instrumentals, on his own Down Home label. Later, Clancy was also featured on vocals with his Washboard Five — a small group drawn from within the larger band — with Watters playing washboard (he was forced to lay off from the trumpet for some time following surgery).

Louis Armstrong and Bunk Johnson

Hot Jazz Society
of San Francisco

July 12, 1943

Sponsors:
BOB BEST
RUDI BLESH
HARRY BRIDGES
BILL COLBURN
ALFRED FRANKENSTEIN
RAY GERALDO
DON HAMBLEY
EMELIA HODEL
TED LENZ
HAL McINTYRE
H. IRVING ROSENBERG, JR.
PETER TAMONY

(A transcription of this is on pages 314/5)

Dear Fellow Member -

The Hot Jazz Society of San Francisco welcomes you into its select fold of devotees of le jazz hot. Your membership card now entitles you to enjoy each Sunday afternoon jazz session in the Chamber Jazz Room at 150 Golden Gate Avenue at the reduced admission price of six bits.

And speaking of last Sunday's opening session, no attempt at words is necessary to describe the exciting music that poured out of Willie "Bunk" Johnson and his ex-Lu Watters stars---because of course, you were there! After hearing Bunk, the real man of jazz, it is easy to understand that chapter on Louis Armstrong from the book "Jazzmen" that quotes as follows:

"....and Louis had talked a lot about Bunk, his idol of earlier days, had tried to tell how beautiful Bunk's tone was, how intense his vibrato, and had sung phrases to Lil (Armstrong) to show the facile, imaginative way Bunk had of embellishing them. Somehow Louis had felt things the same way as Bunk, had the same inborn sense of beauty, the same melancholic and exuberant accents, and naturally adopted a similar mode of expression. A lesson of inestimable importance which Louis absorbed more than anyone else was the way Bunk had of hesitating, always a little behind the beat, a lazy yet most dynamic way of playing which is at the core of all hot jazz."

Bunk himself shared our "high" feelings after last Sunday's clambake, and the stomps, rags and blues of his "Hot Seven" satisfied him. "That was Jazz," said its creator Bunk, "but wait until a few more sessions and my boys will really do it up like gravy." And with this happy thought in mind, let's treat ourselves to the habit of being present at the next and every Sunday afternoon session for more and better jazz.

The Chamber Jazz Room also will be "done up like gravy" with the addition of a public address system. Four lucky people again will win valuable prizes, including collectors' record albums and the books "Jazzmen" and "This is Jazz" by our own Rudi Blesh - a four-bit must item that is selling like mad at all the music counters. The surprise package of last week's session was Bob Best who thrilled with his blues shouting of "Milenburg Joys". Bob will be on deck again, but a new bundle of joy, Miss Stella Brooks, blues singer extraordinary, who has recorded with Stuff Smith, and was the musicians' favorite when she sang with Art Hodes' famous jazz band in New York, will also be in front of the mike to "send" us.

Your friends too are invited to become members of the Hot Jazz Society of San Francisco and enjoy the privileges of dancing, sipping, discussing and listening to "that genius" Bunk Johnson - as Saunders who was up from Los Angeles described him. Bring them along with you and educate them to the righteous jazz, and if you want them to receive the general Hot Jazz announcement, mail their names to the Secretary, Hot Jazz Society, 1317 Grove Street, San Francisco, 17, California, and we'll be glad to do the rest. Also, your comments and criticism of our first session are welcome.

uopwa 34

Hot Jazz Society Newsletter, 1942
(Courtesy Frank Selman / SFTJF)

STARTING SUNDAY, JUNE 27!!

CLANCY HAYES

Talented Singer and Song Writer (Composer of "A Huggin' and a Chalkin'") You will enjoy Clancy's informal style of singing Blues and Folk Songs.

HEAR HIS 2 SHOWS NIGHTLY
AT

HAMBONE KELLY'S

204 SAN PABLO AVENUE, EL CERRITO

Phone LAndscape 6-3161

COMPLETE DINNERS . $1 to $2

BARBECUED DISHES

TO TAKE HOME

LU WATTERS
JAZZ BAND
EVERY NIGHT BUT MONDAY

Hambone Kelly's advertising poster
(Courtesy Stanford University Libraries Archive / SFTJF)

Additional vocal recordings were also made for Norman Granz' Mercury label. Clancy played washboard (uncredited) on some of the instrumental sides for Mercury. These were originally released as 78s and later, taking advantage of the new formats, as 45rpm singles, Extended Play 45rpms, 10" LP albums and finally 12" LPs. Besides the Mercury and Clef releases, the records were issued on other labels in the UK, Sweden and Europe and on the Verve 'Down Home' series in the U.S.

Vogue 78: My Little Bimbo, label
(Author's Collection)

Down Home 78: Auntie Skinner's Chicken Dinner, label
(Author's Collection)

Clancy's second term with Lu Watters' band ended in the spring of 1950 most likely due to the need to cut costs due to falling audiences at Hambone's. But he was loosened up, available (following his leaving the airwaves that year) and ready to sing jazz. On a fateful April night he just happened to drop into an Oakland club where Bob Scobey's band was playing.

Following Clancy's departure, the Yerba Buena Jazz Band reduced to five pieces during its final months at Hambone Kelly's as attendances continued to fall. A remarkable chapter in jazz history finally closed on 1 January 1951 at the end of the New Year celebration. Lu Watters retired from music completely, becoming a carpenter and later a chef. Lu was also able to spend more time on his life-long hobby of mineralogy. He made only one brief return to music in 1963 to record the Blues Over Bodega LP (for Fantasy records). The album was made in successful protest against a proposed nuclear plant at Bodega Bay, to be built close to the earthquake-prone San Andreas Fault.

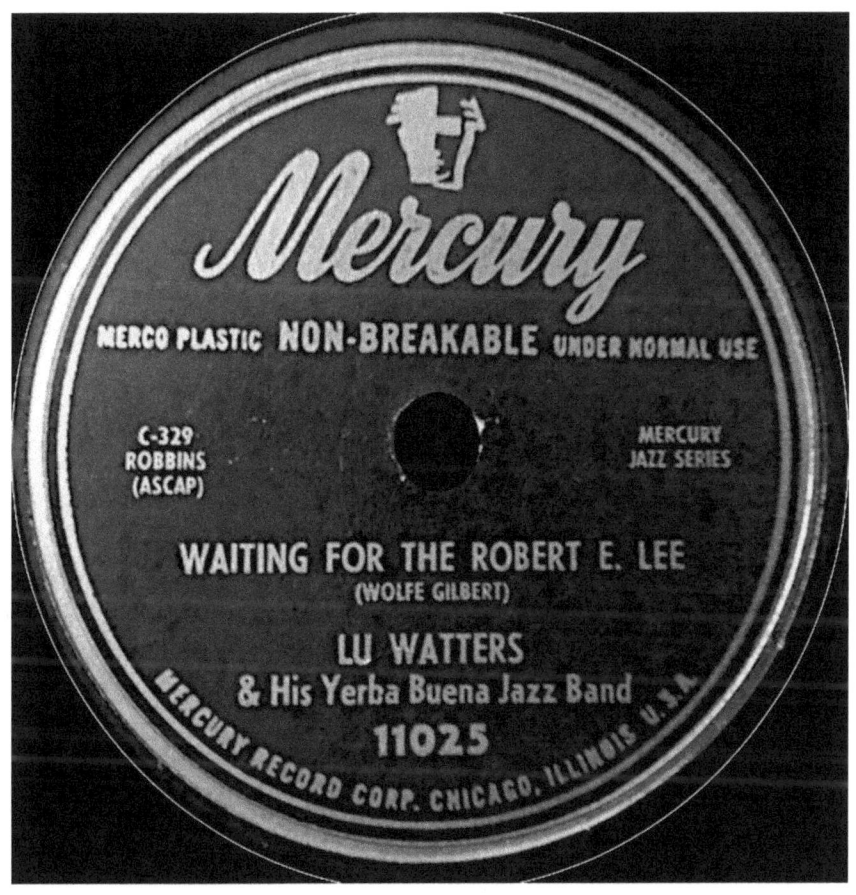

Mercury 78: Waiting For The Robert E. Lee, label
(Courtesy Hal Smith)

The Mid-Late 40s — Clancy's Other Musical Associations

Clancy's jazz activities in the 1940s had been book-ended with involvement in the opening and closing chapters of the Yerba Buena Jazz Band, but the middle years concentrated on other jazz and non-jazz projects.

Clancy's radio work was his 'proper job', but he had considerable extracurricular activities. These included composing songs, writing jingles and playing and recording with the Frisco Jazz Band and others. The Frisco Jazz Band gigs included headlining stints at Club Zanzibar in San Francisco and performing at the Marin County Community Festivals held at Stinson Beach Surf Club on Valentine's Day in 1946 and 1947.

Clancy made a series of records with the band including the original version of his most successful composition *Huggin' And A Chalkin'* issued on the Pacific label. Clancy's friend Hoagy Carmichael covered the song and bagged the hit version. Whether Hoagy's race to the top of the charts was aided by his stardom or the cheaper cost price of his Decca 78 is hard to say; but the $1.05 for Pacific 616 compared to the Hoagy disc at sixty-three cents wouldn't have helped the Frisco Jazz Band with Clancy Hayes sales. Johnny Mercer also recorded the song for his Capitol records and in that version the 'guy comin' around the other way' was Musicians' Union President James Petrillo.

Other vocal recordings with the Frisco Jazz Band in 1946 and 1947 included Clancy compositions *George Washington* and *Gettin' My Boots* as well as three jazz classics *Mamie's Blues / A Good Man Is Hard To Find* and *I Ain't Gonna Give Nobody None Of My Jelly Roll*. The personnel comprised Red Gillham, cornet; Jack Buck, trombone; Jack Crook, clarinet; Ray Jahnigen, piano; Russ Bennett, guitar; Pat Patton, bass; and Gordon Edwards, drums. The band played a public concert at Oakland Library in August 1948 to celebrate the introduction of a record lending library. Unfortunately for jazz lovers, there were no West Coast, Jazz Man or Pacific pressings; most of the records were classical.

The Zanzibar advert for the Frisco Jazz Band
(The Sacramento Bee, 24 March 1947)

In addition to sitting in and recording with the Frisco Jazz Band, in late 1947 Clancy was vocalist on sides recorded by Les Paul for Mercury records. A recording ban, sanctioned by James C. Petrillo, was to start on 31 December. Record companies were stockpiling sessions in the run up to the strike. Clancy described the somewhat strange, and perhaps hurriedly convened, Les Paul session. He was in a booth at the bottom of Paul's garden, while the recording equipment and Les were in the house. Paul observed that Clancy was singing like Nelson Eddy, which is hard to interpret as a compliment on the jazzier sides (*Nobody But You* and *My Extraordinary Girl*). Perhaps the 'Eddy' comment referred to Clancy's very straight rendition of *Now Is The Hour* — a popular song of the day — and the rather serious *Street*

Of Regret. Les Paul also, for no apparent reason, called Clancy 'Sam' throughout the proceedings.

Pacific 78: A Huggin' And A Chalkin', label
(Author's Collection)

In the previous chapter it was noted that Clancy's radio work virtually stopped from spring 1947 to autumn 1948. The evidence suggests that apart from focusing on his song writing (detailed in Chapter 10) he may, witnessing the success of the re-formed Yerba Buena Jazz Band, have been planning to lead his own jazz band. A Christmas tape sent to family and friends in 1971 included two songs from his private tapes with what appears to be a band he had put together around this time; the tape included the following note:

> I put this in particularly to show off the Bay City Boys my little 'misfits' that played better than the 'Fits'. Funny though, when you hear that Burt Bales, I think one of the greatest free hand piano players ever, Vince Dotson what a gutsy little guy on the cornette or do you prefer cornet? Bill Bardin, trombone Ellis Horne, my buddy from the first jazz revival and yours WASHIN' MY SINS AWAY.'

The Bay City Boys play excellent versions of the instrumental *Kansas City Stomp* and *Wolverine Blues* had Clancy on vocal. It is tempting to read between the lines concerning the reference to 'misfits'. It is likely he was referring to the musicians who did not work with the post-war version of the Yerba Buena Jazz Band. In any case Clancy was clearly the driving force behind the Bay City Boys and it shows a desire to lead a band.

Clancy organised numerous practice sessions with a small group of regulars and captured fifteen sessions with his Brush tape recorder. These sessions most likely took place during his 'radio silence' as the Brush tape recorder was released in 1947. Three Clancy compositions were recorded multiple times with varying tempos and different arrangements seeking exactly the right version of each song. Fourteen versions of both *Parsons, Kansas Blues* and *Ten To One It's Tennessee* were recorded along with ten variations of *Otto's New Auto*.

The core group on the recordings consists of: Vince Dotson or Al Zohn, cornet; Bill Bardin or Joe Zohn, trombone; Pat O'Casey or Ellis Horne, clarinet; Burt Bales, piano; and Squire Girsback, bass. Clancy plays drums on most of the sessions and occasionally guitar or washboard. Outside the core group the following musicians occasionally sat in or substituted: Pat Patton, banjo; Ned Dotson, trumpet: Slim Evans, clarinet and Billie Smith, washboard. Full details are in the discography appendix. Clearly these were not relaxed jam sessions, they were very focused.

Other songs recorded multiple times include six versions of *Coquette* and three versions of *At The Angels' Ragtime Ball*, a vintage tune from 1915. With such a limited song list and a relatively steady group Clancy was possibly exploring launching his own band and perhaps seeking to independently release his compositions. Clancy would have been aware that at this time Turk Murphy and Bob Scobey were about to leave Lu Watters to lead their own groups, both made their first records as bandleaders very shortly before the Petrillo recording ban. The momentum and funds from *Huggin' And A Chalkin'* may have tempted Clancy to lead the 'Misfits' to add to the Bay Area bands of Watters, Murphy and Scobey.

Another project around this time involved a pilot radio programme to seek a potential buyer. The fifteen-minute Tempo Train programme is entertaining and includes three good songs with Hayes vocals and two jazz instrumentals — all played in the same rolling train rhythm. An original vocal song *Tempo Train* opens the programme followed by rhyming dialogue explaining the many products the programme could be used to publicise. The band then comes in with the jazz instrumental *Ostrich Walk* followed by more patter before Clancy vocals on *Wolverine Blues* and *I'll Be In My Dixie Home Again Tomorrow*. As Clancy was still working in radio during this period, he no doubt wanted to see if he could write and sell a programme, but it appears there were no takers. It may be that his venture into sales brought him into contact with advertising executive Daphne June King leading to their successful song-writing partnership detailed in Chapter 10.

Any bandleading plans were temporarily shelved in mid-1948. Clancy resumed his radio work, though on a limited basis, leaving his nights free for the regular engagement with Lu Watters' Yerba Buena Jazz Band at Hambone Kelly's. In January of 1949, when Watters had his surgery, Bob Scobey temporarily put aside his own Alexander's Jazz Band to cover for Lu at Hambone's.

In was probably in the late 1940s that Clancy created something of a collector's item; a 78rpm on Ace records of Denver under his own name with a group of non-San Francisco musicians. The record gave him a chance to perform his composition *She's A Good Gal (But 1000 Miles From Home)* coupled with *Blues My Naughty Sweetie Gives To Me*. Apart from the rather unusual band line up, the record is interesting as it features Clancy on *piano*. The saxophone of George Yadon, who played with Art Kassel and his amusingly named Kassels in the Air Orchestra in the late 1930s, is very prominent. Junior

Haworth, who would later become famous in country music circles as 'Speedy' Haworth, takes a guitar solo on *Naughty Sweetie* which Clancy sings at a tempo only he could manage. The record was clearly an attempt to break into another market. It is *not* a jazz record, but its rarity would indicate that the attempt to 'cross over' didn't succeed.

Ace 78: She's a Good Girl, label
(Author's Collection)

Clancy's long and brilliant partnership with Bob Scobey is covered in the next chapter, but it is worth a brief look at Scobey's and Turk Murphy's activities in the period 1947-50. Both men had been associated with Lu Watters since the late-1930s and after almost ten years felt a need to spread their musical wings.

Bob Scobey had made his first records as a bandleader for the Trilon label in December 1947 shortly before the recording ban took effect. His Alexander's Jazz Band was a pick-up group, consisting mostly of Yerba Buena sidemen. Turk Murphy's first recordings were made at the last possible minute - on 31 December 1947. His Bay City Stompers were also drawn from the Yerba Buena ranks — including Scobey on trumpet. Four of the six sides recorded were originally released on the Jazz Man label.

Encouraged by his band's performance, Bob Scobey left Lu Watters around mid 1948 and brought his Alexander's Jazz Band to play at the Melody Club in Oakland. Freeing himself from Lu's not inconsiderable shadow, Scobey wanted to develop his musical ideas using both dynamics and varying rhythms — moving away from Watters' trademark two beat. Perhaps ironically, drummer Bill Dart who had set the Watters beat for many years moved his focus from the woodblocks to the snare drum, tom-toms and cymbals. With Alexander's Jazz Band, Dart developed a new and distinctive style at two Oakland clubs: the Melody Club (3614 Foothill Blvd.) and later at Victor's and Roxie's (551 E.12th St. at 6th Ave.).

ALEXANDER'S JAZZ BAND

Bob Alexander Scobey . Trumpet
Jack Crook . . . . Clarinet
Squire Girsbach . . . Bass

Jack Buck . . . Trombone
Bill Dart . . . . . Drums
Burt Bales . . . . . Piano

at

MELODY CLUB

3614 FOOTHILL BLVD.

Dancing . . . Friday . . . Saturday . . . Sunday Nites

Melody Club advertisement
(Oakland Post Enquirer, 17 November 1948)

As for the other refugee, Turk Murphy overcame some initial struggles in finding suitable gigs and signed with Good Time Jazz in 1949. His first two recording sessions for GTJ included Bob Scobey on trumpet. The overall music scene was not ideal for traditional jazz bands attempting to play regular engagements. Dick Oxtot's report on the state of San Francisco Jazz in the January 1949 *Record Changer* explained the situation:

> Rough days are ahead for local jazz groups or so it would seem, judging by the large crowds NOT seen at the active spots these nights. If anyone has any spare dough it must be in the old Christmas sock, because nobody is spending much to hear jazz bands. Kid Ory was drawing good Friday and Saturday night crowds, but not enough to counteract the weeknight losses incurred by the management at the Venus Club.
>
> Bob Scobey's Alexander's Jazz Band across the bay at the Melody Club was having difficulties cracking a mere three-night nut, with both Friday and Sunday crowds falling off and Saturday's barely taking up the slack. Only Hambone Kelly's with its long time following and its really fine joint is managing to support a band six nights a week...

The following month Dick Oxtot reported that most of the Bay Area musicians were 'feeding on casual dances'.

Hambone's apparent success would of course tail off the following year. Sadly, the same *Jazz Parade* section reported that Ellis Horne had sold his entire New Orleans record collection to Ray Avery, proprietor of Record Roundup in Los Angeles. Dick Oxtot's article did not comment on how Turk Murphy was doing at this time, but Mr Murphy would be around for the next thirty-six years — becoming a San Francisco institution. However, Turk Murphy and Clancy Hayes would not appear together on a regular basis until 1962.

The spring of 1950 marked the end of two eras for Clancy Hayes: his 22-year career in radio as well as his on-again, off-again association with the Yerba Buena Jazz Band. Fortunately, he made a brilliant career move by joining Bob Scobey's band. This alliance would result in bringing a set of new standards to the traditional jazz repertoire and would garner more fans than ever before for Clancy's unique vocal stylings.

5

The Scobey Years Part One 1950 - 1952

Clancy Hayes joined Alexander's Jazz Band in time for the 29 April 1950 recordings with Darnell Howard for Jazz Man records. Again, bearing in mind Clancy's fame in the Bay Area and his years with Lu Watters, his joining the band made quite an impact. According to Scobey's friend and longtime musical associate Jack Buck, the original Alexander's line-up was Bob Scobey, Hots O'Casey, clarinet; Gordon Edwards, drums and Burt Bales on piano. Jack Buck joined the band a little later, playing trombone or piano as the situation required. He explained: 'one night Clancy Hayes strolled by and he stayed to play and sing. Victor heard him and put him on the payroll. Now we were really cooking, rolling and we were getting huge crowds…' Free from the demands of radio work, Clancy had time to concentrate on performing jazz. The appearances with Lu Watters at Hambone Kelly's were a good start, but the Bob Scobey Band was a much better outfit for Clancy's vocals and musical preferences. Having sung thousands of songs over the past twenty-five years, he was now in a position where he could resurrect favourites of the past. Alexander's Jazz Band was still relatively unknown outside of the Bay Area, but the Scobey and Clancy pairing — ably assisted by a superb group of musicians and the recently formed Good Time Jazz record label — would soon expand its horizons.

Another winning aspect of the Scobey and Clancy pairing was a shared approach to their role as entertainers. Undeniably, both had a true love of jazz music, but they also possessed a natural desire to entertain and please audiences. This may explain the variety of material they presented — perhaps leaving some jazz purists 'all shook up.' Based on live recordings from 1956 (Beloit College, Wisconsin); 1957 (Grand Rapids, Michigan) and 1958 (a club date at Madison,

Wisconsin), as well as numerous press reviews, the joy in their live shows was warm and infectious. A Bob Scobey concert was fun, and the jazz was first class.

Victor's and Roxie's, advertisement
(Oakland Tribune, 18 February 1950)

Clancy's first recordings with Bob Scobey in April 1950 for the Jazz Man label were supervised by Nesuhi Ertegun. The band consisted of: Bob Scobey, trumpet; Jack Buck, trombone; Darnell Howard, clarinet; Burt Bales, piano; Clancy Hayes, guitar; Squire Girsback, sousaphone and Gordon Edwards, drums. Presumably for marketing reasons, the four sides were released under the name 'Darnell Howard's Frisco Footwarmers.'

Possibly a version of the House Band at Club Hangover late 1940s:
Left to Right: Paul Lingle, Hots O'Casey, Bob Scobey,
Squire Girsback, Turk Murphy.
(Courtesy Stanford University Libraries Archive / SFTJF)

Darnell Howard was a supremely gifted Chicago-born musician who started as a violinist and gave his first recital in 1902 at the age of seven. He travelled to New York in 1918 to record with W.C. Handy's Orchestra. Upon returning to Chicago he worked with Sidney Bechet, who sold him his first soprano sax. Having mastered this instrument, and the clarinet, he joined the King Oliver band in 1925. He played with Earl Hines' Orchestra in the 1930s and again much later in a small band at Club Hangover in San Francisco. Howard also played extensively with Muggsy Spanier and Kid Ory. In the early 1950s he was based in San Francisco and his impact on the Bob Scobey band produced four timeless recordings that remain fresh and exciting. If there is one very small complaint, the four sides contain no vocals.

Alexander's Jazz Band: Left to Right: Bill Dart,
Burt Bales, Bill Newman, Hots O'Casey, Squire Girsback,
Bob Scobey, Jack Buck, possibly at Cook's Hall or Oakland Public
Library
(Courtesy Stanford University Libraries Archive / SFTJF)

The Jazz Man records were favourably received by the jazz critics, unlike records Scobey had made in the late 1940s for his own Ragtime Label with a Hayes-less band (Ragtime 1050, 1051).[1] A *Record Changer* review of the sides by Bucklin Moon begins with the words 'I don't like to kick people in the teeth...' By contrast, the Scobey / Darnell Howard records were in a different class and enthusiastically received as was virtually everything that Bob Scobey released over the next six years under the name of his Frisco Band, featuring Clancy Hayes. The classic Scobey and Clancy era had begun.

Clancy was a regular performer in the now five-piece Alexander's Jazz Band at Victor's and Roxie's and it was standing room only. The Hayes' vocals and a seemingly limitless collection of songs from the golden age of jazz and popular music blended superbly and the fans loved them. The Scobey and Clancy bandwagon had, as Jack Buck put it, 'started to roll'.

Jazz Man 78: Some Of These Days, label
(Author's Collection)

In February 1951 Bob Scobey again augmented his band to record with another first generation and first-class jazz musician, Albert Nicholas. Born in New Orleans in 1900, Nicholas had played with Buddy Petit, King Oliver, Jelly Roll Morton, Luis Russell and Kid Ory. The musicians were clearly inspired by his presence. The recordings were made for Scobey's own Ragtime label as Alexander's Jazz Band, though the Albert Nicholas name was used when the records were released in Europe. The four sides include Clancy's first vocal with the band on *Beale Street Mama*.

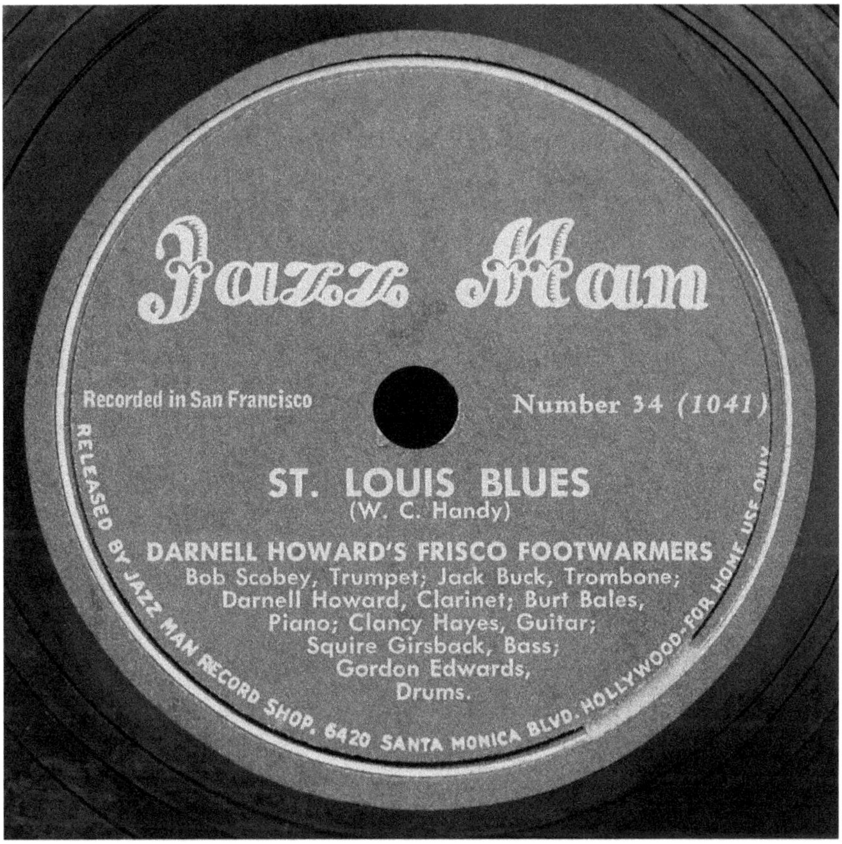

Jazz Man 78: St. Louis Blues, label

(Author's Collection)

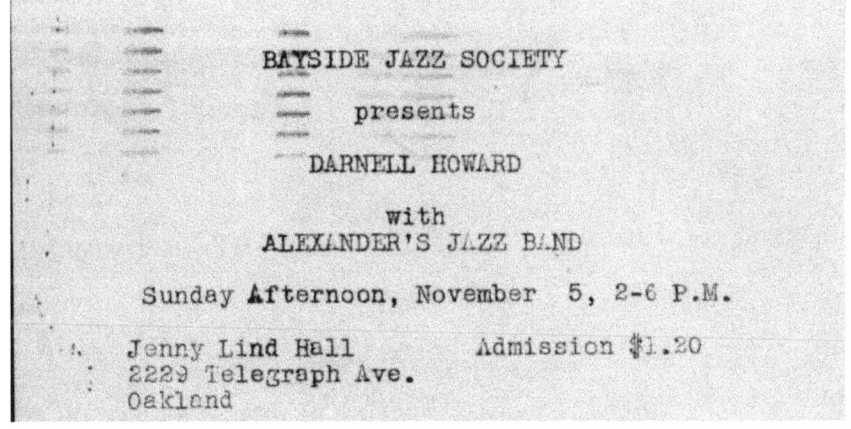

BAYSIDE JAZZ SOCIETY

presents

DARNELL HOWARD

with

ALEXANDER'S JAZZ BAND

Sunday Afternoon, November 5, 2-6 P.M.

Jenny Lind Hall   Admission $1.20
2229 Telegraph Ave.
Oakland

Bayside Jazz Society ticket, Sunday 5 November 1950

(Courtesy Stanford University Libraries Archive / SFTJF)

Victor's and Roxie's Advertisement
(Courtesy Stanford University Libraries Archive / SFTJF)

Alexander's Jazz Band at Victor's and Roxie's, 1950: Left to Right:
Jack Buck, Gordon Edwards, Bob Scobey, Clancy, Burt Bales.
(Courtesy Stanford University Libraries Archive / SFTJF)

Ragtime records 78: Beale Street Mama, label
(Author's Collection)

Despite the successes of the Lu Watters band and others that had taken to 'traditional Jazz', the four major labels (Columbia, Decca, RCA, Brunswick) were largely uninterested in the music. Across America, small independent labels were established to record music the 'big four' wouldn't touch. David Stuart had set up Jazz Man records in 1940, Nesuhi Ertegun had formed Crescent records in 1944 and bands also pressed records on their own labels including Bob Scobey (Ragtime), and the Castle Jazz Band (Castle).

Dixieland Jubilee 78: Coney Island Washboard, label
(Author's Collection)

The four or five piece Alexander's Jazz Band continued at Victor's and Roxie's; its size probably limited by simple economics. In June 1951, the five-piece line-up was Bob Scobey, George Probert, Jack Buck, Wally Rose and Clancy. Come December, the band appeared on KGO TV, San Francisco to positive reviews and in February 1952 the band was again on TV with the Rusty Draper Show.

Returning to Clancy's recordings with Bob Scobey, on Tuesday 6 November 1951 what many Scobey fans regard as one of their finest ever recording sessions took place at Jenny Lind Hall in Oakland. Scobey played gigs, rehearsed and recorded at this venue, including the session with Darnell Howard. He liked the excellent acoustics and natural echo of the large first floor hall and it would serve as the location for many recording sessions throughout the 1950s. In a *Record Changer* review, George Avakian wrote, 'A word about the sound on these records; they are recorded with a big room tone that sounds quite real'.

Alexander's Jazz Band at Alexander's (formerly Hambone Kelly's) 1951. Left to Right: Squire Girsback, George Probert, Fred Higuera, Jack Buck, Bob Scobey, Clancy Hayes (hidden), Wally Rose.
(Courtesy Hal Smith)

Clancy in reflection
(Courtesy Frank Selman / SFTJF)

Four sides, all with superb vocals, were issued: *South / Sailing Down The Chesapeake Bay / Chicago* and *Melancholy*. More is said about the recordings in Chapter 10 (Clancy's Winners) but dear reader, if you don't know these recordings, insert bookmark, put down the book and listen to them now. What makes for any truly exceptional recording is probably something that defies explanation. Much as a sports team can play a one-off unbelievable match or an athlete exceed their personal best, so too must it be the case that everybody in a band excels to create something truly special. I am sure you can think of your own musical and non-musical examples.

Jenny Lind Hall, Telegraph Ave. Oakland (2009)
(Author's Collection)

Jenny Lind Hall Main Hall at first floor level where many recordings took place.
(Author's Collection)

The band that celebrated November day included: Bob Scobey, trumpet; Jack Buck, trombone; George Probert, clarinet/soprano sax; Wally Rose, piano; Clancy Hayes, banjo and vocals; Dick Lammi, string bass; and Fred Higuera, drums. Credit must also go to recording engineer Stan Page who worked on this and several other Bob Scobey sessions; the sound quality is wonderful.

Bob Scobey's Frisco Band 1951
Left to Right: George Probert, Fred Higuera, Jack Buck, Squire Girsback, Bob Scobey, Clancy Hayes, Wally Rose.
(Courtesy Stanford University Libraries Archive / SFTJF)

It is probably worth highlighting one band member, twenty-four-year-old George Probert. Though Bob Scobey had included two original and brilliant clarinettists from the classic era in his previous sessions, for this recording he chose a young musician who plays superbly throughout. Of course, George Probert would go on to be a much-respected musician spending a lifetime in jazz, touring Europe and Japan as well as being a festival favourite for over thirty years. But Bob Scobey gave Probert his initial break and through his clarinet and soprano sax work he returned the favour a million times over. (George Avakian also pointed out that his use of soprano sax on the 1951 recordings was a first in San Francisco Jazz).

Bob Scobey's Frisco Band 1951
(Courtesy Stanford University Libraries Archive / SFTJF)

Something about this particular band and this session encouraged Clancy to achieve truly superb vocals. He made over three hundred commercial recordings during his long career, but many fans agree that these are among his very best. His vocal on *Sailing Down The Chesapeake Bay* was singled out by George Avakian in the January 1953 *Record Changer* review:

> Don't know where Scobey (or Clancy Hayes perhaps) digs up these tunes, but *Chesapeake Bay* is a great stomp in Scobey's hands with the aforementioned Mr Hayes turning in one of his fine vocals once again.

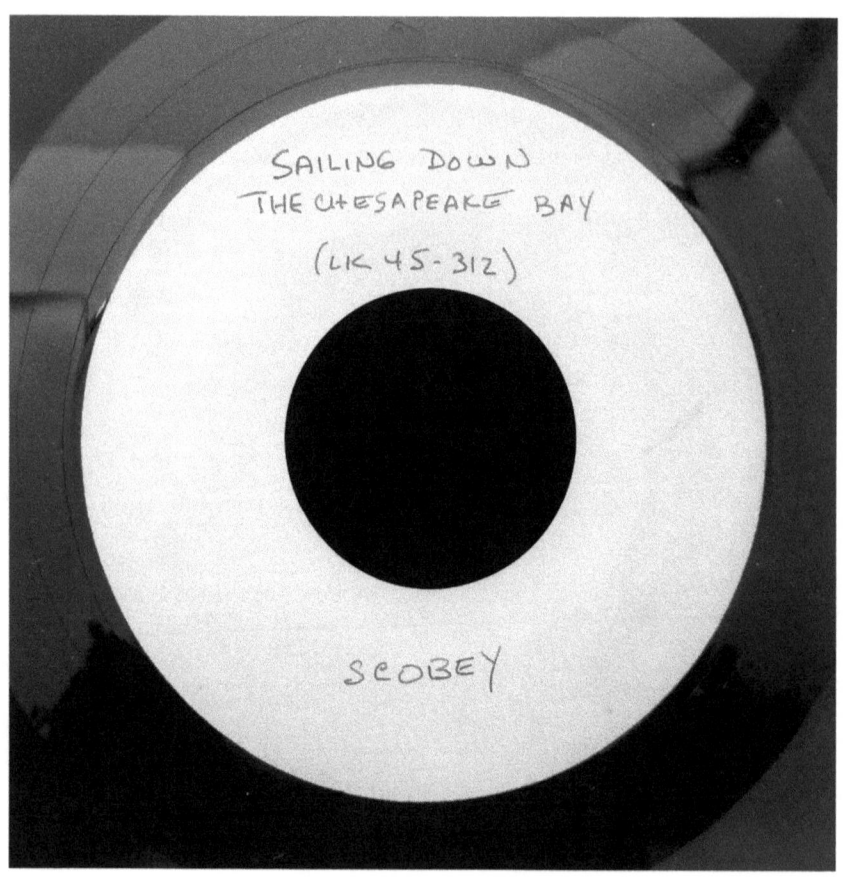

Test Pressing: *Chesapeake Bay / Chicago* LK 45-311/2
(Author's Collection)

But all four sides are excellent. *South* is a traditional jazz standard originally written as an instrumental by Bennie Moten and Thamon Hayes in 1924, and usually performed that way. The lyrics were added much later by the 'other' Ray Charles (Charles Raymond Offenberg — musician, singer and songwriter best known as the organiser and leader of the Ray Charles Singers). The Clancy vocal puts the Scobey version in a different class. His delivery on the solo vocal break '*don't you know you're right next to heaven down South*' is perfection.

Chicago, test pressing
(Author's Collection)

Scobey and Clancy's stars were on the rise. They had a permanent base at Victor's and Roxie's, their records were getting great reviews and selling and they were making TV appearances. In 1952 they signed to Les Koenig's Good Time Jazz record label, established three years earlier specifically to record The Firehouse Five Plus Two. GTJ had also signed the Turk Murphy Jazz Band and Bay Area pianist Burt Bales (his After Hours Piano LP is a masterpiece). As well as making new recordings, Good Time Jazz purchased the catalogues of Jazz Man and Lu Watters' West Coast label. Remastered recordings by the Yerba Buena Jazz Band from 1941-1946 were reissued. Quite a few recordings by other artists were issued either as 45rpm singles or in boxed sets. All records were pressed using high quality vinyl and extended play records were on transparent red vinyl. The album artwork is very distinctive and appealing. San Francisco based Guidi Tri-Arts designed many sleeves; others feature illustrations by the gifted artist Lamartine (Lom) LeGoullon who also produced many memorable covers for the *Record Changer* magazine.

Left to Right: Bob Scobey, Wally Rose, Jack Buck,
George Probert.
(Courtesy Stanford University Libraries Archive / SFTJF)

The Scobey band made four more sides for GTJ on 12 April 1952: *Blues My Naughty Sweetie Gives To Me / Do You Know What It Means To Miss New Orleans / Of All The Wrongs You've Done To Me / Peoria*. All four songs benefit from excellent Clancy vocals. Having a vocalist enabled the repertoire to expand beyond staple traditional jazz tunes. The vocal dexterity shown on *Naughty Sweetie* is something very special; try singing 'there are blues you get from gettin' in a taxi cab and sweatin' every time you hit a bump and jump the clock'. *Peoria* is a fun tune sounding all the more nautical by the use of three trombones (Marshall Ward and Bob Mielke were added for this session). As for *All The Wrongs* and *Do You Know What It Means*, no revivalist jazz band had made comparable recordings of these songs. The superb vocals, accompanied by Scobey's exceptional fills are the essence of the performances.

These tracks were coupled with the November 1951 recordings on the 10 inch Good Time Jazz LP, Bob Scobey's Frisco Band Volume 2. Clancy had a copy of Ralph J. Gleason's enthusiastic review from the *San Francisco Chronicle* [2] in his private papers. It was part of an article covering three GTJ 10 inch releases –Turk Murphy's Jazz Band Vol. 4, Burt Bales After Hours Piano and the Scobey album. Mr Gleason wrote:

> The Scobey LP has Clancy Hayes singing each tune. To me Clancy is, after Louis Armstrong, by all odds the finest singer of traditional jazz tunes. He doesn't shout and he isn't raucous. He just sings simply with warmth and feeling and with a lovely swing. The accompaniment, by Scobey and Co., is top rank too.

In addition to the uplifting nature of Scobey's and Clancy's music and the many positive reviews they received, there is plentiful evidence of their generous nature. Jazz musician Jim Beebe told the story of how in 1952 Bob Scobey had let him sit in with the band at Victor's and Roxie's.

Jim was just out of school and doing military service, stationed at Treasure Island in San Francisco Bay. He and a fellow Private 1st Class Emile Orth would go up every weekend and Jim would sit-in on the vacant trombone chair — Jack Buck was on piano. He always wore his Marine Corps uniform as customers would buy military personnel drinks and the bartender wouldn't get concerned about his age. Clancy's role in the operation — apart from support on the bandstand — was chauffeur. He would collect Jim and Emile en route from San Francisco to Oakland. Occasionally Clancy would be unable to do the chauffeuring which meant that Privates Beebe and Orth had to pay the bus fare to Oakland. Possibly to make up for one of these occasional no-shows, one evening Clancy drove directly into the Treasure Island military base (he may possibly have wanted to reminisce about what went on there thirteen years earlier). In any case, the Military Police were not impressed and issued Clancy with a ticket. Neither the said ticket, nor any fan mail from MPs was found in Clancy's memory box. Jim became good friends with Clancy and his family, visiting his San Francisco apartment for some home cooking.[1]

By 1954, Private Beebe had made the rank of Corporal and in February embarked somewhat hurriedly for Yokohama; he wrote to Clancy and Ann to tell of his experiences:

> Dear Clancy and Mrs Hayes
>
> I hope you will forgive my rude departure without calling you, I got a sudden offer for a ride to LA so I took it without hesitation!
>
> I left the States January 17 and it took us a little over two weeks to get here, the voyage wasn't too pleasant as we managed to hit every storm on the ocean. The ship was very crowded and to make it worse we had rifle inspection and field days every day. However, I managed to escape much of this humdrum activity by organising a ship's band. The special service department had some instruments, so we sent out a call for musicians. About ten guys showed up and claimed that they could play various instruments, but I claim they could not; anyway out of this group we formed a band which was the saddest excuse for a band I have ever heard. Nevertheless, we put on live shows.
>
> The ship docked at Yokohama to let off some army and air force and then came up to Kobe where we got off. I then spent a couple of days shuffling around in trains and trucks and finally arrived here at Camp Shifu. These Jap trains are of about 1800 vintage, I would say that Jessie James robbed better trains than these.
>
> The third Marine Division is split up into five different camps around Japan, the Division band contains about 80 men and is split into three sections. This section I am with is connected with headquarters BTN. They have a warped

conception of band duty here. This band section is a machine gun platoon and we spend most of the time firing and on hikes and field problems. Once in a while we play however. We play retreat a couple of times a week and sometimes colors in the morning.

We just got a new band officer and he says he is going to arrange things so the band plays more often.

Right now there is a lot of activity here — training etc. The whole division is moving out next month for amphibious maneuvres. We're going to Iwo Jima for this.

I'm trying to get together a jazz band of some sort. Found a good trumpet and piano man. We go over to the services club and knock out a few tunes now and then.

I heard a couple of your records on a jap radio station. I wish that I could describe how they pronounced yours and Scobey's names. It was really hilarious. You can hear a lot more good jazz on the radio here than in the States.

I wish you could hear some of this jap music its really weird the whole country is weird. There is a little town right outside of the base. There are a number of jap taverns to accommodate the servicemen and plenty of girls. Jap beer is cheap and good but their whisky is dangerous to fool around with, one guy here almost went blind from it. Jap taverns are completely different from bars in the states, they are very small and their only source of heat is a bowl in the centre of the room which burns charcoal. Almost everyone has an old phonograph and stacks of American records. So far, I haven't found any of yours. It is snowing like hell out and I must close before the mail boy is snowed under, give my regards to Bob, Jack, Darnell etc. drop me a line and let me know what is happening, love and other indoor sports. Jim.[3]

Forty-eight GTJ singles had been issued before the release of GTJ 49 *Coney Island Washboard / Wolverine Blues* by Bob Scobey's Frisco Band in 1952; as with the first Turk Murphy releases on GTJ they were reissues of Jazz Man records. The November 1951 recordings were issued as GTJ singles #60 (*South / Melancholy*) and #71 (*Chicago / Chesapeake Bay*). The story continues in the following chapter with Scobey's next GTJ session.

6

The Scobey Years Part Two: San Francisco and Chicago 1953 — 59

Bob Scobey's next two recording sessions for Good Time Jazz were probably made in early 1953. Unusually for Good Time Jazz (sleeve notes are generally extensive and very informative) recording dates are not given. The text states only that the tracks were recorded under Scobey's supervision in Oakland, making the likely venue Jenny Lind Hall. All eight tunes have a Clancy vocal and were released as singles, a red vinyl double EP and ten inch album. As before, several tunes not associated with traditional jazz bands at the time, such as *Everything Is Peaches Down In Georgia*, were recorded. These sessions also produced versions of *Huggin' And A Chalkin'* and *Ace In The Hole*. The latter title was coupled with *Silver Dollar* on GTJ 78 to become their best-selling single. Fred Reynolds' review in the *Chicago Tribune* on 9 April stated:

> More often than not the best things come in small packages. This is how it is with Good Time Jazz. Somehow you can normally depend on a record original and good from this energetic young company. Perhaps the finest disk Good Time Jazz has ever released is *Ace In The Hole* and *Silver Dollar* by Bob Scobey's Frisco Band with Clancy Hayes singing. In any case it is one of the most wonderful platters I've ever heard. Judging from this record and the others that have come before, banjoist Clancy Hayes is clearly the most underrated vocalist in America today. His style is that of a true minstrel, combining a rich, sincere warmth with a properly rocking beat and superb phrasing...

In the summer of 1953, Scobey and Clancy finished their long residence at Victor's and Roxie's and on 25 July opened at the 500-seat Rancho Grande night club on the Tunnel Strip in Lafayette, where the Scobey family lived. After three years of jazz, Victor's and Roxie's switched their musical menu for a while to Bud McDonald and the Ranch boys, a Western Swing band. However, by October jazz was back in the form of the George Probert Jazz Band (George had left the Scobey band and was replaced briefly by Ellis Horne, followed by Bill Napier — after a period where the band had no clarinettist). Other music on offer in the Bay Area in July 1953 included Dave Brubeck at the Blackhawk, Jesse 'Tiny' Crump at the Mocambo and Buddy De Franco at Club Down Beat.

Strangely, despite the Good Time Jazz records by Bob Scobey's Frisco Band, they were still occasionally billed as Bob Scobey's Alexander's Jazz Band in the Bay Area. A review of their performance on Saturday 19 September confirmed that the Rancho Grande was full to bursting. The band that night included Clancy Hayes, Jack Buck, Burt Bales, Ellis Horne and Bob Hotaling on the drums. (There is no mention of a bass player.)

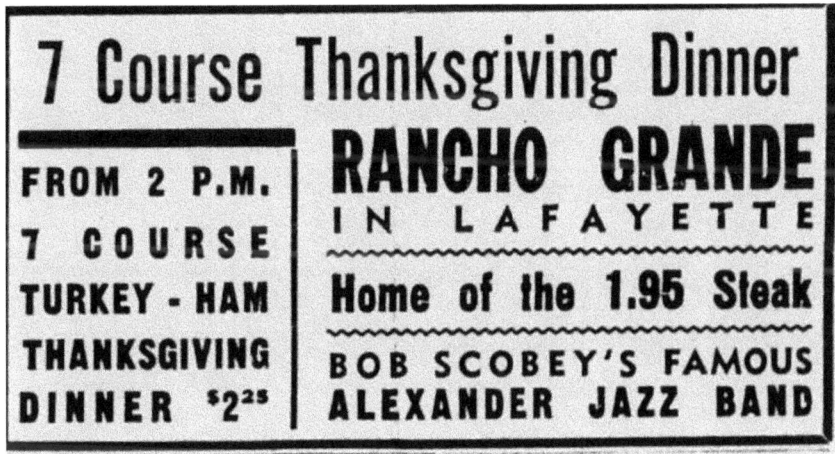

Bob Scobey's band at the Rancho Grande, Lafayette, 1953.
(Oakland Tribune, 24 November 1953)

Clancy Hayes at the Rancho Grande, advertisement
(Contra Costa Times, 5 December 1953)

Such was Clancy's impact with the Scobey band that he won the 1954 *Down Beat* critics' poll for the best new jazz singer — at the age of forty-six! Despite Clancy's prominence as a radio star and band singer for the previous twenty-five years it was the magic of his partnership with Bob Scobey and the excellent musicians within the Scobey band that grabbed the critics' attention.

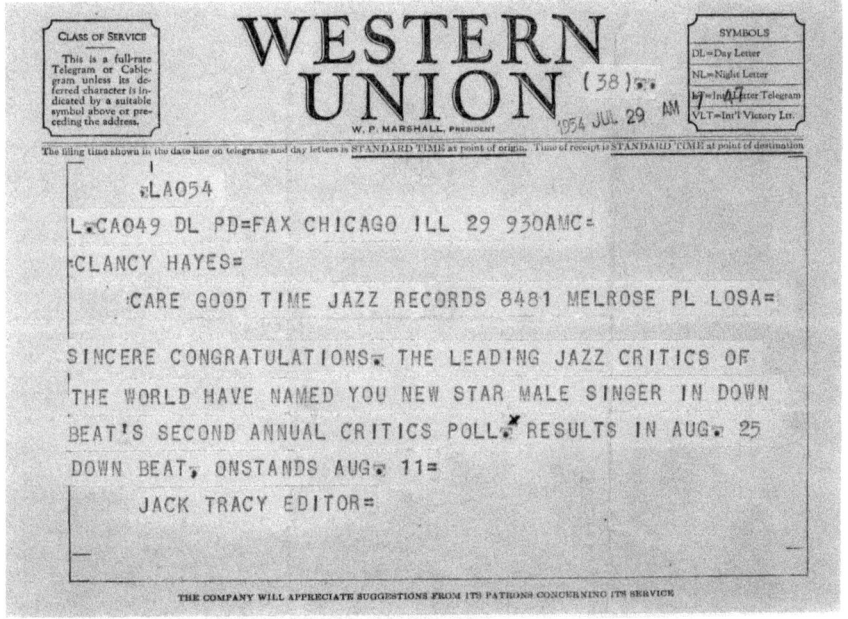

Down Beat's Award telegram
(Courtesy Stanford University Libraries Archive / SFTJF)

At this time Bob Scobey and Clancy Hayes seemingly had equal stardom and were seen by many as partners rather than leader and featured artist; their fifth GTJ album, recorded in 1955, was titled 'Scobey and Clancy'. When interviewed decades later, Pete Clute explained that the Scobey band was less structured than, for example, the Turk Murphy Band (in which Pete played piano from 1955-80). As can be heard on record, Turk Murphy wrote charts for each instrument. These were learned and adhered to, though generally written music wasn't used in performance. There is an anecdote concerning a tuba player who was with the Turk Murphy Jazz Band for only a short time: Pete Clute - 'He added a very slight embellishment in the final couple of bars of an arrangement. After the number, Turk congratulated him for improvising but pointed out that if he'd wanted it played that way he'd have written it that way!'

Bill Napier, Bob Scobey, Clancy Hayes
(Courtesy Stanford University Libraries Archive / SFTJF)

The Scobey band had a much looser style. Pete Clute stated that Clancy would suggest tunes he would like to sing and Scobey would work out an arrangement for the band. These charts were used as guides, but tuba (and other) embellishments were fine. Part of the Scobey and Clancy synergy was their ability to resurrect old tunes and make them sound newly minted: *At The Devil's Ball / I Want To Go Back To Michigan / Somebody Stole My Gal / Everything Is Peaches Down In Georgia / My Gal Sal / Lovey Came Back* and numerous other neglected songs were dusted off and brought to life.

Clancy's Corner and the Black Hole of the Embarcadero.

The Scobey run at the Rancho Grande ended in May 1954 when he moved to the Tin Angel, located on San Francisco's waterfront Embarcadero opposite Pier 23 where Burt Bales was in residence. The Scobey outfit also returned to TV on KPIX in Clancy's Corner, a weekly thirty-minute late-night broadcast from the club. TV exposure was good for record sales of course, but it also encouraged some to seek out the band. The following letter from Mari Ladowski, of Napa, Calif. gives the most wonderful impression of the Tin Angel. Having seen the band on TV, Ms Ladowski was understandably keen to see them in action but was not sure where they were playing — although she knew it was somewhere near Pier 23 on the Embarcadero. The next time she and her husband visited San Francisco they thumbed through the phone book and saw the likely name Tin Angel.

Of all the fan mail Clancy received over the years it is no wonder he kept this gem.

1446 Laurel Street.
Napa, California.
September, 15, 1954.

Dear Clancy and gang,

I've been meanin' to write you ever since I first saw your TV show sometime in July. I just barely caught the last of the show where you were telling about appearing somewhere on the Embarcadero across from pier 23 and I never did hear all of the directions, but I decided right then and there that my husband would have to hear that 'crazy' band. The next time we were in the City we thumbed through the phone book for a logical address on the Emabarcadero across from pier 23 and came up with the 'Tin Angel' of course. We hied ourselves out there posthaste and did a double take when we saw the joint. There was nary a car around there. In fact there wasn't much of anything except a bunch of rubbish and some left-over building material. Since we had already gone that far we decided we may as well do it up brown so we opened the door - ever so quietly and peered into the dimly lit interior which was practically in the same shape as the outside. We were about to depart and call it a day when the clean-up man inform -ed us that the joint would be jumpin' at 9PM. It was then about 8:30PM. By that time my husband was beginning to doubt the existance of a guy named Clancy and whether he would be worth waiting to see if we did wait til 9. I had given you such a buildup though, that he decided to stay out of curiosity. We were the first ones there with only the barkeep for company. When two waitresses came in and start -ed to crowd as many tables to the smallest space possible and the barkeep insisted that they didn't have enough tables, my husband perked up a little. When you boys came at last and gave out with the Dixie-land swing he was completely sold on the first rendition. We stayed til the 2nd intermission and would have stayed on except for the fact we had to drive

Letter from Mari Ladowski
(Courtesy Stanford University Libraries Archive / SFTJF)

back to Napa, and besides only a Rockefeller could afford those drinks all night and we are just working folks. We have been enjoying the weekly broadcasts ever since and if we ever get a phonograph we'll sure buy your new album.

    There's just one thing we would like to know, did you get that halo you wear on your telecast from working at the 'Tin Angel' ? (The halo is formed apparently by the light of the studio shining on your bald spot) No matter where it comes from we like it and you, Bob Scobey and all the boys. Your new ivory tickler is 'real gone'. Of course we liked the other guy too and the way your bass knocks himself out on the ole git-fiddle. We like your drummers friendly smile, your clarinettist' hot licks, the slide trombonists slides, Bob's one-handed trumpeting. Let's see now, did I leave anybody out ? I'll say I did. We forgot to mention ole Clance with his banjo and the trio. I guess you gather by all this that we think you're slightly terrific even if I do have to rassle this typewriter to try to get out a legible letter what with all the mistakes I make. Fo'give me. Just don't leave our dear old San Francisco for long unless you get a bigger audience and a sponsor(making sure of course that you always beam it our way.)

    Pardon the long-winded letter, I just couldn't say all I wanted to say on a measly little postcard.

    By the way, I want you to know that I don't make a practice of writing fan letters least of all one as long as this. The most I ever get out is a short note once in a blue moon. So consider yourselves highly honored.

    Long may you play !!

                  Sincerely

        Mari Ladowski

A transcription of this letter is on pages 316/7

Bob Scobey's Frisco Jazz Band at the Tin Angel, poster
(Courtesy Stanford University Libraries Archive / SFTJF)

At the Tin Angel: Left to Right: Fred Higuera, Bob Scobey,
Dick Lammi, Clancy, Bill Napier
(Courtesy Stanford University Libraries Archive / SFTJF)

Note the advert for 'Clancy's Corner'. And still the pianist, possibly Jack Buck, remains hidden.

A review that left out comments on the locale or drink prices was given by Terence O'Flaherty in the 29 November *San Francisco Chronicle*:

> Radio and Television
>
> If you like jazz and haven't caught 'Clancy's Corner' on KPIX you're missing the best musical program on local television. The music of Bob Scobey's Frisco Jazz Band from the Tin Angel, a waterfront spirit dispensary, is tops. The show is honestly produced, artfully staged, and generally a joy to behold (KPIX 11.00pm) I can't think of a way to improve it — except to make it a full hour.

The Scobey and Clancy LP [1] sleeve notes have a story from this period which shows their popularity in San Francisco. During a break at the Tin Angel, the musicians crossed the Embarcadero for a beer and some Burt Bales piano at Pier 23. Kansas City Kitty, a local entertainer from way-back was there singing and entertaining the patrons. There was no anonymity for the Scobey band and Clancy was soon spotted. Far from taking a break, he was persuaded to give the crowd a song. While drinking his beer, or at least between sips, he and Burt delivered *Ace In The Hole* to the delight of all. The colourful audience of stevedores, business folk and everyone in-between gave a hefty round of applause as Clancy and company went back to work: break over.

Bob Scobey was an energetic leader and operated every aspect of the band management. Surprisingly, it was not until after a full four years of success in the Bay Area that he decided to accept an invitation to take his crew on their first trip east. And what a trip it was! Scobey, Clancy and Co. may have had some doubts about travelling to Chicago's famous Blue Note. The 'windy city's' own style of jazz had evolved from the great originators who headed north from New Orleans in the early 1920s.

However, the ground was well prepared. Nightclub owner Frank Holzfeind discovered the Scobey records, liked what he heard and followed up by bringing the band to the Blue Note. In this extract from his *Chicago Tribune* article of 10 October 1954, Will Leonard wrote:

> The place to look for New Orleans music these days is not in New Orleans, of course, but in San Francisco. Ever since Lu Watters put his Yerba Buena Jazz Band together in 1938, the city of cable cars has been capital of two-beat. One of the best outfits, since Watters' group came apart again, has been Bob Scoby's *(sic)* Frisco band. It's coming to the Blue Note Wednesday, for its first 'eastern' appearance –and that's good news.
>
> This is a Dixieland band with a vocalist and anyone who has heard its numerous records on the Good Time Jazz label knows that Clancy, a portly gent with a bald dome and a rough and ready voice, is just the guy for *Everything Is Peaches Down In Georgia*, *Ace In The Hole* or his own comic classic *Huggin' And A Chalkin*.

The Scobey band was supported by the Original Salty Dogs for whom Clancy was full of praise: a decade later he would record with them.

Clancy described their Blue Note reception in his 1965 interview with Bill Dyer: [2]

> We broke all the records but one; the only other attraction that had ever had a bigger audience than our Friday night audience was Benny Goodman on a Sunday afternoon that ran from about 2:30 in the afternoon 'till about 9:30 at night which was a lot longer than the time that we played.

The Blue Note opened in November 1947 and was a famed Chicago venue. Former railway ticket clerk Frank Holzfeind decided that after twenty-five years of listening to destination requests, he needed a change. He first managed a bowling alley before deciding to operate a jazz club. The Blue Note at Madison and Clark, previously an Elks' clubhouse, was converted to a 'plushy' standard to host jazz. In addition to the liquor crowd, the club had a 'fan club terrace' for youngsters to enjoy a soft drink while watching the proceedings. Mr Holzfeind obviously had a true appreciation of jazz music, as did the audience.

The following year the Scobey band made two return trips, the first from 27 April to 15 May and secondly in August for a two-week Dixieland Festival, again sharing the stage with the Original Salty Dogs. The Chicago fans' reaction to Dixieland was the same. Will Leonard's *Chicago Tribune* review stated:

> No audiences in any Chicago cabaret are quite like those at the Blue Note these nights. The Note's patrons whoop and holler and sing with the band, clap their hands in time with the music and when a number has ended, they shout requests for such exotic items as *Sailing Down The Chesapeake Bay, Peoria, The Parsons Kansas Blues*.....

Bob Scobey's Frisco Band, advertisement, September 1955
(Chicago Tribune, 4 September 1955)

Scobey Joins the RCA Label

Chicago disc jockey and music journalist Fred Reynolds was a staunch Scobey and Clancy fan. When he got the job as Jazz Artists and Repertoire Director with RCA records in early 1956, he was keen to sign them to the label. At the time, *no* traditional jazz bands had signed with RCA. However, Bob Scobey had several recording projects in the works, including two albums for the Norman Granz-owned Down Home label which had been recorded at Jenny Lind Hall in April. Perhaps surprisingly, not least to Mr Reynolds, Scobey was undecided about signing for RCA. He had always personally managed the band and was possibly uneasy about losing total control. Mr. Reynolds must have been incredulous at Scobey's reluctance. He had been a strong supporter of the band and was now offering the position of leading traditional jazz outfit with a major record label.

In a letter, Mr Reynolds sought Clancy's assistance in persuading Scobey to sign and even offered Clancy an exclusive solo contract with RCA if Scobey decided against joining. Eventually, in August, Bob Scobey's Frisco Band — complete with Clancy Hayes — signed with RCA Victor. Scobey appears to have avoided any exclusivity clause in the contract and so continued to also record for other labels including California Records (a Subsidiary of Contemporary/Good Time Jazz).

Bob Scobey's Frisco Band, Las Vegas 1956. Left to Right: Bill Napier, Fred Higuera Bob Scobey, Clancy Hayes, Jack Buck
(Courtesy Stanford University Libraries Archive / SFTJF)

FROM THE CLANCY HAYES
COLLECTION

J. WALTER THOMPSON COMPANY
Public Relations

Chicago 11, Illinois

(A transcription of this letter is on page 318)

410 N. MICHIGAN AVENUE

August 6, 1956

Dear Clancy et al:

I know you've seen it—but I want you to know I read the "trades" too.

So I send the clipping telling about the RCA business.

I really think the biggest thrill about the whole business is to have my two favorite vocalists signed at the same time—Lee Wiley and Clancy Hayes. Oh, no, I'm not forgetting Lizzie Miles. She's my favorite song belter, and I mean there's a difference.

Anyway, don't try to get away with anything, youse guys, because I'm constantly on the prowl and on the watch. Hope to get to San Francisco in person soon for a lot of reasons.

Bud got home from Fort Lee Saturday afternoon after a 29 hours drive. Saturday night was quiet as he slept until Sunday morning. Then the heat was turned on. Nothing but Scobey records throughout the day. He finally went out last evening or he'd still be catching up on some of the later stuff. He particularly likes the Down Home album. Best thing about that one is the bevy of Hayes numbers and the way the band pretty well plays "Stardust" straight. How gorgeous that way.

Have a nice time in L.A. and Vegas.

Best regards to Ann and the band,

RCA Adds 3 to Jazz Roster

NEW YORK — RCA Victor added three names to its jazz roster last week: Lee Wiley, Bob Scobey and Jack Montrose.
Thrush Wiley most recently recorded for Storyville, and previously for Columbia and Liberty Music Shops. Scobey, with his Frisco Dixieland band and vocalist Clancy Hayes, has been with Good Time Jazz. Montrose, tenor saxophonist-arranger, was with Atlantic. Deals were made for the diskery by jazz chief Fred Reynolds.

NEW YORK   DETROIT   CHICAGO   SAN FRANCISCO   LOS ANGELES   DENVER   ATLANTA   LONDON

Letter from J Walter Thompson Co.
(Courtesy Stanford University Libraries Archive / SFTJF)

The Scobey Years 1957-59: Travelin' Shoes

Towards the end of 1957, Bob Scobey made a bold decision to relocate the band. Although by this time he had made seven LPs and was now with RCA, he was struggling financially. In addition to income from record sales, the Scobey band played at least eighty-five gigs in 1957 — including two more very successful runs at the Blue Note. Perhaps it was this experience that encouraged Scobey to head for Chicago. Bob Scobey's Frisco Band had broken attendance records at the Blue Note yet struggled for gigs in the Bay Area. Scobey confessed to being sad about leaving Lafayette. In an interview he explained:

> I've struggled to stay in the Bay Area, in fact the last two years have kept me broke, but we just can't make it out here. On the other hand, the band does fine back east. Our stature is much greater there. We've built up quite a following in such cities as Chicago, Milwaukee, Cincinnati, Cleveland, Columbus and Minneapolis. That means lots of bookings and money.

Bob Scobey was married, had three grade-school children and had been settled in Lafayette for fourteen years. The move was a real upheaval, but necessary. Scobey's relocation was essentially about success for the band and the directly related issue of money. As for the musicians, the proposed move was a major challenge for everyone. Three musicians decided not to go. Jack Buck, who had been with Scobey since 1949, had four children and for him the upheaval was just too great. His decision was undoubtedly a real blow as he was both a superb trombonist and fine piano player, which had been especially useful in the early days at Victor's and Roxie's. Pianist Clyde Pound and bassist Tommy Beeson were West Coast natives and also decided not to leave San Francisco. On the positive side, Dave Black, Pete Dovidio, Doug Skinner and Toni Lee Scott were Chicago bound. But Clancy Hayes was undecided.

Scobey's decision must have created a dilemma for Clancy. A wholesale relocation away from his adored adopted home town of thirty years would be a real wrench. Since settling in the Bay Area,

Clancy had not needed to travel much in his entertainment career. His radio years and Scobey's three-year residence at the bistro of Mr and Mrs Victor Long at Sixth Ave. and E. 12th St. Oakland had allowed him a fairly settled lifestyle; but he would now need his 'travelin' shoes'. Eventually Clancy decided he would head east but only for a while. Vowing to be back soon, he kept his San Francisco home at 702, 46th Ave. As it turned out, his promised quick return would be somewhat delayed. Clancy bought some good winter clothes and left for Chicago on 25 January for the band's opening engagement; a four-week run at The Preview Lounge.

Although the majority of the Scobey band's 1957 gigs had been at the Pioneer Village in Lafayette, by far the most successful engagements were two further Blue Note gigs on 17-28 April and 16-20 October. The band attracted a lot of interest when performing outside of San Francisco. In other locations it had the draw of a visiting band with a strong reputation achieved through its significant and very popular record catalogue. Within the Bay Area there may have been a degree of familiarity that acted against their appeal and the number of suitable night spots was limited. Chicago was of course a larger and busier city with the famous Rush Street entertainment district and business conventions to bring in casual audiences. Scobey's decision proved to be a good one. Having struggled for a couple of years, the band was now in demand and the bookings flowed. After the initial Preview Lounge engagement came two weeks at The Chanticleer in Madison, Wisconsin. Other notable 1958 engagements included:

March 12-16	Wagon Wheel, Rockton, Illinois
April 9-30	Preview Lounge, Chicago
Mid-May	College tour of Illinois and Wisconsin (Chicago, Charleston, Moline, Bloomington, Appleton)
May 23-25	Sinton Hotel, Cincinnati
June 13-26	New Lakeview, Spring Park, Minneapolis, Minnesota
July	A four-week run at the Preview Lounge
August 8 -25	Stateline Lounge, Lake Tahoe, Nevada
August 29-September 17	Stage Bar, Reno
October 21-26	The Villa, Madison, Wisconsin
November 18-30	Crest Lounge, Detroit

In addition, there were gigs in Arlington, Stickney and Wateska, Illinois and on 7 June the Scobey band added an engagement at the Central Plaza Hotel in New York City to an RCA recording session.

At the Sinton Hotel, Cincinnati. Clancy Hayes, Bob Scobey, Brian Shanley.
(Courtesy New Orleans Jazz Club Collection of Louisiana State Library)

A private gig, not in the above list, took place in Toronto on 6 June when George Hulme, a twenty-eight-year-old English chemical engineer with Acorn Anodising (and most importantly a jazz fan) seized an opportunity created by his Canada posting. As part of his professional life George Hulme produced technical documents as both author and editor; he also used his skills to write about jazz as editor of *Matrix* magazine and contributor to *Discophile*, *Jazz Monthly* and *Coda*.[3]

George hired the Scobey band complete with Clancy and Toni Lee Scott for an engagement. At the time, the band was working only 521 miles from Toronto. Photographs from the gig are in this book and I am indebted to George who sent them to me during tape and letter exchanges in the late 1980s. An added bonus was his tape of the after-gig party where Clancy entertained on a piano that had been long estranged from its tuner; Clancy quipped, 'You'd better take this piano with you back to England'. Even after a full club-date, Clancy played Jelly Roll tunes on piano along with two Hayes originals: *Witch Watch* and *When The One You Love Is Gone*. As Clancy admitted many times 'I just like to play'.

Members of the Bob Scobey band at George Hulme's gig:
Left to Right: Rich Matteson, Jim Beebe, Brian Shanley,
Dave Black, Bob Scobey
(Courtesy George Hulme)

Floyd Bean and Clancy Hayes.
(Courtesy George Hulme)

Left, Lizzie Miles; centre, Bob Scobey, right Professor Hayakawa
with two appreciative fans
(Courtesy Stanford University Libraries Archive / SFTJF)

Bob Scobey's Band c. 1957: Left to Right: Clyde Pound (hidden), Bob Scobey, Clancy Hayes, Pete Dovidio, Jack Buck, Doug Skinner
(Courtesy New Orleans Jazz Club Collection of Louisiana State Library)

1958 also saw Clancy on film with Professor S. I Hayakawa for *The Semantics of Popular Song*, an educational programme that was interesting and entertaining enough to be shown on public television.[4] S. I. Hayakawa had toured universities in January and February 1956 (including Beloit, Chicago, Purdue) presenting a lecture-concert on *The Meanings of Jazz* with musical demonstrations by the Bob Scobey band including Clancy and Lizzie Miles.

When it came to making the thirty-minute film, Clancy would have been an obvious choice as musical illustrator. In the programme, Prof. Hayakawa reveals the unreal expectations of love in popular songs (*Dream House / My Ideal / Blue Room / My Blue Heaven*) as opposed to the earthier and more realistic presentation of human emotions in jazz and blues recordings (*A Good Man Is Hard To Find / St. James Infirmary / Nobody Knows You When You're Down And Out*).

Clancy's relaxed style and the obvious friendship with Prof. Hayakawa make this superb viewing. It is also, to date, the only freely available footage of Clancy in performance — apart from glimpses in the very brief Marlboro television commercial mentioned in the next chapter.

If 1958 saw a change in Bob Scobey's fortunes, then 1959 was destined to be even better. A club bearing his name — Bob Scobey's

Bourbon Street — opened on Thursday 22 January in the basement of the Towne Club in Madison, Wisconsin. The band played there from March until mid-April when a surprising change occurred: On 13 April the band switched to the Embassy Room at the Café Continental on Chicago's Rush Street. Although Bob Scobey's Bourbon Street in Madison continued to operate by bringing in name bands, Bob Scobey no longer played there. Instead, the band stayed at the Embassy Room for an eight-month run, winding up on 12 December.

On 19 April Will Leonard wrote in the *Chicago Tribune*:

> Bob Scobey and his Frisco Band seem about to become a Chicago band. The Dixieland trumpeter, who has been a Highland Park resident for the last year, has cast anchor at the Café Continental to play seven nights a week and it looks like being one of the happiest bookings of the season. The big Embassy room jumps as it never has in its ten-month history. Clancy Hayes, happily, still is ensconced on his high stool, strumming banjo and singing verse and chorus of more songs than most folks ever learn in a lifetime. Dave Black is on drums, Rich Matteson is on helicon (bass trumpet), Ron Di Phillips on piano, Brian Shanley on clarinet, and Jim Beebe on trombone, with Toni Lee Scott as vocalist. The sound is solid, so is business, and the outlook is bright.

Mr Leonard updated the band's progress on 12 July:

> Scobey's septet, who start their fourth month on Rush Street tomorrow night, are a diligent bunch who play good arrangements attentively but with spirit, rather than doodling the time away in individual solos. Bob says he doesn't know whether or not it's still his 'Frisco jazz band' because he's a Chicagoan now and doesn't call it that any more, although the recording makers still do. Scobey is in the Embassy Room Mondays through Saturdays…

During this period Bob Scobey used Chicago pianists George Zack and Oro 'Tut' Soper for several months. Jim Beebe communicated with jazz fan and writer Bert Whyatt for an article on Tut Soper and made some interesting comments about the challenge of playing piano with the Scobey band:

> Both Tut and George Zack worked with Scobey's band for several months each, but I can't remember which was first. The piano chair was demanding because of the wide range of material. We did a lot of early jazz classics and Clancy Hayes did a wide range of vocal material. We had a female vocalist, Toni Lee Scott, who had some fancy arrangements on stuff like *Ten Cents A Dance*. Neither Zack nor Tut were show pianists and they had trouble with these arrangements. There was grumbling in the rhythm section and it became apparent they wanted to get rid of Tut. I asked Clancy what the trouble was. He said that Tut was rushing the beat and it was driving everyone in the rhythm section nuts. Well, he was right. Tut was committing the worst sin that a pianist can do. It happens to a lot who single too much; they lose the sense of timing necessary to play in a band. So Scobey finally let Soper go but hired him to play intermission piano at the Café Continental in Chicago. He had Tut out there in the middle of the room with a sort of piano bar and when we were off, Tut would play.

When the Café Continental Embassy Room residence ended that December, the band took a scheduled eight-week break. This included a tour of Las Vegas, time off for the Christmas holiday and a return to the Bay Area for an engagement at Fack's II in Oakland. However, when Bob Scobey's Frisco Band returned to the Embassy Room things would look and sound very different.

7

The Scobey Split: He's A Good Man (But 1,850 Miles From Home) 1960 - 61

The new decade began with something of a shock for fans of Bob Scobey's Frisco Band. The longstanding Scobey and Clancy partnership was finished. When Bob Scobey returned to the Embassy Room on 15 February 1960 there was no Clancy and the band included 'The Idiots' - musicians and comedy entertainers previously with Spike Jones.

Bob Scobey at the Cafe Continental, advertisement
(Chicago Tribune, 4 April 1960)

Clancy left the band at the conclusion of the Facks II engagement. Instead of returning to Chicago, he headed for a two-week job at the Squaw Valley resort in California, playing with pianist Ralph Sutton at the Winter Olympics. He and Ralph were good friends and would play together occasionally for the rest of Clancy's career. From California, Clancy returned to Wisconsin to play weekends at the Towne Club which had operated as Scobey's 'Bourbon Street' the previous year. Having been a Wisconsin and Illinois regular for the past two years there was work available for Clancy both as a single and with local bands. There may also have been contractual obligations to explain a very unusual situation when Scobey and Clancy played opposite each other at the Café Continental's Embassy Room throughout April and May 1960.

One possible reason for Clancy's departure was covered in Bob Scobey's posthumous biography, *He Rambled 'Tll Cancer Cut Him Down* written by his second wife Jan. Her account suggests there was ill feeling concerning the royalty split from a lucrative TV commercial the Scobey band had made for Marlboro cigarettes in 1959.[1] Both Clancy and Toni Lee Scott sang in the commercial.

Whether or not this is so, and whether it was the sole reason for Clancy's departure, is something that remains unanswered. Jan Scobey also mentioned the possibility that Clancy may have been lured away by Joe Glaser's Associated Booking Corporation agency. Glaser handled many of the top names in the music industry, most famously Louis Armstrong. He had tried unsuccessfully to get one of his artists to perform in the Marlboro commercial. Jan Scobey's theory is probably true.

But it is likely that Clancy's decision was based on *several* factors. He may have regretted missing the chance offered by Fred Reynolds to be a solo artist with RCA and perhaps felt it was time to break out of the featured artist role. In any case, he and fellow band members Brian Shanley and Jim Beebe left the Scobey band. Clancy immediately sealed a deal for an album with Audio Fidelity Records.[2]

When Bob Scobey took his band back to the Bay Area for the Fack's II engagement in January, it may have exacerbated Clancy's homesickness and longing to return to his adopted city. His exodus two years earlier was supposed to be a short one. One thing is certain, Clancy loved San Francisco and he no doubt missed the temperate climate of the 'City by the Bay'. His promised return was *long* overdue. Clancy commented in a 1961 interview that, 'One of the graces of a real marriage is that Ann has made us a home wherever we go'. But residing in Chicago at 6200 North Kenmore was definitely not the same as living in San Francisco, as Clancy explained in a later interview, 'My roots are there. I love it. I think we all love our home town. It may be a big city but wherever you are if you're not there, you're not right at home'.[3]

Clancy's Chicago home: 6200 North Kenmore (2023)
(Courtesy Frank Selman)

Musical reasons may also have contributed to Clancy's decision. The Scobey band's style had changed during the Chicago years. In a 1959 interview he commented that he wasn't sure if it was still the 'Frisco' band or a 'Chicago' band. A listen to the 1959 RCA album *Rompin' and Stompin'* would indicate that it was very much the latter. This album was unusual in that it comprised twelve classic New Orleans jazz tunes, quite a departure from the programming on previous Scobey LPs. Most surprisingly, for the first time, it was a Scobey album with no vocals.

Whatever the reason or reasons, it appears there was no insurmountable ill feeling in the breakup between Clancy and Scobey. Within weeks, they shared the bandstand at the Embassy Room and would share other gigs in 1960-61. Moreover, in 1962 Clancy returned to Chicago to fill in at Scobey's new Bourbon Street club on Rush Street while the Scobey band toured Europe with the Harlem Globetrotters. Finally, it is worth noting that in researching for this book, I came across not a single word of criticism from either party. Ten years of close friendship and success had formed a very special relationship that withstood whatever led to the parting of the ways. But if Clancy's plan was for a quick return to California he was to be disappointed; it would be eighteen months before he made it home.

Bob Scobey had been right about the availability of work around Chicago and Madison. Having lost the services of Clancy and the other musicians, he experimented with a Las Vegas type floor show. Scobey's recruitment of the Idiots may have helped put on a show, but it wasn't what a Chicago audience expected, or wanted, from Bob Scobey. The reviewer who described the new act in *Chicago Tribune* of 21 February was less than enthusiastic:

At the Café Continental

> Bob Scobey, once of Lu Watters' Yerba Buena Jazz Band that took its Dixieland seriously, now is in the clowning business, as well as the two-beat trade. New in the line up of his ensemble newly returned to the Café Continental are Freddy Morgan, Elaine Evans and Mack Pearson, formerly of Spike Jones' band who call themselves 'The Idiots' and act as if they believe their billing.

At the beginning of April, Clancy played a Friday and Saturday gig at the Towne Club, Madison and a Sunday night at the Union Hall Club Racine, WI. billed as 'The Barrelhouse Nightingale.' However, Monday night 4 April found him back at the Café Continental's Embassy Room playing with Art Hodes — opposite the Scobey Band. The engagement lasted through April up to the end of May when Art Hodes departed, leaving Clancy to continue as a single opposite the Bob Scobey band.

Clancy with his Vegaphone Deluxe six-string banjo, 1960.
(Publicity photo courtesy New Orleans Jazz Club Collection of Louisiana State Library)

Bob Scobey quickly abandoned his experiment with comedy and returned to a straight jazz band; Las Vegas style entertainment didn't work in Chicago. The refocused band included Dickie Philips, electric bass; Bill Napier, clarinet; Tom Smoot, piano; Richard Nelson, trombone; and the ever-present Dave Black on drums. Scobey was back on track, but it was Clancy who took the stage at the Café Continental Embassy Room as Scobey's band departed for engagements in Minneapolis and Madison.

The somewhat strange arrangements at the Embassy took another turn at the end of June 1960 after both Bob Scobey and Art Hodes had left. The stage was now taken by Clancy Hayes' Dixiecrats for a summer-long engagement playing six nights a week. Clancy was the titular leader of a band which included Nappy Trottier, trumpet; Jim Beebe, trombone; Brian Shanley, clarinet; George Zack, piano; Casey Duda, bass; and Bill Pfeiffer, drums. The final Embassy twist came when the Dixiecrats were bolstered by another Scobey alumnus in early July; enter Toni Lee Scott. The Embassy run ended in September and Clancy's now renamed Dixieland Band (with Floyd Bean replacing George Zack) went on to play engagements at Gallagher's Steak House in Milwaukee and the Boulevard Room in Madison.

Clancy had played with Jim Beebe, Brian Shanley and, for a brief period, George Zack in Bob Scobey bands. As already noted, George Zack had a spell with the band around 1958 or '59; his story is told in *Chicago Jazz — The Second Line* written by Derek Coller and Bert Whyatt.[4] This excellent book shines a deserved light on several of the lesser-known names of white Chicago Jazz including Oro 'Tut' Soper, Floyd Bean, Jack Gardner and Zack. This welcome exposure reveals interesting and illuminating stories about the times, the music, the musicians and their love and appreciation of jazz.

George Zack had suffered a bizarre introduction to the harder side of life when still a child. At a Sunday lunch, his father stood up, announced he was tired of family life and left the room never to reappear. George was born on 20 July 1910 and took piano lessons from an early age, but his teacher soon realised his ability was something special. As with all good stories, there are several entertaining versions as to how he got into jazz. Perhaps the best is that having developed his musical talent at the Chicago Conservatory of Music for four years, he was tiring of bookwork and theory. Walking through the city one day around 1926 he encountered the King Oliver band tailgating to advertise their Sunset Café residence. (Interestingly the famous Sunset Café was managed at the time by Joe Glaser of ABC and Louis Armstrong connection). Pied Piper (or trumpeter) style, George followed the truck and the episode ended his classical studies; he was hooked. He would spend a lifetime in jazz and is probably best known for his recordings with the Muggsy Spanier band in 1939. Regrettably, he made few solo recordings.[5]

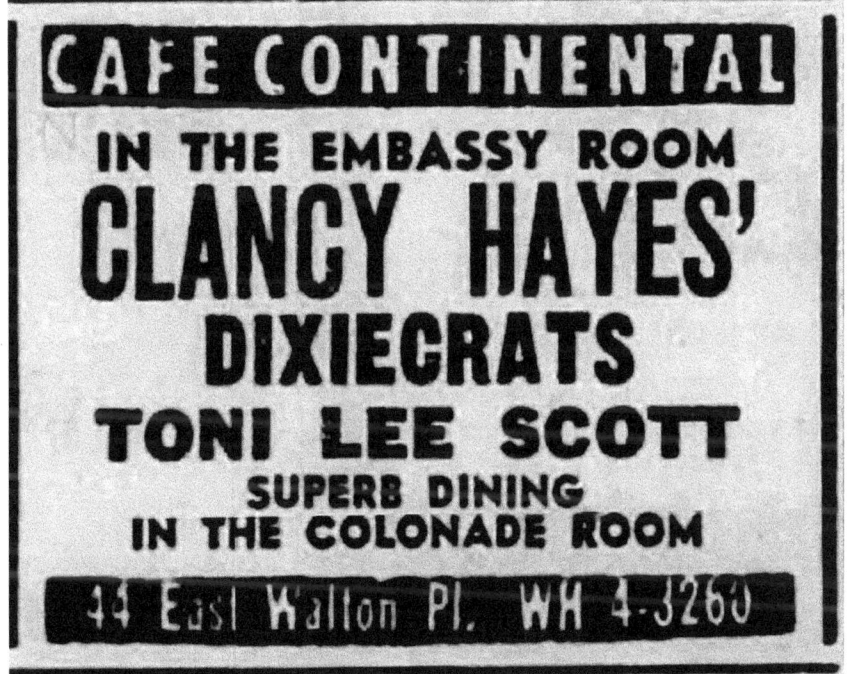

Clancy Hayes' Dixicrats, Café Continental, Chicago IL advertisement
(Chicago Tribune, 24 June 1960)

Clancy Hayes was undoubtedly a man with a multitude of talents, but it is debatable whether at the age of fifty-two he was cut out for the role of bandleader — despite his earlier attempts. He had considered organizing a band as early as 1934, and again with the Bay

City Boys in 1947/8; but his easygoing personality may have been a detriment to the sometimes tough attitude needed to lead a band. It may be that the 'bandleader' designation was window dressing to attract the audience with the Clancy Hayes name. In November, the band played a six-week residency at the Orchard Twin Dixieland Lane (a bowling alley) in Skokie, Illinois. However, the band was now billed as 'Nappy Trottier's Dixieland All Star Band'. Clancy was back to his familiar and probably more comfortable role as featured artist. Otherwise, it was a case of *Same band; different leader*.

During the Orchard Twin engagement, Clancy may have made a New Year resolution to return to his beloved San Francisco. However, that did not happen immediately. He remained actively employed in the Midwest for several more months, including a gig at the Badger Room in Madison that criss-crossed with Bob Scobey's band.

Nappy Trottier's Band with Clancy Hayes advertisement
(Chicago Tribune, 25 December 1960)

The first steps towards a return to San Francisco began in the spring with a three-month residency, playing six nights a week at Kenkel's in Dayton, Ohio. Though Dayton was no closer to San Francisco than the other gigs in the Midwest, it at least offered a break from the

Illinois-Wisconsin circuit of the past three years. Kenkel's was a 450-seat restaurant with top-name entertainment. The bands of Pee Wee Hunt, Billy Butterfield, Kay Winding and Billy Maxted performed there prior to Clancy's appearance.

Kenkel's Dixieland Band, Dayton OH advertisement
(The Journal Herald, Dayton, Ohio, February 1961)

Clancy was involved in assembling the Dixieland band which performed at Kenkel's. The personnel consisted of: Andy Bartha, trumpet; Eddie Hubble, trombone; Brian Shanley, clarinet; Bob Hirsch, piano; Gene Mayl, bass; and Walt Gifford, drums. There is a story behind one band member that shows his generosity and admiration for Clancy...

Andy Bartha was a true friend. A superbly gifted musician, he was a violinist with Arthur Fielder's Orchestra at the time the Japanese attacked Pearl Harbor. Within weeks he was in the U.S. Air Force, having exchanged his violin and bow for an anti-aircraft gun and trumpet — 'because that's what they needed'. (Marching bands in the Armed Services do not have string sections!). Obeying orders, Andy learned to play his new instrument and thus began a musical double life of concert violinist and jazz trumpeter.

After the war, Bartha had a ten-year career with Pee Wee Hunt making over 300 recordings. He settled in Florida in late 1959, having previously bought a house and touring the USA for eighteen months to pay for it. After sanding boats for six months while sweating out his Florida Musicians Union card, he received a call from Clancy. 'Andy the Condor — the mighty midget of the Everglades' as Clancy called him, was Dayton bound for the three-month gig. They were friends indeed, and their paths would cross again.

Clancy's return to the Bay Area was still on 'hold' after he landed a very lucrative contract with the Playboy organization, negotiated through Associated Booking Corporation. Booked as a single, Clancy had an engagement for a club opening at 7701 Biscayne Blvd. Miami starting on 10 May 1961 through to 10 June. The contract also gave Playboy options for three-week engagements over the coming three years. As usual, the schedule was demanding: a seven-day work week with three shows on weekdays and four on Friday and Saturday (plus a late-afternoon rehearsal on the opening day). Clancy was one of five headliners, together with singers Mae Barnes, Johnny Janis and the Starr Sisters. Comedian Don Sherman completed the bill along with the house band 'Movie Biz'. A contemporary press review described Clancy as a 'barrelhouse nightingale acclaimed by jazz buffs as a "hip" Burl Ives'. Of the many names and descriptions bestowed to Clarence Leonard Hayes over the years, 'a hip Burl Ives' may be the most surreal. Despite the questionable label, Clancy's Playboy engagements most likely went very well as he was booked for a nine-week club tour the following year. It is easy to imagine him scanning the Playboy audience as he began to sing *Ace In The Hole* or *Wise Guy*.

Joe Glaser's ABC also secured a lengthy engagement at Jazz Ltd.. Chicago, beginning in August 1961. But there was a two-week gap during the month of July allowing a brief return to San Francisco.

Clancy Hayes with members of his 1960 Dixiecrats which became Nappy Trottier's Dixieland All Star Band: Standing L-R Jim Beebe, Bill Pfeiffer, Nappy Trottier, unknown(possibly Casey Duda), Clancy: seated - Brian Shanley, George Zack.
(Courtesy Frank Selman / SFTJF)

8

(Back Home Again In) San Francisco 1961 — 62

Clancy's opportunity to get back to San Francisco and play — albeit for just two weeks — came via his old Yerba Buena bandmate Turk Murphy. On the basis that absence makes the audience's collective heart grow fonder, Earthquake McGoon's (which Turk ran with partner Pete Clute at 99 Broadway) was just the place. The local press announced that 'bald old Clancy Hayes, the banjo strummer, is to rejoin the Turk Murphy band'.[1] Despite the slight inaccuracy of the report (Clancy was never part of the Turk Murphy band) once again it would seem the thickness of Clancy's skin was being tested. Clancy's baldness was in some respects a trademark and there is affection in the description. Bald, undoubtedly, but old? That sort of 'affection' is something that fifty-three-year-olds can definitely do without!

On 2 July 1961, Clancy opened as the intermission act at Earthquake McGoon's.

Having re-engaged with California sunshine for a mere two weeks, Clancy returned to Chicago for the three-month engagement at Jazz Ltd, 164 East Grand Ave. Like McGoon's, this was a genuine jazz club — no bowling or á la carte. Clarinettist Bill Reinhardt and his wife Ruth opened Jazz Ltd in June 1947. In its early years, the house band included such luminaries as Muggsy Spanier, Sidney Bechet, Doc Evans, Miff Mole, Don Ewell and Sidney 'Big Sid' Catlett. Clancy was scheduled to perform from 9:30 pm until 3:30 am Monday through Wednesday and Friday and Saturday nights until 4:30 a.m. (Fortunately Thursday and Sunday were rest days). Clancy's appearance was greeted with great enthusiasm; one reviewer compared Clancy's fit with Bill Reinhardt to 'ham and eggs'.[2]

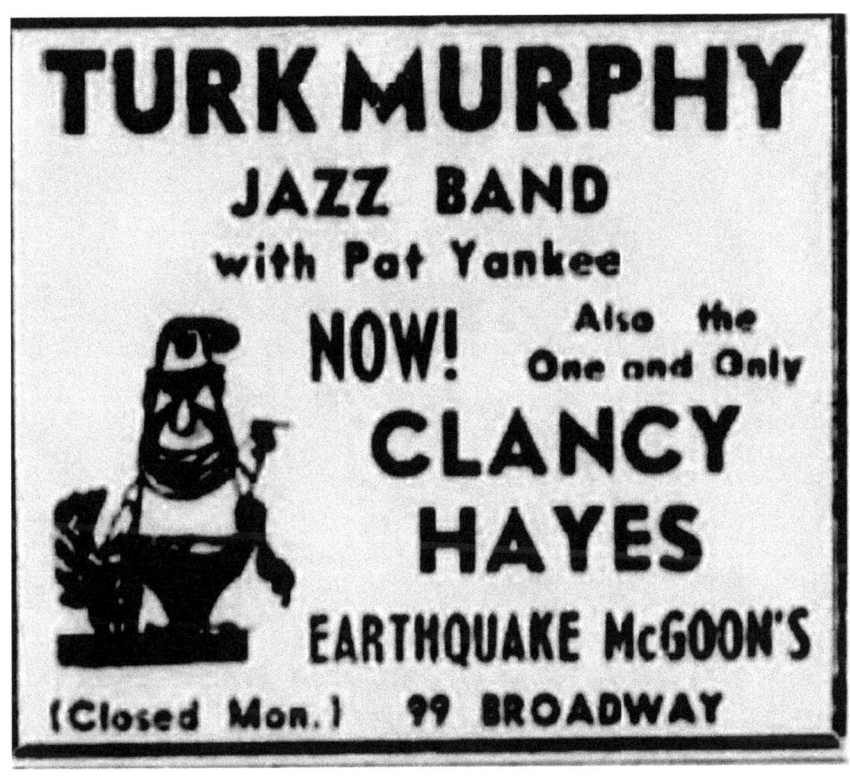

Clancy Hayes at Earthquake McGoon's advertisement
(San Franciso Examiner, 17 December 1961)

Bob Scobey's decision to relocate to Chicago in 1958 was a wise move. There was plenty of work in the area and by 1961 Scobey had his own club on Rush Street. Back in San Francisco, Turk Murphy and Pete Clute's Earthquake McGoon's was also doing good business with a mix of regular jazz fans, visitors in town on business and tourists who were bussed in. When Clancy's engagement at Jazz Ltd finished at the end of October, he was again offered the intermission spot at McGoon's, this time on a permanent basis. The arrangement worked well for both Turk and Clancy, allowing each to travel for out-of-town engagements. When Turk's band was on the road, Clancy took care of the music side of things. Turk and Clancy had of course known each other since the 1930s and Clancy was to be part of the Earthquake McGoon's set-up until illness forced his premature retirement in March 1970.

During Clancy's stay in Chicago, Andy Bartha wrote to say hello and wish him well:

> so its Thursday
>
> Greetings o' Clancey
>
> Just closing after 18 wks. think I have a better spot. Nothing for sure yet, playing a lot of fiddle feels good to get back to it. Got 4 men Piano, Drum, Trombone D. bass myself on Cornet & violin, we get off the ground on occasion, (still cant spell) Teagarden & Don Ewell bought a home in the Pompano area. So I know I'm in the right place — also a couple of Maxted's bunch are going to do the same.

Letter from Andy Bartha
(Courtesy Stanford University Libraries Archve / SFTJF)

Hope everything is O.K. on your end massa Simba, o sage of the pluckers. Shure do miss Geo. Washington, otto, + swingingdoors, meaning, you all — a very happy thing in Dayton. When you left you took me with you.

Hope to hear from you. Give my love to your family, + best regards to Bill + Ruth + all the guys. Tell Bill when he comes down here to bring the clarinet.

The hell with sitting in the sun. Much better to sit on the bandstand. s/o buddy

otto.

(A transcription of this letter is on page 319)

Earthquake McGoon's: Clancy Hayes is Back. advertisement
(San Francisco Examiner, 2 December 1961)

Clancy played at McGoon's throughout December 1961. Turk commented 'He's here on a definite indefinite run, he can stay as long as he wants to'; and he did. Having at last got back to San Francisco, it would be a full six months before Clancy hit the road again in May 1962.

Clancy's first trip away from his new base was to do a favour for an old friend, returning to Chicago to play a six-week engagement at Bob Scobey's 'Bourbon Street' on Rush Street. The Scobey outfit was in Europe, playing intermissions for the Harlem Globetrotters tour. Art Hodes led the band, which also featured vocalist Toni Lee Scott. The gig began on 21 May and followed a two-week stint by Kenny Ball's Jazzmen from the United Kingdom.[3]

> **Bob Scobey Presents**
> **Direct from England**
> # KENNY BALL
> Hit Record—Midnite in Moscow
> Only American Engagement
> **NO COVER**
>
> ---
>
> OPENING MAY 21—
> Bob Scobey's Alumni
> ## CLANCY HAYES
> ## TONI LEE SCOTT
> # BOURBON ST.
> **936 N. RUSH ST.**   **WH 3-2650**

Kenny Ball at Bourbon Street, Chicago IL advertisement
(Chicago Tribune, 18 May 1962)

Clancy returned to McGoon's on 15 July for three weeks before once again donning his travelin' shoes. His next out-of-town trip involved a nine-week tour of Playboy clubs in New Orleans, Chicago and Miami. Clancy may have wondered how a musician associated with San Francisco Jazz would be received in the birthplace of jazz.[4] When word got out of his visit, Harry Souchon, President of the New Orleans Jazz Club, wrote expressing his enthusiasm and extending an invitation to one of their regular Sunday gatherings. Clancy was also asked to open their monthly Jam session at the Grand Ballroom in the Roosevelt Hotel the following night, backed up by Paul Crawford's Levee Stompers.[5] The *Times-Picayune* article promoting his appearance explained that the session would be starting earlier to accommodate the 'full roster' which included the Eureka Brass Band, the Lionel Woods Brothers and Teddy Ludwig's Footwarmers — a teen-age combo.

Ragtime 45 Midnight in Moscow, Bob Scobey's Ragtime Band, label
(Author's collection)

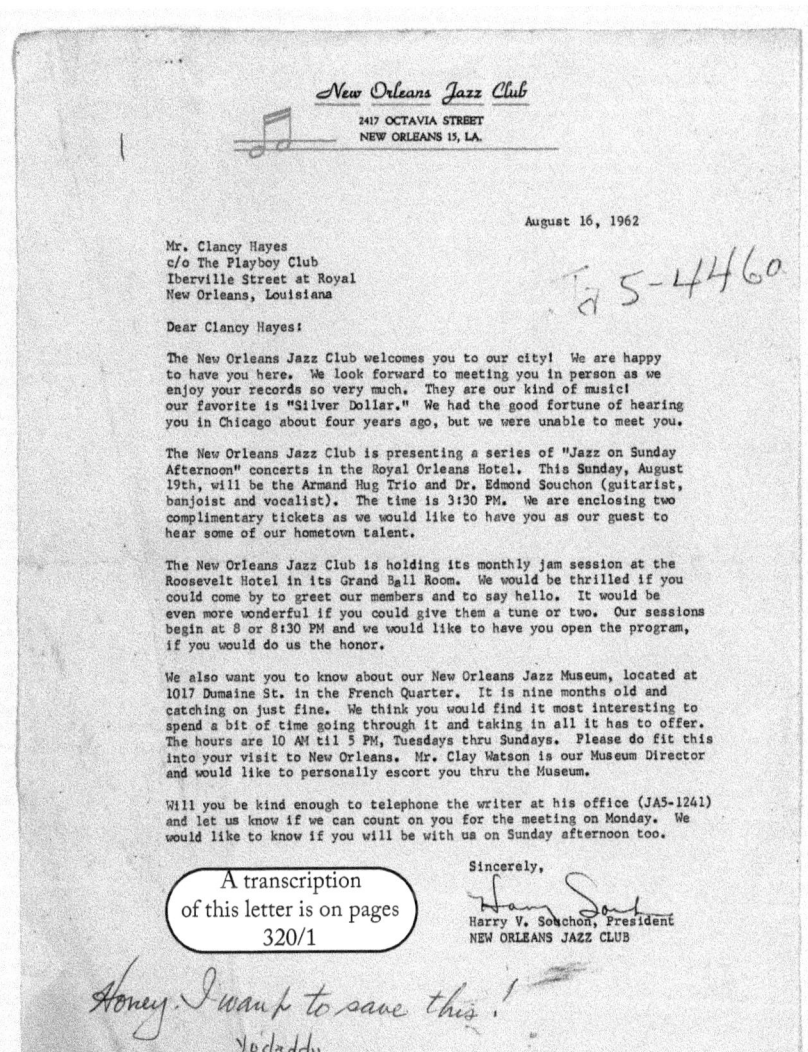

Letter from New Orleans Jazz Club, August 16, 1962
(Courtesy Stanford University Libraries Archve / SFTJF)

This sequence of letters from his collection tell the story and show the appeal of Clancy Hayes as an entertainer and jazz man. Equally they show the generosity and warmth of the New Orleans jazz community and abundant mutual respect. Clancy probably hummed his composition *In New Orleans* for some time after visiting the Crescent City.

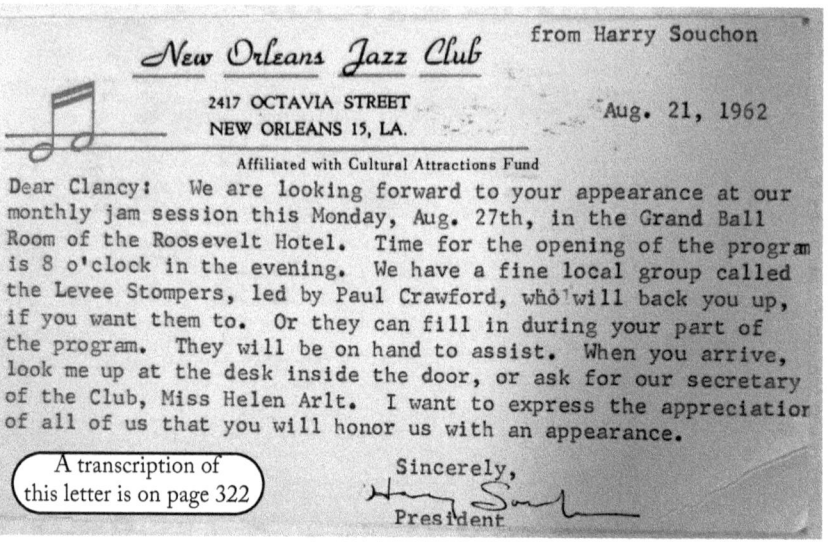

Letter from New Orleans Jazz Club, August 21, 1962
(Courtesy Stanford University Libraries Archve / SFTJF)

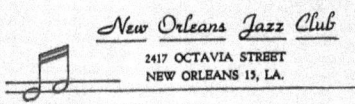

2417 OCTAVIA STREET
NEW ORLEANS 15, LA.

September 11, 1962

A transcription of this letter is on pages 323/4

Dear Clancy:

    Well, who do you think was looking back at us from our TV sets this past Thursday? You! It was an educational station and the program was entitled (I believe) Words in Action. It's subject was the words to love songs and the narration was done by a Japanese fellow. You did the illustrations by singing the words to given songs he wanted illustrated. It was good and we enjoyed seeing and hearing you so soon after the real thing -- your performing in person both at the Play Boy Club and particularly at our own New Orleans Jazz Club August jam session.

    Wanted to write you before now and say "hello" from a southern friend on your opening at the Chicago Play Boy Club, but too much detail and work at the office prevented my doing so. Hope this will make up for the good intention I had. Since you are an "adopted" New Orleans son, we will have to keep in touch. Won't you give us that pleasure? For it was so easy to be with you and know you in such a short time, that we feel like old, old friends.

    Let me convey the thanks of our Board of Directors for your interest in our Club activities and the Jazz Museum at 1017 Dumaine Street. We were honored to have you and we hope you will enjoy receiving our publication, THE SECOND LINE. We look forward to your fulfilling your promise to send us some material to display in our Museum, for we will be mighty proud to have it.

    We feel we are doing the most conscientious job of promoting New Orleans jazz and our people are truly dedicated who are serving the Club with their voluntary time and effort. It would be deeply appreciated if you would endeavor to spread our word around wherever you might find an interested listener. Word of mouth is probably our best means of becoming known. Although our Museum will be one year old on November 12th, we have already done exceptionally well, we feel, in becoming as well known as we are at this point.

    Again let me say thanks, both for performing at our session, and also for letting us get to know you better and be with you that wonderful Saturday night at the Play Boy Club. Our only complaint - your stint was far too short!

    We'll be awaiting word from you - just to keep in touch.

                                            Bye, you all,

Mr. Clancy Hayes
c/o THE PLAYBOY CLUB
Chicago, Illinois

Letter from New Orleans Jazz Club, September 11, 1962
(Courtesy Stanford University Libraries Archve / SFTJF)

At the New Orleans Jazz Museum
(Courtesy of New Orleans Jazz Club Collection of Louisiana State Library)

Clancy's notation on Harry Souchon's August 16 letter shows his delight at the New Orleans welcome.

As for Clancy's performance at the Monday Jam session, the September/October NOJC magazine *The Second Line* reported:

> Banjoist Clancy Hayes, of San Francisco and Chicago, blew into New Orleans for a first visit in August and assessing our town concluded: 'It's a gasser — a seven-ply gasser!'
>
> New Orleans and particularly New Orleans Jazz Clubbers returned the compliment. They took to each other like booze and blues.
>
> Taking a breather from his regular chores at the Playboy Club, Mr. Hayes put in an early evening appearance at the August session of the Jazz club where he was backed up by our own popular Crawford-Ferguson band. The meeting having been advanced half an hour to fit his Playboy show schedule, Mr. Hayes was greeted by only half a house in the Roosevelt Grand Ballroom.
>
> But with characteristic enthusiasm that shines alike for a handful or a house full, he launched into a sparkling slate of standards and novelty numbers, including the nostalgic *Do You Know What It Means To Miss New Orleans*, the rarely sung *Tin Roof Blues* and his own *The Ace in The Hole* and *Silver Dollar*. His presentation was in a pleasant mellow blues voice with an agile well-disciplined accompaniment.
>
> By the time he was half through his stand, the growing crowd was captivated by his warm personality and his obvious delight at performing with an authentic New Orleans Jazz combo — and it is one of the best in the business. Without rehearsal the competent Crawford-Ferguson group gave smooth and solid backing to Hayes' unique arrangements. [6]

Before getting away for his Playboy gig, Clancy was made an honorary member of the New Orleans Jazz Club. Helen Arlt's letter makes it clear that Clancy was now 'an adopted son' of New Orleans. How proud he must have been. The following letter from Clancy to Ann tells of the public response and how he was touched by the Brunies' hospitality. What a pity there is no tape recording of the proceedings. (Maybe a recording will eventually turn up?) Clancy would have almost certainly taken his banjo to the event.

> Wed. 10:25 P.M.
>
> Hi my darlings —
> A sleepy day for me because it was rainy and (HOT) out so I just stayed in the cave and snoozed — watched T.V. and snoozed some more. Just read your letter and am sure I'll enjoy our nice clean apt. Just to be home will suit me fine. That meat loaf sounds wonderful, I think I'll have another slice.
> I am having dinner tomorrow with Harry Brunies, and the whole Brunies family. This is Geo.'s brother I mentioned before. He insisted I come to their home so I could meet the mother.

These are wonderful people in Jazz music — all very gifted and left such tunes as "Tin Roof," "Wish I could Shimmy, Ugly Chile, etc, etc.

Don't know why I should be surprised, after all the records I have made about N.O. but I am about the biggest hero (hear me) since Gen Jackson Fit the Battle of New Orleans. Can't even get thru the lobby without pictures, autographs, and stares.

Finally got my confirmation on a flight to Chicago on Delta Air Line. Will write more soon

All my love
"Yo' daddy"

(A transcription of this letter is on page 325)

Letter to "my darlings"
(Courtesy Stanford University Libraris Archive / SFTJF)

After the delights of New Orleans, the other two Playboy gigs were probably more routine but for sure Clancy would have given his all, whether to a 'handful or a house full'. Clancy was one of a group of artists providing mixed entertainment. The Chicago stage was shared with three comics, three other singers, five instrumental groups, a ventriloquist and a puppeteer. In Miami, he was billed as a 'Dixieland Favorite' and one of six acts. Stage time was probably short, but the nights were long — six shows a night running to 3 am. The late nights and hotel living was probably a challenge but the weekly pay of $600 may have been a consolation, along with the thought of putting away the 'travelin' shoes' in November, for a well-earned rest.

Earthquake McGoon's, advertisements
(Above: Author's collection; below, courtesy Hal Smith)

9

Golden Years 1963 -1969

Clancy's musical activities between 1963 and 1969 followed a steady pattern in what were to prove golden years. Anchored happily in San Francisco he travelled only occasionally for selected out of town gigs.

By the early 1960s, Clarence Leonard Hayes had been in the professional entertainment business for thirty-five years. He had accumulated twenty years of radio fame and a jazz pedigree as a founder member of the great Lu Watters' Yerba Buena Jazz Band and featured artist with Bob Scobey's Frisco Band. Clancy had wide appeal to musicians and jazz fans alike as his reception in New Orleans (and just about everywhere else) showed. He was unique in traditional jazz circles since first and foremost he was a *vocalist*. While other traditional jazz artists may have excellent or even unique voices they are primarily *musicians* rather than *vocalists*. Clancy was the opposite. A wonderful vocalist who just happened to play banjo, guitar and drums. He also possessed an unerring sense of time. This attribute is mentioned in many reviews and liner notes and is evident in just about everything he recorded.

Clancy expressed the view that jazz singing was all about, what he called 'the beat' and one of his many musical gifts was the ability to find the right rhythm for a song. He gave the example of Johnny Mercer, who Clancy felt did not have a great voice, but he had the *beat*. Clancy also felt that it was a vital component for instrumentalists: 'Bands have to have it too, and they have to have a spirit shining through and to have fun — or it isn't any fun for the listener.'

A wonderful example on record is Clancy's spoken introduction to *Mama's Gone Goodbye* leading the Tune Termites in their live and obviously unrehearsed set on the 1968 Blue Angel Jazz Club album.

Clancy kicks off the song rhythmically admonishing, 'Not too fast, not too slow, right in the middle — away we go...' His introduction is temporarily disrupted when clarinettist Matty Matlock asks politely about the key signature. Discussion among the musicians ensues, with Clancy joking: 'Listen. If we get lost, we'll meet at the drug store, OK?' When the musicians finally start playing (in the key of Eb), the performance is truly memorable — with a well-chosen tempo, courtesy of Clancy Hayes.

As a single, and with the security of the McGoon's permanent gig, Clancy's selected musical excursions and associations ranged from spirited amateur bands to some of the best professionals in the business. But each time, it is clear that Clancy had a lot of fun. Detailed below are some of Clancy's memorable gigs and activities which demonstrate his love of jazz music and his ability to 'jazz it'.

The Docs of Dixieland: 1963, 1965, 1966.

In April 1963, Clancy made his first excursion of the year, travelling to Dayton, Ohio to perform in concert with the Docs of Dixieland (the best smiles in jazz). This amateur group of jazz loving dentists was organized in 1959. Each April, beginning in 1960, they played for the Kettering Rotary Club — augmenting their performances with guest artists and bands such as the Salt City Six, Dukes of Dixieland and Dayton's own Dixieland Rhythm Kings. Clancy was hired as the main attraction for their fourth annual event, dedicated to him in recognition of his services to jazz. He returned to perform in 1965 and 1966 when he shared the bill with the Cincinnati-based Gin Bottle Seven. A compilation of recordings from the three concerts was issued on Dox LP 12367.[1] Six tracks from the 1965 concert were issued on a double CD in 2002.

IN CONCERT

THE DOCS of DIXIELAND

and

CLANCY HAYES

**MEMORIAL HALL
SATURDAY,
April 20—8:30 P.M.**

ALL SEATS RESERVED

$2.50 Tax Incl.

*Tickets at Hauer Music Houses
and Mayer's Jewelry*

Docs of Dixieland Concert, 20 April 1963, advertisement
(Dayton Daily News, 17 April 1963)

The Dayton Scene, album cover
(Author's collection)

Oh By Jingo! — Clancy and the Original Salty Dogs 1964

August 1964 was to prove a busy month for Clancy with a month-long engagement at the Plugged Nickel, a weekend performance as a guest artist at Dick Gibson's Aspen Jazz Party, and on the last day of the month he recorded an LP. The Plugged Nickel was a newly opened 'Dixie joint' on Wells Street, Chicago. The house band was led by clarinettist Lance Schulz and included two musicians who had played on Clancy's 1960 Audio Fidelity album: trombonist Bill

Hanck and trumpeter Bob Ballard. The exceptionally gifted Jim Dapogny, later to become Professor Dapogny at the University of Michigan, was on piano.

On the second Saturday night of the engagement, three members of the Original Salty Dogs sat in: cornetist Lew Green, clarinettist Kim Cusack and pianist Johnny Cooper, who also played tuba. The resulting performance was so good that Clancy had a bright idea.

A few days earlier he had wandered into Bob Koester's Jazz Record Mart. In conversation regarding the recently released Swingin' Minstrel album on Good Time Jazz, Mr Koester happened to mention that he also had his own record label and would love to make an album featuring Clancy. Now was the time to test Mr Koester's resolve.

Clancy returned to the Jazz Record Mart and said, 'Look. I know you haven't got any money, but if you can dig up enough for the session to pay the boys, I am willing to split my royalty with them. If you'll let me use the men I want, play the tunes I want, in the way I want and keep out of my hair, I'll make a record for you'.[2]

This incident demonstrates Clancy's willingness to do things on the spur of the moment. Drummer Wayne Jones, an 'original' Salty Dog, from the band's formation at Purdue University in 1947, confirmed that the album was hastily organised. Pete Clute also recalled in a later interview with Dave Radlauer: 'Clancy was always up to doing something on the spur of the moment. He loved to do things just sort of off-the-cuff and was never at a loss for words for anything. And he knew every tune and the verses and the chorus.'

Just a single day (31 August) was available for the recording session. The resulting Delmark album, Oh By Jingo, also issued in the UK on Doug Dobell's 77 label, is a gem that stands the test of time. It is no wonder Clancy chose to record with the Original Salty Dogs as they were one of the best traditional jazz bands to be heard anywhere. The regular personnel was altered slightly for the session with Clancy replacing banjoist Bob Sundstrom and pianist Jim Dapogny switching to cornet (Hal Smith advised that he also added the tagline 'Eight-piece jazz band — the kind men like' on the album cover).

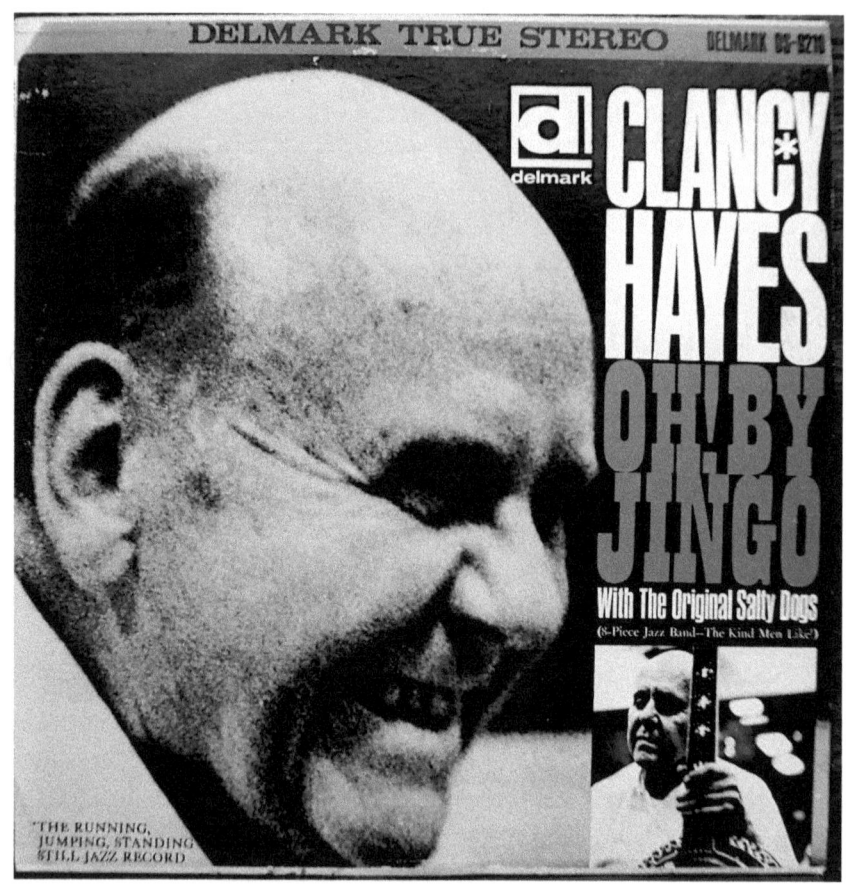

Oh By Jingo! Delmark album cover
(Courtesy Julia A. Miller, Delmark Records LLC)

Wayne Jones' detailed and entertaining album sleeve notes explain that Clancy picked the vocal tracks and the band chose the three instrumentals. The whole episode must have sparked something in Clancy. He dusted off *Oh By Jingo!* and *My Little Bimbo*, songs he hadn't recorded since the last of the Yerba Buena days. In addition, he took the opportunity to sing two songs he'd never recorded — *Wise Guy* and *I'm Coming Virginia*. Clearly, he got great satisfaction playing with such a superb two cornet traditional jazz outfit. The beat, spirit and fun shine throughout.[3]

Clancy in action at Earthquake McGoon's
(Courtesy Julia Carroll and Dom Adinolfi)

Jazz In The Troc and the World's Greatest Jazz Band 1964-69

Starting in 1964, when not handling the intermissions at Earthquake McGoon's, (now at 630 Clay Street, S.F.) Clancy played with Yank Lawson, Bob Haggart and Ralph Sutton in bands that included other true jazz greats.

Their association began when jazz fan, wealthy businessman and investment banker Dick Gibson had a brilliant idea. Mr Gibson moved from New York to Denver in the early 1960s and after a couple of years asked his wife Maddie what she most missed about the East. 'The ocean and jazz' came the reply. In 1963 Mr Gibson brought jazz to Denver in the form of a three-day private party at the Jerome Hotel in nearby Aspen. The event featured ten world class musicians and 200 invited guests. Things went so well that plans were made for a gathering the following year and to invite additional musicians. Among the performers at that first party was ex-Scobeyite and Aspen resident Ralph Sutton. Clancy and Ralph were good friends and Clancy had played at Sunnie's Rendezvous, Aspen (owned by Ralph and his wife Sunnie). Ralph may have suggested Clancy as an ideal addition to the party — or perhaps he was Dick Gibson's choice. Either way, Mr Gibson very much wanted to include Clancy in the programme, despite the conflict with his booking at the Plugged Nickel.

One of the guests at the invitation-only event was Jack Gurtler, co-owner of Denver's historic Elitch Gardens amusement park. Elitch Gardens was built in the late 19th century. In addition to spectacular gardens and rides, it accommodated a huge ballroom — The Trocadero, noted for its period charm. Dancing at Elitch Gardens had been an annual summer event for many years. The best dance bands had played there during the 1930s and 1940s; Isham Jones, Ben Pollack, Benny Goodman, Ray Noble, Tommy Dorsey, among others. Having seen the fun and excitement at the Dick Gibson party, Jack Gurtler wondered if the small jazz band from the party could entertain as many as 2500 dancers at his Trocadero Ballroom?

Still undecided, Mr Gurtler went to see how the band would be received by a young crowd at the Denver Symphony Debutantes' Ball, held in December at the Brown Palace Hotel. The band that evening consisted of Yank Lawson, trumpet; Cutty Cutshall, trombone; Lou McGarity, trombone; Peanuts Hucko, clarinet; Ralph Sutton, piano; Clancy Hayes, banjo and vocal; Bob Haggart, bass; and Cliff Leeman, drums.

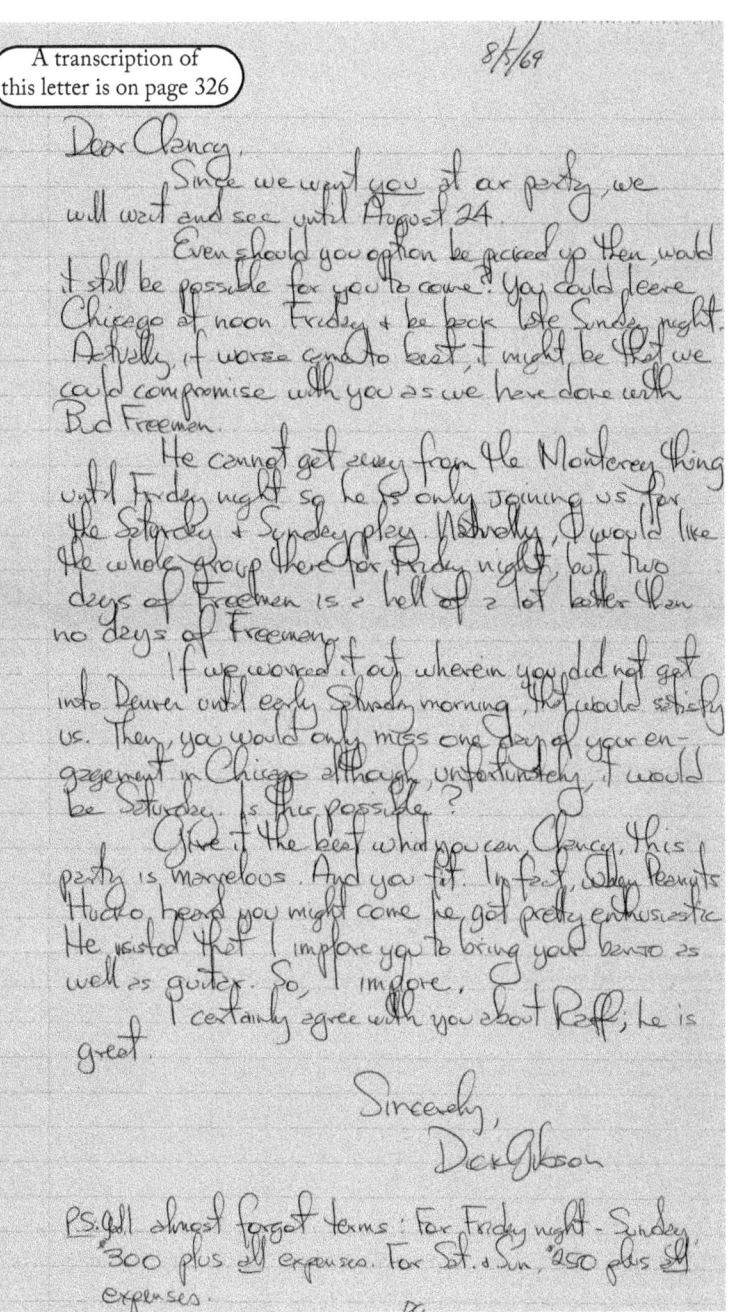

Letter from Dick Gibson
(Courtesy Stanford University Libraries Archive / SFTJF)

Buoyed and reassured by a brilliant performance and crowded dance floor, Mr Gurtler made the decision to bring the band to the Troc, as explained in James D. Shacter's book *Loose Shoes — The Story of Ralph Sutton*.[4] He insisted that he wanted *exactly* the same musicians; and so began 'Jazz in The Troc'. The eight musicians, billed as the Greats of Jazz, played over two July weekends in 1965.

The omens for the very first concert were not good; it was preceded by Denver's worst flood for 100 years. On the opening night, the day after the storm, the venue was exactly 2463 people under capacity. Just thirty-seven people made it to the vast ballroom. Fortunately, Jack Gurtler's gamble eventually paid off. 'Jazz in the Troc' became a successful fixture in the Elitch summer season for the next six years.

Clancy was among the chosen eight who took the Trocadero bandstand that first ill-fated night and remained part of the band for the rest of his career. For the 1966 gig, the eight-piece band expanded to nine with the addition of Bud Freeman on tenor saxophone, while Morey Feld replaced Cliff Leeman on drums. Thankfully, performances from the 1966-69 concerts were captured and issued on Jazz in the Troc LPs. The recordings include six wonderful Clancy vocals with outstanding versions of *Silver Dollar* and *Washboard Blues*.

As for Dick Gibson, his involvement in jazz took a new direction in 1968, switching from party host to band manager of the World's Greatest Jazz Band no less. Impressed by the excellence of the Greats of Jazz who had played at the Trocadero, he was keen to manage them. Aware of his novice status he wrote to all band members seeking their patience as he gained experience in this new role.

New to band management he may have been, but Mr Gibson was a successful businessman. Having established the Waterpik company in 1962, he became a wealthy man when he sold it five years later. For good measure he was also an investment banker and an expert in Oriental rugs! His business perspective and managerial abilities were soon proven when he secured a five-week booking for the band at the prestigious Riverboat nightclub in New York City. (The so-called Riverboat was 'docked' in the driest of places — beneath the Empire State Building).

Bob Haggart was appointed Musical Director of the World's Greatest Jazz Band but in a letter to the musicians, Dick Gibson expressed his personal views regarding the musical goals that the band should aim for:

> In my opinion the basis of any success we enjoy will be in the ensemble parts of the driving jazz standards at which the band excels. Yet, to become a world-famous band, with a broad appeal consonant with its name, we must stretch and update our repertoire as an overall band and soloists. In everything we do, however, we must keep one fixed concept: we are a <u>jazz band</u>. We must be true to that. Everything we do must sound like us and nobody else. It must swing, be creative and represent musicianship of a caliber that no other band can match.

Dick Gibson was clearly serious that the World's Greatest Jazz Band should live up to their name musically. In addition, he expected the band to *look* the part. His letter specified that the band would play in tuxedos and each member would require two tuxes as they were playing six nights a week with four sets — starting at 8:15 pm and concluding at 1:15 am. A six-piece house band led by Big Tiny Little played between sets. Sunday was a rest day, but the band would be available for bookings (one had already been contracted). For the extra engagements and Sundays, dark blue blazers and charcoal slacks were required. Was this not only the World's Greatest Jazz Band but also the Best Dressed?

The World's Greatest Jazz Band 1968
Top - Carl Fontana, Ralph Sutton, Lou McGarity, Morey Feld:
Middle - Billy Butterfield, Bob Wilber, Clancy Hayes:
Bottom - Yank Lawson, Bob Haggart, Bud Freeman.
(Courtesy Sam Linschooten / photographer unknown)

In their Sunday best: Billy Butterfield, Lou McGarity, Carl Fontana
(Courtesy Stanford University Libraries Archive / SFTJF)

Clancy seems to be recalling sweeping up from his radio days
(Courtesy Stanford University Libraries Archive / SFTJF)

The well-dressed man
(Courtesy Frank Selman / SFTJF)

John S. Wilson's review in the *New York Daily News* noted: 'It takes a lot of brass for a group of musicians to bill themselves as The World's Greatest Jazz Band. That is the official name of the ten-man group that has moved into the Riverside under the joint leadership of Yank Lawson and Bob Haggart, both of whom were part of the Bob Crosby band in the 1930s.'

The World's Greatest Jazz Band line-up:

Yank Lawson	trumpet
Billy Butterfield	trumpet
Lou McGarity	trombone
Carl Fontana	trombone
Bob Wilber	clarinet & soprano saxophone
Bud Freeman	tenor saxophone
Ralph Sutton	piano & soloist
Bob Haggart	bass & Musical Director
Morey Feld	drums
Clarence Hayes	banjo & vocal

This formidable line-up was necessary to compete in a music world going through an unprecedented and interminable revolution. Interestingly, the repertoire included pop songs of the day such as *Mrs Robinson / Sunny* and *Up Up And Away*. Were they The Greatest? Of course the claim is infinitely debatable and perhaps a little tongue in cheek, but there is no question that each and every musician had an impeccable jazz pedigree. Clancy was singled out in Mr. Wilson's review for his banjo playing and his 'deep dark bag of old songs singing *Rose Of Washington Square* and *Ragged But Right* in a wonderfully warm and smoky voice' — yet another interesting description of Clancy's singing.'[5] Mr Wilson concluded that the band made a very convincing claim to their title. By the later part of the evening the audience had crowded around the bandstand.

Clancy's Riverboat gig provides a reminder of the trials of the professional musician. In his personal effects is a birthday card from wife Ann and son Bill. Opening night on Friday 8 November 1968 was Clancy's sixtieth birthday and despite the fun at the Riverboat and comforts of his berth at the Roger Williams Hotel on Madison Avenue, it is possible that on this day he perhaps would rather have been elsewhere.

Happy Birthday!
(Courtesy Stanford University Libraries Archive / SFTJF)

In July 1969, Clancy would again join the Greats of Jazz on the Trocadero bandstand, but sadly his association would soon be interrupted by illness. While he is featured on all five Jazz in the Troc LPs (the 1969 issue was a double LP) he isn't on any of the WGJB albums; his name is on the sleeve of their initial album (on Project 3 records) but this was likely an act of kindness to allow him a royalty. Clancy's friends in the WGJB went on to achieve international success throughout the 1970s, recording over a dozen albums.

Jazz in the Troc, album cover
(Courtesy Hal Smith)

Oceania Lounge, Fort Lauderdale, Florida - December 1966, August 1967

In December 1966, Clancy appeared at Jack Wood's Oceania Lounge, where his friend Andy Bartha led his 'Deep South' house band. The Oceania had a policy of bringing in name artists to provide an added attraction to their supremely talented house bandleader. Andy Bartha had, of course, responded to Clancy's call and spent three months with him in Chicago in 1961. This was an opportunity for Clancy to return the favour, spend nine days with his friend, enjoy some Florida sunshine and add 'Clancy Hayes' to the illustrious names (Tex Beneke, PeeWee Hunt and Billy Butterfield) that had appeared there. Clancy played solo sets and also featured with the band delivering favourites such as *Muskrat Ramble / Tin Roof Blues* and his own composition *Swingin' Doors*.

Whether Clancy's nine-day stint hadn't quite settled the debt, or whether the Floridians just wanted more, Clancy was back at the club on 25 August 1967 for another short stay. On this visit, Jack Wood changed the formula using Clancy as a solo artist between the Andy Bartha band sets. As at Earthquake McGoon's, the band joined Clancy on his final number to seamlessly take over the stage.

Blues Alley, Georgetown, Washington DC — September 1967/ March 1968

A gig at an intimate club (capacity 100 patrons) owned by musician Tommy Gwaltney is something Clancy really enjoyed. In an interview with radio host Felix Grant during his stay, he confirmed it was his first visit to the capital.

The American Federation of Musicians contract paperwork in Clancy's collection detailed the booking date as 6 to 16 September. His status was 'Guest Artist' and the type of engagement — 'Entertainment' [for sure!]. Working hours were 9.30pm to 1.30am weekdays; somewhat strangely Saturday hours were 8.30pm to midnight.

Clancy and Tommy were good friends and somewhere during the proceedings plans were made to make an album with Tommy Gwaltney's Blues Alley Cats, but the details remain a mystery.[6] Clancy returned to Blues Alley in March 1968 and it is likely the Mr. Hayes Goes To Washington album was recorded during this second visit. Guitarist on the session, Steve Jordan, wrote about Clancy's time at Jazz Ltd in his book Rhythm Man — Fifty Years in Jazz stating that Clancy apparently looked older than his fifty-nine years and walked as if he had back trouble. Despite his appearance, Mr. Jordan said that 'when he sang in his clear, crisp voice the years faded away and he sounded much younger than his age'. The Clanco recording affirms his opinion.

Jack Wood's Oceania, Fort Lauderdale FL, advertisement
(Fort Lauderdale News, 23 August 1967)

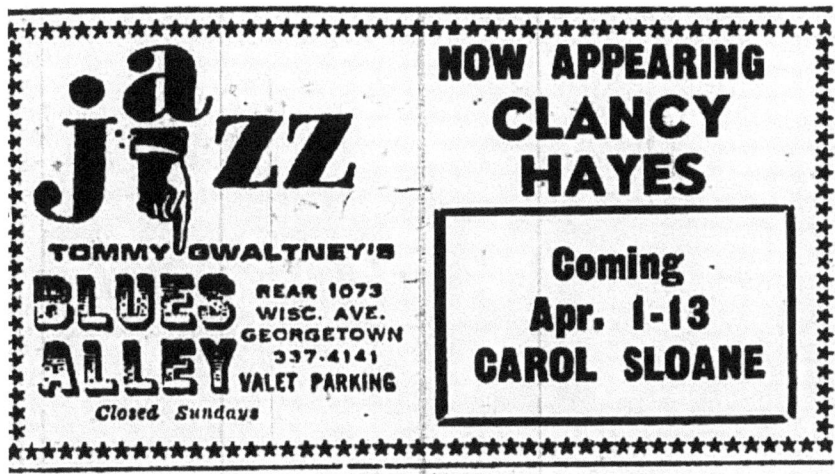

Blues Alley, Washington WA, advertisement
(The Washington Daily News, 18 March 1968)

Tommy Gwaltney, Pee Wee Russell, Clancy
(Courtesy Stanford University Libraries Archive / SFTJF)

Monterey Dixieland Jazz Festival 10/11 May 1968

Staging a large Dixieland Jazz event in 1968 was a brave venture. Promoter Don Lewis and the local business sponsors were hoping inquisitive teenagers would turn up to the Monterey County Fairgrounds Arena along with those who knew the music from the days of the Jazz Revival and before. Many top names in traditional jazz were signed up. The Friday night opening included the Firehouse Five Plus Two (with Scobey alumnus George Probert) and the Dukes of Dixieland. Impresario Bill Bacin of the New Orleans Jazz Club of California assembled a group of legendary jazzmen: Barney Bigard, Alton Purnell, Ed Garland, Ben Pollack, Wingy Manone along with two relatively young musicians, Bob Havens and Dick Cary. Clarinettist Phil Howe led the 'Festival All-Stars', which included pioneer New Orleans bassist Pops Foster as well as former Turk Murphy sidemen Bob Neighbor (trumpet) and Thad Vandon (drums).

The Saturday matinee featured the Turk Murphy Jazz Band, Pat Yankee, Wally Rose, Phil Howe's Festival All-Stars and Clancy as a solo artist. Other performers included Mickey Finn, Barbara Kelly, Sugar Willie Erickson and his Ten Cubes, the South Market Street Jazz Band and a teenage jazz outfit - Pawnticket and the Hockshop Four. Louis Armstrong and his All Stars were the evening headliners.

Sadly, the worst thing that can happen to any outdoor festival occurred — dismal weather. Intermittent rain and a very chilly $50.0\,°F$ limited the audience to an estimated 2500, about one-third capacity. While the conditions kept many away, the hardier fans were given a great show. Reports in the *San Francisco Examiner* and *Oakland Tribune* rated the event a 'hit'.

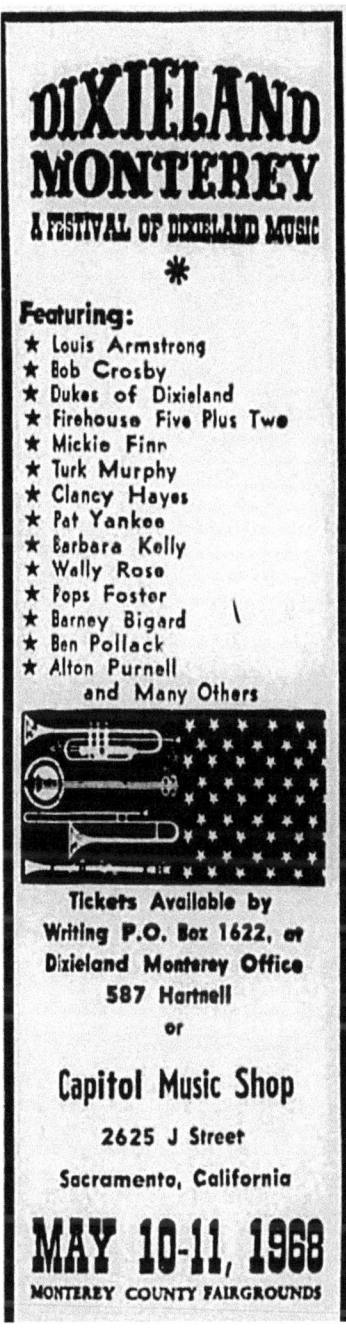

Dixieland Monterey, advertisement
(Courtesy Sam Linschooten)

Pops Foster, Clancy Hayes and two gas heaters!
(Courtesy Stanford University Libraries Archive / SFTJF)

Clancy's afternoon set, rated 'excellent' by Russ Wilson in his *Tribune* review, was recorded by Bill Bacin along with the entire festival. Mr Bacin shared a cassette of Clancy's performance with the author, so a description in the present tense is possible. Starting with emcee Phil Elwood's affectionate introduction:

> I think probably the first of the San Franciscans I ever heard about who had a devotion to jazz and an interest in entertainment, an interest in old music and was playing it certainly in the late twenties as a mainstay of Coffee Dan's[7] in its great days. The first of the radio men that I can ever remember in growing up in the Bay Area who used to play tunes that I learned later on were jazz tunes and classics. Who also was one of the two banjoists who played with Lu Watters' band 1940, 41-42, who taught me more lyrics than any other person I can think of. I always associate one tune with him and I think maybe toward the end we'll hear it. He's been playing with Turk Murphy as intermission and occasional banjoist with the band for years and years at Earthquake McGoon's.

> He makes an annual pilgrimage into the East. He had a wonderful record out with Yank Lawson on, as I remember it, ABC — that's a free plug — a couple of years ago. A fine Dixieland record that didn't get nearly enough attention. A great vocalist, a great minstrel man, a fine guitarist and banjoist and one of the real giants in our Bay Area jazz scene, Clancy Hayes, Clancy Hayes (applause).

Clancy takes the stage, bidding hello to the 'boys and girls of radio land' and continues: 'I just want to make one brief announcement before I start: I have no intention of trying to stop the show but I sure as hell am going to slow it down a little, I'll tell you that'.

Accompanying himself on banjo, he begins with *Sweet Georgia Brown*, followed by *Michigan Water Blues / Blues My Naughty Sweetie Gives To Me* and *Do You Know What It Means To Miss New Orleans*.

Clancy then asks Pops Foster to join him. He takes the stage and the duo open with *Sailing Down The Chesapeake Bay* which is met with applause lasting a full thirty seconds. Then comes *Rose Of Washington Square* and this time applause breaks out *during* the song [Who cares about the weather? -C.R.]

Clancy introduces his finale as follows:

> To wind up my little effort here for you guys, gals, I'd like to lay on you a little blues I made up out of my own ugly head a few years back and see if I can get Phil and the rest of the gang out here to back me up while I take you on a little train ride now. This is what I call my Midwest, railroad type, cowboy and Indian, bossa nova something for everyone blues and I hope that includes you all. In any case, if we can get this train on the track we are going to take you back to Parsons, Kansas for the *Parsons, Kansas Blues*. All aboard you guys, all aboard…

Clancy, Pops and the Phil Howe Festival All Stars deliver a superb four-minute version and the audience appreciates every second. (A press report noted that Clancy's set covered jazz, vaudeville and 'minstrelsy' and that he was in excellent form). Finally, it is worth repeating Bill Bacin's role in supporting the concert and his kindness in sharing the recording of the Clancy set.

The Blue Angel Jazz Club — 1968 and 1969.

The Blue Angel concerts, organized by William MacPherson, M.D. and George Tyler M.D., were held at the University Club of Pasadena. The inaugural event took place on Saturday 28 December 1968. As with the Troc concerts some of the best names in jazz participated including Nappy Lamare, Matty Matlock, Jess Stacy, George Van Eps, Abe Lincoln, and Peanuts Hucko. The BAJC organizers aimed to bring top musicians together for a jazz party, issue records of the proceedings and pass the receipts from record sales to the musicians. The excellent recordings were made by Wally Heider — an attorney turned highly respected recording engineer.

Volume One of the 1968 concert (BAJC LP 502) has a complete side by Clancy Hayes' Tune Termites. The varying line-up includes Jack Coon, trumpet, mellophone; Dick Cary, alto horn; Ward Erwin, bass; Gene Estes, drums; Robin Frost, piano; John Guerin, drums; Abe Lincoln, trombone; Matty Matlock; clarinet; Jack Sperling, drums; Ira Westley, bass; and Stan Wrightsman, piano.

The following extract from William MacPherson's liner notes confirm that he was both fan and true friend:

> Side Two consists of a miniature concert by Clancy Hayes and his 'Tune Termites'. It is at once the most delightful and uproariously informal set of the entire party. With typical modesty, Clancy was reluctant to be so prominently featured. After all, many other fine artists contributed to the success of the party. Perhaps he was thinking wryly of the clinkers which always turn up at an informal session such as this one. You will hear, unexpurgated, all of the many parts that go to make up Clancy Hayes; the humorous announcements, the uncanny ability to select and generate an inspiring beat; the phrasing, projection, and timing and the aged in the wood timbre of a truly great minstrel voice.

This session included the humorous debate concerning the key for *Mama's Gone Goodbye* which, despite the uncertain start, provides a tour-de-force for the Termites.

Proceedings of the Blue Angel Jazz Club, album cover
(Author's collection)

Clancy appeared at the second Blue Angel concert on November 1. Three of his vocals from the proceedings were released on BAJC albums 505 and 506. The liner notes make reference to Clancy's health at the time, noting 'he was really too ill to have any business being out of bed'. Despite his condition, he turns in typical Hayes performances on *Waiting For The Evening Mail* and *Wolverine Blues* but there is genuine pathos in his rendition of *Melancholy*. The joy of the 1951 recording with Bob Scobey just isn't there; as intimated by the sleeve notes, he sounds unwell.

Clancy at the Blue Angel Jazz Club, probably 1968.
(BAJC album photo, photographer unknown)

Manassas Jazz Festival 1968

During his time at the Riverboat with the World's Greatest Jazz Band, Clancy used a rest day to fly to Manassas, Virginia to appear in the 3rd Manassas Jazz Festival. His appearance on Sunday 8 December gives an insight into Clancy's busy schedule: Having flown down from New York, Clancy needed to leave the festival early to return to New York in the early hours, ready for the WGJB's engagement the following day.

Thankfully, proceedings at Manassas were recorded by festival organizer Johnson 'Fat Cat' McRee.[8] Several Clancy numbers were issued on Fat Cat FCJ LP 105. One of the highlights is a triumphant solo version of *Sailing Down The Chesapeake Bay*. The banjo accompaniment provides a driving rhythm and expertly played mixture of chords and runs. Clancy's banjo playing is described by Hal Smith in Chapter 13 and his six string banjo, with guitar tuning, provides the perfect backing on this song. At Manassas he also played and sang with an excellent band consisting of Johnny Wiggs, cornet; Raymond Burke, clarinet; Don Ewell, piano; Van Perry, bass; Zutty Singleton, drums; and trombonist Paul Crawford, who had played with Clancy during his 1962 New Orleans trip.

When not performing out-of-town, Clancy continued as intermission entertainer and name attraction at Earthquake McGoon's. His performances there followed a set routine, accompanying his own vocals on banjo between the Turk Murphy Jazz Band sets. Clancy's repertoire for the intermissions ranged from ragtime-era numbers like *At The Angels' Ragtime Ball* and *Auntie Skinner's Chicken Dinner* to obscure Fats Waller-associated songs such as *Where Were You On The Night Of June The 3rd?*

At the end of his intermission set, Clancy stayed onstage for a final number as the band returned one-by-one following their twenty minutes break. Clancy often brought the Murphy band back to the stage with excellent versions of his tried-and-true repertoire, such as *Ace In The Hole*, *Willie The Weeper* and, naturally, *Parsons, Kansas Blues*. The 1966 ABC-Paramount LP Clancy Hayes Live at Earthquake McGoon's includes several wonderful performances by Clancy on banjo and vocals, accompanied by Squire Girsback on string bass. His renditions of *Tomorrow* and *Blues My Naughty Sweetie Gives To Me* are outstanding. On the other tracks he is accompanied by the full Turk Murphy band.

Sadly, as the November 1969 Blue Angel party heralded, Clancy was developing significant health problems and the new year would bring bad news to the jazz world.

10

Melancholy (Clancy's Illness 1969-1972)

Fans and friends would comment that a conversation with Clancy 'the artist' was like a personal performance. Whether over the airwaves, on record, in the concert hall, night club, coming for dinner or even on a train, he entertained throughout his life.

As much as Clancy had a shining persona when in the spotlight, in private moments, and particularly without his banjo, he came across quite differently, almost a little reserved. It is revealing that when he visited people's homes, no doubt to their delight, he invariably took his banjo — perhaps to shield Clancy 'the man'. From the age of seven Clarence Leonard Hayes had been addicted to music, entertaining and bringing joy to an audience no matter how large or small. Being silenced by his illness must have been difficult to bear though, not surprisingly, he coped well - aided by those who loved him and the many to whom he had given so much pleasure.

The love, affection and respect shown to Clancy in his final years when he battled with cancer provides a testament and eulogy like no other. This chapter in his story will be told not from the perspective of this cruel illness but from that of the people who reached out to him with their support.

Pete Clute spoke about Clancy's illness during his 1998 interview with Dave Radlauer and explained that he, Turk Murphy and Clancy regularly visited the same throat specialist. Sometime in the late 1960s the specialist picked up a 'spot' on Clancy's tongue and suggested it be checked out. It is not known whether he followed the advice but sometime later the problem manifested as cancer of the mouth and jaw. When news of Clancy's illness broke in spring 1970, musicians, fans and friends rallied to help. Countless well-wishing letters attempted to lift his spirits. More practically, three benefit concerts would be held at Earthquake McGoon's to help with medical bills; he was in Stanford Hospital from late March until November.

Clancy was clearly unwell on 1 November 1969, when performing at the BAJC concert at the University of Pasadena Jazz Club. As previously noted, William MacPherson (coincidentally a doctor) wrote 'Clancy's remarkable vibrato and vitality give little evidence of the fact that he was too ill to have had any business out of bed'.[1]

Clancy ceased performing at Earthquake McGoon's in March 1970. As news of his illness began to reach friends and family, messages of love and goodwill deluged the 'ABC' residence at 702 46th Street, San Francisco and Stanford Hospital.

Below are just some of the many letters and messages from friends and family during his two years of illness; some so poignant as to be beyond any attempt to paraphrase.

Letter to Ann Hayes from Bill and Ann MacPherson 23 March 1970:

> Dear Ann, Thank you for your letter. I have not really been soliciting money for Clancy but in mentioning his illness to the head of one of the local jazz clubs I unwittingly set off a chain reaction.
>
> First, Jim Young wasted no time in calling the head nurse on Clancy's ward, then in disturbing the two of you on the solarium the other day. Then Bill Bacin sent the enclosed check and asked me to forward it 'with my best professional manner' and asked for the address, so he could encourage Clancy's friends to write to him. I hope you will find some use for the enclosed twenty (Perhaps a little high-quality mouthwash when the Doctor permits).
>
> Mr. Young states that the nurse told him that part of Clancy's tongue had to be removed and that he was much relieved to hear that Clancy had only a slight impediment to his speech… needless to say I am also much relieved.
>
> Under the circumstances, I believe that a man's fighting spirit and the emotional support of those who love him are his prime weapons. In this case Clancy has an enviable armament. I know how miserable he felt when he came down here last November and my heart wept. Please keep us informed,
>
> Love, Bill and Ann

Jack Gurtler wrote:

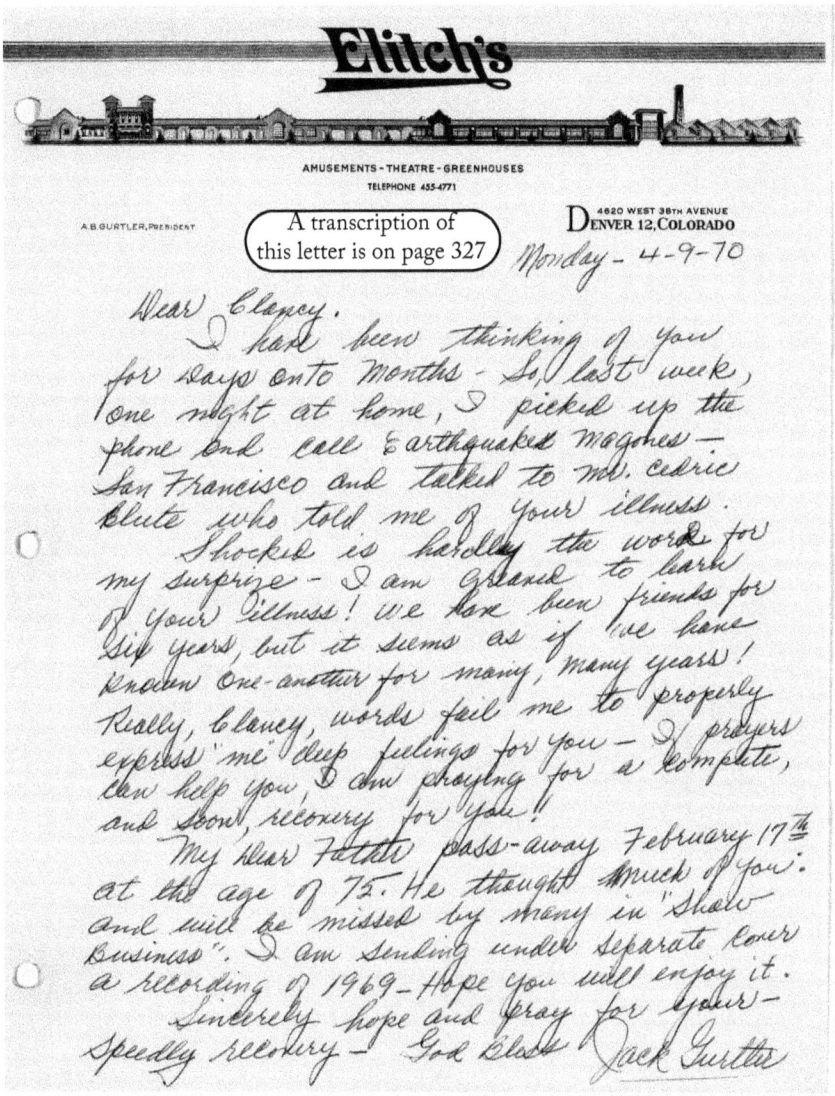

Letter from Jack Gurtler
(Courtesy Stanford University Libraries Archive / SFTJF)

Don Newton of Jackson, MI, (fan/friend) wrote a letter dated 20 April 1970:

> Dear Clancy,
>
> So the doctors finally found out what those of us who have been listening to you for 20-30 years have known all along — you're sick!
>
> Seriously, I learned the address from the Southern California Hot Jazz Society's bulletin. Had heard previously from Dick Gibson (of the World's Greatest) of your physical problem. These and other reports indicate that you'll be back on the bandstand before too long — although if I were in Frisco one more day out would be too long.
>
> After having heard you live in spots such as Eddie Condon's and the Riverboat, and of course on records for many years, it was a genuine pleasure for me to meet and have a couple of little shots with you in Frisco a couple of years ago — in fact on your birthday...There are indispensable men. Django Reinhardt and Charlie Christian have not been replaced. Louis Armstrong will pass on and jazz will continue — but not his brand of it. Zutty Singleton (who has recently had a stroke and won't be able to play again) is indispensable for his brand of drumming.
>
> I suppose steamboats will always have foghorns. But they'll never perfect one to replace the 24-karat perfect pitch foghorn I know by the name of Clancy Hayes. You're the indispensable one-of-a-kind...
>
> In every audience you face there'll be dozens, or hundreds of guys (and gals) like me. WE seldom take time or trouble to express it, but we love you and appreciate you. And please know that at least one of us will tonight say a prayer for your speedy and complete recovery.
>
> Sincerely, Don Newton.

Myrtle Fischbacher of Oakland CA (a relative of Ann Hayes) sent this letter dated 15 May 1970:

> Dear Clarence
>
> It was through Herb Caen's column that I first learned of your illness, (several weeks ago) and at that time I decided to write to you. As you see it took another Caen reminder to give me the push I need to get started.
>
> You know Clarence I have always wished for a short hospitalization, which would give me the time to write what I have learned, whom I have known, experiences I have had etc. One day I realized that I have practically nothing to write. Experiences have been limited to encounters with either bill collectors or customers and all have been so commonplace they don't deserve to appear in writing. My knowledge is limited to what hearsay I get on the radio talk programs the accuracy of which is questionable. The only claim to fame I can boast is: No. 1, I have met and spoken with Norman Thomas and escorted him in my car while he was candidate for president. No. 2, I know and am remotely related (by marriage) to Clancy Hayes. Not a jazz fan myself, I am quick nevertheless to seize upon every opportunity to let it be known that I have this distinction. You are Mr. Jazz himself to every jazz nut I have ever known.
>
> It has occurred to me that you must have so very much to tell that your followers would like to read. You have met so many interesting and prominent people — have participated in so many really big occasions etc. Really Clarence, I think you should put these things on paper. There are so many things about you and your life that your fans would enjoy reading. While I boast about my relationship (by marriage, twice or thrice removed) I must confess that I never really got to know you. Somehow, I always stood in awe of you. Perhaps because of your fame and maybe a little because I have always felt a great awe for people of championship stature.
>
> However, my purpose in writing you is to urge you to use the time you must spend recuperating in the way I have described. You need not have written before. Simply record events and your chronological progress as it comes to you. Name the persons who would be of interest to others, record experiences — especially the ones that turned memorable after time erased the embarrassment or confusion. These are the gems. Don't

think of style or try for words or you'll lose your train of thought. Simply write. You can rewrite and edit when you get home.

I hope I haven't been presumptuous although I know I have. I just feel so strongly that you have a wonderful story to tell, and you should tell it.

In case you don't know who I am, I am Laura's sister Myrtle. You know, of course, that we all have followed your career — and are now following your recovery with love.

Laura is in bed about 23½ hours a day. The doctor can't find any explanation for her tenacity, her hanging on to life in the face of the hopeless prognosis — But the doctors know very little even yet. Frank is still at home. He has had two serious illnesses but still seems to have a little of that old Stuhlmacher grit. Arnold and I are still grinding away at trying to earn a living. I'll be 65 in 1972 — if I make it. Then social security and — heck what is there for anyone after 65? Dreams, indigestion and arthritis.

When you get back home, I should like very much to visit you and see Ann and Bill again.

Most sincerely,
Myrtle Fischbacher.

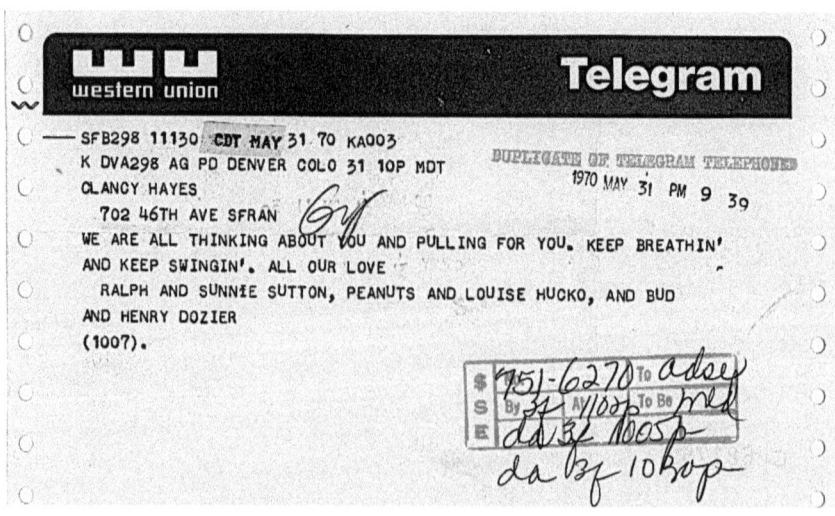

Greetings telegram, May 31, 1970
(Courtesy Stanford University Libraries Archive / SFTJF)

> *A transcription of this letter is on page 328*

May 16 - '70
1144 No. 1st Ave
Tucson. Ariz.
85719

Hiya Clancy:
 Just got back from a three mo. gig in Ill. Maybe more than 3 mos. Left here Jan. 14 to be exact. Joined "Smokey Stover" in Moline. (Trompet). Blew some jazz. (19° below.)
 Done a T.V. shot. An hr. deal. Hour with "Smokey". Had Brownies + Granita on clar. for a couple of dates in Mattoon. Then used them on the last ½ hr. of the T.V. shot, in Davenport. Biographical thing with shots of "Smoke" wandering around the levees of the Ole Missippi. Some of it's good. some of it's bad. Oh well.
 Yeah bein' gone like that, didn't hear about you taking the
(over)

Letter from George Zack, page 1
(Courtesy Stanford University Libraries Archive / SFTJF)

Clancy's Kansas roots were mentioned in several letters. Those that knew him and his brothers from those joyful days, were keen to refresh happy memories. This letter from ex-Iola High School friends raises the poignant question of how anyone could possibly measure the happiness and joy that Clancy spread over his long career?

> May 24, 1970
> 7100 South Street #7
> Lincoln, Nebraska
>
> *(A transcription of this letter is on page 329)*
>
> Dear Clancy:
>
> When we visited with you in October, you told us that you were receiving treatment at the Stanford University Hospital, and now we are sorry to learn that surgery has been necessary. We send you our most sincere wishes for your comfort and recovery— and we are pleased that you are to be honored in San Francisco on May 31st. We wish we could be there.
>
> You know we have been real fans of yours since the days in Iola High School. It was a great joy to find you at Earthquake McGoon's and we have never missed a chance to hear you when we were in San Francisco. We have all but two of your known recordings and spend many hours here at home listening to them. You sing and play "our kind of music"— and so for the many hours and days of pleasure you have given us, we do thank you. It should be a great satisfaction to you to know how much good you have done for your fellow man.
>
> With sincere good wishes,
>
> Esther and Bob
>
> Esther and Bob Garlinghouse

Letter from the Garlinghouses, 1970
(Courtesy Stanford University Libraries Archive / SFTJF)

801 North 12th St.
Rogers, Ark. 72756
May 26, 1970

Mr. Clancy Hays
Earthquake McGoon's
630 Clay St.
San Francisco, Calif.

Dear Clancy:

Can you believe having two admirers .. and fans .. way down in Arkansas?

We have heard that the Mayor of San Francisco has proclaimed May 31 as Clancy Hays Day in honor of your long-time contribution to the music and pleasure of the people around the Golden Gate ... as well as many others living elsewhere that he might not know about. We hope that it will be good therapy for you in the recovery period after your recent surgical experience.

Although we have never had the opportunity to hear your music in person, we have had considerable exposure to it for a long time on numerous visits with my sister and brother-in-law, Esther and Bob Garlinghouse of Lincoln, Nebraska. They have a large collection of your music on tapes and records which they play every time we get together. We also have re-tapes that they have given us, so we listen to Clancy Hays here at home, too.

Needless to say, since I am a sister of Esther's, I remember you from High School days in Iola even though I was a few years behind you in school. You are very personal to us and this brings you our love for old time's sake, memories for the past and present, admiration for years of pleasure to your public, and best wishes for the future.

"Clancy" fans,

Billie and Don Leach

Billie

Letter from Billie and Don Leach
(Courtesy Stanford University Libraries Archive / SFTJF)

From the desk of
EARL WATKINS
Oakland Branch Secretary

MAY 6, 1970

(A transcription of this letter is on page 331)

DEAR CLANCY:

JUST A LINE TO SAY HELLO AND ASK HOW YOU ARE DOING.

MARILYN GAVE ME A CALL AND GAVE ME YOUR ADDRESS SO I'M WRITING. I PLAYED A JOB MONDAY NITE WITH MIKE TILLES, JERRY BUTZEN, VINCE, ERNIE FIGEROA, JOHN FARKAS, RED GILLUM, JACK KNOX, AND JIM CUMMINGS — WHAT A BALL. WE PLAYED FOR BOB COATE, WHO IS RUNNING FOR LEIUTENANT GOVERNOR, AND THE JOB WAS AT THE 'CANNERY' UPSTAIRS.

I ALSO PLAYED AT THE DANVILLE HOTEL WITH TOMMY KAHN AND SAW SAM AND HEIDE THERE. THEY WERE LOOKING SWELL THEY DON'T LOOK A DAY OLDER THAN CHICAGO AND OUR FIRST TRIP TO THE BLUE NOTE. REMEMBER THE PARTY AT THE CONRAD HILTON.

WE ARE PRETTY BUSY HERE AT THE UNION, THE PHONE RINGS OFF THE HOOK ALL DAY, BUT I'M GLAD TO HAVE A GIG. I'LL CONTACT YOU LATER AND TRY TO HAVE A LITTLE GOSSIP FOR YOU.

BYE FOR NOW, GOOD LUCK

Earl Watkins

Letter from Earl Watkins
(Courtesy Stanford University Libraries Archive / SFTJF)

5/28/70

My dear Clancy,
 We know these must be most difficult days for you! We are adding our prayer to those of your innumerable friends who love you — that God will be very near and heal you!
 Love & Kisses
 Peanuts & Louise

P.S. Will be here at Raddisson Hotel for 6 wks.

Letter from Peanuts and Louise Hucko
(Courtesy Stanford University Libraries Archive / SFTJF)

Clancy Hayes Day, 1971 Left to Right: Dick Oxtot, Ray Skjelbred, Bob Neighbor (facing away), Bob Helm, Bob Mielke.
(Courtesy Stanford University Libraries Archive / SFTJF)

Same Group with Bob Neighbor in view. Jim Cumming (bass) and Earl Watkins (drums) are not in the photos
(Courtesy Stanford University Libraries Archive / SFTJF)

Clancy Hayes Day poster
(Courtesy Stanford University Libraries Archive / SFTJF)

Clancy (seated with mask), brother Ashton is to his left and Bill Hayes is standing behind.
(Courtesy Stanford University Libraries Archive / SFTJF)

Faces in the crowd: Phil Howe and Fred Higuera are either side of the lady in the hat.
(Courtesy Stanford University Libraries Archive / SFTJF)

OFFICE OF THE MAYOR
SAN FRANCISCO

JOSEPH L. ALIOTO

Proclamation

Clancey Hayes has long been a much loved San Franciscan who has often contributed his time and talents to countless Bay Area civic and charitable undertakings.

He has been honored throughout the years for his contribution to music and has pioneered his banjo music in engagements, on radio and television and recordings, thereby bringing countless hours of entertainment and enjoyment to thousands.

His music, in its way, has become somewhat of a San Francisco "landmark."

NOW, THEREFORE, I, Joseph L. Alioto, Mayor of the City and County of San Francisco, do hereby join his fellow musicians in paying tribute to him by officially proclaiming Sunday, May 31, as "Clancey Hayes Day in San Francisco."

IN WITNESS WHEREOF I have hereunto set my hand and caused the seal of the City and County of San Francisco to be affixed on this sixteenth day of April, nineteen hundred and seventy.

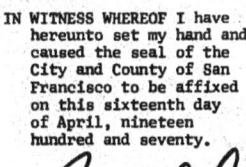

Joseph L. Alioto
Mayor

(A transcription of this is on page 333)

Proclamation of 'Clancy Hayes Day', 1970
(Courtesy Stanford University Libraries Archive / SFTJF)

Such was Clancy's stature as a San Francisco institution for over forty years, Mayor Joseph Alioto officially declared 31 May 1970 'Clancy Hayes Day', on which his musician friends organised a nine-hour fundraising event at Earthquake McGoon's. The benefit was scheduled to run from 3:00pm to midnight. However, an expectant and faithful audience began to gather before 2:00pm. To clear the crowd from the sidewalk, the club opened forty-minutes early, but a line remained in place throughout the day. It was standing room only inside of the club which resembled a packed New York subway train.[2.] An empty seat didn't appear until after 10:00pm.

Musicians and friends were eager to support this marathon with contributions from Norma Teagarden, Burt Bales, Bill Napier, Fred Higuera, the Bay City Jazz Band, Bob Mielke's Bearcats, Bob Helm, Squire Girsback, George Probert, Red Gillham, Ray Skjelbred, Joe Darensbourg, the Jelly Roll Jazz Band, Wally Rose and Spencer Quinn along with Turk Murphy's band and vocalists Pat Yankee and Jimmie Stanislaus.

Particular highlights included an appearance by Hoagy Carmichael who played *Ole Buttermilk Sky* and *Huggin' And A Chalkin'* and sang *Up A Lazy River* with Turk Murphy's Jazz Band. Unable to be there in-person, Clancy's admirer, Bing Crosby, phoned to express his best wishes. Lu Watters sent a letter with get-well wishes, which was read to the audience by former Dawn Club manager Augie Girretto.

The most touching aspect of the day was Clancy's attendance for a couple of hours, accompanied by medical staff from Stanford Hospital. Unable to participate in the musical proceedings, Clancy gave smiles and nods to his fans who responded with cheers and applause.

The Original Salty Dogs, Clancy's good friends from the Chicago days, held their own benefit concert on Sunday 2 August 1970 at the city's Three Fools Hall.

In addition to the celebrations of 'Clancy Hayes Day', the California Legislature Assembly Rules Committee passed a Resolution. recognising Clancy as one of America's greatest folk singers. Clancy was commended for his many contributions to San Francisco and his fellow man. California Governor Ronald Reagan sent a letter acknowledging his own appreciation of Clancy's radio years.

Clancy Hayes Day at McGoon's, ticket
(Courtesy Stanford University Libraries Archive / SFTJF)

McGoon's Club Tent Card
(Courtesy Ray Skjelbred)

Assembly Rules Committee-California Legislature
Resolution

By the Honorable Don Mulford
Sixteenth Assembly District

RELATIVE TO COMMENDING CLANCY HAYES

WHEREAS, The members of the Assembly have learned that Clancy Hayes is to be honored at a benefit dinner on May 31, 1970; and

WHEREAS, Clancy Hayes is a long-time San Francisco resident and musician of great renown; and

WHEREAS, Since his arrival in San Francisco in 1926, Clancy Hayes has become one of that city's best-known entertainment personalities; and

WHEREAS, During an outstanding career in radio and television, as a composer, recording artist and nightclub entertainer, he has gained recognition as one of America's greatest folk singers; and

WHEREAS, Clancy Hayes has given generously of his time to innumerable civic and charitable causes, and has provided much entertainment for members of the California Legislature; and

WHEREAS, May 31, 1970, has been proclaimed by Mayor Alioto as "Clancy Hayes Day in San Francisco"; now, therefore, be it

Resolved by the Assembly Rules Committee, That the Members commend Clancy Hayes for the outstanding contributions which he has made to San Francisco, and congratulate him upon the occasion of the honors bestowed upon him, and extend to him their best wishes for the future; and be it further

Resolved, That the Chief Clerk of the Assembly transmit a suitably prepared copy of this resolution to Clancy Hayes.

Resolution No. 471 approved by the Assembly Rules Committee

By

Eugene A. Chappie
Chairman

Subscribed this 26th day of May, 1970

Bob Monagan
Speaker of the Assembly

Resolution from the California State Assembly
(Courtesy Stanford University Libraries Archive / SFTJF)

State of California
GOVERNOR'S OFFICE
SACRAMENTO 95814

RONALD REAGAN
GOVERNOR

May 27, 1970

Mr. Dana G. Leavitt
President
Transamerica Title Insurance Company
1330 Broadway
Oakland, California 94612

Dear Mr. Leavitt:

Governor Reagan was pleased to prepare the enclosed message for Mr. Clancy Hayes.

Mr. Hayes has been one of my favorite performers since I first heard him on a radio program called "Remember" in 1943, and I have since enjoyed his recordings with the Bob Scobey band. I am indeed sorry to hear of his illness.

Best wishes for a successful event.

Sincerely,

Mrs. Betty Sabourin
Mrs. Betty Sabourin
Administrative Assistant

Enclosure

Letter on behalf of Ronald Reagan
(Courtesy Sam Linschooten / SFTJF)

After eight long months in Stanford Hospital, Clancy at last returned home in November. He visited Earthquake McGoon's on 26 February 1971 to play a set with the Turk Murphy band, but never performed again. Further surgery to his mouth and jaw meant there would be no more wonderful Hayes' vocals for the world to enjoy. His prolonged illness prompted a further McGoon's benefit on Sunday 13 June 1971. In addition to another impressive line-up of bands and guest artists, Lu Watters came down from Cotati, CA to greet his old musical colleague and wish him well.

Once again, an army of musical friends and fans came to show their support. As in the previous year Clancy visited the club during the benefit and this time, he bravely joined the Turk Murphy band on stage. A young Hal Smith, who played at the event with the Fink Street Five recalled: 'Clancy was very ill and his lower jaw had been cut away. He was drinking champagne through a tube, if I remember correctly. He managed to sing *Sunset Café Stomp* with Turk's band, though what came out were sounds more than lyrics. Very sad'.

Pianist Ray Skjelbred performed at both Clancy Hayes Day events and explained that when playing at McGoon's Clancy would send him requests written on a club tent card. I am grateful to Ray for providing this example; the sketch style is unmistakable.

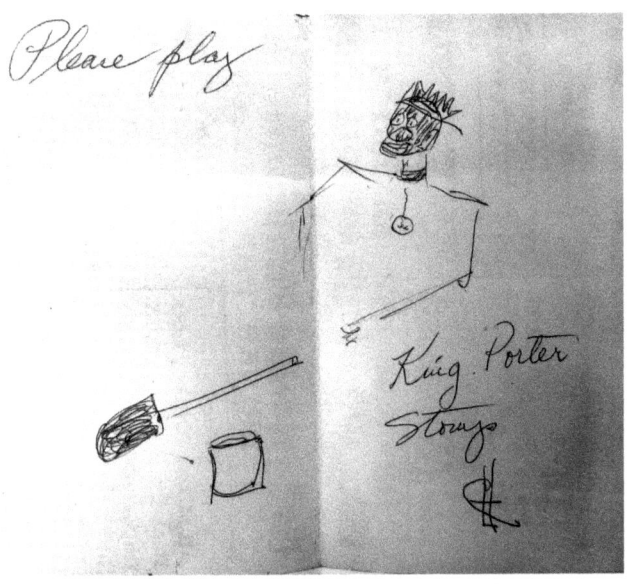

Request to Ray Skjelbred
(Courtesy Ray Skjelbred)

Another of the touching letters sent to Clancy around this period is reproduced in full below; it needs no comment.

June 10, 1971

Mr Clancy Hayes
% Earthquake McGoons

Dear Clancy:

I saw the attached article in the newspaper, but I'm a 66 year old guy on Social Security and not exactly the type to go trotting around to nightclubs — so I'm sending my remembrance in the mail.

Clancy, you simply GOT to get well! There ain't NOBODY who can sing "Ace in the Hole," "Silver Dollar," "Big Butter and Egg," "Do You Know What it Means To Miss New Orleans," "Peoria" — and all them wonderful songs like you do.

I've never seen or heard you IN PERSON, but I've got nearly every phonograph record that BOB SCOBEY'S FRISCO BAND made, and it is your

(continued)

Letter from Ed Watson (page 1)
(Courtesy Stanford University Libraries Archive / SFTJF)

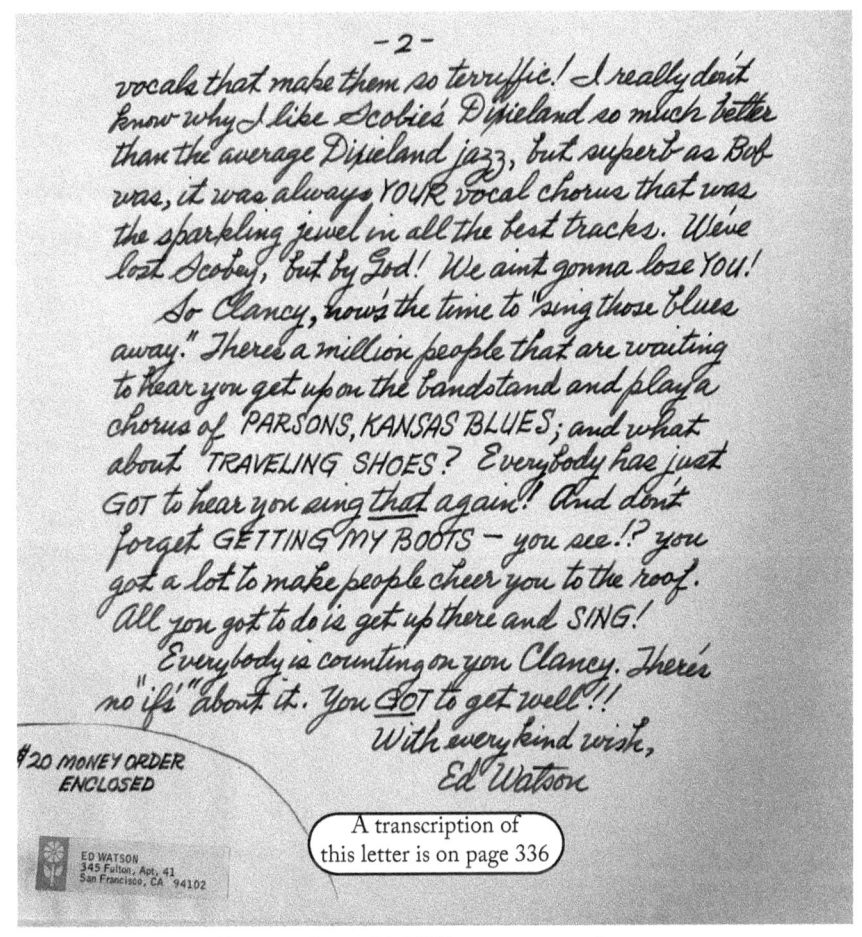

Letter from Ed Watson, page 2
(Courtesy Stanford University Libraries Archive / SFTJF)

Despite his illness, Christmas 1971 saw Clancy spreading seasonal joy with a tape for friends and family - a mixture of historic performances (including the aforementioned Bay City Boys) drawn from his collection and some more recent music by Elitch's Ten Greats of Jazz. Clancy's typed tape-log for Bill Bacin explains the programme:

"Tape Log For Bill Bacin"

Recorded June 6th, 1971.
Sterio. 3;3/4 I.P.S.

SIDE ONE.

(Counter No.) TITLE

1; Billy. Written by Gordon Jenkins for Billy Butterfeild. "W.O.J.B. New York /69

54 I Bubble Gum Strut Written by Bob Haggert same date

100 I Fidgitty Feet. Matty Matlocks Basin Street Patrol. From Blue Angel Jazz Club party 1970

200 I Elder Fatmore's Sermon On "Throwing Stones" Recorded in 1928 by Louis (Satch) and Harry Mills. Original of same was made by Bert Williams, 1912.

275 I Excerpts from Standard School Broadcast 1948. These were made at a one hour rehearsal at N.B.C. Studios S.F. I was the star that year of the series, Broadcast weekly to the school children of the seven Western States by Standard Oil of Calif. I played a mythyical character, sort of a Paul Bunyon type guy, who could live in any age. I was the central character "Jack of All Tunes" along with my buddy Matt the Mapmaker. In any case we had a Show on N.O. Jazz coming up, and I got the producer to hire Louis Armstong and his all Stars, (who were appearing at the Hangover) for one hour. We later only used about three and a half minutes of it on the show but I had them tape the entire hour. This was made on the old Paper Tape before they had Scotch type, so even though I have kept them in metal containers, they have not weathered it too well I have since transfered nearly all of the old gems I want to keep on Mylar Polyester.
Personel; Armstrong, Tmpt. Jack Teagarden, Trom. (a young fellow from the studio orch subbing for Barney Bigard) Ray Daniels on Clar. Earl Fatha Hines Piano, Sid Catlett Drums and Can't remember who the Bass was, I beleive it was Orvil Shaw, Myself sometimes on guitar, when I'm not busy yackkin' with the other people.

980 I Short Snorter from a tape I made for Squirrel Aircraft in 1958. Me on Piano.

Clancy's tape log for Bill Bacin, page 1
(Courtesy Stanford University Libraries Archive / SFTJF)

Re-set Counter.

SIDE TWO Rose of Washington Square. (Myself with the Nine
Greats of Jazz. Recorded at the Famous
old Trocadero, at Flitch Gardens in
Denver Colorado 1966. Personel
Yank Lawson, Tmpt. Lu MacGarrity and
Cutty Cuttshal Trombones, Peanuts
Hucko Clar. Ralph Sutton Piano. Morey
Feld Drums, Bobby Haggert Bas,
Bud Freeman Tenor Sax, myself on Banjo.

57 I   Honky Tonk Train. (Featuring Sutton, Same group)

120 I Stealin' Apples. (Peanuts Hucko with same group).

253 I. Silver Dollar. (Made one year later same spot with
the Ten Greats of Jazz, personel same as
above with Billy Butterfield added.)
Cherry   (Featuring MacGarrity, and Cutty. Same night)

Easy Street
Dixieland One Step.
Careless Love.
Washboard Blues.(These are all cuts from an Album I
made for Audio.Fidelity in 1960,
with the Band I had in Chicago, right
after I broke up with Scobey.
Art Hodes, piano. Bob Ballard, Tmpt.
Bill Henk, Tmb. Lyle Daniels Clar.
Buddy Smith, Drums. Earl Murphy Bass.
Banjo and Vocalist unknown.

Boy From New Orleans.
Bury Me on Basin Street. (From the ABC- Paramount
Album, "Big Yank is Here.
Lawson, Tmpt, Cutty, Tmb.
Bill Stegmeyer, Clar.
Osie Johnson Drums, Dave
MacKenna Piano Haggert Bass
Banjo and Vocalist unknown.

(Surprise Party)
Clancy Hayes Dixieland Jazz Band for Tweed Records.
Recorded in 1960, Chicago for the Republican National
Comittee "Vote For Nixon Lodge" and the instrumental
was called "Elephant Stomp"
(Piano)
Personel; "Judge" Floyd Bean
the only Law West of the Pecos; Jim Beebe, Tromb.
Brian Shanley, Clar. "Nappy" Trotier XX trumpet.
TAUTIER

Bill? (I'll have to think of it later. And "Gypsy Sam" Bacin
Bass All very nice guys that Later play WOW XX
EVER Clancy

Clancy's tape log for Bill Bacin, page 2
(Courtesy Stanford University Libraries Archive / SFTJF)

On 23 January 1972, Clancy's buddies from the World's Greatest Jazz Band flew into San Francisco to play a special two day benefit at Earthquake McGoon's. The group included co-leaders Yank Lawson and Bob Haggart plus Bud Freeman, Bob Wilber, Vic Dickenson, Eddie Hubble, Ralph Sutton, Billy Butterfield and Gus Johnson. Reportedly, one of the highlights of their performances was a Yank Lawson/Bob Haggart duet on Charlie Chaplin's *Smile*. The band played four sets on the Sunday and two on Monday night. Ever since the 1964 Dick Gibson 'Jazz Party' in Aspen, Clancy had felt honoured to be part of this very special group of musicians. However, the respect and admiration was clearly mutual. Clancy had added his own special something to a truly extraordinary jazz outfit.

Just six weeks after the WGJB benefit, Clancy Hayes died at home on Sunday 12 March 1972.

To the very end of his life he had been dealing with music matters and correspondence. Bill MacPherson wrote to Ann Hayes on 16 March referring to a tape Clancy had posted to him only a few days before his death. So sure was Bill that Clancy was on the mend that he apologized for calling him (affectionately of course) 'a broken down cantankerous old goat'. The letter is wonderful and I am sure Mr MacPherson would want to share this extract:

> I am so grateful that I got under the wire and had my chance to hear him and know him because, as I've said many times he was a walking archive and should have been a national monument...
>
> Everything he did will be as fresh and as delightful a hundred years from now as it was the moment he did it. And it should be there for the delight of audiences still unborn.

Fittingly, the most poignant and beautiful tribute came from Ann Hayes. She gave this succinct description of her husband: 'He was great, he was patient, he was wonderful. I loved him very much'. Of all the accolades that could be ascribed to any individual, patience is probably one of the rarest and most precious.

Clancy's private funeral took place at Cypress Lawn Memorial Park, Colma, California on 15 March. His ashes are held, alongside those of Ann, brother Ashton and his wife Jeanne at Santa Rosa Memorial Park, 1900 Franklin Ave. Santa Rosa, CA.

A memorial service attended by family, friends and musicians took place on Friday 17 March at the auditorium of the Asylum Masonic Temple on Van Ness Avenue, San Francisco. Clancy's banjo rested beside his smiling picture as tributes were paid. Turk Murphy's Jazz Band, with Pat Patton as additional banjoist, provided the music. In his eulogy, Reverend Subke said 'The world knew Clancy for his goodness and the joy in his heart came out in his music and enriched the lives of so many'. Burt Bales described Clancy as a 'very human man whose talent wasn't matched by the fame he deserved'. In Burt's undoubtedly biased opinion, 'he was every bit as good as Bing'.

In 1969 Clancy had been hired to entertain delegates travelling by train to a Worldwide Management Conference in Florida. After his death, the unnamed organisers issued A Tribute To Clancy Hayes, a four-LP complimentary gift set comprising GTJ 12006; 12009 and S10050 plus the Clanco LP. Having such an excellent taste in music, the organiser's anonymity is a pity. The notes on the gift box pay their own tribute to Clancy:

> Many of you will recall the first time you saw and heard Clancy Hayes. It was on a train headed for our 1969 Management Conference in Boca Raton. He entertained us then with guitar and his banjo and songs like *Ain't She Sweet*, *Wolverine Blues* and *After You've Gone*.
>
> And if you were like everyone else, his songs made a deep impression. Pianist Jess Stacy once said 'Clancy had the right conception of a song plus an unerring instinct for setting the perfect swinging tempo, which combined to make him a great jazz singer — the best I ever played for. Clancy to us was tops but now he's gone'.
>
> So we thought you might like to have this special collection of four of Clancy's best known record albums to remember him...and old times as well...
>
> Hearing these great recordings now is to realize what we've lost ... though in another sense, we will never lose Clancy Hayes. He lives on - in his music.

A tribute to Clancy Hayes, four LP gift set cover
(Author's collection)

11

Clancy's Legacy

As Bill MacPherson predicted, Clancy's legacy would remain 'fresh and a delight for audiences still unborn'; this coda looks at that legacy. It also reveals some as yet undisclosed aspects of the fun-loving Mr Hayes - including a few non-musical activities.

Clancy Hayes was variously described as, *'A portly gent with a bald dome and a rough and ready voice'*; *'A barrelhouse nightingale'*; *'A hip Burl Ives'* and less politely, a *'Bald old banjo strummer'*.

Leaving aside the last one, let's take a look at each of these descriptions.

'A portly gent with a bald dome and a rough and ready voice'?

Presumably, libel in the 1950s wasn't what it is today. This description also calls into question the sensitivity of the reviewer's ear: 'Rough and ready'? But the *Chicago Tribune's* Will Leonard was a big fan so perhaps I am being hypercritical.

'A barrelhouse nightingale'?

Clancy probably sang in every bar, club and hotel in San Francisco. If there is any accuracy in Mari Ladowski's wonderful description of The Tin Angel (Chapter 5), then this one sticks. In any case, didn't nightingales also sing in fashionable Berkeley Square?

'A hip Burl Ives'?

The richness and timbre of Burl Ives' distinctive voice along with his charismatic stage presence makes this a real compliment, so this is another one that sticks. No 'itty-bitty' tears here. Clancy's good humour would no doubt have allowed him to smile at this description (he got a kick from being nicknamed 'the Murdering Butler' by Lu Watters).

CLANCY HAYES

Barrel House Nightingale

Formerly with the Bob Scoby Dixieland Band

Appearing 1 Night Only

SUNDAY, APRIL 3, 9:00 to 1:00

$1.00 Admission at Door

(Look for the One Flashing Red Arrow)

UNION HALL CLUB

428 Wisconsin Ave.   Racine, Wis.

Barrel House Nightingale, 3 April 1960, poster
(Kanosha News, 30 March 1960)

Clancy's love of music consumed the greater part of his life, but there were moments for other pursuits. For example, on a warm June day in 1930, young Clarence wanted a break from a stuffy radio studio and decided to try his hand at fishing. What could go wrong? It would seem he was very good at it — landing a 160 pounder no less.

Alas, it was neither a Xiphias gladius or a Thunnis or even a member of the order Selachimorpha. The specimen was in fact Homo Sapiens — of the family Hayes, species Clarence. Clancy endured a painful journey from his fishing spot to a doctor who removed a sizeable hook from his earlobe. Thankfully the doc threw him back. Rod for sale.

Clancy attempted something different — if not safer, in 1932. A remarkable coincidence saw sixteen-year-old Turk Murphy, on an outing with his father at Clear Lake, CA, witness a scene which he described as 'a maniac on a speed boat'. The 'maniac' stood on the boat's deck, from which a monstrous World War I 'Liberty' aircraft engine protruded. He was desperately trying to start the engine but, mercifully, without success. The short engine-bursts which preceded its spluttering death saw the lone sailor decked *Oceana Roll* style. He never did get the engine started and eventually rowed safely back to shore. The story came to light many years later when Turk told the tale to Clancy who confessed to being the hapless mariner. He was an infinitely better musician than mechanic. Boat for sale.

Reassuringly, Clancy did participate in safer sports. In June 1941 he was part of an NBC softball match. His all-male team from the KGO-KPO radio station beat their buddies from KFSO by a score of 29-24. However, *Broadcasting* magazine reported: 'the game was so bad that girls on the staff of KFSO challenged their male colleagues and beat them 6-2 in a four-innings game'.

Clancy played golf and was obviously a decent player being among the favourites mentioned in an upcoming spring-1949 musicians' tournament at Harding Park, San Francisco. His friend and occasional Yerba Buenan, Russ Bennett, was also mentioned as a possible winner, although defending champion Dave Lugone was the firm favourite. Despite this, they were all beaten by Buddy Lewis of Oakland. The Pete Clute/Jim Goggin book *Some Jazz Friends*, page 44, has a picture of Clancy on the golf course. Those who know such things will be able to favourably assess Clancy's address and grip; surprisingly he is not dressed in plus-fours as one might expect.

One of Clancy's more idiosyncratic pastimes, apart from (attempted) maniacal speed-boating, was stereoscopic photography, a hobby which he pursued for many years. He was a member of the Stereoscopic Society based in the UK.

```
                    THE STEREOSCOPIC SOCIETY
                           Founded 1893

Hon. General Secretary                                          Hon. American Officers
W. C. DALGOUTTE          Annual Report, Treasurer.         THOMAS PIERCE ROGERS
     England         January 1, though December 31 1970       General Secretary
Hon. Treasurer       January 28,1971.                         RANDOLPH G. WILSON
J. L. COTTER                                                   Transparency Secretary
     England                                                     EUIN SHOOK
                           S.S.B.S                                Treasurer
                                                                Print Secretary
Joseph P. Fallon    $4.00    ,,       Fred Lightfoot    $4.00       ,,
Ralph D. Geiser      6.00             Thomas P. Rogers   4.00       ,,
R. G. Wilson         4.00    ,,       Miss Lucia Brann   7.00       ,,
Euin Shook           4.00    ,,       Dr. Miles R. Markley 4.00     ,,
Elmer A. Ostlund     4.00    ,,       Paul Springer      4.00       ,,
Frank Farrell        4.00    ,,       Clancy Hayes       4.00       ,,
Lloyd W. Dunning     3.00             Dr. Robert E. Markley 4.00     ,,
Hugh M. Stilley     10.00             R. W. Harris     10.00 -1971  ,,
Howard R. Sweezy     4.00    ,,

     Special Subscriptions to the Stereoscopic Society Bulletin.

Professor Harold A. Layer  $3.00    Paul Darnell      $2.00 - 1970-71
H. J. Johnson               1.00    Dr. Paul Milligan  1.00
Vincent McMullen            1.00
W. H. Groves    (P.S.A.)    1.00
Albert L. Sieg    ,,,       1.00
                                    Total Cash Received    $94.00
1969 Cash Balance                                           76.69
                            Total
                                                          $170.69
Expenses For 1970                                           98.25
                                                          -72.44-
Post card and printing(Mr R.G.Wilson)  $36.40
Annual Report printing        Shook     9.34
Postage for letters and the folios     28.51
Sterescopic Society Subscriptions      24.00
                                    ----------
                            total       98.25
Mr R.G.Wilson == Expenses ==

     Prints Folios received from Mr Wearing.
O.A.B.1; Feb.13 1970 .Dispatched to Australia  July 28 1970
O.A.B.2; May 25 1970 .,,,,,,,,,,,,,,,,,,,,,,,  Oct, 28 1970
O.A.B.3, Oct, 20 1970 in circulation here.
```

Stereoscopic Society Annual Report
(Courtesy Stanford University Libraries Archive / SFTJF)

Of course, music was Clancy's passion and his private tapes and the following stories show how happy he was to record when a guest in people's homes. My thanks go to musician Russ Whitman for kindly providing this story which explains the background to private recordings at the Whitman home; warmly recalling how Clancy liked to share his music and his willingness to entertain:

> I was just 22 [in 1961] when the recording was made in my parents' home, north of Chicago in Highland Park. Jim Henman, the son of friends of my parents', was both an investment advisor and a jazz fan. He was apparently giving advice to Clancy and was, by this time, a friend and drinking buddy. Jim arranged the small gathering at the Whitman home so as to include my father (an amateur pianist), my mother (like Clancy from the Nashville, Tennessee, area) and me (a budding young part time musician).
>
> The drummer was Charlie Weeks, a high school friend of mine who lived across the street. He brought over some recording equipment to which Clancy was kind enough not to object. There was no shortage of Clancy's and Jim's favorite beverage, so eventually Clancy was coaxed to play piano. It was my impression at the time that some of what he was playing, aside from the requests, were tunes from a musical show he had written, including *Witch Watch*. I seem to remember his mentioning his show while he was playing, but I haven't been able to find my copy of the recording for verification.
>
> In any case, the gathering was arranged by Jim Henman and recorded by him, with rhythm accompaniment from, Charlie Weeks (who is now regrettably deceased). So, I was just a more than willing bystander and bass sax player. Charlie was a banker and later had his own band, the 'Hornblowers and Weeks' (I think the financial company Hornblower, Weeks, Hemphill Noyes made him change it).

In a 1977 radio broadcast disc jockey Fred Moldenhauer told of a similar home recording event which took place in Denver. Clancy was a dinner guest like no other:

> In 1968 Clancy Hayes, banjo player and vocalist, was playing a kind of a club date with Peanuts Hucko down at the Navarre. One Saturday, early Saturday afternoon, Dad arranged to have Clancy come up to my house and have dinner. I went down to

pick him up. He was staying at a hotel downtown, and I went to pick him up and there he was in his Bermuda shorts and he had that banjo case with him and I figured wow this is going to be more than just dinner!

He came out and we talked a while and finally he said well, why don't you turn on the tape and I'll make some, we'll do some playing and singing here and I really thought that was very nice of him. He was a very wonderful individual and none of us knew at that time of course how really sick he was and I think this session that I have is one of the last things that he ever did. And one of the tunes that he recorded for me was called *The Duke Was Wont To Say* and as I understand it, he never performed it on the West Coast, so I think the tape I have is the only version of him writing this tune and performing it.

So we'll listen to this sequence and see how it all turns out there. It's very good listening; Clancy was a very warm and friendly individual.

Turk Murphy was playing in Denver at this time and later confirmed that *The Duke Was Wont To Say*, a song about a foxhunt, *was* unknown to him as Clancy had never sung it at Earthquake McGoon's. Clancy wrote the tune one afternoon in a hotel room as he was struggling to take a nap while somebody was trying to saw a pipe. What is remarkable about the performance of *The Duke Was Wont To Say* is that Clancy sings in a quasi-Bob Sheridan accent — a little less upper-class, but very British!

Clancy recorded five songs at this memorable session - *The Duke Was Wont To Say / Hassan / She's Just Perfect For Me / Sweet Sue* and *Rose Of Washington Square*. The last two are included on the Satchel of Song CD. Clancy was a dinner guest like no other.

Clancy took little persuasion to buy his own Brush BK 401 reel-to-reel tape recorder when they hit the domestic market in 1947. He used his prize possession to informally record family moments, solo playing for his own amusement and band rehearsal sessions at his home. As noted in Chapter Four, these rehearsals included Bay Area musicians Burt Bales, Bill Bardin, Ellis Horne, Hotz O'Casey, Vince Dotson, Squire Girsback and, on one occasion, Jack and Charlie

Teagarden. He was also happy to make field recordings. Clancy's collection of twenty-three paper and thirty-four conventional polyester tapes (some are duplicates of the paper tapes) is now held by Stanford University as part of the extensive San Francisco Traditional Jazz Foundation archive.[2]

The following note accompanied a copy of a tape sent to a friend. It details Clancy's attempt to capture proceedings at the Ethiopian Baptist Church, in San Francisco. The recording was possibly made on an earlier wire tape recorder.

> Dr. Hamilton
> Etheopian Baptist Church
> Probably - 1944 or early 1945
> Recorded at the church. We were way in the back of the church, Lu Watters, Ellis Horn, Bill Colburn, & Myself. Dr. Hamilton had given me permission to bring my Brush recorder, (on paper tape yet) if we would not make it too obvious to the congregation." The pick up is so bad because I was trying to pick it up from the Monitor Speaker of the Radio Broadcast that was on. Still very interesting though, and beleive me for Real. I shall never forget Rev. Hamilton, taking his big gold watch out of his vest pocket and saying "Now, in about two minutes we are gonna be on The Electric Radio, and I want all you brothers and sisters, to sing out loud and clear, We are praising the Lord - PRAISE THE LORD
> Clancy

(A transcription of this letter is on page 340)

Notes on tape box containing the recording at Ethiopian Baptist Church
(Courtesy Stanford University Libraries Archive / SFTJF)

The following correspondence shows the warmth and kindness that emanated from the ABC family through their countless friendships.

This letter gives another example of the generosity of the Hayes household:

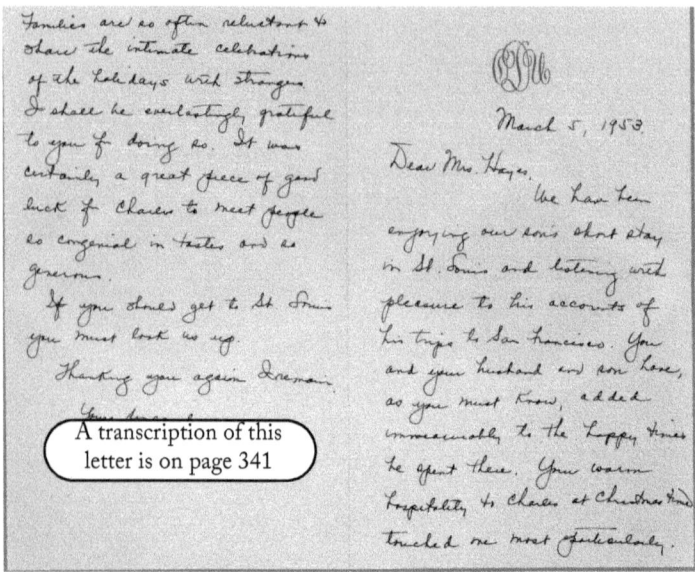

Letter of thanks to the Hayes Family
(Courtesy Stanford University Libraries Archive / SFTJF)

This next letter is from the great jazz and blues vocalist Lizzie Miles to Ann Hayes following the death of Ann's mother. Miss Miles was singing with the Bob Scobey band in Las Vegas at the time:

> A transcription of this letter is on page 342

THE Flamingo HOTEL · LAS VEGAS, NEVADA

Hello Mrs Hayes – Hope you're feeling a little better today. God will help you to overcome your grief as his will must be done. Now here's a prayer to St Anthony that you can get on your knees and say help find your mother's picture. I hope your niece have explained why we ask the saints to help us with our prayers to God. Cause we are all sinners and must be helped along the way to learn God's teachings and live them and become christians if not saints. There is nothing greater than prayers. The more you pray the better you get so pray for your son husband and yourself to become christians and live up to his teachings. I'm tryin hard to be a good christian hope I succeed God is good to me and I hope he continues. I will do all in my power to stay with him. I will pray for your ankle to not give you too much trouble but God never makes our cross heavier

Letter from Lizzie Miles to Ann Hayes page 1
(Courtesy Stanford University Libraries Archive / SFTJF)

Letter from Lizzie Miles to Ann Hayes page 2
(Courtesy Stanford University Libraries Archive / SFTJF)

Pete Clute knew Clancy very well. In his interview with Dave Radlauer, which also included Daphne June King, he responded to Dave's suggestion that Clancy could be described as a 'character':

> Well I wouldn't say that. He was more of an individual than a character. Clancy was just Clancy… like I say, he loved his music and he loved having a good time. Clancy was a true troubadour. He had that knack of being able to put a tune over. Bing Crosby once said of him that he had the best way with words and the best phrasing of anybody he ever knew. Clancy was a one of a kind.

Daphne June King had no problem in talking about Clancy when Dave Radlauer asked her about 'Clancy Hayes the man':

> That's easy, he was absolutely charming. He was tall, well-co-ordinated, always well dressed, very bald and not a handsome man at all. But he was charming and he was funny, and gentle and mostly very, very kind. He had a tremendous wild sense of humor. He had quite a nice social stand. He was not a grubby man by any means. He was quite elegant; wore a lot of silk shirts and things like that - which not everybody was doing in that era. He thought well of himself and he took care of himself. Pete Clute didn't think Clancy was as tall as Daphne suggested. He just seemed shorter, she replied, because he got bigger and rounder.

Daphne King's description of Clancy fits with a comical aside made by Bill Bardin in his extremely entertaining 1993 interview with Dave Radlauer and Bill Carter.[3] He commented 'Clancy and Turk both had the knack of getting along with rich people. Clancy got a few good casuals down at the Peninsular. I remember we played at Ty Cobb's one time; Ty Cobb lived in Atherton — everybody lived in Atherton'.

Pete Clute's memories included a story concerning a prank played on Clancy at Earthquake McGoon's. Clancy drank quite a lot of 'Early Times' Bourbon and kept a supply in a rear storage area at the club. After his set, he would go to that spot for some refreshment. On this particular occasion, one of Turk's band (the prankster was never identified) switched the contents of Clancy's bottle for Worcester Sauce. Apparently, Clancy took a decent gulp and was 'as mad as hell for an hour or so before somebody brought him a good drink'. There was no mention of how his voice sounded in his next set, nor whether it included *Flamin' Mamie*.

Pete also related that Clancy, like many 'star' musicians, needed to have a status symbol:

> ... you had to have a big Cadillac. That showed success ... he (Clancy) had one that was half-a-block long. Clancy used to

drink a lot; he'd go home — he lived out on Balboa and about 41st Street, San Francisco — and it would take him sometimes two or three hours to get home. He would go so slowly in this huge Cadillac. 'Course if anything hit him, he wouldn't have felt it, but he always seemed to make it.

I doubt Pete Clute was condoning drink driving. It appears that the most likely danger was walking into the *back* of Clancy's car! At an approximate distance of eight miles from McGoon's to Clancy's home (on 46th Ave.) it would have been travelling at 4 mph. As to Clancy's status symbol, Pete was not exaggerating. His 1950 Cadillac 60 Special four-door sedan was a stretched-car weighing over 4,000 lbs, with an opulent interior matched by no other model. However, it seems Clancy made little use of its 5.2 Litre V8 engine, which must have purred along at single-digit speeds.

A Cadillac 60 Special
(nakhon100, Wikimedia Commons 2.0)

A number of personal memories, observations and tributes to Clancy were included in the liner notes to the Mr. Hayes Goes To Washington album released after his death:

> Clancy was one of the most talented people it has been my pleasure and honor to work with. Clancy was not only a

great vocalist, entertainer, composer, banjo-guitar player, good drummer, but could also play some very nice piano.

One of my warmest memories is going to his home for dinner and spending several hours sitting around playing piano and clarinet duets. He was one of those rare people whom everybody loved. From my travels around the country I know he left many, many friends who remember him with great warmth and miss him as I do.

George Probert

Another fine showcase of Clancy Hayes' talents: great voice, phrasing, and moving rhythm. I have long considered his sound, reflecting his verve for life and love of his fellow man, the greatest of our time.

Squire Girsback

Clancy was a marvellous original, a delight to be with, a unique entertainer in public and private, a swinging jazz musician, possessor of remarkable time, a prodigious memory for popular songs, a voice of the greatest charm and warmth. On sheer talent he should have been as well-known as Crosby or Sinatra. For over thirty years I felt privileged to be his fan and his friend. There'll never be another Clancy Hayes.

Lester Koenig

Having known and played with Clancy for over forty years, I can say I never knew anyone who loved and enjoyed to sing or play jazz more; it was reflected in his performance. He was a beautiful person and storyteller of song, equal to the best.

Pat Patton

When I told Clancy I was getting off the road to settle in Florida, he presented me with the music and his record of *Travelin' Shoes*. I went to work in a boat yard for six months while sweating out my union card. The same day I got my card I got a phone call: Clancy was putting a band together in Dayton. I left town two days later. Clancy will never be forgotten. He called me 'Andor the Condor, the mighty midget of the Everglades' and was going to write a parody on it. I am proud to have been his friend.

Andy Bartha

237

Saying a few words about Clancy Hayes is like writing a biography on Jelly Roll Morton and merely calling him a piano player. Although I met Clancy in the mid-thirties and listened to him for years on the radio and with various orchestras, we first worked together when I joined the Yerba Buena Jazz Band in 1942. We remained understanding friends for thirty years. During that time we worked with almost every jazz band in the Bay Area.

To say that working with Clancy was always a pleasure is a massive understatement. It was a joy; but my fondest memories are the many conversations we had driving to and from work and at home talking and listening to records or recording for our own amusement. So I am really looking forward to hearing Clancy sing again.

Burt Bales

In 1955-6 I had the pleasure of accompanying the Bob Scobey Frisco Band with Clancy Hayes on a lecture-concert tour of colleges and universities in the West and Midwest. It was during the lecture-concerts that I learned fully to appreciate the richness and nuances of Clancy's voice. He was no crooner; he has no affectations, he didn't try to be operatic — he was just a man, a real man, singing and communicating, telling a story, philosophizing on life, love and women with effortless, colloquial American humor. The more I listened, the more enchanted I became. Clancy's death in March 1972 was an irreplaceable loss to American music, and a great personal loss to me.

Professor S. I. Hayakawa

One of Clancy's many albums was entitled Swingin' Minstrel — I don't know who coined the phrase or title but I cannot think of two words that describe the man and his music more beautifully…with maybe the exception, to me personally, of friend, raconteur, jazzman — single words that describe the pleasure the man brought into my life on so many occasions… his improvisational ability and his deep knowledge and love of people was also reflected in his conversation…talking with

Clancy was equal to his giving a private performance for your entertainment.
Bill Bacin

It is often said that someone is 'One of a Kind' or that 'after making him they broke the mold.' Often this is purely emotional, but in the case of Clancy Hayes I must stand up on my hind legs and say this is not only that but objective and true. There is not going to be another Clance, and anyone who attempts similarity will suffer greatly by comparison to a truly great and good man. I can say no more. I don't like writing about dead friends. I am not puddling up, but the grooves on Clancy's records tell more than I possibly can.
John Dengler

Guitarist Steve Jordan who played on the Clanco LP wrote about Clancy in his book Rhythm Man — Fifty Years In Jazz. [4:]

> Clancy was a walking encyclopaedia of old songs. He seemed to know them all, verses included. I've never heard anyone sing *I Ain't Gonna Give Nobody None Of My Jellyroll / Hindustan / Silver Dollar / Ace In The Hole / Rose Of Washington Square / Oh By Jingo!* or *Down In Jungle Town* the way he did. His phrasing was marvellous. They said he was irreplaceable when he was alive, and they were right.

Writing to the letters page of Jazz Report magazine in the early 1960s, one time president of the New Orleans Jazz Club and part time musician Dr. Edmond Souchon said:

> I thoroughly enjoyed the Paul Lingle article (Vol.6 #2), especially the Clancy Hayes remarks. I LOVE that Hayes.. he should go down in history as one of the greatest jazz singers, and certainly one of the All-Time, All-American 6 string banjo players. I think he's terrific. And he's written and collaborated on several wonderful tunes…..

British musician Spats Langham provided these interesting contemporary comments:

Clancy Hayes - An appreciation and comment on his legacy in the United Kingdom:
I find it fascinating that in the 1940s a few groups around the world started playing the music of Oliver, Armstrong, Morton etc. They were not interested in the modern developments of jazz music for their mission was to keep this music alive. In my opinion, they are the grandfathers of what we call traditional-classic jazz.

Australia had the Graham Bell band, here in the UK we had George Webb's Dixielanders and the USA had Lu Watters. These bands forged the way for us all to enjoy and discover the beautiful thing that is early jazz. Characters emerged from these three bands - Lazy Ade Monsburgh, Humphrey Lyttleton and of course our hero, Clancy Hayes.

As a young banjo player, I was obsessed with early jazz, but growing up in rural England in the 1970s meant there was limited access to such recordings, although our local record store stocked the usual 'popular' jazz material. Then one day a record appeared in the 'nostalgia' section - Lu Watters. Not only was this an American band (exciting), I didn't recognise some of the tunes (good), but best of all, there were *two* banjos (ecstatic!), or, as the late Professor Stanley Unwin would declare, 'deep joy'!

The first thing that attracted me to Clancy was the banjo and his subtle use of the bass strings on his 6-string instrument to cut through the strident powerhouse sound of the Watters band. Like Johnny St. Cyr, Bud Scott and others, he did this always in the right place and never over employed.

I loved Clancy's songs and immediately started copying them. I have to say however, that every band I played in at that time gave me a funny look whenever I suggested we play *Oh By Jingo!* or *Saloon!* This was all to change.

When I left school and began to play professionally, it soon became clear that nearly all the traditional jazz bands I played with had a Clancy song in their repertoire. It seemed that Clancy had definitely made an impact on the UK scene through his records with Lu Watters and Bob Scobey.

Over the years we have had several fine Frisco style bands in the UK which have featured many of Clancy's songs. The most prominent being the Merseysippi Jazz Band from Liverpool; the band started in 1949 and is still going!

But I would like to highlight two British individuals, Tommy Burton and Keith Nichols, - both piano players, exceptional at what they did and sincerely in love with early jazz. I have spent much of my career playing with these two gentlemen who I believe put Clancy's songs *out there* more than anyone else. They told audiences about his mercurial character and role as a troubadour of lost gems from the past, passing on the greatest of tips - 'Listen to Clancy'.

Their enthusiasm rubbed off on me. I found my old Watters record and set-to digging deeply into Clancy's recorded repertoire and studying his singing style. The best singers, I always think, sound relaxed and cool; Bing Crosby did ok! Clancy's story telling style was warm, engaging and always had a lilt and swing to it. The old music hall phrase, 'He knows how to put a song over', of course applies to him, but it's more than that. It's natural, never forced and has an enviable laid-back feel to it.

Sadly, we no longer have Keith or Tommy on our shores to champion Clancy, while many bands that once featured his songs have now retired. However, life rolls on and we now have a very strong scene of young and exceptionally talented musicians who concentrate on early jazz and ragtime. Whenever I play with these chaps and suggest playing a ragtime song from Clancy's book, I'm always delighted to find that everyone either already knows it or that they want to learn and play it. This makes me very happy.

Anyone who's ever played a banjo and sung a few songs in a traditional jazz band will recognise that Clancy was *the* man, a kindred spirit.

Thomas Spats Langham, July 2024

Bandleader, multi-instrumentalist and arranger John Gill, a great authority on San Francisco jazz, never met Clancy, but has intricate knowledge of his music. He has recorded, performed and sung Clancy's numbers with his own bands as well as those of Turk Murphy, Bob Schulz and many others. John has kindly provided these comments:

Just yesterday [5 Nov.2023] I was on a gig and a customer came up to me out of the blue and asked me if I could play any Clancy Hayes songs! I was, as they say in your country, gobsmacked. It was the first time in many years that I've been asked that question. So we gave him *Oceana Roll*, *My Little Bimbo* and a few others. So maybe there's some hope for the sorry state of traditional jazz after all. The first Clancy record I ever heard was Live at Earthquake McGoons that I found in a cut out record bin for about 50 cents and I've been listening ever since.

I never got to meet Clancy, he died a few years before I joined Turk Murphy. As I said, I think he was a fine singer and banjo/guitar player. Also good on the drums and piano. Very relaxed and easy to listen to. Apparently, Bing Crosby was a frequent visitor to McGoon's to listen to Clancy and spend some time chatting between sets. I've been told that Bing always showed up alone, without his hairpiece but with his pipe and hat. I would have loved to eavesdrop on their conversations. I've also enjoyed the various airchecks of Clancy vocalizing on the radio in his pre-Yerba Buena days. In a word he was just wonderful. I wish that I could have met him.

Dear reader, thank you for your interest in the life of Clancy Hayes. I hope this book will encourage you to explore further the joy that lies within the grooves — or 'bytes'– of his recordings; the enduring legacy of a remarkable man.

Let's leave the final words to the man himself:

'Who can take life seriously? Anyone who does is a nut'.[5]

'I like all music. I think that all sound has a correlation to your feelings. Some like it hot, some like it cold, some like it sweet, some like it modern, some like it old-fashioned but it all adds up really to sound and there's a little bit of something there for all of us'.[6]

12

An Appreciation of Clancy Hayes' Singing

By Hal Smith

At the request of author Chris Reid, I would like to share a few thoughts regarding Clancy Hayes and his music...

My first exposure to Mr. Hayes' great talent was the same recording that hooked Chris Reid: The 1951 Bob Scobey session which produced *South*, *Sailing Down Chesapeake Bay*, *Chicago* and *Melancholy*. I was already familiar with the recordings by Lu Watters' Yerba Buena Jazz Band, Turk Murphy's San Francisco Jazz Band and the Firehouse Five Plus Two (plus live performances by Turk and the FH5+2).

But as great as all that music sounded, there were no standout vocalists other than Turk and an occasional solo vocal by the Firehouse Five's cornetist Danny Alguire. Hearing Clancy Hayes' engaging vocals on the four sides mentioned above was an eye-and-ear-opening experience! His sunny voice and bouncy delivery were a delight to hear on those four songs — and on the subsequent recordings by Scobey from the early 1950s.

As my record collection expanded, I enjoyed many more Clancy Hayes performances: the DOWN HOME and MERCURY 78s by Lu Watters; the GOOD TIME JAZZ LPs by Bob Scobey; "Oh, By Jingo" with the Original Salty Dogs; GTJ's "Swingin' Minstrel" LP; and numerous private recordings. As I remember how Clancy sang on the various sessions, an adjective comes to mind: *Effortless*. His vocals seemed to float in the air, whether it was over the heavy two-beat of Watters' band on *Frankie And Johnny*, a gentle duet on *Indiana* with the wonderful Lee Wiley, or the speed-of-light Scobey treatment of *Down In Jungletown* Clancy's voice always sounded natural and his timing was unhurried.

That same effortless quality was in evidence when I heard Clancy performing the intermissions at Earthquake McGoon's. Accompanied only by his own six-string banjo, singing an impressive repertoire from *At The Angels' Ragtime Ball* to *Where Were You On The Night of June the 3rd?* his vocals charmed the audience. On the last song of each intermission, the Turk Murphy band joined him onstage — one or two musicians at a time until the whole band was present. But even with the full, brassy sound of the Murphy band behind him, Clancy's vocals always sounded relaxed.

On my second visit to McGoon's, I appropriated a table tent and collected the band's autographs during Clancy's intermission. When the band resumed their performance, I took the paper to Clancy, who was sitting alone at a balcony table. When his autograph was requested, he looked up and in a very soft voice asked, "Any ole place?" His speech was just like his singing!

I am grateful for having been able to hear Clancy Hayes perform those intermissions at McGoon's. Who else could have come up with such a wide variety of material and performed it so confidently as a soloist in a low-key, folksy image? The versions of *Willie The Weeper, Auntie Skinner's Chicken Dinner* and his own *Parsons, Kansas Blues* with the Murphy band were also memorable, as was his duet with the great bassist Pops Foster at the ill-fated "Dixieland Monterey" in 1968.

The last time I heard Clancy Hayes was at the second benefit for him which was organized by Turk Murphy. Turk's band, Wally Rose, Bob Mielke's Bearcats, Ted Shafer's Jelly Roll Jazz Band and others performed. Turk also invited a young group from Southern California called the Fink Street Five to play at the benefit and I was honored to be included with the band. We played our hottest numbers (and were complimented by none other than Lu Watters, who had driven down from Cotati to wish Clancy well). The performers were inspired and the atmosphere in McGoon's was upbeat when Turk's band returned to the stage for their second set. Then, as the band tore into *Sunset Café Stomp*, the guest of honor made his way to the stage.

After years of listening to his easygoing Southwestern vocals, it was a shock to hear Clancy *struggling* to sing. He managed to make it through an entire 34-bar chorus, forcing out the sounds (his lower jaw had been cut away to stop the spread of cancer). It was a sad performance to witness, but it was also an incredible display of determination in the face of adversity and an unyielding sense of professionalism. I only wish that, for Clancy's sake, it could have been another effortless vocal for him.

Clancy with Dick Lammi. Photo taken at Hambone Kelly's
(Courtesy Stanford University Libraries Archive / SFTJF)

Clancy in action, 1958.
(Courtesy New Orleans Jazz Club Collection of Louisiana State Library)

13

Clancy Hayes in the Rhythm Section

By Hal Smith

Clancy Hayes' singing is discussed at length in this volume. But what about his performances as a banjoist, guitarist and percussionist?

Reading through Chris Reid's narrative, we know that Clancy's original instrument was drums and we can see when and where he took up the other instruments. But *how* did he play?

After listening to Clancy's many recordings on banjo with Lu Watters, Bob Scobey and in various bands it is safe to say that he did not view himself as the primary timekeeper in the rhythm section. With Watters, he was usually playing alongside Russ Bennett, Harry Mordecai or Pat Patton — all of whom laid down a rock-solid, highly supportive 4/4 beat. When listening to the later Watters recordings where the fidelity allows the listeners to hear the two banjos clearly, Clancy tended to emphasize beats 2 and 4 while Patton played an unaccented 4/4. With Bob Scobey — and as a soloist — Clancy tended to accent phrases, leaving the time keeping to the other rhythm men.

This approach was particularly effective alongside drummer Fred Higuera, in the early 1950s editions of the Scobey band. Higuera's looseness on the drums was an excellent match for the bouncy accents on the banjo. On some occasions, you can actually hear a "meeting of the minds" where Clancy and Fred play the same accents at the same time.

When accompanying himself on solo performances (and sometimes on brighter tempos with bands), Clancy often played a bass note on the six-string banjo, followed by a run of single notes and/or chords. This effect is similar to the way New Orleans banjoists Johnny St.

Cyr and Bud Scott used the six-string banjo as a full rhythm section. From time to time, Clancy also played random accents behind ensembles and solos, emphasizing four or eight-bar phrases with the same rhythm that Jelly Roll Morton incorporated between the band choruses on *Kansas City Stomp* and *Georgia Swing*. Clancy continued to use this approach throughout his time with Bob Scobey's bands, as a soloist, as a guest with other groups and even later with the Ten Greats of Jazz/World's Greatest Jazz Band.

We might wonder why Clancy did not play another of his instruments — acoustic guitar — with groups such as the WGJB. Possibly, by that stage of his career he was identified so closely with the banjo and songs like *Silver Dollar* and *Rose of Washington Square* that the saloon vocals and the banjo were viewed as a matched set.

There are fewer examples of Clancy's guitar playing on record. A 1940s-era photo exists of Clancy in a ten-gallon hat and Western clothes; it looks as though he was posed for a publicity still in the role of a "singing cowboy." No recordings of this type of performance have surfaced, but it is easy to imagine how Clancy would have approached a Gene Autry-Tex Ritter repertoire.

The first record of Clancy on guitar in a jazz band is the 1950 JAZZMAN session by Scobey's "Alexander's Jazz Band" (originally issued under clarinetist Darnell Howard's name), where he adds even more propulsion to an already-forceful rhythm section. Clancy played guitar on at least one occasion the listener would expect to hear a banjo: A 1951 concert with a band that included Scobey and Don Kinch on trumpets, Turk Murphy on trombone, Bob Helm on clarinet and Bill Dart on drums. The more dynamic banjo might have helped in this situation, as the rhythm section seemed incapable of holding the tempos.

While he was still performing regularly with Scobey, Clancy organized a recording session under his own name in 1956. He alternated between guitar and drums in a small group which also featured Bill Napier, clarinet; Ralph Sutton, piano; and Bob Short, tuba. (These sides were not released at the time, but were combined with a second session to make up the "Swingin' Minstrel" LP which was issued by GTJ in 1963). Clancy's guitar rhythm on this date is as casual as his banjo playing with Scobey. No Freddie Green-like 4/4; just accents as he felt like. However, he was capable of playing straight-ahead rhythm guitar, as heard on the 1957 "Bing With a Beat" record, with Scobey fronting a band full of stellar jazz and studio musicians. (We can only wish that an enlightened A&R man might have suggested a vocal duet with Clancy and Mr. Crosby)!

As mentioned above, Clancy played drums on some of the tracks which became the "Swingin' Minstrel" LP. For the most part, he limited himself to some light brushwork and choked cymbal at the end of phrases. However, earlier non-commercial recordings illustrate the techniques he learned in the 1920s. This type of drumming is very effective on recordings by two versions of the Wartime Yerba Buena Jazz Band: the 1942 airshots with Benny Strickler on trumpet and the 1944 records with Bunk Johnson. On all the sides, Clancy was playing a drum style very similar to the YBJB's Bill Dart, with extensive use of the woodblock and choked cymbal.

Clancy drumming, a study in concentration
(Courtesy Stanford University Libraries Archives / SFTJF)

There are more examples of Clancy's "old-time" drumming on the "Tempo Train" audition and on nearly all his home recordings with Vince Dotson, Bill Bardin, Ellis Horne, Burt Bales, Squire Girsback et. al. Besides his excellent technique as a drummer, Clancy's time was very accurate on every one of these recordings. Tubist/bassist Gene Mayl, who worked with Bob Scobey in the early 1950s, recalled that Clancy was in a rotation of drummers which also included Gordon "Gramps" Edwards, Bill Dart and Fred Higuera at a time when Scobey was unable to pin any of them down to work regularly with his fledgling band.

No doubt Clancy Hayes will be remembered primarily as an outstanding jazz vocalist. But his unique contributions to the rhythm section should not be overlooked!

Clancy circa mid 1950s
(Courtesy Stanford University Libraries Archives / SFTJF)

14

Clancy's Banjos

Clancy Hayes used four banjos during his jazz years; the instruments are pictured below. Thanks go to John Gill for his advice, for identifying the various models and also for providing the image of the restored Bacon Peerless.

Clancy's first banjo-guitar was a Bacon and Day Montana 4, seen in the well-known picture from the Big Bear roadhouse in the late 1930s and with the Yerba Buena Jazz Band at the Dawn Club and Hambone Kelly's. Used for most of the 1940s, its theft from his car ended a beautiful friendship. The replacement, a Bacon Peerless, probably dating from the late 1920s, came courtesy of Harry Mordecai.

Clancy played the Peerless for the next decade firstly with Lu Watters at Hambone Kelly's in 1949/50 then throughout the 1950s with Bob Scobey and on his own Swingin' Minstrel recordings. The instrument is seen in the Bob Scobey's Frisco Band photographs in Chapters 5 and 6. The Peerless was retired around the time Clancy left the Scobey outfit. It later came, via Clancy's daughter in law Joan Hayes, to Pete Clute who kindly donated it to the San Francisco Traditional Jazz Foundation. In 1998, Foundation member Lue D. Cramblit generously paid for its complete restoration.[1] When the SFTJF ceased operation, the instrument fittingly passed to John Gill.

Clancy switched to a Vegaphone Deluxe in 1960 and it is proudly displayed on the cover of his Audio Fidelity LP recorded in April of that year. The Vegaphone was followed in 1964 by his last instrument - a Weymann model pictured on the cover of the Oh By Jingo album (Delmark 1964) and Happy Melodies (ABC Paramount 1965). The banjo had a detachable resonator seen in the final image from Blues Alley probably in 1968.

Jamming at the Big Bear c. 1939; Bacon and Day Montana.
Wally Rose, Clancy, Turk Murphy
(Courtesy of Stanford University Libraries Archive / SFTJF)

Yerba Buena Jazz Band members at the Dawn Club, early 1940s:
Left to Right: Bob Scobey, Lu Watters, Clancy Hayes,
Turk Murphy, Ellis Horne.
(Courtesy of Stanford University Libraries Archive / SFTJF)

The Bacon Peerless, still from The Semantics of Popular Song
(Courtesy Indiana University Libraries - Moving Image Archive)

The Restored Instrument
(Courtesy John Gill)

Clancy with The Vegaphone Deluxe, 1960.
(Courtesy Julia Carroll and Dominic Adinolfi)

The Weymann with resonator, Blues Alley.
Steve Jordan, Clancy, Pee Wee Russell circa 1968
(Courtesy Frank Selman / SFTJF)

15

The Songs Of Clancy Hayes: Winners and Compositions.

Clancy's many commercial recordings, radio airshots, private tapes and various interviews reveal his obsession with music. This chapter looks at some of the songs associated with Clancy and explores his compositions.

Clancy's uniqueness as a traditional jazz entertainer was, as already noted, in part due to fact that he was first and foremost a vocalist. He had a wonderful voice that over the years covered virtually every style. In his teen years with the King Tut Tooters and Harmony Aces he performed the popular songs of the day, which of course included jazz songs. As was the fashion in the 1930s, Clancy crooned — as exemplified by his work with the Bob Beale-Herb Taylor Orchestra in 1934 and, strangely enough, with Les Paul as late as 1947. Clancy's jazz singing came to the fore with Lu Watters' Yerba Buena Jazz Band in the 1940s and found fame throughout the 1950s with Bob Scobey. Clancy remained a *jazz* vocalist and instrumentalist for the rest of his career.

It was regularly asserted by others that Clancy knew the verse and chorus to more songs than anyone else. Modestly, he would always play this down but in the 1965 Bill Dyer interview [1] he did admit:

> I am either blessed or cursed with almost total recall. Sometimes it's a blessing — like remembering lyrics and things you haven't heard for fifteen years — and other times it can be rather depressing because you think of all the things you wish you'd done different.

It would, of course, have been impossible to remember lyrics to the thousands of songs performed during his career, particularly those from the radio days, but without a doubt he knew a great many.

Clancy had a particular liking for old songs from the first and second decades of the twentieth century and enjoyed bringing them to his audience, complete with verse. An example of his deep appreciation for music comes across in a description of the instrumental performance of the song *Dinah* on the Happy Melodies album (ABC LP 591) recorded shortly before the Bill Dyer interview. Clancy explains:

> We made a brand-new record of *Dinah* that you'll hardly recognize as, for so many years, it's been sung in a jazzed-up *'hotcha hotcha'* sort of way. But it really is a pretty tune if it's approached from a pretty angle because it has one of the prettiest verses of any tune for a so-called pop tune. During the days of the razz-a-ma-tazz 'Russian Joe' bit they lost the verse completely. I'll wager to say that there isn't one per cent of the people in the whole of the United States that ever heard the verse to *Dinah* ... its very sweet and very beautiful played in that nice easy soft tempo. Cutty Cutshall plays the verse on that trombone and it makes you either want to cry or your hair just stands up right on end. He plays it very straight in his inimitable style; straight in the sense that he's not just slurring and sliding around like a guy doing acrobatics....

Home recording remained one of Clancy's favourite pastimes from the moment he acquired his Brush BK 401 reel-to-reel tape recorder in 1947. His private tapes are now part of the San Francisco Traditional Jazz Foundation collection at the Stanford University Library and form the primary source of information for his non-commercial recordings. Given his admiration for Jelly Roll Morton and Hoagy Carmichael, it is no surprise that the collection has him playing many of their songs for his own amusement, often with piano accompaniment. Clancy explained that he had learned piano largely to attempt Jelly's compositions. (The discography appendix includes all known vocal recordings).

Dick Gibson's sleeve notes to the 1968 Jazz in the Troc LP tell us that of the hundreds of songs in his 'jazz book', Clancy regarded four as 'winners': *Rose Of Washington Square / Ace In The Hole / Silver Dollar* and his own *Huggin' And A Chalkin'*. Of course, many other songs are pure Clancy in terms of style, fit and the fact that he was the only person to sing them, but he regarded these four as special.

The Clancy Winners:

Rose Of Washington Square **(Ballard Macdonald and James Hanley) 1920**

This song fits Clancy like an Armani suit. It simply works and that's all there is to it; he recorded the song eight times. In a 1967 interview with Washington DJ Felix Grant, Clancy discussed the version he'd recorded with the Nine Greats of Jazz at the Elitch Gardens Trocadero the previous year:

> **FG**: I don't believe I have ever heard the verse to that song. Are you one of those people who know the verses to all these songs? You know so many...
>
> **CH**: No one knows all the verses, but I have a theory that lyrics to a song — if you are going to have lyrics — should mean something and usually the verse is like the opening scene; it sets the scene and without the verse you sometimes don't get the import of what the man is trying to say. If I can, I like to play the verse.

Rose Of Washington Square dates from 1920, introduced by Fanny Brice in Ziegfield's Midnight Frolic at New York's New Amsterdam theatre. Clancy's view on the importance of a verse is certainly apt here. The song has two different verses which completely change its meaning. The first is a very straight ballad version with the titular rose of the horticultural variety. The second is a comedy version which describes a young lady who wanders from the Bronx to the Bohemian honky tonks of Washington Square. There, she is asked to 'pose for a picture on the cover of Jim Jam Jems'.[2] In the sheet music, there are two choruses: one to follow the straight verse and another for the comedy verse.

The comic version of the song was revived with great success in the 20th Century Fox film of the same name released in 1939 with Alice Faye, Tyrone Power and Al Jolson. The plot closely resembles the life story of Fanny Brice and includes *My Man*, her theme song. *Rose* was a regular in Clancy's solo performances; he delivered it to great applause in his set at the Monterey Dixieland Jazz Festival in 1968. Vocalist Pat Yankee (and sometimes drummer Thad Vandon) also sang the comedy lyrics with Turk Murphy's San Francisco Jazz Band for many years.

Jazz in the Troc, album cover
(Author's collection)

Ace In The Hole (George Mitchell and James Dempsey) 1909

I tried for many years, without success, to find the history of this classic barroom jazz standard, played by almost every traditional jazz band. It was with a degree of relief that I eventually found an article in *The Capital Times*, Madison, WI, in which Clancy himself admitted: 'No one really knows who wrote *Ace in the Hole*'. I am pleased to say that light is shed on the mystery in the footnotes.[3]

This song is a fantastic jazz vehicle and the wry lyric can't help but make you smile. A privately recorded acetate dating back to 1942 has survived, of Clancy singing the number with the wartime Yerba Buena Jazz Band, led by Benny Strickler. He subsequently recorded *Ace In The Hole* with Bunk Johnson and the wartime YBJB in 1944 and with Lu Watters' Jazz Band in 1950. Following the success of the 1952 Bob Scobey-Clancy recording, *Ace In The Hole* was a natural inclusion at all live engagements with the Scobey band. In total, there are fifteen versions of the song listed in the discography.

Silver Dollar (Jack Palmer, Clark Van Ness) 1939

In some ways this song is also a little mysterious in that in Clancy's hands — or voice — it sounds like a turn of the twentieth-century barroom ditty, but actually dates from 1939. It's not a jazz standard by any means and to make the song work in a jazz setting, it needs an outstanding vocal. In 1950 Clancy recorded it with the Washboard Five (a combination drawn from the Watters Band). However, the version he recorded in April of 1952 with Bob Scobey is the definitive one. Clancy also performed the song with real feeling on the 1966 Jazz in The Troc album, giving it a very melancholic mood. Surprisingly for one of the 'winners', there are only six recorded versions of *Silver Dollar*. All but one have band accompaniment, the only solo performance with banjo was taped at Earthquake McGoon's in the mid 1960s. The 1952 Bob Scobey Good Time Jazz single (GTJ 78), which coupled the song with *Ace In The Hole*, was estimated to have sold over a million copies and a GTJ sleeve note states that it was on half the jukeboxes in the U.S.A. during the mid-1950s.

Ace In The Hole, label
(Author's collection)

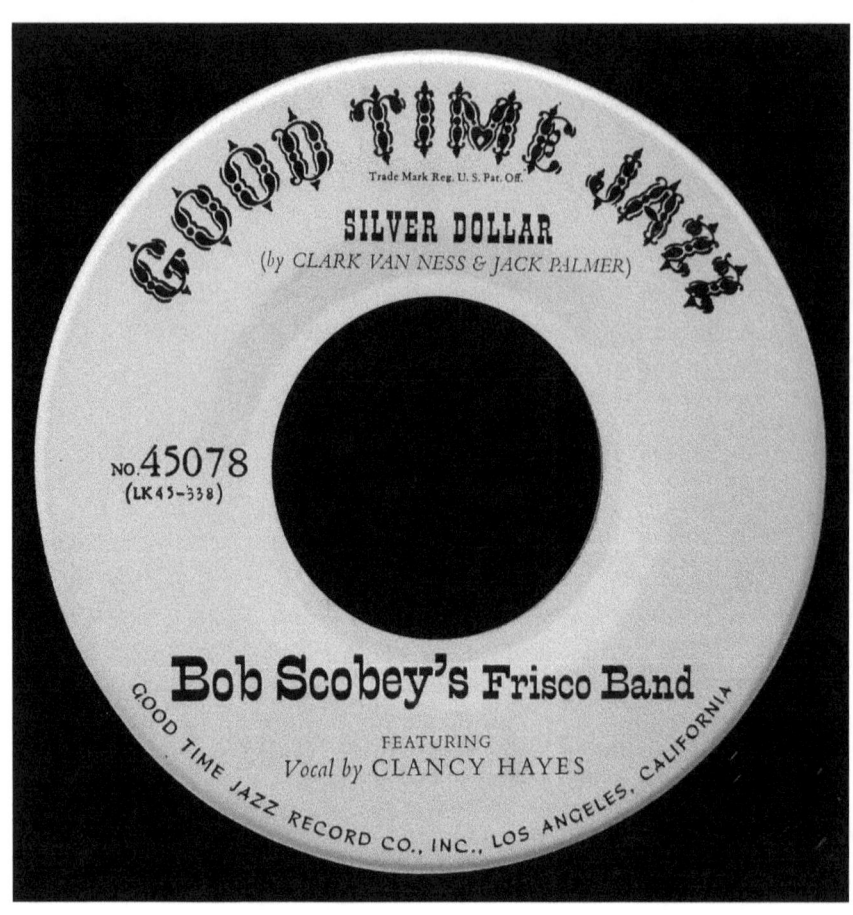

Silver Dollar, label
(Author's collection)

Huggin' And A Chalkin' (Clancy Hayes and Kermit Goell)
Hudson Music 1946

Clancy's own composition and biggest 'hit' by some margin was composed with Kermit Goell, making the Billboard top 20 in 1947. The fine melody and amusing lyric made it very popular. 'Name' artists including Hoagy Carmichael (whose top-selling version was on Decca with Vic Schoen's Orchestra), Bing Crosby, Les Elgart, Kay Kyser and Johnny Mercer also recorded the song. Smokey Rogers even recorded a Country & Western version and it was revived in later years by Clinton Ford (1962) and Jerry Reed (1972). Clancy's own 1947 version with the Frisco Jazz Band is mentioned in Chapter 4.

It is odd that the ridiculous lyrics caused the song to be banned by Clancy's employer — NBC — as 'potentially offensive'. Co-composer Kermit Goell, who was not affiliated with NBC, fought the ban. He managed to get clearance for an instrumental version plus a letter of support from the Legion of Decency — which approved the song complete with lyrics!

Clancy wrote a version of the tune in the early 1920s whilst still a teenager in Iola. He carried the tune around for many years and made a home recording in 1942 with a slightly different lyric and less subtle title. In 1946 songwriter and publisher Kermit Goell, seeking new songs, got in touch with Clancy who offered it for publication. Goell wrote a verse, rewrote a few words in the chorus and then worked with Clancy on a title for the song. Goell's Hudson Music Company published the song and introduced it to Hoagy Carmichael. In 1975, three years after Clancy's death, his fifty per cent rights to the song were assigned to his wife and son.

Sheet music for Huggin' And A Chalkin'
(Author's collection)

Clancy's Compositions

Although a jazz musician, it is interesting that Clancy's compositions are *not* jazz tunes. Most fit the classification of popular, novelty or comedy songs and for this reason some were never performed in jazz settings. Even the open-minded Bob Scobey, who included many Clancy compositions in his 'band book', did not use such favourites as *She's A Good Gal, Weddin' Day, Otto's New Auto* or *Witch Watch*.

Clancy's sixteen known compositions (listed below) never reached the popularity of *Huggin' And A Chalkin'*. Nevertheless, they are good songs and deserve wider exposure. Most were written in collaboration with others including the San Francisco based Daphne June King, who composed music and jingles as a side-line to her job as an advertising copyrighter. She and Clancy worked together from the late 1940s to the early 1950s — with Daphne composing the music to Clancy's lyrics.

Ms King explained their working relationship in a 1999 letter to Dutch 'Frisco Jazz' fan Sam Linschooten:

> To the best of my knowledge, with the possible exception of *Parsons Kansas Blues*, I doubt Clancy ever wrote any published music. He was a lyricist and an absolutely superb one. But he did not, repeat NOT, write music. As a writer I can turn out a decent professional quality lyric, but I could never begin to touch Clancy's genius. I was able to churn out the lyric to *Broken Promises* but that one automatically wrote itself.

Despite Ms King's assertion, Clancy *did* compose music and lyrics to several songs that both pre-date and post-date their song writing association; perhaps Ms King was unaware of them.

Clancy with camera and companion
Courtesy Frank Selman / SFTJF

The Clancy Hayes Compositions

Year	Title	Co-Composers	Publisher (Publication Date if known)
c.1942	She's A Good Gal (But A Thousand Miles From Home)	Stanley Smith	Hudson Music Corp. (1948)
c.1945	I've Been A Fool About Love	Newell Chase, Charles Conlin	Unpublished
1946	Huggin' And A Chalkin'	Kermit Goell	Hudson Music Corp. (1946)
1947	Gettin' My Boots	none	Beechwood Music Corp. (1947)
1947	George Washington, Abraham Lincoln, Ulysses S. Robert E. Lee	Kermit Goell	Hudson Music Corp. (1947)
1948	Ten To One It's Tennessee	Charles Conlin	Lutz Bros. Corporation (1948)
c.1948	Otto's New Auto	none	Unpublished
1949	Weddin' Day	Carl Kalash	Famous Music Corp. (1949)
1949	Broken Promises	Daphne June King	Unpublished
c.1950	Travelin' Shoes	Daphne June King	Beechwood Music Corp.
c.1950	In New Orleans	Daphne June King	Beechwood Music Corp.
c.1950	When The One You Love Is Gone	Daphne June King	Beechwood Music Corp.
c.1950	I'm Happy Go Lucky	Daphne June King	Martin Music (Unknown)
c.1950	On The Midway	Daphne June King	Bourne Inc.(unknown)
c.1952	Swingin' Doors	Daphne June King	Beechwood Music Corp. (1952)
c.1953	Parsons Kansas Blues	Charles Conlin	Ardmore Music Corp.
1958	Glad To Be Me	none	Unpublished
1958	Hassan	none	Unpublished
c.1961	Witch Watch	none	Unpublished
c.1967	The Duke Was Wont To Say	none	Unpublished

She's A Good Gal (But A Thousand Miles From Home) (Clancy Hayes and Stanley Smith) Hudson Music Co. 1948

Although the Library of Congress copyright for this song is dated February 1948, the song had been around for a while and featured in Clancy's billing with the wartime Yerba Buena Jazz Band in 1942. It was no doubt known to the Dawn Club audience. However, it was not widely recorded and apart from Clancy's 78 rpm on the ACE label the other three known recordings are all non-commercial. [4]

I've Been A Fool About Love (Clancy Hayes, Newell Chase and Charles Conlin) unpublished c.1945

This song dates from 1945 or possibly even earlier, since there is an incomplete version by Clancy with orchestra in his Mother's Cakes and Cookies radio programme broadcast in that year. Clancy's personal papers name the songwriters but no publisher details. However, in the 1958 private recording of the song made for Russ Whitman, Clancy says, 'I'm gonna give you a copy of this tune.'

The lyric from this recording is shown below, except for one small section that is unclear. Despite the missing words, the lyrics are truly poetic and worth sharing:

> Verse
>> I had designs for living, love wasn't in my plan;
>> I thought I was wise, 'till I looked in your eyes,
>> And the fireworks began.
>
>> Chorus
>> I've always been such a fool about love,
>> Never could see romance;
>> I stayed at home with a ??? (unclear lyric)
>> Never would take a chance;
>> I was so happy in my way,
>> Never a heartache night or day;
>> That was the life for me,
>> So careless and fancy free;

When accidentally I gazed in your eyes,
As now and then one will;
Heaven came tumbling right out of the skies,
My universe stood still;
Then over went my apple cart,
Why didn't I realize from the start?
You were the words to the song in my heart,
And I've been a fool about love.

Gettin' My Boots (Clancy Hayes) Beechwood Music Corp. c.1947: *Glad To Be Me* (Clancy Hayes) unpublished, c.1958

These two songs are grouped together as neither were covered by other artists. The Clancy versions are excellent. *Gettin' My Boots* was released with the Frisco Jazz Band in 1947 on Pacific records and with Bob Scobey on the 1956 Dixieland Jazz LP on Verve. These are Clancy's only recordings of the song. I could not find sheet music, but the Verve LP credits the song solely to Clancy with Beechwood Music Corporation listed as the publisher.

It has not been possible to locate either sheet music or publisher details for *Glad To Be Me*. The song, with a trademark Hayes lyric, is sung as a duet by Clancy and Toni Lee Scott on Bob Scobey's 1958 RCA album Something's Always Happening On The River. Clancy made a private recording, accompanying himself on piano, for his friend Squirrel Ashcraft, possibly a short time before the LP release. The song reflects Clancy's philosophy on life but with one minor inconsistency. The line 'Why should I long for a Cadillac? I'll get along with a Pontiac' was untrue.

George Washington, Abraham Lincoln, Ulysses S. Robert E. Lee (Clancy Hayes and Kermit Goell) Hudson Music Corp. 1947

Another Hayes/Goell composition recorded by Clancy with the Frisco Jazz Band in 1947 on the Pacific label. The eponymous character with the All-American names, is about to get into a fight with 'Big

Foot Joe, a so and so, tough and mean as he can be'. However, George warns him off: 'Don't you mess around with me'. The warning has the desired effect. The Frisco Jazz Band version was not a big seller, but the song attracted the attention of Phil Harris who recorded a Dixieland version for RCA (78rpm 20-2301-B).

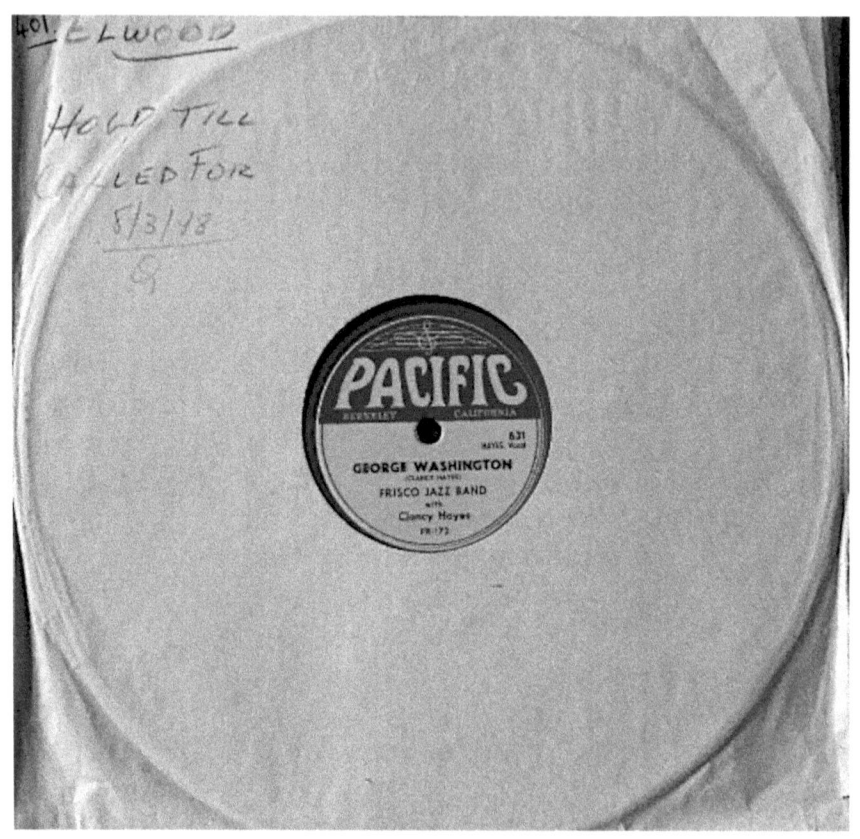

78 George Washington, label.
(Note the sleeve writing - presumably holding for the noted DJ and music critic Phil Elwood)
(Author's collection)

Ten To One It's Tennessee. UK 78 rpm release coupled with Clancy's In New Orleans
(Author's collection)

Ten To One It's Tennessee (Clancy Hayes, Charles Conlin) Lutz Bros. Music Co.1948

This song was Hoagy Carmichael's follow up to *Huggin' And A Chalkin'* attempting to capitalise on his success but it failed to catch the record buying public's attention. Clancy's 1956 recording with Bob Scobey's Band[5] far better captured the spirit and charm of the song, something missing in Hoagy's version. Clancy and Hoagy were friends and he apologised to Clancy saying, 'I should have kept my big mouth shut'. For Clancy the lyrics are certainly appropriate to someone once billed as 'The Voice of the South'…

>When the smell of roastin' possum mixed with
>>honeysuckle blossom and a welcome mat,
>
>Means there's room on the rack for one more hat,
>Ten to one it's Tennessee.

Otto's New Auto (Clancy Hayes) unpublished c. late 1940s

This catchy and lyrically dexterous composition was probably written in 1947 as part of the continuing search for another hit. 'Otto' never made it to record but there is a private tape version on the Satchel of Song CD.[6] It is clearly a number that Clancy enjoyed as he privately recorded ten versions, in different tempos, in the search for the perfect one. The image below shows Clancy's updated lyric bringing a 1960s model to market. Later, Clancy may have performed this as an intermission number at McGoon's but all the private recordings have band accompaniment.

☺ OTTO ☹ *(A transcription of this letter is on page 343)*

OTTO McNAUGT, Tho somewhat ~~Tight~~ Taut, Feelin' Like an Astronaut, Glidin' as he's ridin' down that 'ol main street — Gadgets here and gadgets there, you push a button everywhere, for Automatic Windows and a push pull seat —

LO☺K
MA
NO FEET

There was Uncle Futz in his Bearcat Stutz, And that, Fag With the Bag in his Beatup Jag

Otto's New Auto, handwritten lyrics
(Courtesy Stanford University Libraries Archives / SFTJF)

Wedding Day, sheet music
(Author's collection)

Weddin' Day (Clancy Hayes and Karl Kalash) Famous Music Corp. 1949

This song was probably Clancy's second biggest selling composition, but one *he* never recorded commercially. Throughout his career, Clancy showed a gift for words, whether writing rhyming scripts for the Tune Termites, radio scripts, jingles or lyrics. This country/novelty song has the premise that a young man wants to marry a country gal, but her father demands that any prospective suitor must first acquire some "farmin' land". The groom sings this happy chorus after rising to the challenge:

> Got a Pig, got a cow, got a horse and buggy now,
> and soon I'll be drivin' down the old highway.
> got a farm, got a plow, got a heart for workin' now,
> tomorrow morning is my weddin' day.

Jack Kilty recorded the most popular version of the song on MGM records. It was also recorded for Brunswick by Bing Crosby with the Andrews Sisters. Again, it shows Clancy's compositional leaning towards popular and comedy tunes.

The King / Hayes Compositions[7]:

Broken Promises unpublished

Broken Promises, written as a Western tune, was probably the first King/Hayes collaboration which Clancy introduced to the Lu Watters band in 1949. The Yerba Buenans spotted the 'trail dust' and were not happy about recording what they regarded as a 'cowboy song'. With typical humour, in a private recording of the band rehearsing the song, Clancy lets out a full-throated 'Yee-haa' halfway through the vocal (Head 'em up and move 'em out)![8] The Watters band subsequently relented and recorded the tune, minus the 'Yee-haa', for Norman Granz. It resurfaced in the late 1980s/early 1990s with excellent renditions by third generation San Francisco Jazz bands.[9]

Travelin' Shoes (Composers Music): _In New Orleans_ (Ardmore) both tunes c.1950

Travelin' Shoes and *In New Orleans* were registered with the Songwriters Protection Association on May 4, 1956 together with *When The One You Love Is Gone*. However, all three songs were composed several years earlier. The songs were managed by Beechwood Music Corporation for a joint royalty advance of one dollar, of which Clancy received 57½ per cent and Ms King 42½.

Daphne June King had already written part of *Travelin' Shoes* but needed help to finish it. She explained, 'I got stuck. Clancy came over and twenty minutes later it was all done; he had that kind of incredible ability. Genius, I guess you'd call it.' Issued on the Scobey LP Direct From San Francisco, it is one of Clancy's jazzier compositions.

In New Orleans started out as a Caribbean tune titled *Chee Chee Bonga*. The introduction was borrowed from something Daphne June King heard clarinettist Slim Evans play and opens with a minor strain to which she added a Latin bridge. Clancy completely rewrote the lyric, relocating it about 1,000 miles north-west of the Caribbean. 'It pleased me very much,' said Daphne.[10]

When The One You Love Is Gone unpublished c.1950

There is something very special about the poetic lyric and mournful melody to this song. It is yet another in the long list of songs that inexplicably fail to get the attention they deserve. Although not a jazz tune, the Bob Scobey band recorded it as one of four Clancy originals on the Down Home album for Verve in 1956. Scobey featured additional brass and reed players for the session and named the ensemble as Bob Scobey's Band with no mention of 'Frisco Jazz' anywhere on the album. The treatment on *When The One You Love Is Gone* is closer to that of a jazz orchestra than a traditional jazz band.

> Spring sunrise smiles on my pillow,
> The robin sings to cheer the weeping willow;
> But he's silent for me,
> 'Cause the one I love has gone.

Warm winds sweet scented with laughter,
Should whisper winter is what spring comes after;
But there's no spring you see,
'Cause the one I love has gone.

(Chorus)
Riding a cloud I was swept on,
Blind that my heart would be stepped on;
When will a new love bring back
That April feeling;
I pray some day it will find me,
And where my heart is broken, tie and bind me;
Ending this misery
'Cause the one I love has gone.

Swingin' Doors Beechwood Music 1952

The lyric on this Hayes/King gem is pure fun and the song really should have received more attention. Once again, perhaps the problem is that this tune is equally novelty and western, but not jazz. It was another of the Clancy originals on the 1956 Down Home 1 album. A live version made during a rehearsal at the Jenny Lind Hall is included on the Unheard Bob Scobey CD GHB BCD 283.

Apart from their recorded compositions, Clancy and Daphne June King also wrote two songs, registered in the Library of Congress copyright office, which do not appear to have been issued:

I'm Happy Go Lucky (Clancy Hayes and Daphne June King) Martin Music.1950
On The Midway (Clancy Hayes and Daphne June King) Bourne Inc.1950

Clancy did sing *I'm Happy Go Lucky* on the June 1958 Bob Scobey RCA recording session (Something's Always Happening On The River), but it was one of six unissued tracks.[11]

The Hayes/King collaboration also produced several children's songs (*Bow Legged Bill* and *The Christmas Mouse*) and jingles. One such, written for Horse Trader Ed's Used Car Lot, 790 Van Ness Avenue, San Francisco, 'got him more business than he could handle,' recalled Daphne June King. Other products benefiting from the Hayes' jingle pen included Tut Tut Tuttles Cottage Cheese and NoDoz caffeine pills to prevent drowsiness — 'as harmless as coffee'.

Parsons Kansas Blues (Clancy Hayes, Charles Conlin) Ardmore Music Corp. 1953

This song is hard to classify. The beat is close to Rhythm and Blues *and* early Rock 'n' Roll, but all the available recordings by Clancy are with jazz groups. From the 1955 recording with Bob Scobey's Frisco Band to the late-1960s session with Tommy Gwaltney, all versions really swing. The song is Clancy's nod to his early years in Kansas and his father's work as a railroad ticket agent. Unsurprisingly, it was especially popular with the people of Parsons and throughout the years there were many references to Clancy and the song in the local press. It was one of his most requested numbers and I guess anyone with a connection to the Sunflower State would have enjoyed hearing it.

In addition to the commercial releases, there are twenty-two private recordings of the song. It lends itself to 'jamming' and there are several extended versions. At the 1968 Dick Gibson Jazz Party, Clancy performed the song as a tribute to a Parsons native — trumpeter Buck Clayton, in a version lasting nearly *nine* minutes. As he was going onstage, Clancy remarked, 'It was like being fed to the lions in the arena'. Fortunately, on this occasion he received a thumbs-up rather than becoming a meal for the lions.[12]

Bob Scobey's Frisco Band. Left to Right: Jack Buck, Clancy Hayes,
Fred Higuera, Bob Scobey, Hal McCormick, Bill Napier,
Jesse 'Tiny' Crump
(Courtesy The Parsons Sun, 22 Nov.1955)

Hassan (Clancy Hayes) c.1958
Witch Watch (Clancy Hayes) 1958

These two later songs, with words and music by Clancy, again show a true aptitude for wordplay, to the extent that no one else appears to have attempted to sing them.

Hassan was recorded with the Bob Scobey band during a marathon 1957 recording session for RCA. Between December 10 and 14 the band cut thirty-one tunes for two albums (LPM 1567 and LPM 1700). *Hassan* didn't make it to vinyl and was one of six unissued sides.[15] The song was included in their set at Grand Rapids, MI (shortly before the RCA session) and Bob Scobey announces:

> Here's one he wrote about a month ago and we are going to record this in New York in a couple of weeks — a little novelty selection called *Hassan, What a Man*. We are going to

let Clancy tell you all about *Hassan*, give you a little preview of our next recording. He wrote it and he's entirely responsible for everything that happens.

Witch Watch was not recorded commercially, but three Clancy versions have been preserved in private tapes — including an intermission performance at Earthquake McGoon's in 1966.[14] The song is a tongue-twister with 'witches watching witches watching watches' (and lots more besides). One might assume that sobriety was an absolute prerequisite in attempting to sing this one, but Clancy performed it faultlessly in 1958 at the George Hulme after-gig party in Toronto.

The Duke Was Wont To Say unpublished c 1967

It is probable that the only performance of Clancy's final composition took place at the home of the Moldenhauer family as explained in Chapter 11.[15]

Other Possible Compositions

For the sake of completeness, it is worth detailing information from the Satchel of Song CD. The sleeve notes credit five songs to Clancy from a 1939 Tune Termites radio broadcast. Although it is likely that he would have been involved in these compositions, it has not been possible to verify this or establish whether the songs were published. The five songs are detailed in the discography appendix along with the other songs from radio programmes, some of which Clancy may have been involved in.

Satchel of Song also has two instrumental tracks titled *Clancy's Piano Rag* and *Clancy's Last Rag* which may well have been his compositions and recorded during his illness; again it has not been possible to positively establish the composer.

16

The Scobey and Clancy Recordings — An Overview

Any attempt to review Clancy's vocal recordings with Bob Scobey would require a book of its own. However, I have attempted to summarize some key aspects of their special partnership which blessed us with so much musical art. Bob Scobey released fifteen albums under his own name in his all too short life, including a flurry of nine releases between 1956 and 1958. All but two albums feature vocals by Clancy Hayes. In addition, three LPs and two CDs of private and unissued recordings were released posthumously giving a total of 135 commercially issued vocal recordings with Bob Scobey's excellent bands. Thankfully, there are also eighty-nine vocals from private concerts. It is a thrill to hear this band live.

Bob Scobey was a remarkable trumpet player and bandleader, undoubtedly one of the finest in traditional jazz. Charlie Crump, the internationally respected jazz aficionado and sound restorer of classic recordings, once opined that Scobey's standing as a jazz artist was hampered by Clancy's prominence with the band. Their close association influenced the repertoire which included many popular and vaudeville tunes; for some this may have detracted from Scobey's status as a 'serious' jazz trumpeter. Indeed, I have read reviews of Bob Scobey recordings that warn of the presence of vocals! Nevertheless, despite Mr Crump's astute observation, many jazz fans (me included) regard Bob Scobey as a true jazz great who possessed a unique tone, fluent technique and great sensitivity in his playing. It is my unquestionable belief that, but for his premature death from cancer at the age of forty-six on 12 June 1963, he would have achieved the broader legendary status he deserves.

Bob Scobey, August 1953
(Courtesy Stanford University Libraries Archives / SFTJF)

Scobey and Clancy, mid 1950s, location unknown.
(Courtesy Stanford University Libraries Archives / SFTJF)

The superb Good Time Jazz recordings of *South* and *Chesapeake Bay* (recorded 16 Nov. 1951) are mentioned in Chapter 5 and in Hal Smith's observations in Chapter 12. It is no surprise that the remaining two titles from that session — *Chicago* and *Melancholy* — are also outstanding performances. *Chicago*, written by German-born composer Fred Fisher, was a top selling song of 1922 and has been sung by just about every performer of popular music. The song is not a staple of traditional jazz (it was not included in the repertoire of Lu Watters, Turk Murphy or Louis Armstrong), but was a perfect vehicle for Clancy's playing and singing with the Scobey band. In addition to Scobey's forceful lead, an enthusiastic sounding ensemble and a delightful vocal chorus, there are excellent solos by George Probert and Wally Rose.

By contrast *Melancholy* is of course a jazz classic, recorded in 1927 by Louis Armstrong's Hot Seven and also Johnny Dodds' Black Bottom Stompers. The song receives a sympathetic and lyrical treatment from the Scobey band. Clancy's vocal is sublime; particularly when delivering these lyrics:

Like the flowers need the sun,
Crave the dew when day is done,
I need someone to tell my troubles to…

Many fans of Scobey and Hayes regard the Good Time Jazz recordings with a special affection and as close to the magic that the association was able to achieve. By comparison, the later RCA recordings were an attempt by a major label, having signed Scobey as their leading traditional jazz 'flag-waver', to make records for a wider audience. When Dutch Frisco Jazz fan Sam Linschooten first obtained the private tape recording of the Bob Scobey Band in concert at Grand Rapids from December 1957, he was thrilled and surprised to hear the band playing in what he regarded as the 'Frisco style' — close to the Good Time Jazz sound. Sam pointed out that the concert took place in the same month as the marathon session that produced the tracks for the Between 18th and 19th on Any Street and College Classics LPs for RCA. But the music style on the albums is quite different from how the band played in concert.

The Something's Always Happening on the River album from June 1958 may have been a near return to the San Francisco sound but the other RCA albums were closer in style to the East Coast than the West. The comparison between Scobey's Victor and Good Time Jazz recordings in the following (anonymous) review, printed in the *Virginia Pilot and Portsmouth Star* of 1 December 1957, makes the point well:

Bob Scobey, Clancy Hayes Are Restored To Eminence

Bob Scobey and Clancy Hayes will be relieved to learn that there is still material being released from the not-so-distant past. Recent Scobey recordings for Victor have been marred by a soupy artificiality that gives no hint of the band's vigor. Now on GTJ L12032 the Scobey crew is restored to eminence by virtue of a release recorded back in *March 1956* (author's italics). Hayes the itinerant banjo plucking blues singer, who many including this reviewer regard as the finest white jazz singer working today is in his usual spirits for *Michigan Water Blues* and *Travelin' Shoes* among others…

It is important that we come to our own view regarding the merits and high spots of the Scobey and Clancy recordings. As Sam Linschooten noted, the band's live performances in the RCA period were excellent both musically and in terms of putting on a show for the audience. There are many gems within the RCA records. Fun tracks like *The Five Piece Band / Let's Dance The Ragtime Darlin'* and *My Bucket's Got A Hole In It* are terrific. The title track from Something's Always Happening on the River is excellent, as are Clancy's own *Glad To Be Me* (a duet with Toni Lee Scott) and his heartfelt vocal on *River Stay 'Way From My Door* from the same album. If we let ourselves go, and suspend any analytical jazz pretensions, the College Classics album is pure fun. Please investigate and come to your own view.

An LP that probably only a Bob Scobey band could pull off was their Scobey and Clancy Raid The Jukebox, recorded for the Stereo Records/California labels in 1958. The album consists of twelve hits from the pop charts of 1957. As luck would have it the charts contained a couple of genuine jazz tunes (*See See Rider* and *Yellow Dog Blues*) which are stand out band/vocal tracks. But *Love Letters In The Sand, Round And Round* and, wait for it, *All Shook Up* are also performed with real style. To borrow an expression from Clancy, the LP 'is a gasser' and Bob Scobey and the band shine on the instrumental numbers.

I hope this brief resumé of some of Clancy's vocal efforts with Bob Scobey will encourage you to search and listen to his wonderful voice, style and the personality he brings to a song. This author sincerely thanks Clancy, Scobey (and all the members of one of the best bands that ever went under the Dixieland/Traditional banner) for all the enjoyment their music has provided.

17

Clancy's Albums (And Four Rare Songs From The Satchel)

This chapter details the eight LPs issued under Clancy's own name, some of which are described in earlier chapters. In addition, there are comments on four songs from his private tapes that never made it to band performances but are good examples of his interest in music from the early part of the 20th century.

The first three albums were released/recorded during the Lu Watters and Bob Scobey years. To avoid the over-use of superlatives, I make no comment as to how good each of these albums is. Suffice to say that they are all excellent in their different ways.

Clancy Hayes and His Washboard Five: Down Home 1004 (early 1950s)

The arrival of the long-playing record in 1949 allowed Lu Watters to use the new format to reissue the 78 rpm Down Home recordings. Also on the Down Home imprint, the first two ten-inch albums featured the Yerba Buena Jazz Band. The third (DH 1003) was a Ralph Sutton album comprising six piano solos and the fourth featured reissues of Clancy Hayes' Washboard Five recordings. Such was the newness of the LP format that the rear covers were blank and there were just six tracks on each album. The Clancy recordings are discussed in Chapter 4.

Clancy Hayes and His Washboard Five, album cover
(Author's collection)

Clancy Hayes and His Washboard Five, record label
(Author's collection)

Clancy Hayes Sings: Down Home MG D-3; Verve MG — V 1003 (1956)

Another collection of recordings Clancy had made with his Washboard Five and the Yerba Buena Jazz Band in 1949/50 reissued of the Down Home label. The label was purchased by Norman Granz in 1953 and the album reissued on his Verve label. Those who had worn out, broken or lost their original 78s must have been thrilled to hear these numbers in High Fidelity sound.

Swinging Minstrel: Good Time Jazz M12050/S12050 (1963)

An outstanding LP released in 1963 and comprising two small band sessions recorded on 29 October 1956 and 18 January 1958. It marks a departure from revivalist jazz and as the title announces, it swings! With his wide musical tastes and knowledge, Clancy was no doubt keen to experiment with smaller units to allow more freedom for the vocals.

The first session features Bill Napier, clarinet; Ralph Sutton, piano and Bob Short, tuba. Clancy plays guitar on two tracks *When You And I Were Young Maggie* and *Willie The Weeper* and drums on three-*Honeysuckle Rose, Limehouse Blues* and *Wolverine Blues*.

On the second session Clancy is accompanied by Pud Brown, clarinet; Jess Stacy, piano; Bob Short, tuba and Shelly Manne, drums. Clancy plays banjo on all tracks.

The reasons why GTJ chose to delay the release of these tracks is open to debate. Perhaps they thought that the record buying public wasn't ready for the different style at the time of their recording. Or perhaps they were simply short of suitable material - the initial session had only enough tracks for an EP.

No matter. It is fair to say that almost seventy years later, the recordings have a freshness that gives them a newly minted quality in every respect and each musician excels. If ever there is a 'must listen to' Clancy album, this is it. Hal Smith's comments (Chapter 13) on Clancy's drumming style make listening to the album all the more enjoyable. You will have noted that Shelly Manne plays drums on the second session.

Clancy Hayes' Dixieland Band: Audiofidelity AFLP/AFSD 1937 (1960)

Recorded in April 1960, shortly after his break with Bob Scobey, this album shows Clancy's style outside of the Scobey band. The inclusion of two 'new' songs to the Clancy songbook, *Easy Street* and *Washboard Blues*, sit alongside ten familiar jazz standards and give this album a special interest.

Oh By Jingo!: Clancy Hayes with the Original Salty Dogs - Delmark LP DL 210 (CD reissue DE 210) (1964)

The background to this album is covered in detail in Chapter 9. Congratulations to Delmark records, still going strong sixty years later.

Happy Melodies: Clancy Hayes with Yank Lawson and His Yankee Clippers - ABC 519 (1965)

Clancy's association with the Greats of Jazz at the Trocadero was no doubt behind this album with musicians drawn from the Greats line-up.

It includes two contemporary songs, *Fickle Finger Of Fate* and *Don't Forget 127th Street*, which were issued as a 45 rpm single. At the same sessions Yank Lawson recorded the Big Yank Is Here album (ABC Paramount 518) leading his Yankee Clippers with Clancy on banjo and two vocals.

Live At Earthquake McGoon's: Clancy Hayes with The Turk Murphy Jazz Band and Squire Girsback - ABC 591 (1966)

This follow-up album for ABC, recorded 23 September 1966, showcased Clancy in his setting as intermission entertainer at Earthquake McGoon's. Five vocal numbers are performed as a duo with Clancy on banjo and Squire Girsback on string bass. On another five vocal tracks he is accompanied by Turk Murphy's Jazz Band.

Whether there was any staging to the repeated calls for *Tomorrow*, from a customer who appears to have had plenty of 'refreshment', is unknown. Thankfully, he is silenced when Clancy obliges with a wonderful version (accompanied by Mr Girsback) giving us the second of his two recorded versions of this song (the other was part of the Tempo Train pilot radio programme).

Mr Hayes Goes To Washington: Clancy Hayes with Tommy Gwaltney and the Blues Alley Cats - Clanco (1972)

This LP is another mentioned in the text of the book (Chapter 9). It is worth repeating that the vitality and freshness in the recordings is incredible. The band format is similar to that of the second Swingin' Minstrel session, creating an exciting and lean accompaniment that brings Clancy's vocals to the fore. In addition, two instrumental numbers, *Capitol City* and *Trip To Rio*, really swing.

When Clancy announces 'All Aboard' at the beginning of *Parsons Kansas Blues*, the sense of mutual respect and bond of friendship between the musicians really comes through. Please excuse me for straying from my avowed commitment not to use superlatives, but this track is a stunner.

Four Songs From The Satchel

Clancy's love of old and obscure songs led to him resurrecting many forgotten popular tunes including *Oh By Jingo!*, *My Little Bimbo*, *Long Gone*, *Peoria*, *Auntie Skinner's Chicken Dinner*, *At The Angels' Ragtime Ball*, *Sailing Down The Chesapeake Bay*. These and many others were brought to public attention when Clancy performed them with the Lu Watters and Bob Scobey bands. Apart from the songs included in Clancy's commercial recordings, the following excellent songs from private tapes are worthy of a mention, further exemplifying his fondness for the songs of his youth.

Many of his private recordings, including those described below, are posted on the Clancy Hayes Jazz YouTube channel (and all are detailed in the discography appendix). Each has a special magic that makes them well worth a listen, as are the original versions (also available on YouTube):

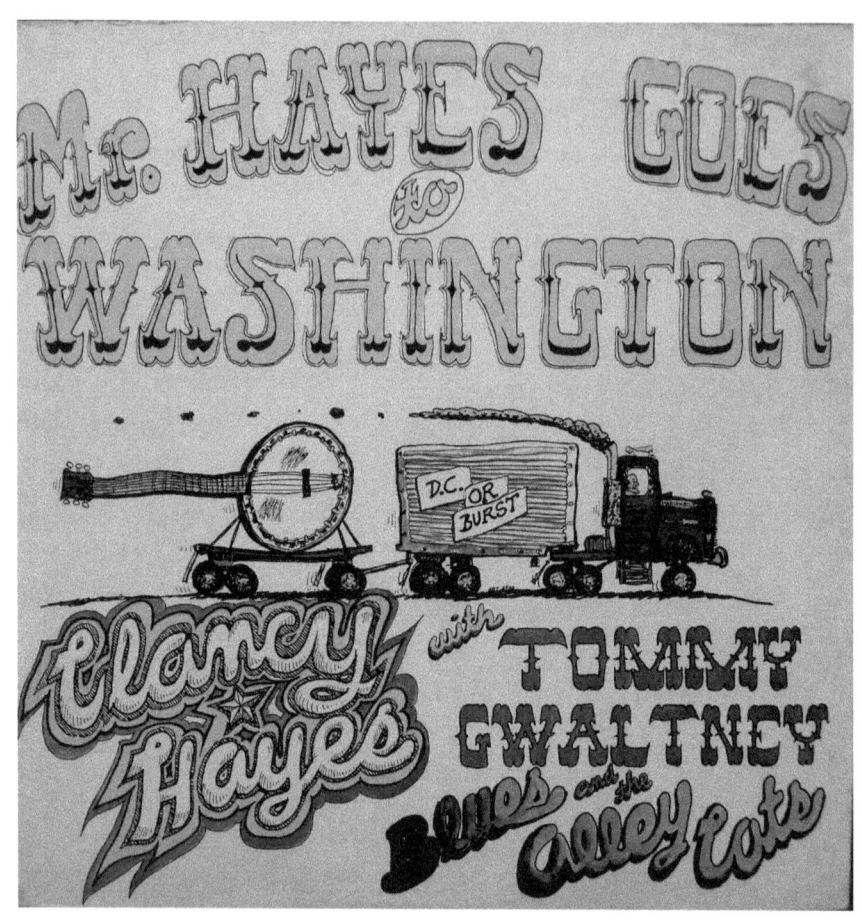

Mr Hayes Goes to Washington, album cover
(Author's collection)

Stavin' Change (Alfred Bernard) 1923

A song with an amusing lyric written and recorded by Alfred Aloysous Bernard (1888-1949), a vaudeville entertainer billed as 'The Boy from Dixie'. Bernard started his prolific recording career in 1916 and was one of the first white men to sing the blues. He is credited with bringing *St. Louis Blues* to public attention, recording many versions of the song for different labels. Composer W.C. Handy regarded Bernard's 1918 Victor record (18772A) with the Original Dixieland Jazz Band as the best.

Stavin' Change sung as *Chain* by Clancy is a perfect fit for the Hayes delivery as the excerpt below shows. Clancy made three private recordings of the song:

> He has a knife long enough to row a boat,
> A big 44 underneath his coat,
> Looking for a scuffle at a fish fry every night;
>
> Mustard brown, they loved the tiger in his eye,
> In satin blacks, they used to feed him rocks and rye,
>
> He said there's changes in the ocean, changes in the sea,
> Never gonna be any change in me;
> 'Cause I'm Stavin' Chain, meanest man in New Orleans

It is likely that the published version was inspired or based on an original jazz/blues song. In his recordings for the Library of Congress in 1938, Jelly Roll Morton referred to an individual named 'Stavin' Chain' in the lyrics of *Winin' Boy*. The connotation in Morton's song seems to be completely different from the published version. In any case, Clancy's versions incorporate melodic fragments of *Winin' Boy*.

YouTube has a piano roll version of *Stavin' Change* posted by 'pianmn199' complete with lyrics and 78 versions posted by 'phonodaze' and 'VictrolaJazz.'

What A Life When Nobody Loves You (Little, Goodwin, Shay) 1925

The hit version of this number was released by Gene Austin with ukulele accompaniment on Victor 19677-A in 1925. There are several postings on YouTube including Clancy's only version recorded in 1942. It is a simple song, but one Clancy obviously liked. His delivery is superb.

When He's All Dolled Up (Monty C. Brice and Walter Donaldson) 1917

This comedy song from is another from Clancy's 1942 home

recordings. It fits the Hayes vocal style perfectly. YouTube has a 1917 version by Byron G. Harlan on Victor 18303 — described on the label as 'Rube song with orchestra' posted by 'recordsrob.' The song, performance and humour are timeless and wonderful.

Deep Elm Blues (Willard Robison) J.W. Jenkins Sons 1925

An excellent blues written by Willard Robison, composer of *A Cottage For Sale* and *Old Folks*. Robison was a friend of Clancy's and taught him the song, Clancy explained:

> *Deep Elm Blues* was never published[1], this would be circa 1921 when he (Robison) had the Deep River Jazz Band … this was later made by Busse's Buzzards when Busse was working with Whiteman. The other side of that record is the first one that I was on — *I'm Gonna Charleston Back To Charleston* — with Coon Sanders. [2]

I encourage you to search and listen to these and other private recordings which are so accessible via YouTube. Clancy's legacy of recordings from the 1934 broadcasts to his final commercial recording at the Blue Angel Jazz Club in 1969, give us so much to enjoy. As his long-standing friend and fan Pete Clute put it, 'Clancy's voice is just happiness, pure happiness'.

18

A Jazz Journey: Encountering Clancy Hayes

By Frank Selman

While doing my school homework on a dreary day around 1958 in the Netherlands I fiddled around with my radio.

I hit the Jazz Program of the *Voice of America* beaming from Frankfurt their weekly Jazz Hour by Willis Connover.

Along came Jelly Roll with Dr. Jazz and Hyena Stomp.

I can still feel the impact to this day.

Next day I hurried to the local record store to buy my first vinyl with more Red Hot Peppers. From the corner of my eyes I noticed some Jazz EPs that took my fancy: Good Time Jazz was the label, great artwork and moreover red vinyl. GTJ EP 1018 - 'Bob Scobey and his Frisco Band with vocals by Clancy Hayes'.

My love for the music, the performers and moreover the unique minstrel story telling by Clancy has never left me.

Of course I wanted to share my musical treasure trove with others. That was not an easy task.

In the Netherlands I was an ardent member of the Dutch "Dr Jazz Society", in his heyday counting well over 1,000 Jazz Afficionados,

Around 1975 I met Sam Linschooten, a longtime member, selling Jan Scobey's Bob Scobey book and the Jansco Scobey records.

He was the one who compiled the Lu Watters, Bob Scobey and Clancy Hayes discographies. This got me in some serious Frisco Style Record collecting, even going after YBJB acetates.

It was Sam who started the "Bob Scobey Society" attracting other Frisco Traditional Style Jazz Fans.

What was a musical hobby of mine became a Jazz passion for the rest of my life.

To cut my story short: thanks to a visit with Hal Smith in New Orleans in 1990 I did attend the San Diego Traditional Jazz Fest for some 30 years and listened to and recorded more Frisco Style Jazz than I ever could have wished for.

Wonderful people I met and befriended, just to name a few:

Hal Smith, Bob Helm, Wally Rose, Dave Radlauer, Leon Oakley, Robbie Rhodes, Tom Bartlett, Mike Walbridge, Terry Waldo, Carol Leigh, Robin Wetterau, Charlie Sonnanstine, Bob Schulz, John Gill and so many more. All of whom kept the YBJB fire burning.

I am delighted that Clancy Hayes' enormous contribution to jazz music has been captured in this book and congratulate Chris Reid for his energy and perseverance to realize the biography of our beloved Minstrel. Hats off, my Frisco Friend.

To end my story:

On a visit to Earthquake McGoon at the Embarcadero in San Francisco many years ago I met Wally Rose and asked him to sign the red vinyl EP that started it all.

He quipped: "so you saw red eh?".

I still do, unashamedly.

Frank Selman.

19

My Uncle Clancy

By Melissa Phillippe

When I was growing up, I had a favorite uncle. I didn't know, at the time, he was many people's favorite.

Clancy was my mother's uncle, making him (technically) my great uncle. But in our house, and in my heart and mind, he's always been, and will always be, My Uncle Clancy.

I was only 14 years old when Clancy died. Unfortunately, this means I never saw him on stage doing his music with a band. But I saw him regularly, in our house, with his banjo and that big beautiful voice of his. It was my very favorite thing.

My family was actually filled with musicians. Many of them were professional. But they were classical musicians. Clancy was the only one playing music that was just downright fun!

And it wasn't just his music. *He* was fun.

When he would visit, I preferred to sit right next to him. That way I could *feel* his laughter, as well as his wonderful voice (whether speaking or singing) reverberate through me. He had a magical voice, and a contagious joy.

We had family gatherings fairly often. Clancy wasn't always able to be there. I didn't fully understand all that he was up to, keeping him away and busy, until these recent years.

I knew that Clancy had a following in San Francisco. I knew this because I remembered that San Francisco had had "Clancy Hayes Day" when he was sick. I knew that a city didn't have such a thing for just any old person.

But it wasn't until I got to talking more with Chris Reid — the author of this book — about Clancy's body of works and his life of music that I really understood. I'd had *no idea* just how well-known my Uncle Clancy actually was.

He was so unassuming. I mean, he was unforgettable. His voice, and his joy, and the imprint of his goodness in my mind and heart. But I never would have guessed he was so well-known and celebrated.

Decades after his passing, I was playing music with a guy I'd been singing with for years. For some reason, I mentioned my Uncle Clancy. It was the first time I heard the response, practically screamed at me, "Wait. *Your uncle* was *Clancy Hayes?!*"

It turned out that his dad had played trumpet with Clancy for years at Earthquake McGoon's. He used to go and watch them play sometimes. He told me that his biggest memory of Clancy, besides that amazing voice, was his banjo playing. He said Clancy was doing things on that banjo that no one had ever done.

As I've gotten to know Chris, I've also gotten to know the professional side of my sweet, Uncle Clancy. It's been amazing to learn so much more about him.

Through Chris, and all the material he's managed to amass in the preparation for this book, I have been re-introduced to the man I only half-knew growing up. Clearly, Clancy's music was his passion.

Now I understand more fully who I was sidling up to at those family gatherings. I thought I was drawn to his joy and his fun music. But it was also his passion.

I now see that his passion for music was a blessing to many. I didn't realize, then, that he belonged to the world. Not just our family.

Turns out, he passed along that love of music to me. Obviously, it was also in my genes, from his brother Ashton — my grandfather. Ashton and my grandmother met because of music. She stopped to ask a friend if he could help her read a melody she was trying to learn. Ashton was visiting his friend at the time, and sang her the melody. They were married two weeks later!

I'll never really know how much of my own joy and passion for music was fortified by those wonderful visits when Uncle Clancy would laugh and play and sing for us. I think being near him when he was around was like being infected with joy and love for music.

I am grateful for my own life in music. It's been an amazing life filled with laughter, fun and, of course, music. And I am eternally grateful for my Uncle Clancy. For his introducing me to the possibility of a life so completely filled with joy and music.

What a life well-lived!

Afterword

It was my good fortune to hear the recordings of Clancy Hayes singing with Bob Scobey's band when I was just a child growing up in Brixton, South London.

From a very early age I incessantly played the family's modest 78rpm record collection of British popular music; every aspect of playing records fascinated me. Family parties were a particular thrill as Uncle Jock would always bring a large box of 78s and other people would bring along one or two latest hit records. We danced to the sounds of Fats Domino, Bill Haley, Lonnie Donegan, Fats Waller, Jimmy Durante, Bob Crosby and Humphrey Lyttelton; none of these records were in my family's collection. If luck was on my side Uncle Jock's 78s would be left for several days after the party. (He eventually made me a gift of the whole collection when I was around nine years old, one of the happiest days of my life).

At one fateful party (probably in 1957) another uncle, George, brought along his latest purchase - a ten-inch Bob Scobey LP on Good Time Jazz LDG 109. The proud owner of a new Philco Hi-Fi, he purchased only LPs (which he was kind enough to lend to a certain pestering child). As the opening notes of *South* burst from the loudspeaker my world changed forever, even more so when Clancy's vocal began. The next track, *Sailing Down The Chesapeake Bay* had the whole family dancing in a Conga line. *Melancholy* was greeted with some relief, allowing people to find a partner and enjoy a slow dance. Apart from their excellence as jazz numbers these songs were very easy to dance to; for many years Uncle George livened parties with his treasured Scobey LP.

From my first hearing of the Scobey and Clancy records that was it; I was hooked and for over fifty years have enjoyed seeking Bob Scobey and Clancy Hayes recordings. The quest of course had the added benefit of bringing me into contact with many interesting, entertaining, knowledgeable, generous and helpful jazz friends. I fairly quickly learned that there were so many wonderful jazz artists and records to be discovered, but the music of Scobey and Clancy and the artists of the Great Jazz Revival were (are!) tops.

Full credit goes to Bob Scobey and his constantly remarkable band personnel, but for me there is something in the vocals that make the music so very special. That November 1951 session which produced *South, Sailing Down The Chesapeake Bay, Chicago* and *Melancholy* is one of the best sessions in music history; the angels were in Jenny Lind Hall that day.

Clancy's voice and delivery has an indefinable *something* that brings happiness to the listener. It is Happy Music for sure but it is also *real* jazz, there are no straw hats or striped vests. As Hal Smith commented, Clancy's singing also seems effortless. He had a true love of music and a desire to bring songs from the past to new generations — complete with verse. Renowned semanticist Professor S. I. Hayakawa put it like this:

> He was no crooner, he had no affectations; he didn't try to be operatic — he was just a man, a real man, singing and communicating telling a story, philosophizing on life, love and women with effortless colloquial, American humour.

Musician and jazz club owner Pete Clute was also very young when he first heard Clancy on the radio. He described Clancy's voice in this way, 'it was just happiness, pure happiness'. No wonder "the Old Groaner", Bing Crosby, cited Clancy as his favourite traditional jazz singer'.

I acquired the two 'Scobey Story' 12-inch albums as presents when they were released in the early 1960s but it wasn't until I started work a decade later that record hunting began in earnest. Thankfully in the early seventies Good Time Jazz reissued its LP catalogue and other labels such as Homespun and Dawn Club issued early and private recordings of Lu Watters, Bob Scobey and other West Coast revivalists.

Jazz Record Fairs and Vintage Jazz Mart were also a source of records and contacts. But as you will no doubt know, it is the people one meets along the way that make the real difference. Sharing and celebrating music with the friends mentioned throughout the book, and many others not mentioned, has been a joy and privilege.

Fifty-plus years on, I have been fortunate to hear virtually everything Clancy recorded thanks to those generous enough to share music and of course the San Francisco Traditional Jazz Foundation, the Charles N. Huggins Project and Stanford University Libraries.

Mindful of the enormous work done by others to record the history of the Great San Francisco Jazz Revival of the 1940s, especially in relating the pre-eminent roles of Lu Watters, Turk Murphy and Bob Scobey, it seemed to me important to write Clancy's biography. A man of multiple talents who loved music above all else, Clancy spent a remarkable forty-five-year career entertaining his audience, a period spanning the early days of radio to the break-up of The Beatles.

Setting out Clancy's story has allowed me to part repay a debt of gratitude for the immeasurable joy his music has given over a lifetime of listening. May I also thank Jazz musicians past and present, and all those involved with the creative process, for bringing us what is known interchangeably as revivalist jazz, traditional jazz, New Orleans Jazz or perhaps better still, *the* original American Music.

When the next Jazz Revival comes along, I hope this book will be a source of information and inspiration.

Chris Reid

Transcriptions

Spelling and other errors in the following transcriptions are as in the original texts and have not been identified or corrected. The texts are as written.

Aunt Jemima Boy

ANNOUNCEMENTS AND DESCRIPTIONS
THE AUNT JEMIMA BOY
WEDNESDAY, APRIL 30, 1930.

7.45 to 8.00 A.M.

ANNOUNCER: You will now be entertained by the Aunt Jemima Boy.
ROOSTER CROW.
ALARM CLOCK.
YAWN.
OPENING SONG.
Mornin, folks. How is you all dis nice, bright, sunshiny mornin?
It sho am a joy to get up dese mornins. Eh? No, ah didn't get all mah sleep last night. You see it was dis way: Bud Judson an his gal, and me and mah gal went on a moonlight picnic last night in Bud's car. Yes, sah, and it was a real picnic with real eats. When we got to de shores of de lake de gals said dey had a surprise for us. And it sho was a surprise. Dey each had a fryin pan and a package of Aunt Jemima's Pancake Flour. And did dose gals know how to cook pancakes? Um, um! Well, Bud and I got to racin, and we was a-runnin neck-and-neck, but we jest had to quit, 'cause if we didn't there would a-bin none left for de gals. After we was through eatin dose delicious, golden browns Bud's gal sang us a couple o' songs. While ah's waitin for mah stack ah'll sing one of 'em for you. SHAW!

Down Among The Sugar Can

Bud's gal was telling us about takin her little sister to de circus last week. Her name am Nanny. Ah means de sister's name am Nanny. Dey calls her Nanny 'cause it am easy to get her goat. Well, when day came out o' de side show Nanny kicked 'cause she hadn't seen de "Also." Bud's gal got sore and said, "Dere aint no Also in dat shaw. "Yes dere am," said Nanny. What makes you all tink dere's

[Page 2 is missing]

said: "Yes, mother, ah sho was good, a man offered me a big plate full of money an ah said 'no thank you!" SHAW!

Well, Dad, ah tinks you had better wipe off your chops and tear yoself away from dose light, flaky, golden browns, or you'll be late for work. Jes hand me de paper over here an ah'll give it de once-over, and see what's goin on.

SONG ..... I SEE BY THE PAPERS

Well, folks, now dat Tillie is at liberty to go to work cookin me a couple o' stacks of dose luscious Aunt Jemima hot cakes ah'll get busy with these two sets of white ivories of mine a-masticatin of 'em

CLOSING SONG.

Fan Mail from a devoted blonde'

Gilroy, Calif.
June 5, 1930

Dear Pancake Boy,
    I listen to your program every morning.
You have a wonderful voice, and are very entertaining.
  My "pet hobby" is collecting radio stars pictures. I am willing to pay for them. Sometimes I don't have to. I would like very much to know your real name and to have a picture of you.
  Just about the time you dive into your ten-foot stack of hot cakes I finish mine. You ought to get up earlier.
    How long have you been on KGO.
    I never heard you until about two months ago.
     Wishing you every success in the world and hoping I get my picture.

A devoted blonde
Marguerite Sween
Gilroy Calif.

P.S. If you have to, send the picture C.O.D.

Letter from Albers Milling Co.

Albers Bros Milling Co.
Cereal and Flour Millers
Stock and Poultry Feeds
San Francisco, Cal.

Mr. Clarence Hayes,
1129 Neilson St.,
Berkeley, Calif.

Dear Sir:-
Knowing of your interest in the proposed broadcasting to transpire later, and desiring to acquaint you with our various products, we are taking the liberty to address you with the object of enquiring if you would care to designate the kind of Albers' cereals you would prefer, whether it would be Waffle Flour, Flapjack Flour, etc.?
Carnation Milk will accompany delivery of cereals.
At your leisure please advise the writer your preference of the following and oblige:
Carnation Wheat Flakes
Carnation Oats
Carnation Waffle Flour
Pearls of Wheat
Peacock Buckwheat Flour
Cornmeal - White and Yellow
Graham Flour
Rye Flour
Fluff Cake Flour
Instant Tapioca
Pearl Barley

Yours very truly
Albers Bros. Milling Co. - Carnation Co.
K.L.Dial, Manager

Letter from Three Girls in Seattle

Seattle Washington,
October 20 1932

Dear Mr. Hayes

We're sitting here listening to your three o'clock broadcast with the Buccaneers and your "<u>Please</u> Mr. Hemmingway, compelled this note of appreciation.

We're a bunch of radio fans and listen to the popular programs on both national chains and we are unanimously of the opinion that your jazz singing is the most perfect jazz rhythm we ever heard. We've decided you have "Jazz It". Bing, Russ, Rudy croon but you sing jazz.

Maybe you've guessed by this time that we think your "Good". Well you're exactly right. Will you sing "When Uba Plays the Rumba On the Tuba", and "Is I In Love, I Is," sometime please.

   Thanks for the pleasure received,
Sincerely yours, Three Girls in Seattle.
P.S. We're having fits over your "Goofus"

M.A.

Letter from B.L. Frank, Manager Ambassador Hotel, Los Angeles

October 26, 1934

Mr. Clarence Hayes
2355 Bay Street,
San Francisco, Calif.

Dear Clarence,

I am in receipt of your letter of October 8th and must apologize for this tardy reply.

However during the past month I have been devoting practically all my time to the Liquor questions coming before the voters on November 6th and have neglected all other work. I realize that your letter required a prompt reply but so much work was needed to be done to defeat these proposed Local Option Laws that I felt it necessary to devote all possible time to it. If we are not successful in our efforts we may not need any band, as you can well imagine.

Now regarding your band. It is impossible to consider it now Clarence, as I am under contract for many months to come so could not use them in the Grove. So far as being interested in placing them outside the Grove, I just could not undertake this as running the Ambassador is about all I can manage. No doubt your band is all that you say it is but it is just impossible to consider at this time.

With my kindest regards to you, I am

Sincerely yours,

Ben

Letter from Hank Mingie

San Jose, Calif.
June 26 — 33

Dear Clarence,

    I was just sitting here listening to the Rythm Vendors so thought I'd drop you a line. I generally hunt up your programs.

I've been down here around San Jose for about a year now before that I was in L.A. Looked up Max Robinson while there.

I haven't been around the old home town for about two years, but every thing remains about the same there. Its been quite a few years since I saw you, but I suppose your memory will recall me. Thought I might look you up the next time I am in the City and say hello. I enjoy your programs, and some how it brings back the old "Harmony Aces" wasn't it?

Claire, Porter, yourself and Kenneth Smith don't remember who else.

    In the mean time I remain,

as ever,
"Hank" Mingie
Campbell, Calif.
13#, Box 172

Letter from San Francisco Chronicle

San Francisco Chronicle
THE CITY'S ONLY HOME-OWNED NEWSPAPER
FIFTH AND MISSION STREETS
SAN FRANCISCO, CALIF.
July 12, 1933

Mr. Clarence Hayes
National Broadcasting Company
111 Sutter Street
San Francisco, California

Dear Mr. Hayes,

 May I take this opportunity of expressing my appreciation for your splendid work in making the Chronicle Inaugural Program a success.
 You put over your numbers in fine style and they are still whistling around the Chronicle offices— "Let's all sing like the birdies sing."
 Again, many thanks,

      Sincerely,
      James Adam,
      Director of Radio Activities
      The Chronicle.

Letter from Dorothy Wickman

Dear Mr. Hayes,

I suppose to you this will be just another "fan" letter to deposit in the waste basket.

I listen to you sing with the "Rhythm Venders" every chance I get - which isn't very often because I'm usually not home when you're on the air.

I have, what I suppose would be called a "crush", on your voice.

It has such a lighthearted carefree note in it and it certainly cheers me up in my "blue moments".

In case you have a small photo of yourself somewhere, please, will you honor me by sending it to me?

I'd love to see what you look like and I hope I won't be disappointed. Thank you for bothering to read this (if you did).

Sincerely,
Dorothy Wickman,
Rt 1, Box 244,
Healsburg, Calif.

P.S.

I forgot to mention that I'm only an infant of sixteen, but infants can have "crushes" on voices, too, Can't they? "Dot"

Letter from Lena and Louise Lerza

Lodi, California
July 15, 1931

Mr. Clarence Hayes
Radio Station K.G.O.
Oakland, California

Dear Mr. Hayes:
    My sister and I have been listening to your singing for quite some time. We never fail to tune in when the "Vagabonds" are on the air. We were certainly surprised to hear you sing with Jesse Stafford and his orchestra several months ago.
    Mr. Hayes, do you appear on any other program besides with Mahlon Merrick and the "Vagabonds?" Another question, you play some instrument, do you not? We enjoy your singing so very much—maybe because it's such a different type of singing. "The Hour of Parting" is, at present, the number we would like to hear you repeat. Could you state a definite day when you could do this number for us? Maybe this is asking too much--how we hope it isn't!
    One more favor, and that is, do you send out photographs of yourself to fans?
    We would appreciate it very much if you would send us any picture of yourself.

Two sincere admirers,
Misses Lena & Louise Lerza
Box 546
Lodi, California

Hot Jazz Society Newsletter, 1942

Hot Jazz Society
of San Francisco
July 12, 1943

Sponsors:
BOB BEST
RUDI BLESH
HARRY BRIDGES
BILL COLBURN
ALFRED FRANKENSTEIN
RAY GERALDO
DON HAMBLEY
EMELIA HODEL
TED LENZ
HAL McINTYRE
H. IRVING ROSENBERG. JR.
PETER TAMONY

Dear Fellow Member -
The Hot Jazz Society of San Francisco welcomes you into its select fold of devotees of le jazz hot. Your membership card now entitles you to enjoy each Sunday afternoon jazz session in the Chamber Jazz Room at 150 Golden Gate Avenue at the reduced admission price of six bits.

And speaking of last Sunday's opening session, no attempt at words is necessary to describe the exciting music that poured out of Willie "Bunk" Johnson and his ex-Lu Watters stars—because of course, you were there! After hearing Bunk, the real man of jazz, it is easy to understand that chapter on Louis Armstrong from the book "Jazzmen" that quotes as follows:

"...and Louis had talked a lot about Bunk, his idol of earlier days, had tried to tell how beautiful Bunk's tone was, how intense his vibrato, and had sung phrases to Lil (Armstrong) to show the facile, imaginative way Bunk had of embellishing them. Somehow Louis had felt things the same way as Bunk, had the same inborn sense of beauty, the same melancholic and exuberant accents, and naturally adopted a similar mode of expression. A lesson of inestimable importance which Louis absorbed more than anyone else was the way Bunk had of hesitating, always a little behind the beat, a lazy yet most dynamic way of playing which is at the core of all hot jazz."

Bunk himself shared our "high" feelings after last Sunday's clambake, and the stomps, rags and blues of his "Hot Seven" satisfied him. "That was Jazz," said its creator Bunk, "but wait until a few more sessions and my boys will really do it up like gravy." And with this happy thought in mind, let's treat ourselves to the habit of being present at the next and every Sunday afternoon session for more and better jazz.

The Chamber Jazz Room also will be "done up like gravy" with the addition of a public address system. Four lucky people again will win valuable prizes, including collectors' record albums and the books "Jazzmen" and "This is Jazz" by our own Rudi Blesh - a four-bit must item that is selling like mad at all the music counters. The surprise package of last week's session was Bob Best who thrilled with his blues shouting of "Milenburg Joys". Bob will be on desk again, but a new bundle of joy, Miss Stella Brooks, blues singer extraordinary, who has recorded with Stuff Smith, and was the musicians' favorite when she sang with Art Hodes' famous jazz band in New York, will also be in front of the mike to "send" us.

Your friends too are invited to become members of the Hot Jazz Society of San Francisco and enjoy the privileges of dancing, sipping, discussing and listening to "that genius" Bunk Johnson - as Saunders who was up from Los Angeles described him. Bring them along with you and educate them to the righteous jazz, and if you want them to receive the general Hot Jazz announcement, mail their names to the Secretary Hot Jazz Society, 1317 Grove Street, San Francisco, 17, California, and we'll be glad to do the rest. Also, your comments and criticism of our first session are welcome.

uopwa 34

Letter from Mari Ladowski

1446 Laurel Street.
Napa, California.
September, 15,1954.

Dear Clancy and gang,

    `I've been meanin' to write you ever since I first saw your TV show sometime in July. I just barely caught the last of the show where you were telling about appearing somewhere on the Embarcadero across from pier 23 and I never did hear all of the directions, but I decided right then and there that my husband would have to hear that 'crazy' band. The next time we were in the City we thumbed through the phone book for a logical address on the Emabarcadero across from pier 23 and came up with the 'Tin Angel' of course. We hied ourselves out there posthaste and did a double take when we saw the joint. There was nary a car around there. In fact there wasn't much of anything except a bunch of rubbish and some left-over building material. Since we had already gone that far we decided we may as well do it up brown so we opened the door -- ever so quietly and peered into the dimly lit interior which was practically in the same shape as the outside. We were about to depart and call it a day when the clean-up man informed us that the joint would be jumpin' at 9PM. It was then about 8:30PM. By that time my husband was beginning to doubt the existance of a guy named Clancy and whether he would be worth waiting to see if we did wait til 9. I had given you such a buildup though, that he decided to stay out of curiosity. We were the first ones there with only the barkeep for company. When two waitresses came in and started to crowd as many tables to the smallest space possible and the barkeep insisted that they didn't have enough tables, my husband perked up a little. When you boys came at last and gave out with the Dixie-land swing he was completely sold on the first rendition. We stayed til the 2nd intermission and would have stayed on except for the fact we had to drive back to Napa, and besides only a Rockefeller could afford those drinks all night and we are just working folks. We have been enjoying the weekly broadcasts ever since and if we ever get a phonograph we'll sure buy your new album.

There's just one thing we would like to know, did you get that halo you wear on your telecast from working at the 'Tin Angel'? (The halo is formed apparently by the light of the studio shining on your bald spot) No matter where it comes from we like it and you, Bob Scobey and all the boys. Your new ivory tickler is 'real gone'. Of course we liked the other guy too and the way your bass knocks himself out on the ole git-fiddle. We like your drummers friendly smile, your clarinetist' hot licks, the slide trombonists slides, Bob's one-handed trumpeting. Let's see now, did I leave anybody out? I'll say I did. We forgot to mention ole Clance with his banjo and the trio. I guess you gather by all this that we think you're slightly terrific even if I do have to rassle this typewriter to try to get out a legible letter what with all the mistakes I make. Fo'give me. Just don't leave our dear old San Francisco for long unless you get a bigger audience and a sponsor (making sure of course that you always beam it our way.)

Pardon the long-winded letter, I just couldnt say all I wanted to say on a measly little postcard.

By the way, I want you to know that I don't make a practice of writing fan letters least of all one as long as this. The most I ever get out is a short note once in a blue moon. So consider yourselves highly honored.

Long may you play !!
Sincerely
Mari Ladowski

Letter from J. Walter Thompson Company

J. WALTER THOMPSON COMPANY
Public Relations
Chicago 11, Illinois

August 6, 1956

Dear Clancy et al,

I know you've seen it—but I want you to know I read the "trades" too.

So I send this clipping telling about the RCA business.

I really think the biggest thrill about the whole business is to have my two favorite vocalists signed at the same time — Lee Wiley and Clancy Hayes.

Oh no, I'm not forgetting Lizzie Miles, she's my favorite song belter, and I mean there's a difference.

Anyway, don't try to get away with anything, youse guys, because I'm constantly on the prowl and on the watch. Hope to get to San Francisco in person soon for a lot of reasons.

Bud got home from Fort Lee Saturday afternoon after a 29 hours drive. Saturday night was quiet as he slept until Sunday morning. Then the heat was turned on. Nothing but Scobey records throughout the day. He finally went out last evening or he'd still be catching up on some of the later stuff. He particularly likes the Down Home album. Best thing about that one is the bevy of Hayes numbers and the way the band pretty well plays "Stardust" straight. How gorgeous that way,

Have a nice time in L.A. and Vegas.

Best regards to Ann and the band.

(?)Meyla.

NEWSPAPER CUTTING: RCA ADD 3 TO JAZZ ROSTER

New York - RCA Victor added three names to its jazz roster last week: Lee Wiley, Bob Scobey and Jack Montrose.

Thrush Wiley most recently recorded for Storyville, and previously for Columbia and Liberty Music Shops. Scobey, with his Frisco Dixieland band and vocalist Clancy Hayes has been with Good Time Jazz. Montrose, tenor saxophonist-arranger, was with Atlantic. Deals were made for the Diskery by jazz chief Fred Reynolds.

Letter from Andy Bartha

so its Thursday
Greetings o' Clancy
Just closing after 18 wks. think I have a better spot.

Nothing for shure yet. playing a lot of fiddle feels good to get back to it. Got 4 men Piano, Drum, Trombone, D.Bass myself on cornet & violin. we get off the ground on occasion, (still cant spell) Teagarden and Don Ewell bought a home in the Pompona area. So I know I'm in the right place -- also a couple of Maxted's bunch are going to do the same.

Hope everything is O.K. on your end massa Simba, o sage of the pluckers. Shure do miss Geo. Washington, otto, and swinging doors, meaning, you all -- a very happy thing in Dayton. When you left you took me with you.

Hope to hear from you. give my love to your family. & best regards to Bill & Ruth & all the guys. Tell Bill when he comes down here to bring the clarinet.

The hell with sitting in the sun. Much better to sit on the bandstand. Yo buddy Andy.

Letter from New Orleans Jazz Club,, August 16, 1962

New Orleans Jazz Club
2417 OCTAVIA STREET
NEW ORLEANS 15, LA.
August 16, 1962

Ja5-4460

Mr. Clancy Hayes
c/o The Playboy Club
Iberville Street at Royal
New Orleans, Louisiana

Dear Clancy Hayes:

The New Orleans Jazz Club welcomes you to our city! We are happy to have you here. We look forward to meeting you in person as we enjoy your records so very much. They are our kind of music! our favorite is "Silver Dollar." We had the good fortune of hearing you in Chicago about four years ago, but we were unable to meet you.

The New Orleans Jazz Club is presenting a series of "Jazz on Sunday Afternoon" concerts in the Royal Orleans Hotel. This Sunday, August 19th, will be the Armand Hug Trio and Dr. Edmond Souchon (guitarist, banjoist and vocalist). The time is 3:30 PM. We are enclosing two complimentary tickets as we would like to have you as our guest to hear some of our hometown talent.

The New Orleans Jazz Club is holding its monthly jam session at the Roosevelt Hotel in its Grand Ball Room. We would be thrilled if you could come by to greet our members and to say hello. It would be even more wonderful if you could give them a tune or two. Our sessions begin at 8 or 8:30 PM and we would like to have you open the program, if you would do us the honor.

We also want you to know about our New Orleans Jazz Museum, located at 1017 Dumaine St. in the French Quarter. It is nine months old and catching on just fine. We think you would find it most interesting to spend a bit of time going through it and taking in all it has to offer. The hours are 10 AM til 5 PM, Tuesdays thru Sundays. Please do fit this into your visit to New Orleans. Mr. Clay Watson is our Museum Director and would like to personally escort you thru the Museum.

Will you be kind enough to telephone the writer at his office (JA5-1241) and let us know if we can count on you for the meeting on Monday. We would like to know if you will be with us on Sunday afternoon too.

Sincerely,
Harry V. Souchon, President
NEW ORLEANS JAZZ CLUB

Honey. I want to save this!
Yodaddy

Letter from New Orleans Jazz Club, August 21, 1962

from Harry Souchon
New Orleans Jazz Club
2417 OCTAVIA STREET
NEW ORLEANS 15, LA.
Aug. 21, 1962

Affiliated with Cultural Attractions Fund

Dear Clancy: We are looking forward to your appearance at our monthly jam session this Monday, Aug. 27th, in the Grand Ball Room of the Roosevelt Hotel. Time for the opening of the program is 8 o'clock in the evening. We have a fine local group called the Levee Stompers, led by Paul Crawford, who will back you up, if you want them to. Or they can fill in during your part of the program. They will be on hand to assist. When you arrive, look me up at the desk inside the door, or ask for our secretary of the Club, Miss Helen Arlt. I want to express the appreciation of all of us that you will honor us with an appearance.
   Sincerely,
   President

Letter from New Orleans Jazz Club, September 11, 1962

2417 OCTAVIA STREET
NEW ORLEANS 15, L.A.
September 11, 1962
Dear Clancy:

Well, who do you think was looking back at us from our TV sets this past Thursday? You! It was an educational station and the program was entitled (I believe) Words in Action. It's subject was the words to love songs and the narration was done by a Japanese fellow. You did the illustrations by singing the words to given songs he wanted illustrated. It was good and we enjoyed seeing and hearing you so soon after the real thing --your performing in person both at the Play Boy Club and particularly at our own New Orleans Jazz Club August jam session.

Wanted to write you before now and say "hello" from a southern friend on your opening at the Chicago Play Boy Club, but too much detail and work at the office prevented my doing so. Hope this will make up for the good intention I had. Since you are an "adopted" New Orleans son, we will have to keep in touch. Won't you give us that pleasure? For it was so easy to be with you and know you in such a short time, that we feel like old, old friends.

Let me convey the thanks of our Board of Directors for your interest in our Club activities and the Jazz Museum at 1017 Dumaine Street. We were honored to have you and we hope you will enjoy receiving our publication, THE SECOND LINE. We look forward to your fulfilling your promise to send us some material to display in our Museum, for we will be mighty proud to have it.

We feel we are doing the most conscientious job of promoting New Orleans jazz and our people are truly dedicated who are serving the Club with their voluntary time and effort. It would be deeply appreciated if you would endeavor to spread our word around wherever you might find an interested listener. Word of mouth is probably our best means of becoming known. Although our Museum will be one year old on November 12th, we have already done exceptionally well, we feel, in becoming as well known as we are at this point.

Again let me say thanks, both for performing at our session, and also for letting us get to know you better and be with you that wonderful Saturday night at the Play Boy Club. Our only complaint - your stint was far too short!

We'll be awaiting word from you - just to keep in touch.
Bye, you all,

Mr. Clancy Hayes
c/o THE PLAYBOY CLUB
Chicago, Illinois

Clancy's Letter to Ann and Bill Hayes

Wed. 10:25 p.m.

Hi my darlings –

A sleepy day for me because it was rainy and (HOT) out so I just stayed in the cave and snoozed — watched T.V. and snoozed some more. Just read your letter and am sure I'll enjoy our nice clean apt. Just to be home will suit me fine. That meat loaf sounds wonderful, I think I'll have another slice.

I am having dinner tomorrow with Harry Brunies, and the whole Brunies family. This is Geo's brother I mentioned before. He insisted I came to their home so I could meet their mother.

These are wonderful people in Jazz music — all very gifted and left such tunes as Tin Roof, Wish I could Shimmy, Ugly Chile, etc. etc.

Don't know why I should be surprised, after all the records I have made about N.O. but I am about the biggest hero (hear me) since Gen Jackson Fit the Battle of New Orleans. Can't even get through the lobby without pictures, autographs, and stares.

Finally got my confirmation on a flight to Chicago on Delta Air Line.

Will write more soon,
all my love
   "Yo daddy"

Letter from Dick Gibson regarding the 1964 Aspen jazz party

8/5/64

Dear Clancy,

Since we want <u>you</u> at our party we will wait and see until August 24th.

Even should you option be picked up then, would it still be possible for you to come? You could leave Chicago at noon Friday & be back by late Sunday night. Actually, if worse came to best, it might be that we could compromise with you as we have done with Bud Freemen.

He cannot get away from the Monterey thing until Friday night so he is only joining us for the Saturday & Sunday play. Naturally, I would like the whole group there for Friday night, but two days of Freemen is a hell of a lot better than no days of Freemen.

If we worked it out wherein you did not get into Denver until early Saturday morning, that would satisfy us. Then, you would only miss one day of your engagement in Chicago, although, unfortunately, it would be Saturday. Is this possible?

Give it the best which you can, Clancy, this party is marvelous. And you fit. In fact, when Peanuts Hucko heard you might come he got pretty enthusiastic. He insisted that I implore you to bring your banjo as well as guitar. So, I implore.

I certainly agree with you about Raff, he is great.

Sincerely,

Dick Gibson

P.S. Gad, I almost forgot about terms: for Friday night–Sunday 300 plus <u>all</u> expenses. For Saturday & Sunday 250 plus <u>all</u> expenses.

DG

Letter from Jack Gurtler

Monday 4-9-70

Dear Clancy,

    I have been thinking of you for days onto months — So, last week, one night at home, I picked up the phone and call Earthquake Magones — San Francisco and talked to Mr. Cedric Clute who told me of your illness.

    Shocked is hardly the word for my surprise — I am greaved to hear of your illness! We have been friends for six years, but it seems as if we have known one-another for many, many years! Really, Clancy, words fail me to properly express "me" deep feelings for you — If prayers can help you, I am praying for a complete, and soon, recovery for you!

    My dear Father pass-away February 17th at the age of 75. He thought much of you: and will be missed by many in "Show Business". I am sending under separate cover a recording of 1969 — Hope you will enjoy it.

    Sincerely hope and pray for your speedy recovery - God Bless

                              Jack Gurtler

Letter from George Zack

H'ya Clancy, just got back from a three-month gig in Ill.-maybe more...Joined Smokey Stover, had [Georg] Brunies and [Jimmy] Granata [Granato] for a couple of dates in Mattoon. Then used them for the last ½ hour of the TV shot in Davenport. Biographical thing with shots of 'Smoke' wandering around the levees of the old Mississippi. Some of it's good some of it's bad. Oh well.

Yeah, being gone like that didn't hear about you taking the count. Received a note from Bob Howno and he filled me in.....

Was listening to a bunch of your recordings not too long ago, friend of mine has got 'em all Al Saunders. He's comin' home tonite has been in KC this week. He's been up to S.F. to catch you a couple of times. He's chief at the Tucson Airport (Ex banjo). Remember Hick my ole-lady? She's in the kitchen — shakin' like this — makin a lemon pie! Yeah. She wishes you were here to have some. Wish I could get up there for your benefit. But No-way.... It seems all I do is exist from one yr. to the next, Well all our love from everyone here. Let me know if you want any more of these ramblin' notes,

your friend, G.

Letter from the Garlinghouses, 1970

May 24, 1970
7100 South Street # 7
Lincoln, Nebraska

Dear Clancy:

When we visited with you in October, you told us that you were receiving treatment at the Stanford University Hospital, and now we are sorry to learn that surgery has been necessary. We send you our most sincere wishes for your comfort and recovery— and we are pleased that you are to be honored in San Francisco on May 31st. We wish we could be there.

You know we have been real fans of yours since the days in Iola High School. It was a great joy to find you at Earthquake McGoon's and we have never missed a chance to hear you when we were in San Francisco. We have all but two of your known recordings and spend many hours here at home listening to them. You sing and play "our kind of music"— and so for the many hours and days of pleasure you have given us, we do thank you. It should be a great satisfaction to you to know how much good you have done for your fellow man.

With sincere good wishes,
Esther and Bob Garlinghouse

Letter from Billie and Don Leach

801 North 12th St.
Rogers, Ark. 72756
May 26, 1970

Mr. Clancy Hays
Earthquake McGoon's
630 Clay St.
San Francisco, Calif.

Dear Clancy:

Can you believe having two admirers .. and fans .. way down in Arkansas?

We have heard that the Mayor of San Francisco has proclaimed May 31 as Clancy Hays Day in honor of your long-time contribution to the music and pleasure of the people around the Golden Gate ... as well as many others living elsewhere that he might not know about. We hope that it will be good therapy for you in the recovery period after your recent surgical experience.

Although we have never had the opportunity to hear your music in person, we have had considerable exposure to it for a long time on numerous visits with my sister and brother-in-law, Esther and Bob Garlinghouse of Lincoln, Nebraska. They have a large collection of your music on tapes and records which they play every time we get together. We also have re-tapes that they have given us, so we listen to Clancy Hays here at home, too.

Needless to say, since I am a sister of Esther's, I remember you from High School days in Iola even though I was a few years behind you in school. You are very personal to us and this brings you our love for old time's sake, memories for the past and present, admiration for years of pleasure to your public, and best wishes for the future.

"Clancy" fans,
Billie and Don Leach

Letter from Earl Watkins
From the desk of
EARL WATKINS
Oakland Branch Secretary
MAY 6, 1970

DEAR CLANCY:

JUST A LINE TO SAY HELLO AND ASK HOW YOU ARE DOING.

MARILYN GAVE ME A CALL AND GAVE ME YOUR ADDRESS SO I'M WRITING. I PLAYED A JOB MONDAY NITE WITH MIKE TILLES, JERRY BUTZEN, VINCE, ERNIE FIGEROA, JOHN FARKAS, RED GILLUM, JACK KNOX, AND JIM CUMMINGS - WHAT A BALL. WE PLAYED FOR BOB COATE, WHO IS RUNNING FOR LEIUTENANT GOVERNOR, AND THE JOB WAS AT THE 'CANNERY' UPSTAIRS.

I ALSO PLAYED AT THE DANVILLE HOTEL WITH TOMMY KAHN AND SAW SAM AND HEIDE THERE. THEY WERE LOOKING SWELL THEY DON'T LOOK A DAY OLDER THAN CHICAGO AND OUR FIRST TRIP TO THE BLUE NOTE. REMEMBER THE PARTY AT THE CONRAD HILTON.

WE ARE PRETTY BUSY HERE AT THE UNION, THE PHONE RINGS OFF THE HOOK ALL DAY, BUT I'M GLAD TO HAVE A GIG. I'LL CONTACT YOU LATER AND TRY TO HAVE A LITTLE GOSSIP FOR YOU.

BYE FOR NOW, GOOD LUCK

Letter from Peanuts and Louise Hucko

5/28/70

My dear Clancy!

We know these must be <u>most</u> <u>difficult</u> days for you! We are adding our prayer To those of you innumerable friends who love you -- that God will be very near and <u>heal</u> you!

Love and Kisses

Peanuts & Louise

P.S.

We'll be here at Radisson Hotel for 6 wks.

Proclamation of 'Clancy Hayes Day', 1970

Proclamation

Clancey Hayes has long been a much loved San Franciscan who has often contributed his time and talents to countless Bay Area civic and charitable undertakings.

He has been honored throughout the years for his contribution to music and has pioneered his banjo music in engagements, on radio and television recordings, thereby bringing countless hours of entertainment and enjoyment to thousands.

His music, in its way, has become somewhat of a San Francisco "landmark."

NOW, THEREFORE, I, Joseph L. Alioto, Mayor of the City and County of San Francisco, do hearby join his fellow musicians in paying tribute to him by officially proclaiming Sunday, May 31, as "Clancey Hayes Day in San Francisco."

IN WITNESS THEREOF I have
hereunto set my hand and
caused the seal of the
City and County of San
Francisco to be affixed
on this sixteenth day
of April, nineteen
hundred and seventy.

Joseph L. Alioto
Mayor

Text of Assembly Rules Committee—California Legislature

By the Honorable Don Mulford,
16th Assembly District

RELATIVE TO COMMENDING CLANCY HAYES

WHEREAS: The members of the Committee have learned that Clancy Hayes is to be honored with a benefit dinner on 31 May, 1970; and

WHEREAS: Clancy Hayes is a long-time San Francisco resident and musician of great renown; and

WHEREAS: Since his arrival in San Francisco in 1926, Clancy Hayes has become one of the City's best-known entertainment personalities: and

WHEREAS: During an outstanding career in radio and television, as a composer, recording artist and nightclub entertainer he has gained recognition as one of America's greatest Folk singers: and

WHEREAS: Clancy has given generously of his time to innumerable civic and charitable causes and has provided much entertainment for members of the California legislature, and:

WHEREAS: May, 31st, has been proclaimed by Mayor Alioto as "Clancy Hayes Day"; now, therefore, be it

Resolved by the Assembly Rules Committee, That the Members commend Clancy Hayes for the outstanding contributions which he has made to San Francisco, and congratulate him on the occasion of the honors bestowed upon him, and extend to him their best wishes for the future; and be it further

Resolved, That the Chief Clerk of the Assembly transmit a suitably prepared copy of this resolution to Clancy Hayes

Resolution 471 approved by the Assembly Rules Committee

By Eugene A. Chappie
Chairman,
Subscribed this 26th day of May, 1970.

Letter on behalf of Ronald Reagan

State of California
GOVERNOR'S OFFICE
SACRAMENTO 95814

May 27, 1970
Mr. Dana G. Leavitt:
President
Transamerica Title Insurance Company
1330 Broadway
Oakland, California 94612

Dear Mr. Leavitt:
Governor Reagan was pleased to prepare the enclosed message for Mr. Clancy Hayes.

Mr. Hayes has been one of my favorite performers since I first heard him on a radio program called "Remember" in 1943, and I have since enjoyed his recordings with the Bob Scobey band. I am indeed sorry to hear of his illness.

Best wishes for a successful event.
Sincerely,
Mrs. Betty Sabourin
Administrative Assistant

Enclosure *[missing]*

Letter from Ed Watson

June 10, 1971
Mr Clancy Hayes,
c/o Earthquake McGoons

Dear Clancy:
    I saw the attached article in the newspaper, but I'm a 66 year old guy on Social Security and not exactly the type to go trotting around to nightclubs -- so I'm sending my remembrance in the mail.
    Clancy, you simply <u>GOT</u> to get well! There ain't <u>NOBODY</u> who can sing "Ace in the Hole", "Silver Dollar", "Big Butter and Egg", "Do You Know What It Means To Miss New Orleans", "Peoria" -- and all them wonderful songs like you do.
    I've never seen or heard you IN PERSON, but I've got nearly every phonograph record that BOB SCOBEY'S FRISCO BAND made, and it is your vocals that make them so terriffic! I really don't know why I like Scobie's Dixieland so much better than the average Dixieland jazz, but superb as Bob was, it was always YOUR vocal chorus that was the sparkling jewel in all the best tracks. We've lost Scobey, but by God! WE ain't gonna lose YOU!
    So Clancy, now's the time to "sing those blues away". There's a million people that are waitingto hear you get up on the bandstand and play a chorus of PARSONS, KANSAS BLUES; and what about TRAVELING SHOES? Everybody has just Got to hear you sing <u>that</u> again! And don't forget GETTING MY BOOTS -- you see!? you got a lot to make make people cheer you to the roof. All you got to do is get up there and SING!
    Everybody is counting on you Clancy. There's no "if's" about it. You <u>GOT</u> to get well!!

With every kind wish
Ed Watson

#20 MONEY ORDER ENCLOSED

Clancy's tape log for Bill Bacin

"Tape Log For Bill Bacin"
Recorded June 6th, 1971.
Sterio. 3;3/4 I.P.S,

SIDE ONE.

(Counter No.)	TITLE	NOTES
1;	Billy.	Written by Gordon Jenkins for Billy Butterfield. "W.S.G.B. New York /69
54 I	Bubble Gum Strut	Written by Bob Haggert same date
100 I	Fidgitty Feet.	Matty Matlocks Basin Street Patrol. From Blue angel Jazz Club party 1970
200 I	Elder Eatmore's Sermon On "Throwing Stones"	Recorded in 1928 by Louis (Satch) and Harry Mills. Original of same was made by Bert Williams, 1912

275 I   Excerpts from Standard School Broadcast 1948. These were made at a one hour rehearsal at N.B.C. Studios S.F. I was the star that year of the series, Broadcast weekly to the school children of the seven Western States by Standard Oil of Calif. I played a mythyical character, sort of a Paul Bunyon type guy, who could live in any age. I was the central character "Jack of All Tunes" along with my buddy Matt the Mapmaker. In any case we had a Show on N.O. Jazz coming up, and I got the producer to hire Louis Armstrong and his all Stars, (who were appearing at the Hangover) for one hour. We later used only about three and a half minutes of it on the show but I had them tape the entire hour. This was made on the old Paper tape before they had Scotch type, so even though I have kept them in metal containers, they have not weathered too well. I have since transferred nearly all of
 .   the old gems I want to keep on Mylar Polyester. Personel; Armstrong, Tmpt. Jack Teagarden, trom.

(a young fellow from the studio orch subbing for Barney Bigard) Ray Daniels on Clar. Earl Fatha Hines Piano, Sid Catlett Drums and Can't remember who the Bass was, I beleive it was Orvil Shaw. Myself sometimes on guitar, when I'm not busy yackkin' with the other people.

980 I Short Snorter from a tape I made for Squirrel Ashcraft in 1958. Me on piano.

Re-set Counter

SIDE TWO Rose of Washington Square. (Myself with the Nine Greats of Jaxzz. Recorded at the Famous old Trocadero, at Flitch Gardens in Denver Colorado 1966. Personel Yank Lawson, Tmpt. Lu McGarrity and Cutty Cuttshal Trombones, Peanuts Hucko Clar. Ralph Sutton Piano. Morey Feld Drums, Bobby Haggert Bas, Bud Freeman Tenor Sax, myself on Banjo.

57 I Honky Tonk Train. (Featuring Sutton, Same group.)

120 I Stealin' Apples. (Peanuts Hucko with same group).

253 I. Silver Dollar. (Made one year later same spot with the Ten greats of Jazz, personel same as above with Billy Butterfeild added.)
Cherry (Featuring MacGarrity, and Cutty. Same night)

Easy Street
Dixieland One Step.
Careless Love.
Washboard Blues. (These are all cuts from an Album I made for Audio Fidelity in 1960, with the band I had in Chicago, right after I broke up with Scobey. Art Hodes, piano. Bob Ballard, Tmpt. Bill Henk, Tmb. Lyle Daniels Clar. Buddy Smith, Drums. Earl Murphy Bass. Banjo and Vocalist unknown.

Boy from New Orleans
Bury Me on Basin Street. (From the ABC-Paramount Album
"Big Yank is Here. Lawson, Tmpt,
Cutty, Tmb. Bill Stegmeyer, Clar. Osie
Johnson Drums, Dave MacKenna Piano
Haggert Bass Banjo and Vocalist
unknown.

(Surprise Party)
Clancy Hayes Dixieland Jazz Band for Tweed Records.
Recorded in 1960, Chicago for the Republican National
Comittee "Vote for Nixon Lodge" and the instrumental
was called "Elephant Stomp"

(Piano)
Personel; "Judge" Floyd Bean the only
Law West of the Pecos; Jim Beebe,
Tromb. Brian Shanley, Clar. "Nappy"
Tro(t)tier, trumpt.

Bill? (I'll have to think of it later, and "Gypsy Sam" Bacin
Bass All very nice guys that Later play
[Sketches]

Letter to Dr Hamilton, Ethiopian Baptist Church

Dr. Hamilton, Etheopian Baptist Church, Probably - 1944 or early 1945

Recorded at the church. We were way in the back of the church, Lu Watters, Ellis Horn, Bill Colburn, & Myself. Dr Hamilton had given me permission to bring my Brush recorder, (on paper tape yet) if "we would not make it too obvious to the congregation". The pick up is so bad because I was trying to pick it up from the Monitor Speaker at the Radio Broadcast that was on. Still very interesting though, and believe me for Real. I shall never forget Rev. Hamilton, taking his big gold watch out of his vest pocket and saying "Now, in about two minutes we are gonna be on the Electric Radio, and I want all you brothers and sisters, to sing out loud and clear, we are praising the Lord -- <u>PRAISE THE LORD</u>. Clancy

Letter from Olive U.D.

March 5, 1953
Dear Mrs. Hayes,
    We have been enjoying our son's short stay in St. Louis and listening with pleasure to his accounts of his trips to San Francisco. You and your husband and son have, as you know, added immeasurably to the happy times he spent there. Your warm hospitality to Charles at Christmas time touched me most particularly.

    Families are so often reluctant to share the intimate celebrations of the holidays with strangers. I shall be everlastingly grateful to you for doing so. It was certainly a great piece of good luck for Charles to meet people so congenial in tastes and so generous.

    If you should get to St. Louis you must look us up
              Thank you again I remain
              Yours Sincerely
                  Olive U. D???

Letter from Lizzie Miles to Ann Hayes

The Flamingo Hotel Las Vegas, Nevada
Hello Mrs Hayes --
Hope you're feeling a little better today. God will help you to over come yout grief as his will must be done. Now here's a prayer to St Anthony that you can get on your knees and say help find your mother's picture. I hope your niece have explained why we ask the saints to help us with our prayers to God. Cause we're all sinners and must be helped along the way to learn God's teachings and live them and become christians if not saints. There is nothing greater than prayers. The more you pray the better you get so pray for your son husband and yourself to become christians and to live up to his teachings. I'm tryin' hard to be a good christian hope I succeed God is good to me and I hope he continues. I will do all in my power to stay with him. I will pray for your ankle to not give you too much trouble but God never makes our cross heavier than we can bear but you must pray. Hope you will read prayer and not cast it aside as an old piece of paper as some day you might wish for any kind of prayer to take you out of your suffering. I'll be prayin for you. God bless you.
Lizzie Miles

Otto's New Auto, handwritten lyrics

OTTO

OTTO McNAUGT, Tho somewhat taut, Feelin' Like an astronaut, Glidin' as he's ridin' down that 'ol main street -- Gadgets here and gadgets there, you push a button everywhere, for Automatic Windows and a push pull seat --
LOOK
MA
NO FEET
There was Uncle Futz in his Bearcat Stutz, And that, Fag with the Bag in his Beatup Jag

Notes

Acknowledgements

1 The Hal Smith Discography compiled by Gerard Bielderman details his many recordings and musical associations.

Chapter 1

1 The Iola Register 14 July 1905
2 Undated press clipping in Clancy's papers held in the SFTJF collection at Stanford University
3 The Iola Register 30 Oct. 1922
4 Stanford University / SFTJF Charles Huggins Project (b068_09) Bill Dyer Interview
5 The Iola Register 26 October 1923
6 Clancy Hayes private tape recorded at Bill Priestley's home August 1959

Chapter 2

1 The song is posted on YouTube Clancy Hayes Jazz channel
2 These tracks are posted by on YouTube by 'princecastle'

Chapter 3

1 Satchel of Song Clancy Hayes' Private Collection, 1939-72 SFTJF CD 108. 2001
2 Private recordings from the Dawn Club are listed in the discography appendix
3 San Francisco Examiner 28 April 1943
4 San Francisco Examiner 16 April 1943
5 Stanford University / SFTJF Charles Huggins Project (b109_04)
6 Stanford University / SFTJF Charles Huggins Project (b068_22)
7 The broadcast is available on the Old Time Radio website (otrcat)
8 Fifteen Standard Oil programmes from the 1949/50 season are available on the Old Time Radio website (otrcat)
9 Louis Armstrong featuring Jack Teagarden and Earl Hines — Standard Oil Sessions CD (SKU DT8005); 2017

Chapter 4

1. 'A Conversation with Lu Watters part 1' YouTube — uploaded by Jazz Pagoda
2. Oakland Post Enquirer 14 July 1930
3. Dave Radlauer's Jazz Rhythm website; Clancy Hayes Archive 2A
4. Oakland Tribune 27 January 1938
5. as 1 above
6. Dave Radlauer's Jazz Rhythm website; Bob Helm Interview 1993
7. Tracks from this session are on the San Francisco Traditional Jazz Foundation CD 105 Lu Watters- Yerba Buena Jazz Band Volume 1
8. Cary Ginell, Hot Jazz For Sale: Hollywood's Jazz Man Record Shop, Amazon, 2010
9. The 16 August performance was issued on Riverside RLP 2513. The full broadcast is available on the Internet Archive — programme 28
10. Dave Radlauer's Jazz Rhythm website; Dave Radlauer and Bill Carter interview with Bill Bardin (interview 2) 1993

Chapter 5

1. Ragtime 1050 - Wang Wang Blues / How Come You Do Me Like You Do; Ragtime 1051 - Clarinet Marmalade / Alcoholic Blues
2. Dixieland jazz: Sitting in with Bob Scobey and Clancy Hayes JimDBB@aol.com 5 Dec. 2002
3. Jim Beebe developed a habit for letter writing and was a natural raconteur — as well as a superb musician. Terkel interviews Jim Beebe in the Studs Terkel Radio Archive

Chapter 6

1. Scobey and Clancy GTJ LP L12009
2. Stanford University / SFTJF Charles Huggins Project Clancy Hayes interview with Bill Dyer (b068_09)
3. George Hulme wrote two excellent books: *Mel Torme: A Chronicle of His Recordings, Books and Films* and, with joint author Bert Whyatt, *Bobby Hackett: His Life In Music*. George also wrote the LP sleeve notes for two LPs of Lu Watters' 1950s recordings with Clancy's vocals that were issued in the early 1970s on the Dawn Club label.
4. It was a delight when in autumn 2021 I received a very positive and unbelievably helpful reply to my query to Indiana University Libraries-Moving Image Archive which held a copy of the 16mm film. Yes, they had a copy in a remote storage facility and it would take a couple of weeks to retrieve and digitize it. The film was soon available on-line and even better the film was in the public domain; it is now on YouTube — Clancy Hayes Jazz channel. My

gratitude and thanks go to Rachael Stoeltje, Director of IULMIA for her help in making the film available

Chapter 7

1 The Marlboro commercial is posted on YouTube; see 'Dobie Gillis closing 2' uploaded by James Craig
2 'Clancy Hayes' Dixieland Band' (AFSD 5937) was released later that year and Glaser's ABC secured bookings for Clancy at Jazz Ltd. in Chicago and at Playboy clubs across the USA in 1961 — 62
3 1967 interview with Washington DJ Felix Grant
4 *Chicago Jazz: the Second Line* by Derek Coller and Bert Whyatt.
5 George's reconnection with Clancy as one of the 'Dixiecrats' led to a longlasting friendship. There is a touching 1970 letter from George to Clancy in Chapter 11 which shows their closeness; no doubt the families had got together during the Chicago years

Chapter 8

1 San Francisco Examiner 26 June 1961
2 Will Leonard, Chicago Tribune 30 July 1961
3 Bob Scobey recorded a superb version of Kenny Ball's hit Midnight In Moscow released as a 45rpm single (backed with Panama) on his Ragtime label. The looser, more swinging Scobey version deserved as much attention as Kenny Ball's hit recording. Unfortunately the Scobey single is, disappointingly, yet another rarity
4 The regionality of music in the United States, and across the globe, is very real. I first visited The United States in 1988 taking two very excited young children to Disneyland, Florida then spending a week driving to Newark, New Jersey to meet friends. Their equally excited father was keen to track down second hand record stores during the trip convinced that the jazz sections would be piled high with Scobey and Clancy records. Entering a Richmond, Virginia record store I will never forget the look on the owner's face when I enquired where the Scobey, Murphy and Watters records were; explaining that I was particularly interested in 45rpm singles for a jukebox. The store owner let me down gently, tactfully pointing out that these were west coast artists and I was in the east. In my head I was thinking 'but the records have had 40 years to make the journey'. Feeling very deflated I simply said 'Oh'. The owner knew his business, Good Time Jazz records were in short supply out east. It would be 14 years until I got the opportunity to ask the same question at Jack's Record Cellar, 254 Scott Street, San Francisco. In response Jack smiled and handed me a large stack of singles. I knew I was in the right place; no-one could fail to spot a 6 x 6 feet photo of Clancy adorning the shop's back wall

5 The Times — Picayune, August 27th 1962
6 The Second Line, New Orleans Jazz Club magazine September-October 1962, p.19

Chapter 9

1 The Dox LP The Dayton Scene has two excellent Clancy solos from 1963 plus three vocals with the Docs Of Dixieland from later concerts. The Docs were also assisted on 5 other tracks by guest musicians including ex Scobeyite Brian Shanley and Clancy's friend Andy Bartha. The album sleeve notes observed: 'Clancy Hayes has spent his entire life in music. Although never a great commercial success he is to people all over the world a living legend of jazz. In appreciation of Clancy as a composer, performer and most of all a man, the Docs of Dixieland and Vadhere records are privileged to dedicate this record to him.'
2 SFTJF Charles Huggins Project at Stanford University: Bill Dyer interview with Clancy Hayes 1965 (b068_09)
3 The album was issued on CD in 1997 with a bonus of 5 alternate takes (Delmark DE-210)
4 Loose Shoes — The Story of Ralph Sutton: James D. Shacter; Jaynar Press
5 New York Daily News 20 Nov 1968
6 Despite my best efforts I have been unable to find out when the Mr Hayes Goes To Washington album was recorded but it is likely to have been during Clancy's second visit in 1968. The album was not issued until 1972 but must have been made several years before and of course prior to the onset of illness in the autumn of 1969. For sure on the wonderfully energetic tracks Sweet Georgia Brown and Way Down Yonder In New Orleans Clancy sounds like a twenty something; in fairness he comes across in character as a mature and world-weary individual on Lonesome Road!
7 Coffee Dan's was a colourful all-night restaurant on O'Farrell Street in San Francisco which in later years expanded into a small chain. In the mid 1920s it boasted — 'There will be dancing to the tinkle of a piano, there will be songs and it will never close, not even for fire…'
8 The Phil Howe Festival Band consisted of: Phil Howe, leader, clarinet; Bob Neighbor, trumpet; Mike Starr, trombone; Art Nortier, piano; Ted Shafer, banjo; Pops Foster, string bass; Thad Vandon, drums
9 Johnson McCree is another of the many colourful characters of jazz. He is described by Derek Coller in his excellent Fat Cat Discography and Biography as a born enthusiast who would sing with any band at the drop of a hat. As a young man he'd been keen to be a professional singer, but his father was less enthusiastic, steering him to a highly successful career as a Certified Public Accountant. However, Johnson's enthusiasm for jazz led him to a significant sideline as concert organizer and record label owner (Fat Cat Records issued over 100 LPs as well as many cassette tapes) and a guest singer at any opportunity

Chapter 10

1. Blue Angel Jazz Club LP — Jazz at Pasadena Vol. 2 BAJC 506
2. Russ Wilson article, Oakland Tribune 2 June 1970

Chapter 11

1. SFTJF at Stanford University: 'Requiem for Paul Lingle' identifier ars0030_b066_23. The programme tells the story of a remarkable musician and is well worth a listen. It includes interviews with drumming ace Fred Higuera (who as a young man played with Lingle for seven years and later with Scobey and Clancy) and Turk Murphy — as well as the reading of a very amusing letter sent by Lu Watters
In any reference to Paul Lingle it would be remiss not to mention the brilliance of his (regrettably relatively few) recordings. His eight tracks recorded for the GTJ ten-inch Paul Lingle At The Piano album (L13) in February 1952 were reissued along with Burt Bales' equally sublime 1949 After Hours recordings. The Bales and Lingle They Tore My Playhouse Down is an absolutely must have LP or CD (GTJ CD 12025-2)
2. Thanks to the generosity of Charles Huggins, former owner of See's Candies, 2,000 items from the SFTJF collection are digitized and form the 'Charles Huggins Project.' The website is an amazing resource. The 'Great Jazz Revival' video written by Clint Baker and Margaret Moos Pick is a must-watch item with Hal Smith, Clint Baker and Jim Cullum entertainingly telling the Revival story. The Charles Huggins Project includes many of Clancy's tapes; details of those that are available are in the discography appendix. A general search and wander through the SFTJF/Stanford website is like landing on Jazz Island, seeking musical treasure — and finding it!
3. Jazz Rhythm website: Bill Bardin Interview (2) with Dave Radlauer and Bill Carter.
4. Rhythm Man — Fifty Years In Jazz, Steve Jordan with Tom Scanlan, The University of Michigan Press 1993
5. Stanford University / SFTJF Charles Huggins Project Interview with Phil Elwood for a tribute programme to Paul Lingle, December 1962 (b066_23). Further extracts from the interview are in Chapter twelve
6. Stanford University / SFTJF Charles Huggins Project; Clancy Hayes Interviews 1954 and 1965 (b068_09)

Chapter 14

1. SFTJF Frisco Cricket article; Winter 1998

Chapter 15

1. Stanford University Libraries Archive / SFTJF Charles Huggins Project: Clancy Hayes Interviews 1954 and 1965 (b068_09)
2. Contrary to what the name may imply, Jim Jam Jems was a serious magazine, published from 1912 — 1924, that addressed corruption in local and national government across the U.S. The subtitle of each issue was 'A Volley of Truth'.
3. The mystery surrounding Ace In The Hole is partly solved thanks to information given to the School of Anthropology Vaudeville Archive at the University of Arizona by Susan Dempsey — granddaughter of James Dempsey, one of the credited composers. James Dempsey was born around 1880 to a Scottish father and Irish mother both of whom emigrated to the USA. At a young age he became involved in vaudeville in Boston, Mass. Around 1914 James Dempsey moved to New York and opened a club where he and others entertained; he was also part of the original Tin Pan Alley group of composers. Married with a family, his occupation and weakness for drink and gambling did not fit well with home life so in 1916 he decided to make a fresh start. Moving to Carney's Point, New Jersey, Mr Dempsey took a job as a day labourer with the Dupont Corporation where over the years he made the position of senior manager. He died in 1931, so his most famous song predates this period and is most likely from the first decade of the century. Sheet music of the song from 1934 gives an original copyright date of 1909, a year in which James Dempsey had success with one of his published songs A Beautiful Garden of Roses. However, why Ace in the Hole was not published or recorded by the artists of the day — it is not difficult to imagine Campbell and Burr, Billy Murray or the American Quartet singing it — remains a mystery.
4. Burt Bales GHB BCD - 13 (Private recordings; released in 1994); Stanford University Libraries Archive / SFTJF (b109_07); A live 1966 intermission performance at Earthquake McGoon's posted on YouTube — Clancy Hayes Jazz channel
5. The Scobey version on the 1956 Down Home LP was issued in the UK on a Columbia 78 rpm record coupled with In New Orleans.
6. Thanks go to Dave Radlauer who included a late 1940s version on the SFTJF Satchel of Song CD-108 making it available to the music buying public for the very first time
7. Details of the King / Hayes compositions are drawn from Dave Radlauer's 1998 interview with Daphne June King and Pete Clute. The Interview and programme are available on his excellent Jazz Rhythm website, Clancy Hayes Archive.
8. The recording is posted on YouTube - Clancy Hayes Jazz channel.
9. Broken Promises resurfaced in later years on three superb Stomp Off LPs/CDs. The South Frisco Jazz Band used the song on their 1987 album of the same name (LP/CD 1180). The Down Home Jazz Band recorded it, with

a vocal by Bob Schulz, on Dawn Club Joys (Stomp Off CD 1241) and Mr Schulz recorded it with his own Frisco Jazz Band on Remembering Clancy (Stomp Off CD1349).

10 In New Orleans was released on the Down Home 1 LP and an alternate take is on the Bob Scobey Jansco LP JLPS 6252.

11 Bob Scobey: A Bibliography and Discography by Jim Goggin (self-published) San Leandro, California, 1977).

12 Article by Gilbert M. Erskine — Downbeat (autumn, 1968).

13 Bob Scobey: A Bibliography and Discography by Jim Goggin (self-published) San Leandro, California, 1977).

14 Stanford University / SFTJF Charles Huggins Project Video and Audio No.10: McGoon's Intermission and Feature Act

15 Bob Scobey: A Bibliography and Discography by Jim Goggin (self-published) San Leandro, California, 1977).

Chapter 17

1 Clancy Hayes' recollection, disclosed on a private tape recorded at Bill Priestley's Home, Lake Forest, Illinois; August 1959, appears to be incorrect. Deep Elm Blues was published in 1925.

2 I'm Gonna Charleston Back To Charleston, Clancy's first appearance in a band recording, was released in 1925 on Victor 19726-B

Reference Sources

Magazines:

The Record Changer
The Syncopated Times
International Association of Jazz Record Collectors
The Second Line magazine (New Orleans Jazz Club)
Variety

Books

John Buchanan, *Emperor Norton's Hunch*, Hambledon Productions, 1996
Pete Clute and Jim Goggin, *The Great Jazz Revival*, Donna Ewald, 1994
Pete Clute and Jim Goggin, *Meet Me At McGoon's*, Trafford Publishing, 2004
Pete Clute and Jim Goggin, *Some Jazz Friends*, Trafford Publishing, 2005
Derek Coller and Bert Whyatt, *Chicago Jazz: The Second Line*, Hardinge Simpole, 2018 ISBN 9781843822271
Derek Coller with Gene Hyden and David Griffiths, *Fat Cat's Jazz - A Label Discography and Biography*, Self Published, 2021
K.O. Eckland, *Jazz West 1945 To 1985*, Cypress, 1986. ISBN 978 0938995036
K.O. Eckland, *Jazz West 2*, Donna Ewald, 1995. ISBN 978 09064106710
Cary Ginell, *Hot Jazz For Sale - Hollywood's Jazz Man Record Shop*, Amazon, 2010
Jim Goggin, *Turk Murphy Just For The Record*, San Francisco Traditional Jazz Foundation, 1982
Steve Jordan with Tom Scanlon, *Rhythm Man - Fifty Years In Jazz*, University of Michigan Press, 1991 ISBN 978 0472 10256 3
James D. Shacter, *Loose Shoes - The Story Of Ralph Sutton*, Jaynar Pr, 1994. ISBN 9780963910103
Jan Scobey, *He Rambled 'Till Cancer Cut Him Down*, Pal Publishing, 1976. ISBN 9780918104014

Gallery 2

Three unknown lads but possibly Wallace, Clancy and Ashton?
(From Clancy Hayes' personal collection, courtesy Julia Carroll and Dom Adinolfi)

Clancy and John Wolfe c.1930
(Courtesy Stanford University Libraries Archive / SFTJF)

Clancy and a young admirer
(Courtesy of Julia Carroll and Dominic Adinolfi)

The great Bob Scobey.
(Courtesy Stanford University Libraries Archive / SFTJF)

Clancy waiting for a haircut?
(Courtesy Stanford University Libraries Archive / SFTJF)

Tex Hayes
(Courtesy Stanford University Libraries Archive / SFTJF)

Another cowboy outfit
(Courtesy Stanford University Libraries Archive / SFTJF)

Wally Rose, for once not obscured by a piano
(Courtesy Stanford University Libraries Archive / SFTJF)

Jack Buck, a wonderful musician and stalwart of the Bob Scobey
band for ten years
(Courtesy Stanford University Libraries Archive / SFTJF)

The final chorus
(Courtesy Stanford University Libraries Archive / SFTJF)

A clear view of Dick Lammi, with Bob Helm on clarinet
(Courtesy Stanford University Libraries Archive / SFTJF)

Bob Scobey's Frisco Band c.1958. Left to right: Rich Matteson (playing helicon and holding a bass trumpet), Jim Beebe, Brian Shanley, Bob Scobey, Clancy Hayes.
(Courtesy Frank Selman / SFTJF)

Rehearsal Time; Bob Scobey's Frisco Band, late 1957.
Left to Right visible: Bob Scobey, tp; Pete Dovidio,cl;
Tom Beeson, b; Clyde Pound, p; Dave Black, d; Clancy Hayes, bj;
probably Doug Skinner and Jack Buck, tb.
(Courtesy Stanford University Libraries Archive / SFTJF)

Clancy, Ann and Wallace Hayes
(Courtesy Stanford University Libraries Archive / SFTJF)

On the bandstand
(Courtesy Stanford University Libraries Archive / SFTJF)

Clancy and Ann at home - 702 46th Ave., San Francisco
(Courtesy Frank Selman/SFTJF)

American Federation of Radio Artists Honorable Withdrawal Card
(Courtesy of Julia Carroll and Dominic Adinolfi)

American Federation of Musicians Life Member Card
(Courtesy of Julia Carroll and Dominic Adinolfi)

New Orleans Jazz Club Honorary Life Membership - Ann Hayes
(Courtesy of Julia Carroll and Dominic Adinolfi)

Coon-Sanders Original Nighthawks Club Honorary Member Card
(Courtesy of Julia Carroll and Dominic Adinolfi)

Discography of Vocal Recordings

Clint Baker (left) receives the collection from Frank Selman
(Courtesy Frank Selman)

Introduction

(This introduction is an updated version from my self-published vocal discography of 2021. Newly discovered songs are included in the listings.)

Clancy Hayes: The Complete Commercial and Non-Commercial Vocals.

The purpose of this document is to ensure a complete reference of Clancy Hayes' vocal output, for the benefit of us and for Jazz fans of the future. It details all his commercially issued and non-commercial vocal recordings; that is until the happy day when more turn up.

With the wonders of the internet, eBay, Discogs and record dealers, all commercially issued records should be available, although some may be harder to find.

The non-commercial recordings came from two sources. Firstly, my own collection of recordings amassed over a period of almost 40 years through a network of friends, jazz fans and dealers. Special thanks and acknowledgements are due to Sam Linschooten, Hal Smith, William Carter, Dave Radlauer, Frank Selman, Phil Elwood, Pete Clute, George Hulme, Clarrie Henley, Jack Retter, Bill Bacin and "princecastle" on YouTube for making a lot of the private material available. But thanks are due to everyone who has generously shared recordings.

The second source, from which over half of the non-commercial recordings came, is the San Francisco Traditional Jazz Foundation collection (SFTJF) at the Stanford Archive of Recorded Sound, Stanford University Libraries, Stanford, California. Two thousand items from this enormous collection have been digitized and made available through the "Great Jazz Revival-Charles Huggins Project". Many digitized tapes, photographs, sheet music and other memorabilia are publicly available (the available Clancy tapes are shown in bold in the discography, others require a Stanford login).

The quality of the recorded sound derived from the original tapes - including paper tapes - is wonderful. For some tapes there is detailed information on band personnel, locations and dates etc. In addition to The Charles Huggins Project material there is an even larger SFTJF archive held at Stanford. The Collection is a treasure trove and can be accessed through url:

https://oac.cdlib.org/findaid/ark:/13030/c8vt1zt8/.

As part of the work to produce this vocal discography, I was granted access to the non-public Clancy Hayes related items within the Charles Huggins project plus an additional 45 tapes from the archive. I am indebted to Stanford University Library for their expertise, hard work, support and co-operation in making the recordings available. Particular thanks are due to Nathan Coy and Jerry McBride.

How the SFTJF collection actually came about over a period of almost 50 years is entertainingly summarised in Hal Smith's article in the Syncopated Times (an excellent publication) of 20 Feb 2020. We owe Jim Goggin, the SFTJF and the successive keepers of the archive (including Hal) a real debt.

If you are new to the music of Clancy Hayes, take a look at the Jazz Rhythm web page of Dave Radlauer. It is an amazing jazz website and includes six half hour radio programmes which tell the story of Clancy's career and contains many of his excellent commercial and non-commercial recordings.

The Non-Commercial Recordings: A Few Comments.

The radio recordings remind us that Clancy was a radio personality both prior to and during his involvement in the Great Jazz Revival. Also, it is interesting that Clancy composed a significant amount of material in the earlier part of his career and through to the early '50s.

The earliest recording (Sweetie Pie) is from a YouTube posting by "princecastle" of a young "Clarence Hayes" singing on radio in 1934 with the Bob Beale Orchestra. The 1942 solo home recordings made by Clancy are of particular note as they cover several excellent and rarely heard songs including Stavin' Chain, All Dolled Up and Deep Elm Blues. I have posted these on a YouTube channel called Clancy Hayes Jazz. Burt Bales' comments on the sleeve notes of the Mr. Hayes Goes To Washington LP refer to the fun he had playing and recording at Clancy's home; what a pleasure it is that some of this music has been preserved.

The vocals from the three concerts of the Bob Scobey Band are pure Clancy and also capture the warmth and brilliance of the Scobey bands. It is impossible to meaningfully summarise the recordings, suffice to say that all of Clancy's material is worth listening to and is excellent in many and different ways.

For completeness, details of radio interviews and surviving TV/film appearances are included at the end of the non-commercial section.

Sam Linschooten (31 July 1932—19 November 2015)

Finally, I would like to dedicate this discography to my dear friend Sam Linschooten, who was part of the Bob Scobey Society–Holland, set up in the 1970s. Society members, there were seven, met to enjoy, share and discuss the music of the Jazz Revival — and the music and bands that followed.

They also wished to learn more about the musicians as people and to obtain unissued recordings. Members, including Sam, Frank Selman, Pim van Nieuwkerk and Fré Bok, made contact with artists and collectors across the United States and Europe. Sam's hard work and true devotion to the music of the San Francisco jazz revival included producing hand-written discographies of Lu Watters' Yerba Buena Jazz Band, Bob Scobey's Frisco Band and Clancy Hayes.

I first heard from Sam in 1980 in response to my "wants ad" in Vintage Jazz Mart. Thereafter our many joint record hunting excursions in the UK and The Netherlands, and the swapping of tapes and CDs, was a source of great joy.

Sam once told me of his experience in 1954 listening for the very first time to the Scobey and Clancy Good Time Jazz EP 1018 in a record shop at Leiden. The thrill he got from that first encounter with the wonderful voice of Clancy Hayes, and the Scobey band, stayed with him forever. I hope you do, or will, understand why. This discography is dedicated to Sam, his wife Elly and their family.

Chris Reid,
Streatham, London.
June 2021, revised March 2025.

Clancy Hayes: Commercially Issued Vocal Recordings

Clancy Hayes (bj, g, p d; with 1.Vince Dotson, cnt; Bill Bardin, tb; Ellis Horne, cl; Burt Bales, p; Clancy Hayes, wbd. 2. Tune Termites Broadcast; Glen Hurlburt, p.)

Recording locations and dates vary.

(a) Alexander's Ragtime Band   SFTJF CD-108
(b) Birth Of The Blues
(c) George Washington
(d) Hassan, The One Man Caravan
(e) Huggin' And A Chalkin'
(f) I Can't Remember To Forget (2)
(g) I Just Want To Live (2)
(h) It Seems Like A Month Of Sundays Since I Saw You Saturday Night (2)
(i) Mobile
(j) Oceana Roll
(k) Oh By Jingo!
(l) Otto's New Auto
(m) Rose Of Washington Square
(n) Sweet Sue
(o) Ten To One It's Tennessee
(p) That's For Me (2)
(q) The Storybook Ball
(r) Travelin' Shoes
(s) Willie The Weeper
(t) Wolverine Blues (1)
(u) Zizzy-Zizzy Zum Zum Zum

CD title: Satchel of Song. Compilation of radio broadcasts and private recordings from 1939-1971. Produced by Dave Radlauer for the San Francisco Traditional Jazz Foundation; released 2001.

The CD has two solo piano tracks by Clancy Hayes - Clancy's Piano Rag and Clancy's Last Rag presumably recorded c.1971 after his operations.

Bunk Johnson and the Yerba Buena Jazz Band (Bunk Johnson, t; Turk Murphy, tb; Ellis Horne, cl; Burt Bales, p; Pat Patton, bj; Squire Girsback, b, sous; Clancy Hayes, d.)

Recorded San Francisco, 1944

(a) 2.19 Blues   Good Time Jazz GTJ LP-17
(b) Ace In The Hole

Album title: Bunk Johnson and the Yerba Buena Jazz Band. The ten inch GTJ LP-17 was released in the early 1950's. This album and the first eight Lu Watters' Yerba Buena Jazz Band recordings from December 1941 were coupled on a twelve inch LP titled Bunk and Lu (GTJ L-12024) released in 1957. This album was issued on CD GTJCD 12024-2 in 1990.

The Frisco Jazz Band with Clancy Hayes
1. Red Gillham, cnt; Jack Buck, tb; Jack Crook, cl; Ray Jahnigen, p; Russ Bennett, bj; Pat Patton, b; Gordon Edwards, d.;
2. Eddie Smith, t; for Gillham; Clancy Hayes, bj; for Bennett.)

Recorded California, c.1946

(a) A Good Man Is Hard To Find (1)	Dawn Club 12005
(b) Huggin' And A Chalkin'	(1)
(c) George Washington	(2)
(d) Gettin' My Boots	(2)
(e) I Ain't Gonna Give Nobody None Of My Jelly Roll	(2)
(f) Mamie's Blues (2.19 Blues)	(2}

Album title: The Frisco Jazz Band with Clancy Hayes. All titles were originally released on Pacific label 78s.

Les Paul with Clancy Hayes (Les Paul, guitar; p, b, d, unknown)

Location unknown, 1948

(a) Now Is The Hour	Mercury 78 5103
(b) My Extraordinary Girl	Mercury 78 5103
(c) Nobody But You	Mercury 78 5137
(d) Street Of Regret	Mercury 78 5137

Lu Watters' Yerba Buena Jazz Band (Lu Watters, t; Don Noakes, tb; Bob Helm, cl; Wally Rose, p; Clancy Hayes and Pat Patton, bj; Dick Lammi, b; Bill Dart, d.)

Hambone Kelly's El Cerrito, 1949-50

(a) Alcoholic Blues	MMRC CD-10
(b) Doctor Jazz	
(c) Frankie And Johnny	
(d) My Little Bimbo	
(e) Oh By Jingo!	
(f) Roll Jordon Roll	
(g) St. James Infirmary	
(h) Sweet Georgia Brown	

CD title: Live At Hambone Kelly's, released 1995. The CD comprises air shots compiled by the San Francico Traditional Jazz Foundation, issued by the Merry Makers Record Company.

Lu Watters' Yerba Buena Jazz Band (Lu Watters, t, wbd; Warren Smith, tb; Bob Helm, cl; Wally Rose, p; Clancy Hayes, Pat Patton, bj; Dick Lammi, b, tu; Bill Dart, d. Don Noakes, tb; replaces Smith on Homespun 104.)

Hambone Kelly's, El Cerrito CA 1949-50

(a) Bill Bailey Won't You Please Come Home	Homespun 101	
(b) Ace In The Hole	Homespun 101	DC 12010
(c) St. Louis Blues	Homespun 101	DC 12010
(d) Broken Promises	Homespun 101	DC 12010
(e) Waiting For The Robert E. Lee	Homespun 101	DC 12010
(f) When The Saints Go Marching In	Homespun 102	DC 12010
(g) Oh By Jingo!	Homespun 104	
(h) Ballin' The Jack	Homespun 106	
(i) Doctor Jazz	Homespun 106	DC 12010

Album titles: All albums are titled Lu Watters' Yerba Buena Jazz Band — Clancy Hayes Vocals (volumes 1, 2, 4 and 6). The LPs were issued in the early 1970s. About the same time, George Hulme coordinated the release of two volumes of 1950s recordings for Dawn Club records on DC 12010 and DC 12011. The thirty-two tracks on the albums - titled The 50s Recordings Volumes one and two - included twelve vocals.

These recordings, and those listed in the next section(MG D-3) were originally released on Down Home and Mercury 78s; eleven were issued on early ten inch LPs on the Down Home Label and two on ten inch Clef/Mercury albums. Down Home LP 1001(g); DH LP 1004(h). Mercury LP MGC 503(f): MGC 510(i).

Some were issued also on Mercury 45s, EPs.

Clancy Hayes with Lu Watters' Yerba Buena Jazz Band (1 Bob Helm, cl; Wally Rose, p; Dick Lammi, b; Clancy Hayes, bj, Lu Watters, wbd. All other tracks add Lu Watters, t; Warren Smith, Don Noakes, tb; Pat Patton, bj; Bill Dart, d.)

Hambone Kelly's, El Cerrito CA 1949-50

(a) Alabamy Bound	(1)	Down Home MG D-3
(b) Alcoholic Blues	(1)	DC 12011
(c) Auntie Skinner's Chicken Dinner	(1)	
(d) Frankie And Johnny		DC 12011
(e) My Little Bimbo		DC 12011
(f) Nobody Knows You When You're Down And Out	(1)	
(g) Peoria		DC 12010
(h) Ragtime Rufus	(1)	
(i) Roll Jordon Roll		DC 12010
(j) Sailing Down The Chesapeake Bay	(1)	
(k) Silver Dollar	(1)	
(l) St. James Infirmary		DC 12011

Album Title: Clancy Hayes Sings. The album comprises recordings by Clancy Hayes' Washboard Five, marked(1); the other tracks are with the full band. The original twelve inch Down Home album was re-released on Verve MGV 1003. The Dawn Club(DC 12010/11) tracks are explained above. The first LP issues on ten inch Down Home were: DH LP 1001(b)(i): DH LP 1002(g)(e): DH LP 1004(a)(c)(f)(h)(j).

Lu Watters' Yerba Buena Jazz Band (Lu Watters, t; Don Noakes, tb; Bob Helm, cl; Wally Rose, p; Clancy Hayes, bj; Dick Lammi, tu, Bill Dart d.)
Hambone Kelly's, El Cerrito CA 1950
Tradjazz CD TJP3
(a) South
(b) Sister Kate
CD title: Lu Watters at Hambone Kelly's.

Bob Scobey's Frisco Band (Personnel from: Bob Scobey, t; Jack Buck, Bob Mielke, Marshall Nichols, tb, Darnell Howard, Bob Helm, Ellis Horne, Bill Napier, cl; George Probert, cl, ss; Burt Bales or Wally Rose, p; Clancy Hayes, bj; Dick Lammi or Hal McCormick, b; Squire Girsback, b, sous; Bob Short, tu; Fred Higuera, d.)

Recorded San Francisco CA 1950-1957

(a) 2.19 Blues   GHB CD BCD-285
(b) A Good Man Is Hard To Find
(c) Ace In The Hole
(d) At The Devil's Ball
(e) Chicago
(f) Down By The Riverside
(g) Hindustan
(h) Memphis Blues
(i) Of All The Wrongs You've Done To Me
(j) Swingin' Doors
(k) At The Angels' Ragtime Ball

CD title: The Unheard Bob Scobey and his Frisco Jazz Band. Tracks(b)(f)(h) recorded 1950;(c)(g)(i)(j)(k), recorded 1952-1956;(a)(d)(e) recorded 1957. CD produced by the San Francisco Traditional Jazz Foundation - William Carter Chairman - and the George H. Buck Jr Jazz Foundation. Album producer - Hal Smith; released 2007.

Bob Scobey's Frisco Band (Bob Scobey, t; Jack Buck, tb; George Probert, cl; Wally Rose, p; Clancy Hayes, bj; Dick Lammi, b; Fred Higuera, d.(1) Albert Nicholas for Probert, Burt Bales for Rose, Squire Girsback for Lammi; *Band vocal.)

Recorded Oakland, CA 1950-1951

(a) Beale Street Mama(1)   GTJ L-12032 / GTCD-12032-2
(b) Chicago
(c) Coney Island Washboard*
(d) Melancholy
(e) Sailing Down The Chesapeake Bay
(f) South

Album title: The Scobey Story Volume 1. This album and the second volume(see below) were issued in 1959 and brought together the band's first 24 recordings from 1950-1952 on two twelve-inch LPs. All recordings had been issued as singles, EPs and ten-inch LPs:
EP issues: EPG* 1249(a)(c); GTJ-1008/EPG*-1166(b)(d)(e) and(f). *UK Vogue/GTJ
LPs GTJ L9/LDG054*(a); GTJ L-14/LDG109*(b)(d)(e) and(f). *UK Vogue/GTJ
The CD number does not include the letter J as one might expect.

Bob Scobey's Frisco Band (Bob Scobey, t; Jack Buck, tb; George Probert, cl; Wally Rose, p; Clancy Hayes, bj; Dick Lammi, b; Fred Higuera, d.(1) Add Bob Mielke, Marshall Nichols, tb. *Ellis Horne for George Probert.)

Recorded Oakland, CA 1952-1953

(a) Ace In The Hole GTJ L-12033 / GTCD-12033-2
(b) Big Butter And Egg Man
(c) Blues My Naughty Sweetie Gives To Me (1)
(d) Do You Know What It Means To Miss New Orleans (1)
(e) Everything Is Peaches Down In Georgia
(f) Huggin' And A Chalkin'*
(g) Hindustan
(h) Long Gone
(i) Of All The Wrongs You've Done To Me (1)
(j) Peoria (1)
(k) Silver Dollar

Album title: The Scobey Story Volume 2.
EP issues: GTJ-1018/EPG 1012(c)(d)(i)(j): all other tracks on GTJ double EP 2-22.
LP issues GTJ L-14/LDG109(c)(d)(i)(j): all other tracks on GTJ L-22/LDG 155

Bob Scobey's Frisco Band (Bob Scobey, t; Jack Buck, tb; Bill Napier, cl; Ernie Lewis, p; Clancy Hayes, bj; Dick Lammi, b; Earl Watkins, d.)

Recorded Los Angeles, 17, 20, 21 January 1955

(a) Battle Hymn Of The Republic GTJ L-12006 / GTJCD-12006-2
(b) Beale Street Blues
(c) Bill Bailey
(d) Careless Love
(e) Down In Jungletown
(f) Memphis Blues
(g) Mobile
(h) Parsons Kansas Blues
(i) Someday Sweetheart
(j) Sweet Georgia Brown

Album title: Bob Scobey's Frisco Band Vocals by Clancy Hayes vol. 4. The album followed the three ten inch LP releases, hence volume 4.
EP issues: GTJ-1026(a)(d)(g)(j): GTJ-1037(b)(e)(f): GTJ 1038(c)(h)(i).
The CD number includes the letter J.

Bob Scobey's Frisco Band (Bob Scobey, t; Jack Buck, tb; Bill Napier, cl; Ernie Lewis, p; Clancy Hayes, bj; Dick Lammi, b; Earl Watkins, d.)

Recorded Los Angeles, CA 6-7 July 1955

(a) Angry GTJ L-12009 / GTCD-12009-2
(b) At The Devil's Ball
(c) I Ain't Gonna Give Nobody None Of My Jelly Roll

(d) I Want To Go Back To Michigan
(e) Lights Out Blues
(f) St. James Infirmary
(g) When The Midnight Choo Choo Leaves For Alabam
Album title: Scobey and Clancy.

Wally Rose and his Band — featuring Clancy Hayes (Wally Rose, p; Jack Minger, t; Jerry Butzen, tb; Vince Cattolica, cl; Norman Bates, b, Cuz Cousineau, d.)

Recorded at The Chukka, San Mateo, CA 1955

(a) Ballin' The Jack   Columbia CL 782
(b) Black Bottom
(c) Charleston
(d) The Varsity Drag
Album title: From Cakewalk To Lindy Hop. The album was also issued as a triple EP on Col B-782.

Bob Scobey's Frisco Band (Bob Scobey, t; Jack Buck, tb; Bill Napier, cl; Jesse "Tiny" Crump, p; Clancy Hayes, bj; Bob Short, tu; Hal McCormick, b; Fred Higuera, d.)

Recorded Oakland, CA 13-15 March 1956

(a) Curse Of An Aching Heart   GTJ L-12023 / GTJCD-12023-2
(b) Doctor Jazz
(c) Indiana
(d) Jada
(e) Michigan Water Blues
(f) Travelin' Shoes
Album title: Direct From San Francisco.

Bob Scobey's Band (Bob Scobey, Frank Snow, tp; Jack Buck, Will and Jack Sudmeier, tb; Bill Napier, Leon Ratsliff, cl; Jesse "Tiny" Crump, p; Clancy Hayes, bj, g; Bob Short, tu; Hal McCormick, b; Fred Higuera, d.)

Recorded Jenny Lind Hall Oakland, CA April 1956

(a) In New Orleans   Down Home MG D-1
(b) Lazy River
(c) Stars Fell On Alabama
(d) Swingin' Doors
(e) Ten To One It's Tennessee
(f) When The One You Love Is Gone
Album title: Bob Scobey's Band. The album sleeve notes confirm the venue as Jenny Lind Hall. The album was reissued on Verve MGV 1001 and released in the UK on Columbia 10058.

Bob Scobey's Band (Bob Scobey, t; Jack Buck, tb; Bill Napier, cl; Jesse "Tiny" Crump, p; Clancy Hayes, bj; Bob Short, tu; Hal McCormick, b; Fred Higuera, d.)

Recorded Jenny Lind Hall Oakland, CA April 1956
Verve MGV 1011

(a) Ain't She Sweet
(b) Five Foot Two
(c) Gettin' My Boots
(d) Lovey Came Back
(e) My Gal Sal
(f) Somebody Stole My Gal
(g) Stumbling
(h) Trouble In Mind

Album title: Dixieland Jazz. Released in the UK on Columbia 10089 and reissued in the USA on the American Recording Society label ARS G-408.

Bob Scobey and his Frisco Band (Bob Scobey, t; Jack Buck, tb; Bill Napier, cl; Ralph Sutton, p; Clancy Hayes, g, bj; Bob Short, tu; Hal McCormick, b; Fred Higuera, d.)

Recorded Jenny Lind Hall, Oakland, CA 1956

(a) I Can't Give You Anything But Love   Jansco JLPS 6250/Jazzology JCD-275
(b) I'll See You In C.U.B.A
(c) Mack The Knife
(d) My Honey's Lovin' Arms
(e) Then I'll Be Happy

Album title: The Great Bob Scobey and His Frisco Band Volume 1. The Jansco LPs (see below) were released posthumously c.1966 by his widow, Jan Scobey. Reissued on Jazzology CD JCD-275 with 6 tracks from the 1960 LP on Ragtime made after Clancy Hayes had left the band. Titles (a), (d) and (e) are played by a quintet – the rhythm section with Scobey and Clancy on guitar.

Bob Scobey and his Frisco Band (Bob Scobey, t; Jack Buck, tb; Bill Napier, cl; Ralph Sutton, p; Clancy Hayes, g, bj; Bob Short, tu; Hal McCormick, b; Fred Higuera, d.)
Track (c) quintet (as JLPS 6250)

Recorded Jenny Lind Hall, Oakland, CA 1956
Jansco JLPS 6252 / Jazzology JCD-285

(a) In New Orleans*
(b) Five Foot Two
(c) I'm Sorry I Made You Cry

Album title: The Great Bob Scobey and His Frisco Band Volume 2.
*In New Orleans has the same personnel as Down Home MG D-1 and is an alternate take. The album sleeve notes confirm the venue as Jenny Lind Hall.

Bob Scobey's Frisco Jazz Band featuring Clancy Hayes (Bob Scobey, Mannie Klein, t; Jack Buck, Warren Smith, Elmer Schneider, tb; Bill Napier, Matty Matlock, Wayne Songer, cl; Ralph Sutton, p; Clancy Hayes, bj; Bob Short, tu; Phil Stephens, b; Fred Higuera, d.)

Recorded Los Angeles, CA 13 August 1956

(a) Alice Blue Gown   RCA LPM 1344
(b) Calico Sal
(c) Linda
(d) Lulu's Back In Town*
(e) Miss Annabelle Lee
(f) You Must Have Been A Beautiful Baby

Album title: Beauty and the Beat. *Track (d) was recorded at a session on 14th August 1956. All tracks except (d) included on ten inch LP HMV DLP 1116 released in UK.
EP Issues RCA EPC 1334-1(c)(e): RCA EPC 1344-2(a)(b): RCA EPS 1344-3(d)(f).
All EPs were foreign issues (Denmark, Germany, UK).

Bob Scobey's Frisco Jazz Band with Clancy Hayes (Bob Scobey, Dick Cathcart, t; Matty Matlock, cl; Abe Lincoln. Warren Smith, Jack Buck, tb: Ralph Sutton, p; Clancy Hayes bj, g; Red Callender, b; Bob Short, tu; Sammy Goldstein, d. *Mannie Klein, replaces Cathcart; Phil Stephens, replaces Callender.)

Recorded Los Angeles, CA 21 and 22 January 1957

(a) Carolina In The Morning*   RCA LPM 1448
(b) I Can't Get Started
(c) It Happened In Sun Valley
(d) Let's Dance The Ragtime Darlin'
(e) Wabash Cannonball
(f) Waiting For The Robert E. Lee*

Album title: Swingin' On The Golden Gate. Released in the UK as RCA RD27031. EP issues: RCA EPA 1448-1(a)(c): RCA EPA 1448-2(b)(e): RCA EPA 1448-3(d)(f). The above EPs were USA issues; and were also issued in Denmark, Germany and the UK with the EPC prefix.

Bob Scobey's Frisco Jazz Band with Clancy Hayes (Bob Scobey, t; Jack Buck, tb; Pete Dovidio, cl; Clyde Pound, p; Clancy Hayes, bj; Tom Beeson, b; Dave Black, d.)

Recorded Los Angeles 10-14 December 1957

(a) Between 18th and 19th On Chestnut Street   RCA LPM 1567
(b) Cakewalkin' Babies From Home
(c) Medley: My Extraordinary Girl/Little Girl
(d) My Bucket's Got A Hole In It
(e) Struttin' With Some Barbecue
(f) The Five Piece Band

Album title: Between 18th and 19th On Any Street.

Bob Scobey's Frisco Jazz Band with Clancy Hayes (Bob Scobey, t; Jack Buck, tb; Pete Dovidio, cl; Clyde Pound, p; Clancy Hayes, bj; Tom Beeson, b; Dave Black, d.)
Recorded Los Angeles 10-14 December 1957
(a) Absinthe Frappé   RCA LPM 1700 / LSP 1700
(b) I've Been Floating Down That Old Green River
(c) I've Been Working On The Railroad
(d) Let Me Call You Sweetheart
(e) Let The Rest Of The World Go By
(f) Put On Your Old Grey Bonnet
(g) Shine On Harvest Moon
(h) The Whiffenpoof Song
(i) There's A Long Long Trail
(j) Wedding Bells Are Breaking Up That Old Gang Of Mine
(k) We'll Build A Bungalow
(l) You Tell Me Your Dream, I'll Tell You Mine

Album title: College Classics. This album was the first to also be issued in RCA's 'Living Stereo'.

Bob Scobey's Frisco Jazz Band with vocals by Clancy Hayes (Bob Scobey, t; Jack Buck and Doug Skinner, tb; Pud Brown, cl; Stan Wrightsman, p; Bob Short, b, tu; Dave Black, d.)

Recorded Los Angeles 19 and 20 January 1958

(a) Blueberry Hill   California Records M 1501/Stereo Records S7013
(b) C.C. Rider
(c) Love Letters In The Sand
(d) Round And Round
(e) Yellow Dog Blues
(f) All Shook Up
(g) Singing The Blues

Album title: Scobey and Clancy Raid The Juke Box. The mono version was released on California Records, the stereo version on the Stereo Records label. Both companies were a division of Contemporary Records.

Bob Scobey and his Frisco Jazz Band (Bob Scobey, t; Ralph Hutchinson, Doug Skinner, tb; Jack McConnell, cl; Floyd Bean, p; Clancy Hayes, bj: Bob Short, tu; Dave Black, d.)

Recorded New York NY 18 and 19 February 1958

(a) Don't Count Your Kisses   SESAC N2251/52
(b) Too Much Mustard

Album title: Bob Scobey and his Frisco Jazz Band featuring Clancy Hayes. Track(b) was included on Sesac EP AD.28.

Bob Scobey and his Frisco Jazz Band featuring Clancy Hayes (personnel as SESAC N2251/52.)

Recorded New York NY 18 and 19 February 1958

(a) Don't Count Your Kisses   Sounds of Yesteryear CD DSOY817
(b) Strawberry Time
(c) Too Much Mustard (take four)
(d) Too Much Mustard (take five)
(e) While You Are Far Away

CD title: Feelin' The Spirit, released 15 June 2010.

Bob Scobey's Frisco Band with Clancy Hayes (Bob Scobey, v, t; Jim Beebe, tb; Brian Shanley, cl; Gene Schroeder, p; Clancy Hayes, bj; Rich Matteson, tu, bass trumpet; George Duvivier, b; Dave Black, d, Toni Lee Scott, vocal.)

Recorded Webster Hall New York NY 2, 3, 4, 5 June 1958

(a) Alexander's Ragtime Band   RCA LPM 1889 / LSP 1889
(b) Down By The Riverside
(c) Floatin' Down To Cotton Town
(d) Glad To Be Me
(e) Mississippi Mud

(f) River Stay 'Way From My Door
(g) Something's Always Happening On The River

Album title: Something's Always Happening On The River. Track(a) has a vocal trio - Clancy Hayes, Bob Scobey and Toni Lee Scott. Clancy Hayes sings duets with Bob Scobey on track(c) and Toni Lee Scott on track(d).

Will Bradley-Johnny Guarnieri Band (Johnny Guarnieri, p; Bernie Glow, Charles Shavers, Carl Severinsen, James Maxwell, Joe Wilder, t; Will Bradley, Lou McGarity, Richard Hixson, Urban Green, tb; George Berg, Hyman Schertzer, Livio Fresk, Ray Beckenstein, Sam Donohue, Walter Levinsky, sax; Barry Galbraith, Mundell Lowe, g; Bob Carter, b; Don Lamond, d; Charles Shirley, conductor)

Recorded New York and Chicago June 1959

(a) Beat Me Daddy Eight To The Bar   RCA   LPM   2098
(b) Down The Road A Piece

Album title: Live Echoes Of The Best In Big Band Boogie. The Clancy Hayes vocals were dubbed onto the recordings on 8 July 1959.

Clancy Hayes' Dixieland Band (Bob Ballard, t; Bill Hanck, tb; Lyle Daniels, cl; Art Hodes, p; Clancy Hayes, bj; Earl Murphy, b; Buddy Smith, d.)

Recorded Chicago IL 11 and 12 April 1960

(a) Baby Won't You Please Come Home   Audio Fidelity AFLP 1937 / AFSD 1937
(b) Ballin' The Jack
(c) Blues My Naughty Sweetie Gives To Me
(d) Careless Love
(e) Easy Street
(f) Huggin' And A Chalkin'
(g) Nobody Knows You When You're Down And Out
(h) Original Dixieland One Step
(i) Sweet Georgia Brown
(j) Up A Lazy River
(k) Washboard Blues
(l) Willie The Weeper

Album title: Clancy Hayes' Dixieland Band. The album was released in mono and stereo.

Clancy Hayes' Dixieland Band (Nappy Trottier, t; Jim Beebe, tb; Brian Shanley, cl; Floyd Bean, p; Clancy Hayes, bj; Gypsy Sam, b; unknown, d.)

Recorded Chicago IL 1960

(a) Go Vote Nixon - Lodge   Tweed 45 rpm single

Recorded for the Republican National Committee. The 'b side' is an instrumental - Elephant Stomp.

Clancy Hayes (tracks a-e: Bill Napier, cl; Ralph Sutton, p; Bob Short, tu; Clancy Hayes, g, bj, d: tracks f-k: Pud Brown, cl; Jess Stacy, p; Bob Short, tu; Clancy Hayes, bj; Shelly Manne, d.)

Recorded Los Angeles CA 29 October 1956 and 18 January 1958

(a) Honeysuckle Rose   Good Time Jazz GTJ 12050 / GTJS10050
(b) Limehouse Blues   GTJCD-10050-2
(c) When You And I Were Young Maggie

(d) Willie The Weeper
(e) Wolverine Blues
(f) After You've Gone
(g) Ain't She Sweet
(h) Dancing Fool
(i) Oceana Roll
(j) Waiting For The Evening Mail
(k) You Took Advantage Of Me

Album title: Swingin' Minstrel. Although the tracks were recorded in 1956(a-e) and 1958(f-k) the album was not released until 1963. The CD was released in 1995.

Docs of Dixieland with Clancy Hayes (1. Herm Lehman, t; Paul McFall, tb; Jack Halstead, cl; Jim Triffon, p; Bob Deebach and Harry Schlafman, bj; Denny Snyder, tu; Ambrose Johnson, d. 2. Herm Lehman, t; Paul McFall, tb; Brian Shanley, Jack Halstead, cl; Jim Campbell, bass sax; Bob Hirsch, p; Harry Schlafman, bj; Denny Snyder, tu; Walt Gifford, d. 3. Clancy Hayes solo banjo and vocal.)

Recorded at the Memorial Hall, Dayton OH April 1963, 1965 and 1966

(a) Dr. Jazz Stomp (1)   DOX Records LP-12367
(b) Michigan Water Blues (2)
(c) Royal Garden Blues (2)
(d) Waitin' For The Evening Mail (3)

Album title: The Dayton Scene. The dates of the individual recordings are unknown but all took place in April. The LP has eleven tracks in total and other guest artists are: Brian Shanley, Jim Campbell, Walt Gifford, Bob Hirsch, Jim Porter, Harry Schlafman and Andy Bartha.

Docs of Dixieland with Clancy Hayes (personnel as above)

Memorial Hall Dayton OH April 1965
(a) Keeping Out Of Mischief Now   CD number unknown
(b) Huggin' And A Chalkin'
(c) Saloon
(d) Medley: Paddlin' Madeline Home / Baby Face / Five Foot Two /
    Yes Sir! That's My Baby
(e) Rose Of Washington Square
(f) Michigan Water Blues

CD title: Gin Bottle Seven and Friends — Live at the Hitching Post 1957 / Memorial Hall Concert 1965. The second disc includes the above tracks from Clancy Hayes' 1965 set; tracks b and c are solos with banjo. The CD, released in 2001 following discovery of a private tape, was produced by Joe Lehman, brother of Herman Lehman, and Carl Halen - leader of the Gin Bottle Seven.

Clancy Hayes with The Original Salty Dogs (Lew Green, cnt; Jim Dapogny, cnt, valve tb; Jim Snyder, tb; Kim Cusack, cl; Johnny Cooper, p; Clancy Hayes, bj; Mike Walbridge, tu; Wayne Jones, d.)

Recorded Chicago, IL 31 August 1964

(a) Beale Street Blues Delmark DL-210 / DS-210
(b) Cakewalkin' Babies CD   DE-210
(c) I'm Comin' Virginia
(d) Michigan Water Blues
(e) My Little Bimbo
(f) Oh By Jingo!
(g) Rose Of Washington Square
(h) Tin Roof Blues
(i) Wise Guy
(j) Tin Roof Blues (alternate)
(k) Rose Of Washington Square (alternate)
(l) Michigan Water Blues (alternate)
(m) I'm Coming Virginia (alternate)

Album title: Oh By Jingo! The album was released in the UK on the 77 label(LA12-30) - mono only. The CD, with the four alternate takes, was issued in 1997.

Yank Lawson and his Yankee Clippers (Yank Lawson, t; Cutty Cutshall, tb, Bill Stegmyer, cl; Dave McKenna, p; Clancy Hayes, bj; Bob Haggart, b; Osie Johnson, d.)

Recorded New York 30 March 1965

(a) Boy From New Orleans ABC Paramount ABC 518 / 518S
(b) Bury Me On Basin Street

Album title: Big Yank Is Here.

Clancy Hayes with Yank Lawson and his Yankee Clippers (Yank Lawson, t; Cutty Cutshall, tb, Pee Wee Russell, cl; Dave McKenna, p; Clancy Hayes, bj; Bob Haggart, b; Osie Johnson, d.)

Recorded New York 30 March 1965

(a) A Good Man Is Hard To Find ABC Paramount ABC 519 / 519S
(b) Basin Street Blues
(c) Don't Forget 127th Street
(d) Fickle Finger Of Fate
(e) I Ain't Got Nobody
(f) Nobody's Sweetheart
(g) She's Just Perfect For Me

Album title: Happy Melodies.

The Nine Greats of Jazz (Yank Lawson, t; Cutty Cutshall, Lou McGarity tb, Peanuts Hucko, cl; Bud Freeman, ts; Ralph Sutton, p; Clancy Hayes, bj; Bob Haggart, b; Morey Feld, d.)
        Recorded Elitch Gardens Trocadero Ballroom, Denver CO 27 July 1966
(a) Rose Of Washington Square   Troc   WCS-1769
Album title: Jazz in the Troc. Clancy Hayes is accompanied by Cutty Cutshall, Ralph Sutton, Bob Haggart and Morey Feld.

Clancy Hayes (Clancy Hayes, bj; with Turk Murphy's Jazz Band: Bob Neighbor, t; Turk Murphy, tb; Jack Crook, cl, bass sax; Pete Clute, p; Frank Haggerty, bj; Bill Carroll, tu; Thad Vandon, d. Squire Girsback, b.)
        Recorded Earthquake McGoon's San Francisco CA 23 September 1966
(a) Ace In The Hole   ABC-591 / 591S
(b) Auntie Skinner's Chicken Dinner
(c) Blues My Naughty Sweetie Gives To Me

(d) Coney Island Washboard
(e) I Ain't Gonna Give Nobody None Of My Jelly Roll
(f) Medley: Pretty Baby, If I Could Be With You, Jada,
      Oh You Beautiful Doll, Mother To Me
(g) Medley: Paddlin' Madeline Home, Baby Face,
      Five Foot Two, Yes Sir, That's My Baby
(h) My Little Bimbo
(i) Tishomingo Blues
(j) (I'll Be In My Dixie Home Again) Tomorrow

Album title: Live At Earthquake McGoon's. Clancy Hayes and Squire Girsback on tracks(c)(f)(i); Clancy Hayes solo track(g). All other tracks with the Turk Murphy Jazz Band.

The Ten Greats of Jazz (Yank Lawson, Billy Butterfield t; Cutty Cutshall, Lou McGarity tb, Peanuts Hucko, cl; Bud Freeman, ts; Ralph Sutton, p; Clancy Hayes, bj; Bob Haggart, b; Morey Feld, d.)
          Recorded Elitch Gardens Trocadero Ballroom, Denver CO 21 or 22 July 1967
(a) Peoria   Troc   WCS-2831

Album title: Jazz in the Troc. Clancy Hayes is accompanied by Ralph Sutton, p; Bob Haggart, b; Morey Feld, d.

The Ten Greats of Jazz (full band personnel as above).
          Recorded Elitch Gardens Trocadero Ballroom, Denver CO 19 or 20 July 1968
(a) Silver Dollar   Troc   WCS-3853

Album title: Jazz in the Troc. Clancy Hayes is accompanied by Ralph Sutton, p; Bob Haggart, b; Morey Feld, d.

Clancy Hayes and his Tune Termites (1. Jack Coon, t; Abe Lincoln, tb; Robin Frost, p; Clancy Hayes, bj; Ira Westley, b; John Guerin, d. * Matty Matlock, cl. 2. Jack Coon, t; Stan Wrightsman, p; Clancy Hayes, bj; Ira Westley, b; Ward Erwin, b**; Jack Sperling, d*; Gene Estes, d.**)
          Recorded at University Club of Pasadena December 28 1968
(a) Mama's Gone Goodbye(1)*   Blue Angel Jazz Club BAJC 502
(b) Michigan Water Blues(1)
(c) Rose Of Washington Square(1)
(d) Tin Roof Blues(2)*
(e) Willie The Weeper(2)**

Album title: The Blue Angel Jazz Club. The tracks above occupy all of side two.

Clancy Hayes and his Tune Termites / Levee Loiterers (Jack Coon, t; Abe Lincoln, tb; *Dick Cary, ph; Matty Matlock, cl; Robin Frost, p; Clancy Hayes, bj; **Chuck Berghoffer, b; **John Guerin, d.^ unknown bass and drums.)
          Recorded at University Club of Pasadena, 28 December 1968
(a) Basin Street Blues^   Blue Angel Jazz Club BAJC 513/514

(b) Beale Street Blues*^
(c) She's Just Perfect For Me*
Album title: The Blue Angel Jazz Club — The Private Jazz Party — 'Don't Call It Dixie'.
This double album comprises unreleased material from five BAJC events from 1968, 1970, 1971, 1972 and 1974. These three tracks are all from 1968. Track(a) is credited to Abe Lincoln's Barefoot Dixieland Philharmonic with Clarence Hayes; track(b) to Clancy Hayes' Levee Loiterers and track(c) to Clancy Hayes' Tune Termites.

The Wiggs-Burke Crescent City Stompers with Clancy Hayes, Zutty Singleton and Don Ewell (Johnny Wiggs, cnt; Paul Crawford, tb; Raymond Burke, cl; Don Ewell, p; Clancy Hayes, bj; Van Perry, b; Zutty Singleton, d.) Clancy Hayes, solo vocal and banjo on all tracks except(e) and(h).

Recorded Manassas, VA 8 December 1968

(a) Do You Know What It Means To Miss New Orleans

Fat Cat Jazz FCJ-105

(b) Floatin' Down To Cotton Town / Alabama Jubilee
(c) Huggin' And A Chalkin'
(d) My Little Bimbo
(e) Put On Your Old Grey Bonnet
(f) Sailing Down The Chesapeake Bay
(g) She's Just Perfect For Me
(h) Yellow Dog Blues

Album title: More of Manassas. As detailed above, Clancy Hayes sings with band on tracks(e) and(h) only; all other tracks are solo with banjo. The Wiggs-Burke Crescent City Stompers have two instrumental tracks - Bugle Boy and At the Jazz Band Ball. Concert organiser and label owner Johnson 'Fat Cat' McCree sings with the band on My Memphis Baby.

The Ten Greats of Jazz (Yank Lawson, Billy Butterfield t; Cutty Cutshall, Lou McGarity tb, Peanuts Hucko, cl; Bud Freeman, ts; Bob Wilber, sop. sax; Ralph Sutton, p; Clancy Hayes, bj; Bob Haggart, b; Morey Feld, d.)

Recorded Elitch Gardens Trocadero Ballroom, Denver CO 18 and 19 July 1969
(a) Ace In The Hole   Troc   WCS-3330
(b) Washboard Blues
(c) Willie The Weeper

Album title: Jazz in the Troc. Despite the band name there are eleven musicians: Peanuts Hucko is drawn on the cover saying, 'me too'. All three tracks have Clancy Hayes banjo and vocal and include Ralph Sutton, Bob Haggart and Morey Feld. Although not credited it is assumed the soprano saxophone on Willie The Weeper is played by Bob Wilber. Although Gus Johnson Jr. is illustrated on the album cover, Morey Feld is the drummer on the recording.

The Blue Angel Jazz Club (Dick Cary, t; Bob Havens, tb; Matty Matlock, cl; Marvin Ash, p; Clancy Hayes, bj; Ray Leatherwood, b; Jack Sperling, d.)
 Recorded at University Club of Pasadena November 1 1969
(a) Wolverine Blues BAJC 505
Album title: The Blue Angel Jazz Club: Jazz at Pasadena '69 vol 1.

The Blue Angel Jazz Club (Abe Lincoln, tb; Matty Matlock, cl; Jess Stacy, p; Clancy Hayes, bj; Morty Corb, b; Panama Francis, d.)
 Recorded at University Club of Pasadena November 1 1969
(a) Melancholy BAJC 506
(b) Waitin' For The Evening Mail
Album title: The Blue Angel Jazz Club: Jazz at Pasadena '69 vol. 2.

Clancy Hayes with Tommy Gwaltney and the Blues Alley Cats (Tommy Gwaltney, cl, vibes; John Philips, p; Clancy Hayes, bj; Steve Jordan, g; Billy Taylor Jr., b; Bertell Knox, d.)

Recorded, Washington DC(circa 1968)
Clanco Records

(a) Sweet Georgia Brown
(b) Lonesome Road
(c) Tin Roof Blues
(d) Ballin' The Jack
(e) Parsons Kansas Blues
(f) Poor Butterfly
(g) Way Down Yonder In New Orleans

Album title: Mr. Hayes Goes To Washington. The sleeve notes contain no information as to the recording date. Clancy appeared at Blues Alley with Tommy Gwaltney in 1967 and 1968; it is likely the recordings were made during one of these visits. The album was released in 1972 after Clancy's death, the sleeve notes include tributes from musicians and associates.

Clancy Hayes: The Private Vocal Recordings

Clancy Hayes' non-commercial private recordings are set out as follows:
• Recordings with the Lu Watters' Yerba Buena Jazz Band
• Recordings with Bob Scobey
• Recordings where Clancy Hayes is solo, leader or member of a band
• Recordings from TV and Radio Broadcasts
• Radio Interviews

Rating or grading of the recordings has generally been avoided. Sound quality varies between excellent and poor, but most tracks have good sound quality. A few tunes have skips, and on some the vocal is faint. Where songs have a missed start or finish this is shown; "part" shows a missed start and finish.

The objective was to detail all of Clancy's vocal recordings but some instrumentals have been included where they are in context or give background atmosphere.

The many private recordings from the San Francisco Traditional Jazz Foundation collection at Stanford University are identified in two categories. Firstly references in bold plain text show the Charles N. Huggins Project recordings digitized from the extensive SFTJF collection. These bold selections are publicly accessible by putting the prefix ars0030_b in the search field: for example ars0030_b070_22. Secondly there are plain(non bold) selections which are not publicly available and require permission to access.

Although the majority of the SFTJF / Stanford tapes have information on artists, fewer have details on locations and dates. In some cases the information is clearly incorrect; presumably over the years the tape logs may have been incorrectly written or lost. Where the information appears to be reliable it is included; where it is incorrect or there is uncertainty this pointed out.

As explained in the introductions, all other selections (i.e. those without a Stanford reference) are in my own collection and a large number are posted on the Clancy Hayes Jazz YouTube channel. As shown in the text, most private tapes came to me via Dutch Frisco Jazz fan Sam Linschooten who in turn received a great many of them from Hal Smith. Others came courtesy of musicians and jazz fans as shown in the listings. It is worth repeating my gratitude to everyone who made the music available.

The Recordings:

Clancy Hayes with Lu Watters' Yerba Buena Jazz Band

Lu Watters' Yerba Buena Jazz Band (Lu Watters – cnt, leader; Bob Scobey, t; Turk Murphy, tb; Ellis Horne, cl; Wally Rose, p; Russ Bennett, Clancy Hayes, bj; Dick Lammi tuba; Bill Dart, d. Bob Best announcer.)
Dawn Club, San Francisco, CA: KYA broadcast 1941

(a) A Good Man Is Hard To Find	3.02
(b) St. James Infirmary	2.49
(c) Willie The Weeper	2.52
(d) Careless Love	2.21
(e) Darktown Strutters' Ball	2.26
(f) Royal Garden Blues	3.04
(g) Melancholy	3.21

Private tape title unknown; from the collection of Sam Linschooten.

Lu Watters' Yerba Buena Jazz Band (Benny Strickler, t; Bill Bardin, tb; Bob Helm, Ellis Horne, cl; Burt Bales, p; Russ Bennett, bj; Clancy Hayes, d.)
Hambone Kelly's, El Cerrito, CA: KYA broadcast Aug.1942
(a) Ace In The Hole   3.22

Private tape title unknown; from the collection of Sam Linschooten. Lu Watters is absent, Benny Strickler is on trumpet.

Lu Watters' Yerba Buena Jazz Band (Lu Watters, t, wbd, leader; Bob Scobey, t; Turk Murphy, tb, wbd, v; Bob Helm cl, wbd; Johnny Wittwer, p; Harry Mordecai, bj, v; Dick Lammi, tu; Bill Dart, d.)
Hambone Kelly's, El Cerrito, CA. c.1948
(a) Coney Island Washboard   2.56

Private tape title unknown; from the collection of Sam Linschooten. Turk Murphy and Harry Mordecai were the original vocalists; Clancy Hayes overdubbed his vocal later. Watters, Murphy and Helm all play washboards after the vocal.

Lu Watters' Yerba Buena Jazz Band (Lu Watters, t, leader; Turk Murphy, tb, wbd; Bob Helm, cl, wbd; Johnny Wittwer, p; Harry Mordecai, bj; Dick Lammi, tu, b; Clancy Hayes, wbd.)
Recorded Hambone Kelly's El Cerrito, CA. 1948 or early 1949
(a) Cakewalkin' Babies 5.01 **070_11**
(b) South 3.52 **070_11**
(c) Blues My Naughty Sweetie Gives To Me 3.51 **070_11**
Private tape title: **070_11** Clancy Hayes undated, reel K. Turk Murphy plays washboard behind vocal on Cakewalkin' and Bob Helm plays washboard behind the vocal on South.

Lu Watters' Yerba Buena Jazz Band (Lu Watters, t, leader; Turk Murphy, tb, wbd; Bob Helm, cl; Johnny Wittwer, p; Harry Mordecai, bj; Dick Lammi, b; Clancy Hayes, wbd.)
Recorded Hambone Kelly's, El Cerrito CA. early 1949
(a) Cakewalkin' Babies 4.53
Private tape title unknown; from the collection of Sam Linschooten. Turk Murphy plays washboard behind vocal.

Lu Watters' Yerba Buena Jazz Band (Lu Watters, t, leader; leader; Don Noakes, tb; Bob Helm, cl; Wally Rose, p; Pat Patton, Clancy Hayes, bj; Dick Lammi tuba; Bill Dart, d.)
Hambone Kelly's, El Cerrito, CA. Rehearsal for recording session 1949
(a) Oh By Jingo! 2.52
(b) Ding Dong Daddy From Dumas 2.07
(c) Hot Time In The Old Town Tonight 3.49
Private tape title unknown; from the collection of Sam Linschooten.

Lu Watters' Yerba Buena Jazz Band (Lu Watters, t, leader; Don Noakes, tb; Bob Helm, cl; Wally Rose, p; Pat Patton, Clancy Hayes, bj; Dick Lammi, tuba; Bill Dart, wbd.)
Recorded Hambone Kelly's, El Cerrito, CA. 1949
(a) Coney Island Washboard 2.34 **070_14**
Private tape title: **070_14** Clancy Hayes undated reel N.

Lu Watters' Yerba Buena Jazz Band (Lu Watters, t, leader; Don Noakes, tb; Bob Helm, cl; Wally Rose, p; Clancy Hayes, bj; Dick Lammi, tu; Bill Dart, d.)
Recorded Hambone Kelly's El Cerrito, CA. mid-to-late 1949
(a) You Gotta See Your Mama 2.44 **065_15**
(b) Roll Jordan Roll 3.06 **065_13**
(c) Waiting For The Robert E. Lee 2.48 **065_12**
Private tape titles: 065_15 Lu Watters 1950, reel D; 065_13 Lu Watters, Reel B: 065_12 Yerba Buena Jazz Band, Hambone Kelly's broadcast reel A2.

Lu Watters' Yerba Buena Jazz Band (Bob Scobey, t; Bob Helm, cl; Burt Bales, p; Clancy Hayes, bj; Dick Lammi, b; Lu Watters, wbd, leader.)
Recorded Hambone Kelly's, El Cerrito, CA. 1949
(a) Angry   4.39   **070_22**
(b) Jada   4.04
(c) Ain't She Sweet   3.15
(d) Some Of These Days   3.43
Private tape title: 070_22 Clancy Hayes undated, reel 2E

Lu Watters' Yerba Buena Jazz Band (Lu Watters, t, leader; Don Noakes, tb; Bob Helm, cl; Wally Rose, p; Pat Patton, Clancy Hayes, bj; Dick Lammi, tu; Bill Dart, d.)
Hambone Kelly's rehearsal for recording session, 1950
(a) Broken Promises (poor quality)   3.15   070_17
(b) Broken Promises   3.12   070_17
Private tape title: 070_17 Clancy Hayes' tapes reel Q undated.

Lu Watters' Yerba Buena Jazz Band (Lu Watters, t, leader; Don Noakes, tb; Bob Helm, cl; Wally Rose, p; Clancy Hayes, bj; Dick Lammi, tu, b; Bill Dart, d.)
Recorded Hambone Kelly's El Cerrito CA. 1950
(a) Baby Won't You Please Come Home   3.11   **065_14**
(b) Cakewalkin' Babies   3.21   **065_14**
(c) St. James Infirmary   3.14   **065_14**
(d) See See Rider   4.07   **065_14**
(e) After You've Gone   4.16   066_07
(f) Darktown Strutters' Ball   2.28   066_07
Private tape titles: **065_14** Lu Watters 1950, reel C; 066_07 Hambone Kelly's, 3-4 sessions undated.

Lu Watters' Yerba Buena Jazz Band (Lu Watters, t, leader; Don Noakes, tb; Bob Helm, cl; Wally Rose, p; Clancy Hayes, bj; Dick Lammi, tu, b; Bill Dart, d.)
Recorded Hambone Kelly's 1950
(a) Waiting For The Robert E. Lee   3.06   **065_05**
(b) Weary Blues   5.09
(c) Alcoholic Blues   3.24
(d) Doctor Jazz   3.58
(e) Roll Jordan Roll   3.13
(f) When The Saints Go Marching In   3.24
Private tape title: 060_05 Hambone Kelly's KLX airshots 1950 Vol. 1

Lu Watters' Yerba Buena Jazz Band (Lu Watters, t, leader; Don Noakes, tb; Bob Helm, cl; Wally Rose, p; Pat Patton, Clancy Hayes, bj; Dick Lammi, tu; Bill Dart, d.)
    Recording location Hambone Kelly's, El Cerrito, CA. 1949
(a) Oh By Jingo!   2.56 **068_01**
Private tape title: **068_01** Lu Watters' Sweets Ballroom undated Vol. 2. The tape contains only this one vocal track which is clearly by the Lu Watters Yerba Buena Jazz Band; this is a rehearsal for a recording session.

Clancy Hayes with Bob Scobey

Alexander's Jazz Band (Bob Scobey, t; Jack Buck, tb; Ellis Horne, cl; Burt Bales, p; Clancy Hayes, bj; Dick Lammi, tu; Bill Dart, d. *Band vocal.)
    Recorded at Melody Club Oakland early 1950
(a) 2.19 Blues   4.24 103_02
(b) When The Saints Go Marching In*   4.53
Private tape: 103_02 Clancy Hayes paper tape 2 of 23.

Bob Scobey's Frisco Band (Bob Scobey, t; Jack Buck, tb; George Probert, cl, ss; George Miller, p; Clancy Hayes, bj; Gene Mayl, tu; Fred Higuera, d.)
    Recorded at the Southern California Hot Jazz Society meeting, c. 1951
(a) Careless Love   4.21 080_05
(b) I Ain't Gonna Give Nobody None Of My Jelly Roll 2.42
(c) Beale Street Mama   4.03
(d) Wolverine Blues   3.37
(e) Bill Bailey   2.59
(f) Memphis Blues   3.08
(g) Peoria   2.22
(h) Melancholy   4.44
(i) Blues My Naughty Sweetie Gives To Me   3.24
(j) 2.19 Blues   6.01
(k) South   3.12
Private tape: 080_05 Bill Miskell tape Bob Scobey dub, undated reel no.38.

Bob Scobey's Frisco Band (Bob Scobey, t; Jack Buck, tb; George Probert, cl; Wally Rose, p; Clancy Hayes, bj; Gene Mayl, tu; Fred Higuera, d.)
    Recorded at The Greenwich Village, Palo Alto, 1951
(a) Nobody Knows You When You're Down And Out   3.33
(b) Hindustan   3.21
(c) Silver Dollar   3.21
(d) San   3.29
(e) Of All The Wrongs You've Done To Me   3.28
Private tape title: unknown; from the collection of Sam Linschooten.

Bob Scobey's Alexander's Band at Jenny Lind Hall (Bob Scobey; Jack Buck, tb; Darnell Howard, cl; Burt Bales, p; Clancy Hayes, bj; Squire Girsback, b; Fred Higuera.)
Recorded at Jenny Lind Hall, Oakland CA, 5th November 1950
(a) A Good Man Is Hard To Find (cut off) 4.31
(b) Memphis Blues 4.01
(c) Careless Love 6.18
Private tape title: unknown. This tape is from the collection of Sam Linschooten.

All Star Band (Bob Scobey, t; Don Kinch, t; Turk Murphy, tb; Bob Helm, cl; Bill Mulhern, p; Clancy Hayes, gtr; Bob Hoskins, tu; Bill Dart, d. Track (b) Scobey out; track (d) Wally Rose replaces Bill Mulhearn.)
Bayside Jazz Society Concert, probably Cook's Union Hall, Oakland, CA. 1951
(a) My Bucket's Got A Hole In It 4.02
(b) Shake That Thing 2.53
(c) Waiting For The Robert E. Lee 4.08
(d) Mecca Flat Blues 6.26
Private tape title: unknown. This tape is from the collection of Sam Linschooten.

Bob Scobey's Frisco Band (Bob Scobey, t; leader; Jack Buck, tb; Albert Nicholas, cl; Burt Bales, p; Clancy Hayes, bj; Squire Girsback, b; Fred Higuera, d.)
Rehearsal Jenny Lind Hall, 1951
(a) Beale Street Mama 4.24 070_15
(b) Beale Street Mama 2.56
Private tape title: 070_15. Track (b) is an edit of track (a) from the collection of Sam Linschooten.

Bob Scobey's Frisco Band (Bob Scobey, t; Jack Buck, tb; George Probert, cl; Wally Rose, p; Clancy Hayes, bj; Gene Mayl, tu, b; Fred Higuera, d.)
Location Victor's and Roxie's c.1951
(a) Waiting For The Robert E. Lee (poor quality) 2.28 109_20
(b) Swingin' Doors 4.17
(c) Do You Know What It Means To Miss New Orleans 4.34
Private tape: 109_20 Clancy Hayes live with Bob Scobey's Band. Track (a) has poor sound quality.

Bob Scobey's Frisco Band (possible personnel: Bob Scobey, t; Jack Buck, tb; George Probert, cl; Burt Bales. p; Clancy Hayes, bj; Fred Higuera, d.)
Recorded Victor's and Roxie's, Oakland, c.1951
(a) Do You Know What It Means To Miss New Orleans   3.33
(b) Peoria   2.24
(c) Melancholy   5.02
(d) Coney Island Washboard   3.07
(e) St. Louis Blues   4.44
Private tape: from the collection of Sam Linschooten.

Bob Scobey's Frisco Band (Bob Scobey, t; Jack Buck, tb; George Probert, cl; Wally Rose, p; Clancy Hayes, bj; Fred Higuera, d.)
Possibly Greenwich Village, Palo Alto CA. 1951 or 1952
(a) How Come You Do Me Like You Do   4.35   103_11
(b) Shake That Thing   5.46
(c) Beale Street Mama   4.16
(d) Down By The Riverside   4.28
(e) Parsons Kansas Blues (missed start)   2.28
Private tape: Clancy Hayes paper tape no. 11 of 23.

Bob Scobey's Frisco Band (Bob Scobey, t; Jack Buck, tb; George Probert, cl; Wally Rose, p; Clancy Hayes, bj; Dick Lammi, b; Fred Higuera, d.)
Recorded Jenny Lind Hall, Oakland CA c.1952
(a) Everything Is Peaches Down In Georgia
(b) Long Gone
Private tape title: unknown. This tape is from the collection of Sam Linschooten.

Bob Scobey's Frisco Band (Bob Scobey, t; Jack Buck, tb; Bill Napier, cl; Don Ewell, p; Clancy Hayes, bj; Hal McCormick, b; Earl Watkins, d: Lizzie Miles, Claire Austin vocal on Bill Bailey.)
Location unknown, jazz lecture tour by Prof. Hayakawa circa 1955
(a) Chicago   3.29
(b) Ace In The Hole   3.17
(c) Bill Bailey*   3.06
Private tape title: unknown. This tape is from the collection of Sam Linschooten.
*Lizzie Miles, Claire Austin and Clancy Hayes all take a solo on Bill Bailey.

Bob Scobey's Frisco Band (personnel unknown)
Live radio broadcast, Showboat, San Francisco, 31 December 1955
(a) Someday Sweetheart   3.44
This track was included in Dave Radlauer's 1998 Clancy Hayes Story broadcast. It is from a nationwide NBC New Year's Eve show.

Bob Scobey's Frisco Band (Bob Scobey, t; Jack Buck, tb; Bill Napier, cl; Clancy Hayes, bj; Hal McCormick, b; Fred Higuera, d. Unknown, p.)
Unissued recording for Good Time Jazz or Verve c.1956
(a) Dancing In The Moonlight
Private tape title: unknown. This tape is from the collection of Sam Linschooten.

Bob Scobey's Frisco Band (Bob Scobey, t; Jack Buck, tb; Bill Napier, cl; Jesse "Tiny" Crump, p; Clancy Hayes, bj; Hal McCormick, b; Fred Higuera, d.)
Recorded at Beloit College, WI 24 January 1956
(a) Huggin' And A Chalkin'   3.08
(b) South   3.58
(c) Do You Know What It Means To Miss New Orleans   4.01
(d) Peoria   2.16
(e) Ace In The Hole   3.06
(f) Coney Island Washboard   2.46
(g) Parsons Kansas Blues   4.31
Private tape title: unknown. This tape is from the collection of Sam Linschooten. The concert was part of Prof. Hayakawa's concert and lecture tour with the Bob Scobey band.

Bob Scobey's Frisco Band (Bob Scobey, t; Jack Buck, Doug Skinner, tb; Pete Dovidio, cl; Ralph Sutton, p; Clancy Hayes, bj; J. Lenhart, b; Dave Black, d.)
Recorded at the Blue Note, Chicago IL April 1957
(a) South   3.40   032_02
(b) Do You Know What It Means To Miss New Orleans   1.55
 (fade out)
(c) Bill Bailey   3.25
(d) Do You Know What It Means To Miss New Orleans   3.31
(e) Chicago   3.36
Private tape: 032_02 Blue Note Chicago Air Check.

Bob Scobey's Frisco Band (Bob Scobey, t; Jack Buck, Doug Skinner, tb; Pete Dovidio, cl; Clyde Pound, p; Clancy Hayes, bj; Tom Beeson, b; Dave Black, d; Toni Lee Scott, v.)
Recorded at Grand Rapids, MI c.1957
(a) Floatin' Down To Cotton Town   1.36
(b) Silver Dollar   3.09
(c) South   3.59
(d) Sweet Georgia Brown   3.05
(e) Do You Know What It Means To Miss New Orleans   4.44
(f) Royal Garden Blues   5.21
(g) Ace In The Hole   2.49
(h) St. James Infirmary   3.44

(i) Parsons Kansas Blues	4.26
(j) Huggin' And A Chalkin'	2.55
(k) I Want To Go Back To Michigan	2.52
(l) Beale Street Blues	5.18
(m) Bill Bailey	3.12
(n) High Society*	3.05
(o) Memphis Blues	4.32
(p) Blues My Naughty Sweetie...	3.32
(q) Coney Island Washboard	2.34
(r) Chicago	3.18
(s) Peoria	2.14
(t) Hassan	3.01
(u) I Can't Get Started	5.06
(v)(Concert Close)	1.16
(w) When The Saints Go Marching In	3.11

Private tape title: Bob Scobey at Grand Rapids Michigan capturing a full concert including announcements. This tape is from the collection of Sam Linschooten.
*Duet with Toni Lee Scott

Bob Scobey's Frisco Band (Bob Scobey, t; Clancy Hayes, bj; Dave Black, d; the other personnel are unknown but it is likely to be the Grand Rapids band detailed above.)

Bourbon Street Club, Madison Wisconsin c.1958

(a) Tennessee Medley:	
Memphis Blues, Beale Street Blues	6.51
(b) Chinese Medley: Chinatown My Chinatown,	
China Boy*, San*, Limehouse Blues	6.33
(c) River Stay 'Way From My Door	4.45

Album title: Bob Scobey, Bourbon Street, Madison. An acetate of live recordings including a Dave Black drum solo on Down In Jungle Town. Bob Scobey and Clancy are on the album and as detailed above, based on the date, it is possibly the same band as the Grand Rapids concert. *China Boy and San are instrumentals.

Bob Scobey's Frisco Band (Bob Scobey, t; Jim Beebe, tb; Rich Matteson, bass tp, tu; Brian Shanley, cl; Gene Schroeder, p; Clancy Hayes, bj; Dave Black, d).

Art Ford TV Show, Chicago 4 June 1958

(a) Ace In The Hole	3.29

Recorded from a T.V performance. Toni Lee Scott sang After You've Gone.

Bob Scobey's Frisco Band (personnel unknown)

Recorded at Soldier Field, Chicago 1 September 1959

(a) Huggin' And A Chalkin'	-
(b) Bill Bailey	-

Private tape title: unknown. These recordings are held by the Library of Congress.

Bob Scobey's Frisco Band (personnel unknown)
Playboy Penthouse TV show, 12 December 1959
(a) Travelin' Shoes   2.45
(b) Ace In The Hole   2.49
Private tape title: unknown. This tape is from the collection of Sam Linschooten.

Clancy Solo, Leader and with Friends.

Clancy Hayes (guitar, banjo, unknown d.)
Recording location unknown. 1942
(a) When He's All Dolled Up   2.11
(b) Stavin' Chain   2.09
(c) Stavin' Chain   2.59
(d) Deep Elm Blues   2.51.
(e) Sailing Down The Chesapeake Bay   1.26
(f) Medley; Louisville Lou, Flamin' Mamie,   2.58
    Sob Sister Sadie
(g) The Tattooed Lady   2.18
(h) The Fat Girl (Huggin' And A Chalkin')   3.22
(i) What A Life When Nobody Loves You   1.39
(j) Alexander's Ragtime Band   1.09
(k) Alabama Jubilee   1.14
(l) Down At The Husking Bee   1.04
(m) Sailing Down The Chesapeake Bay   1.06
(n) Brown Skin Gal   2.39
(o) Sensation   2.12
(p) Sailing Down The Chesapeake Bay   2.06
(q) Just A Cousin Of Mine   2.29
(r) Down and Out   1.21
(s) Seven Or Eleven   1.52
(t) Beale Street Mama   2.01
(u) Oceana Roll   2.58
(v) Ace In The Hole   2.24
(w) Long Gone   1.34
(x) If He Comes In   1.41
Private tape: From the collection of Fré Bok (a member of the Bob Scobey Society — Holland). These are home acetate recordings from 1942 transferred to tape. Steve Abrams introduces several of the tunes.

Clancy Hayes with Unknown Band (Clancy Hayes, unknown t; tb; p; d.)
Recording location and date unknown
(a) Shake That Thing   3.04
(b) The Fat Girl   2.37
Private tape: from the collection of Ate van Delden. The sound would indicate these are early recordings circa. 1947 or possibly earlier. It is not known if Clancy Hayes is playing drums (there is no banjo or guitar) and it is not him playing piano. The Fat Girl is the original title of what became Huggin' And A Chalkin'.

Clancy Hayes (guitar, unknown violin)
Recording location and date unknown
(a) Weddin' Day   2.11   070_17
(b) Weddin' Day   2.57
(c) Weddin' Day   2.42
Private tape: 070_17 Clancy Hayes' tapes reel Q undated. The three versions are in different tempos.

Clancy Hayes (piano)
Recording location and date unknown
(a) Piano Solo unknown / I Ain't Working No More   5.16   **070_14**
(b) Piano solo unknown / I Haven't Got A Ring   4.26
Private tape: **070_14** Clancy Hayes; undated reel N.

Clancy Hayes (guitar)
Recording location and date unknown
(a) Your Always Hanging 'Round My Man   2.41   **103_21**
(b) Otto's New Auto   1.49
Private tape: **103_21** Clancy Hayes paper tapes no. 21 of 23

Clancy Hayes' Rehearsal Group (Vince Dotson, t; Joe Zohn, tb; Ellis Horne, cl; Burt Bales, p; Squire Girsback b; Clancy Hayes, d.)
Recording location unknown, c. 1947
(a) Home Again Blues   1.21   **070_11**
(b) Otto's New Auto   2.41   **103_10**
Private tapes: **070_11** Clancy Hayes; undated, reel K. **103_10**: (Clancy Hayes paper tapes) no. 10 of 23.

Clancy Hayes' Rehearsal Group (Vince Dotson, t; Bill Bardin, tb; Ellis Horne, cl; Burt Bales, p; Pat Patton, bj, Squire Girsback, b; Clancy Hayes, d.)
Recording location unknown, c. 1947
(a) Ten To One It's Tennessee   5.25   **103_13**
(b) Ten To One It's Tennessee   5.17
(c) Otto's New Auto   4.17
(d) Coquette   3.47
Private tape: **103_13** (Clancy Hayes paper tapes) no. 13 of 23.

Clancy Hayes' Rehearsal Group (Vince Dotson, t; Al Zohn, tb; Pat O'Casey, cl; Burt Bales, p; Squire Girsback, b; Clancy Hayes, g, d.)
Recording location unknown, c. 1947,
(a) Ten To One It's Tennessee 3.56 **103_05**
(b) Willie The Weeper 6.02 **103_05**
(c) Otto's New Auto 2.52 **103_05**
(d) Auntie Skinner's Chicken Dinner 3.17 **103_05**
(e) Cakewalkin' Babies 8.01 **103_08**
(f) Parsons Kansas Blues 10.47 **103_08**
(g) Otto's New Auto 3.36 **103_08**
Private tapes: **103_05** (Clancy Hayes paper tapes) no. 5 of 23: **103_08**(Clancy Hayes paper tapes) no. 8 of 23.

Clancy Hayes' Rehearsal Group (Vince Dotson, t; Bill Bardin, tb; Ellis Horne, cl; Burt Bales, p; Squire Girsback, b; Clancy Hayes, d.)
Recording location unknown, c. 1947,
(a) Coquette 4.27 **103_07**
(b) Parsons Kansas Blues 5.59
(c) At The Angels' Ragtime Ball 3.37
Private tape: **103_07** (Clancy Hayes paper tapes) no. 7 of 23.

Clancy Hayes' Rehearsal Group (Ned Dotson, t; Slim Evans, cl; Burt Bales, p; Pat Patton, b; Clancy Hayes, d.)
Recording location unknown, c. 1947,
(a) Down By The Riverside 4.31 103_03
(b) Parsons Kansas Blues 7.07
(c) Coquette 3.51
(d) Buddy Bolden Blues 5.22
Private tape: 103_03 (Clancy Hayes paper tapes) no. 3 of 23.

Clancy Hayes' Rehearsal Group (Slim Evans, cl; Bill Bardin, tb; Burt Bales, p; Squire Girsback, b; Billie Smith, wbd; Clancy Hayes, d.)
Recording location unknown, c. 1947,
(a) Ten To One It's Tennessee 3.11 103_04
(b) Ten To One It's Tennessee 4.03
(c) Ten To One It's Tennessee 4.04
Private tape: 103_04 (Clancy Hayes paper tapes) no. 4 of 23.

Clancy Hayes with Johnny Wittwer (Clancy Hayes, g; Johnny Wittwer, b.)
Recording location and date unknown
(a) She's A Good Gal (But A Thousand Miles From Home) 3.24
Private tape: from the collection of Sam Linschooten. Ray Skjelbred kindly provided the information on the identity of the previously unknown string bass player.

Clancy Hayes' Rehearsal Group (Vince Dotson, t; Al Zohn, tb; Ellis Horne, cl; Burt Bales, p; Clancy Hayes, g, d; Squire Girsback, b; Billie Smith, wbd. Add Pat Patton, bj; on tracks e-i)

Recording date c. 1947, location unknown

(a) Blues — untitled	8.27	103_09
(b) Wolverine Blues	4.57	103_09
(c) Cakewalkin' Babies	5.45	103_09
(d) At The Angels' Ragtime Ball	3.29	103_09
(e) Coquette	4.42	103_12
(f) St. James Infirmary	5.57	103_12
(g) Baby Won't You Please Come Home	4.53	103_12
(h) Ten To One It's Tennessee	6.16	103_12
(i) Parsons Kansas Blues (cut off)	4.37	103_12

Private tapes: 103_09 (Clancy Hayes paper tapes) no. 9 of 23; 103_12 (Clancy Hayes paper tapes) no. 12 of 23.

Clancy Hayes' Rehearsal Group (Pat O'Casey, cl; Burt Bales, p; Squire Girsback, b; Clancy Hayes, d.)

Recording date c. 1947, location unknown

(a) At The Angels' Ragtime Ball	5.35	103_14
(b) Otto's New Auto	4.38	
(c) Otto's New Auto	4.41	
(d) Parsons Kansas Blues	6.02	

Private tape: 103_14 (Clancy Hayes paper tapes) no. 14 of 23.

Clancy Hayes' Rehearsal Group (Vince Dotson, t; Al Zohn, tb; Pat O'Casey, cl, v; Burt Bales, p; Clancy Hayes, g, d; Squire Girsback, b; Billie Smith, wbd.)

Recording location unknown, c.1947,

(a) 2.19 Blues	8.57	103_15
(b) Long Gone(part)	1.45	103_15
(c) Long Gone	4.05	103_15
(d) Otto's New Auto (part)	3.06	103_15
(e) Parsons Kansas Blues	6.38	103_17
(f) When The Saints....	5.14	103_17
(g) Otto's New Auto	4.22	103_17
(h) At The Angels' Ragtime Ball	5.29	103_18
(i) Coquette(missed start)	3.26	103_18
(j) Parsons Kansas Blues	6.37	103_18
(k) Cakewalkin' Babies	6.57	103_18
(l) Someday Sweetheart	9.04	103_20

Private tapes: **103_21** (Clancy Hayes paper tapes) no. 15 of 23; 17 of 23; 18 of 23; 20 of 23. Clancy Hayes and Pat O'Casey duet on track(l).

Clancy Hayes with Burt Bales (Burt Bales, p; Clancy Hayes, d, unknown bass on tracks b - f.)
Recording location Clancy's home, c.1947/8

(a) Parsons Kansas Blues - snippet	0.37	070_17
(b) You Took Advantage Of Me	2.38	070_17
(c) Lulu's Back In Town	2.44	070_17
(d) Ten To One It's Tennessee	3.02	103_19
(e) Everything Is Peaches Down In Georgia	3.11	109_02
(f) Parsons Kansas Blues	6.29	109_02
(g) Coquette	4.19	109_02
(h) How Come You Do Me Like You Do	4.24	109_02
(i) Somebody's Wrong	2.05	109_02
(j) She's A Good Gal (But 1000 Miles From Home)	3.17	109_07
(k) Willie The Weeper	4.43	109_07

Private tapes: 070_17 Clancy Hayes tapes reel Q; 103_19 Clancy, Burt no. 19 of 23; 109_02 Clancy, Burt; 109_07 Reel T. 1950's. Clancy Hayes plays guitar on (j).

Clancy Hayes with Jack Teagarden (Charlie Teagarden, t; Jack Teagarden, tb, vcl*; Burt Bales, p; Pat Patton, b; Clancy Hayes, g, d.)
Recorded at Clancy's home, San Francisco CA c.1948

(a) Coquette*	6.22	103_06
(b) Down By The Riverside	5.12	103_06
(c) Unknown Blues*	8.52	103_06
(d) Parsons Kansas Blues	5.13	103_16
(e) Rockin Chair*	4.56	
(f) Ten To One It's Tennessee	4.17	070_19
(g) St. James Infirmary*	4.25	070_19
(h) Stardust*	6.07	070_19
(i) Three Little Words	2.31	070_19

Private tapes: 103_06 (Clancy Hayes paper tapes) no. 6 of 23; 103_16 no. 16 of 23; 070_19 Clancy Hayes' tapes reel 2B undated. Track (e) is from the collection of Sam Linschooten. All tracks from the same informal session at Clancy's home

Clancy Hayes with Les Paul (Les Paul, g; Clancy Hayes, v; unknown piano, bass.)
Recording location and date unknown.

(a) Where Flamingos Fly	2.31	103_22
(b) Once And For Always	2.41	

Private tape: (Clancy Hayes paper tapes) no. 22 of 23.

Clancy Hayes (Clancy Hayes, p; unknown bass)
Recording location unknown, late 1940s

(a) Stavin' Chain	5.36	109_03
(b) Sidewalk Blues	4.29	

(c) Down And Out 3.57
(d) Auntie Skinner's Chicken Dinner 2.11
(e) I Ain't Working No More 4.06

Private tape: 109_03 Paper 7 Clancy Hayes / Bob Scobey 1950s (sic). This tape is incorrectly named; it does not feature Bob Scobey and on these tracks Clancy Hayes plays piano with unknown bass. Sidewalk Blues has scat singing by Clancy Hayes.

Clancy Hayes (Clancy Hayes, g; unknown clarinet; family singalong vocal)
Recording locations unknown and Clancy's home; dates unknown
(a) I'll Introduce You To Those Southern Gals 2.11 104_03
(b) Cakewalkin' Babies (part) 1.08 104_03
(c) Darktown Strutters' Ball 3.05 109_04
(d) I've Been Working On The Railroad 1.55 109_04

Private tapes: 104_03 Watters Band no. 3 Clancy Solo with guitar; 109_04 Reel L 1950's. Tracks (a) and (b) are solo performances from a concert; (c) and (d) are singalongs with family and friends; all tracks have Clancy on guitar.

Clancy Hayes with Unknown Band (Clancy Hayes, unknown t, cl, p, b, wbd.)
Recording location unknown, c. 1947
(a) Dallas Blues 6.02 104_03

Private tape: 104_03 - Watters Band no. 3, Clancy Solo with guitar. The Lu Watters Band play instrumentals at the beginning of the tape (Emperor Norton's Hunch, New Orleans Joys, High Society). This track sounds very much like a rehearsal session but the band line up matches none of those listed; it is therefore listed separately. It is not the Lu Watters band.

Clancy Hayes (piano)
Recorded at an after-gig party, Toronto 6 June 1958
(a) My Home Is In A Southern Town 1.21
(b) Why 2.24
(c) Mr. Joe 3.01
(d) Witch Watch 3.16
(e) Medley: I Thought I Heard Buddy Bolden Say / 4.17
     Don't You Leave Me Here
(f) When The One You Love Is Gone 3.48
(g) Piano Instrumentals-end of party 5.29

Private tape: from the collection of George Hulme. On track (g) Clancy Hayes can be heard in conversation, it is likely the piano stool is occupied by another guest.

Clancy Hayes (piano)
Recorded for Squirrel Ashcraft, Chicago IL 1958
(a) Of All The Wrongs You've Done To Me　　　2.33
(b) It Seems To Be Spring　　　3.03
(c) Glad To Be Me　　　3.53
(d) Nothing's Gonna Stop Me Now　　　2.47　　068_03
(e) Getting Ready For Eddie　　　1.51　　068_03
(f) Hassan　　　4.12　　068_03
(g) In New Orleans　　　3.36　　068_03

Private tape: 068_03 Bob Scobey's Frisco Band, Darnell Howard etc. This tape comprises commercial recordings by Bob Scobey's Frisco Band plus the four titles detailed above. All the above recordings, including (a) – (c), which are not on the SFTJF/Stanford tape, are in the collection of Sam Linschooten.

Clancy Hayes and Lee Wiley (Clancy Hayes, g; Lee Wiley, vocal; Frank Chace, cl; Bud Wilson, valve tb; Bill Priestley, g.)
Recorded at Bill Priestley's Home, Park Forest, IL 30 August 1959
(a) Somebody Loves Me
(b) A Cottage For Sale
(c) Indiana.
(d) Old Folks At Home

Private tape: from the collection of Hal Smith. Clancy Hayes sings with Lee Wiley on all tracks.

Clancy Hayes (piano; unknown percussion.)
Probably recorded at Clancy's Home, San Francisco CA c.1959
(a) Washboard Blues
(b) It Happened In Sun Valley
(c) Deep Elm Blues
(d) Jolene

Private tape: from the collection of Sam Linschooten.

Clancy Hayes, Jimmy McPartland, Ralph Sutton, Marty Grosz (Clancy Hayes, p; Jimmy McPartland**, cnt; Ralph Sutton^, p; Marty Grosz*, bj.)
Recorded at Bill Priestley's Home, Park Forest, IL August 1959
(a) Whispering*　　　2.01
(b) Make Me A Pallet On The Floor　　　2.57
(c) Deep Elm Blues　　　2.38
(d) Blues My Naughty Sweetie Gives To Me** ^　　　2.48
(e) Jelly Roll Medley: Winin' Boy / Michigan　　　5.53
　　Water Blues / Don't You Leave Me Here
(f) In New Orleans　　　2.01

Private tape: from the collection of Sam Linschooten. Track (a): Clancy Hayes vocal, Marty Grosz, banjo. Tracks (b), (c) and (f), Clancy Hayes piano and vocal. Track (d) Hayes, Sutton, McPartland. Track (e) Hayes and McPartland duet.

Clancy Hayes with Tut Soper's Band (Tut Soper, p; Jack Howe, Bill Priestley, Clancy Hayes, Ed Tilden, Spencer Clark, Jim Lanigan)

Recording location unknown, 29 May 1960

(a) Willie The Weeper 7.22

Private tape: held by Louisiana Digital Library. The website gives only the musicians' names.

Clancy Hayes and Don Ewell (Clancy Hayes, d; Don Ewell, p.)

Recorded at Doc Pruitt's Home, St. Louis. 1960

(a) St. Louis Blues	4.21
(b) A Good Man Is Hard To Find	3.36
(c) Tonight At The Jazz Band Ball	2.46
(d) Tonight At The Jazz Band Ball	3.27
(e) Tonight At The Jazz Band Ball	3.01
(f) My Home Is In A Southern Town	3.05

Private tape: from the collection of Sam Linschooten.

Clancy Hayes, Art Hodes, Lee Wiley (Clancy Hayes, Art Hodes, p; Lee Wiley* duet.)

Recorded in Chicago IL 1960

(a) Lazy River	3.42
(b) Dream A Little Dream Of Me	4.07
(c) Rain	2.51
(d) Sleepy Time Gal	3.05
(e) Wrap Your Troubles In Dreams	3.05
(f) Baby Won't You Please Come Home	3.13
(g) Lonesome Road*	3.57

Private tape: from the collection of Sam Linschooten.

Clancy Hayes, Russ Whitman, Charlie Weeks (Clancy Hayes, p; Russ Whitman, bass sax; Charlie Weeks, d.)

Recorded at the Whitman home, Chicago IL February 1961

(a) I've Been A Fool About Love	3.57
(b) Melancholy	3.08
(c) Baby Won't You Please Come Home	3.09
(d) Medley: Baby You Please Come Home, Tea For Two, Darktown Strutters' Ball, The One I Love Belongs To Somebody Else	3.51
(e) Witch Watch	3.32
(f) Blues My Naughty Sweetie Gives To Me	3.52
(g) Basin Street Blues	4.43

Private tape: from the collection of Sam Linschooten.

World's Greatest Jazz Band (Yank Lawson co-leader, t; Lou McGarity, tb; Peanuts Hucko, cl; Lou Stein, p; Clancy Hayes, bj; Bob Haggart co-leader, b; Morey Feld, d. *Clancy Hayes, bj; unknown, g.)
Recorded Aspen CO, 1964
(a) St. James Infirmary　　　　　　　　　　　　6.14
(b) Michigan Water Blues　　　　　　　　　　　3.39
Private tape: from the collection of Sam Linschooten.

Clancy Hayes (Clancy Hayes, bj; Unknown, g.)
Recording location and date unknown
(a) Original Dixieland One Step　　　　　　　　2.34
Private tape: from the collection of Sam Linschooten.

Clancy Hayes — Intermission performances Earthquake McGoon's (Clancy Hayes, banjo; *with the Bay City Jazz Band.)
Recorded at Earthquake McGoon's San Francisco CA 1965
(a) Long Gone　　　　　　　　　　　　　　　　2.21　　032_18
(b) Ace In The Hole　　　　　　　　　　　　　　1.27
(c) Medley: Do You Know What It Means To　　5.24
　　Miss New Orleans, Angry, Sister Kate
(d) Ugly Child　　　　　　　　　　　　　　　　0.48
(e) Peoria　　　　　　　　　　　　　　　　　　1.38
(f) Bill Bailey　　　　　　　　　　　　　　　　　2.23
(g) Medley: Pretty Baby / If I Could Be With　　3.31
　　You / Jada, Mother To Me
(h) Silver Dollar　　　　　　　　　　　　　　　2.28
(i) Paddlin' Madeline Home　　　　　　　　　　0.55
(j) Jealous　　　　　　　　　　　　　　　　　　1.37
(k) Witch Watch　　　　　　　　　　　　　　　2.14
(l) When The Midnight Choo Choo…..　　　　　2.23
(m) She's A Good Gal　　　　　　　　　　　　　3.52
(n) Keepin' Out Of Mischief Now*　　　　　　　4.29
(o) Rose Of Washington Square　　　　　　　　2.11
(p) Keepin' Out Of Mischief Now*　　　　　　　3.25

Private tape: 032_18 At Earthquake McGoon's 1965. This tape is not publicly available. However the eleven tracks from Lone Gone (a) to Witch Watch (k) are available on the SFTJF Stanford website under 'Great Revival, Video and Audio 10 McGoon's Intermission and Feature Acts'. The Bay City Jazz Band personnel are not known.

Clancy Hayes — Intermission performances Earthquake McGoon's (Clancy Hayes, bj.)
　　　　　　　　　Recorded at Earthquake McGoon's San Francisco CA July 1966
(a) Something's Always Happening On The River　　2.45
(b) Medley: Paddlin' Madeline Home / Baby Face　　3.21
　　/ Yes Sir, That's My Baby / Five Foot Two
(c) Lazy River　　3.16
(d) She's A Good Gal　　3.22
(e) Huggin' And A Chalkin'　　2.34
(f) Coney Island Washboard*　　4.36
Private tape: recorded by Bill Bacin. *With Turk Murphy's Jazz Band.

Clancy Hayes (banjo).
　　　　　　　　　Recorded at the home of Fred Moldenhauer, Denver CO 1968
(a) The Duke Was Wont To Say　　3.12　　068_18
(b) She's Just Perfect For Me　　3.05
Private tape: 068_18 Clancy Hayes, Denver. The tape includes three other songs recorded during the visit - Sweet Sue / Rose Of Washington Square / Hassan, The One Man Caravan; these are on the Satchell of Song CD.

Clancy Hayes at Monterey (Clancy Hayes, banjo; *Pops Foster, bass; **Phil Howe Festival Band.)
　　　　　　　　　Recorded at the Dixieland Monterey Festival, Monterey CA 10 May 1968
(a) Sweet Georgia Brown　　2.11
(b) Michigan Water Blues　　2.14
(c) Blues My Naughty Sweetie Gives To Me　　2.18
(d) Do You Know What It Means To Miss New Orleans　　2.32
(e) Sailing Down The Chesapeake Bay*　　2.48
(f) Rose Of Washington Square*　　4.03
(g) Parsons Kansas Blues**　　4.59
Private tape: recorded by Bill Bacin. The recording includes an introduction by Phil Elwood. Clancy Hayes is joined on Parsons Kansas Blues by the Phil Howe Festival Band — Phil Howe, leader, cl; Bob Neighbor, t; Mike Starr, tbn; Art Nortier, p; Ted Shafer, bj; Pops Foster, b; Thad Vandon, d.

Clancy Hayes with Turk Murphy's Jazz Band (Likely personnel: Turk Murphy, tb; Leon Oakley, cnt; Jack Crook, cl, sop. sax; Bill Carroll or Mike Walbridge, tu; Smokey Stover, d. *Clancy Hayes solo with banjo.)
　　　　　　　　　Recorded at Earthquake McGoon's, San Francisco CA 1969
(a) Ace In The Hole　　4.11
(b) Willie The Weeper　　3.38
(c) Tishomingo Blues　　3.13
(d) Paddlin' Madeline Home*　　0.59

(e) Coney Island Washboard   3.41
(f) Auntie Skinner's Chicken Dinner   3.35
(g) Your Always Messin' 'Round My Gal*   2.39

Private tape: from the collection of Sam Linschooten. Clancy Hayes was never part of the Turk Murphy Jazz Band so it is possible this tape is a collection of the end of set performances when the Turk Murphy jazz band would join Clancy Hayes on stage. This is very evident on tracks (b) and(e) where musicians come in one by one. However, on Tishomingo Blues the band opens the tune and on (g) the whole band comes in after an opening solo chorus. The likely personnel are based on the regular band members in this period.

The World's Greatest Jazz Band (Yank Lawson, tp; Peanuts Hucko, clt; Lou McGarity, tbn; Lou Stein, p; Clancy Hayes, bj; Jack Lesberg, b; Morey Feld, d.)
Recorded Denver Colorado 1969
(a) St. Louis Blues*   8.36
(b) Keepin' Out Of Mischief Now
(c) Lazy River
(d) St. James Infirmary

Private tape: These tracks are from a YouTube posting by Davey Tough who confirms there are a total of 13 tracks on the reel to reel tape including these four vocals. * Only St. Louis Blues has been posted to date.

Clancy Hayes (piano)
Recording location possibly Clancy Hayes' home, date unknown.
(a) Oh By Jingo!   2.32
(b) Jada   1.06
(c) Chilli Bean   1.09
(d) Ten To One It's Tennessee   3.27
(e) My Home Is In A Southern Town   2.01
(f) Stavin' Chain   5.36
(g) Unknown piano instrumental   1.25
(h) Ten To One It's Tennessee   3.11

Private tape: from the collection of Sam Linschooten. A home recording entertaining family and friends.

Clancy Hayes — Intermission performance at Earthquake McGoon's (Clancy Hayes, banjo.)
Recorded at Earthquake McGoon's, San Francisco CA 2 January 1970.
(a) At The Angels' Ragtime Ball   2.28   085_35

Private tape: 085_35 Turk Murphy's Jazz Band at Earthquake McGoon's, 2 January 1970.
This is Clancy Hayes' last known recording.

Radio Recordings

Bob Beale — Herb Taylor Fairmont Hotel Orchestra (personnel unknown; Clarence Hayes, vocal; *Marjorie Beattie, vocal; Jay Livesy, vocal track b only.)

Broadcasts from Fairmont Hotel, San Francisco CA 1934

(a) Sweetie Pie	2.56	
(b) Dames*	3.05	
(c) You're A Builder Upper	2.36	
(d) How's About Tomorrow Night*	3.04	
(e) Moonglow*	4.34	
(f) It's All Forgotten Now	4.23	
(g) My Whole Day Is Spoiled*	-	
(h) Memphis Blues	-	
(i) Pardon My Southern Accent	-	
(j) My Hat's On The Side Of My Head	-	

These titles are NBC radio broadcasts from the Fairmont Hotel, San Francisco between August and early October 1934. The recordings are from Titan Recording Studio discs. Tracks(a) –(f) are available as YouTube postings by 'princecastle'; the remaining tracks have yet to be posted.

Tune Termites Broadcast (Clancy Hayes, drums; Glen Hurlburt, piano.)

The Tune Termites Radio programmes, c.1938

(a) Let's Dream This One Out	2.44	068_22
(b) What Good's The Moon	2.37	
(c) I Give You My Word	1.54	
(d) I Hear A Rhapsody	3.51	
(e) I'm Waiting For Ships	1.52	

Private tape: 068_22 Clancy Hayes, Christmas 1971. These recordings are on a tape made by Clancy Hayes and sent to friends and family.

Swinging on the Golden Gate Broadcast (NBC Studio Orchestra; Clancy Hayes, musical director, v; *with the Mad Hatters vocal group.)

NBC Broadcast December 1945

(a) My Dearest Darling	2.28	068_22
(b) Martha	2.29	
(c) It's Never Too Late To Pray*	3.01	
(d) Lucky To Be Me	3.37	

Private tape: 068_22 Clancy Hayes, Christmas 1971.

Mother's Cakes and Cookies Broadcast (Clancy Hayes, unknown piano; *with Orchestra.)

Broadcast 1945

(a) If I Didn't Care	1.52	109_04
(b) I've Been A Fool About Love*	3.01	
(c) I Had A Wonderful Time In Columbus	0.47	
(d) I Love You Truly	1.43	
(e) I'm So Right Tonight (cut off)	2.19	

Private tape: 109_04 Reel L 1950s. The tape name is confusing and probably relates to the home recordings on the same tape — these are elsewhere. These recordings are from the 1945 radio broadcast and include Clancy Hayes voicing three characters.

Clancy Hayes — Band Recording for a Radio Pilot (Al Zohn, t; Bill Bardin, tb; Ellis Horne, cl; Squire Girsback, b, sous; Clancy Hayes, d.)

Recording location unknown, c. 1946

(a) Tempo Train	1.41
(b) Wolverine Blues	3.10
(c) Tomorrow	2.08

Private tape: Tempo Train, from the collection of Hal Smith. These three vocals are part of a fourteen-minute pilot programme based on a musical train ride on the 'Rhythm City Line'. Maple Leaf Rag and Ostrich Walk are also played - all the music is in the same 'rolling train' tempo. Between the songs Clancy Hayes and an unknown male deliver entertaining patter — in rhyme — and jokes. There are no commercial shows using this format, so it appears the pilot wasn't taken up.

Clancy Hayes with Unknown Orchestras

Recording dates and locations unknown

(a) True	3.43	103_01
(b) My Romance	3.59	103_15
(c) Theresa	2.01	103_17
(d) South	2.01	103_19
(e) If I Love Again	3.56	109_07

Private tapes: 103_01(Clancy Hayes paper tapes) no. 1 of 23: 103_15 no. 15 of 23; 103_17 no. 17 of 23; 103_19 no. 19 of 23; 109_07 Reel T 1950's.

These recordings are from various programmes, all tracks feature Clancy Hayes singing with a full orchestra.

Clancy Hayes (Unknown, p; Unknown, g.)
Recording location and date unknown
(a) The Hermit Song   2.14
(b) At The Angels' Ragtime Ball   2.18
Private tape: untitled from the collection of Sam Linschooten. No information is available on the origin of these two recordings, both are clearly part of radio broadcasts.

NBC: Jack Webb Show, 1946. (Phil Bovero Orchestra; *Clancy Hayes conducting the Studio Orchestra.)
(a) Indiana   2.11
(b) My Baby Just Cares For Me*   2.17
Source: The programmes are available from the Old Time Radio website.

Candy Matson Show - Yukon 28209 (Clancy Hayes, guitar.)
Recorded San Francisco CA, 1946
(a) Unknown Cowboy Song   0.40
Clancy Hayes acted in this 30 minute detective show playing 'Jess', a shady bartender. He also delivered this brief unknown song.

Standard Oil Schools' Broadcasts 1950 (Orchestra conducted by Carmen Dragon, *duet with Laura Murphy.)
Recorded in San Francisco, 1950

(a) Dixie	1.11	#11 Civil War
(b) Ta Ra Ra Boom De Ay	1.06	#12 Alaska
(c) Kentucky Babe	1.59	#12 Alaska
(d) At Pierrot's Door	1.11	#14 Western Hemisphere
(e) Star of Me	1.35	#18 Music of Time
(f) Waiting For The Robert E. Lee	1.38	#19 Music Map of America
(g) Chicago	0.56	#20 Chicago
(h) Lullaby Of Broadway	1.12	#21 New York
(i) Just One Way To Say I Love You	1.02	#21 New York
(j) Wunderbar	0.49	#21 New York
(k) Some Enchanted Evening	1.05	#21 New York
(l) Yodel Blues	1.13	#21 New York
(m) Baby It's Cold Outside*	1.26	#22 Hollywood
(n) That's For Me*	1.59	#22 Hollywood
(o) Laura	2.43	#22 Hollywood
(p) San Francisco	0.41	#23 San Francisco
(q) Down Among The Sheltering Palms	0.59	#23 San Francisco

Source: from the 1950 Standard Oil Schools' Broadcasts; individual show numbers and names are detailed above. Clancy Hayes performed as Jack of All Tunes - narrator and vocalist; Jack Cahill partnered him as Matt the Mapmaker. The programmes are available from the Old Time Radio website.

TV Educational Film : The Semantics of Popular Song (Clancy Hayes, bj.)
KQED series for Educational TV and Radio Centre: Language In Action program 10 - The Semantics of the Popular Song, 1958.

(a) Dream House   0.43
(b) My Ideal   0.27
(c) My Heart Stood Still / You Were Meant For Me   0.39
(d) Broken Promises   0.49
(e) The Curse Of An Aching Heart   0.27
(f) Paper Doll   0.26
(g) St James Infirmary   1.22
(h) A Good Man Is Hard To Find   0.39
(i) Bill Bailey   0.45
(j) Nobody Knows You When You're Down And Out   0.58
(k) Parsons Kansas Blues   1.06

Source: The film was kindly made available by Indiana University Library — Moving Image Archive and is posted on YouTube, Clancy Hayes Jazz channel. The programme is presented by Professor S.I. Hayakawa, semanticist and later US Senator for California (1977-83). Clancy Hayes performs as musical illustrator showing the unrealistic expectations of life and love in popular songs (a-f) contrasted with the realism of blues and jazz music (g-j). He closes the film with his own Parsons Kansas Blues which falls somewhere between the two genres.

Radio Interviews

Interview - with Bill Dyer (Bill Dyer interviews Clancy Hayes.)
Broadcast by KRE Berkeley CA 1954 and 1965
Private tape: **068_09** Clancy Hayes Interview 1954. The tape also includes an interview from 1965; running times are 31 mins and 49 mins. respectively.

Requiem for Paul Lingle (Phil Elwood interviews Betty Lingle, Turk Murphy, Clancy Hayes.)
Broadcast by KFPA San Francisco, December 1962
Private tape: **066_23** Requiem for Paul Lingle.

Interview with Felix Grant (Felix Grant interviews Clancy Hayes.)
Broadcast from WMAL-AM Washington, 1967
Private tape: from the collection of Sam Linschooten. The Felix Grant Jazz Archive is held at the University of the District of Columbia.

Discography: Song Title Index

Symbols
2.19 Blues (see also Mamie's Blues) 372, 373, 376, 398, 406

A

A Cottage For Sale 409
A Good Man Is Hard To Find 373, 376, 388, 395, 399, 410, 417
A Huggin' And A Chalkin' (see Huggin' And A Chalkin')
Absinthe Frappe 383
Ace In The Hole 372, 374, 376, 377, 389, 391, 395, 400, 401, 402, 403, 404, 411, 412
After You've Gone 387, 397
Ain't She Sweet 379, 387, 397
Alabama Jubilee 391, 403
Alabamy Bound 374
Alcoholic Blues 345, 373, 374, 397
Alexander's Ragtime Band 372, 384, 403
Alice Blue Gown 382
All Shook Up 384
Angry 377, 397, 411
At Pierrot's Door 416
At The Angels' Ragtime Ball 376, 405, 406, 414, 416
At The Devil's Ball 376, 377
Auntie Skinner's Chicken Dinner 374, 389, 405, 408, 413

B

Baby Face 387, 390, 412
Baby It's Cold Outside 416

Baby Won't You Please Come Home 385, 397, 406, 410
Ballin' The Jack 374, 378, 385, 393
Basin Street Blues 388, 390, 410
Battle Hymn Of The Republic 377
Beale Street Blues 377, 388, 391, 402
Beale Street Mama 376, 398, 399, 400, 403
Beat Me Daddy Eight To The Bar 385
Between 18th and 19th On Chestnut Street 382
Big Butter And Egg Man 377
Bill Bailey 374, 377, 398, 400, 401, 402, 411, 417
Birth Of The Blues 372
Blueberry Hill 384
Blues My Naughty Sweetie Gives To Me 377, 385, 389, 396, 398, 402, 409, 410, 412
Boy From New Orleans 388
Broken Promises 349, 374, 397, 417
Buddy Bolden Blues 405
Bury Me On Basin Street 388

C

Cakewalkin' Babies 382, 388, 396, 397, 405, 406, 408
Calico Sal 382
Careless Love 338, 377, 385, 395, 398, 399
Carolina In The Morning 382
C.C. Rider 384, 397
Charleston 378
Chesapeake Bay (see Sailing Down The Chesapeake Bay)

418

Chicago 376, 400, 401, 402, 416
Chilli Bean 413
China Boy 402
Chinatown My Chinatown 402
Clancy's Last Rag 372 (instrumental)
Clancy's Piano Rag 372 (instrumental)
Coney Island Washboard 376, 390, 395, 396, 400, 401, 402, 412, 413
Coquette 404, 405, 406, 407
Curse Of An Aching Heart 378, 417

D

Dallas Blues 408
Dames 414
Dancing Fool 387
Dancing In The Moonlight 401
Darktown Strutters' Ball 395, 397, 408, 410
Deep Elm Blues 403, 409
Ding Dong Daddy From Dumas 396
Dixie 416
Doctor Jazz 373, 374, 378, 387, 397
Don't Count Your Kisses 384
Don't Forget 127th Street 388
Don't You Leave Me Here 408, 409
Down And Out 403, 408
Down At The Husking Bee 403
Down By The Riverside 376, 384, 400, 405, 407
Down In Jungle Town 377
Down The Road A Piece 385
Do You Know What It Means To Miss New Orleans 377, 391, 399, 400, 401, 411, 412
Dream A Little Dream Of Me 410
Dream House 417

E

Easy Street 385
Everything Is Peaches Down In Georgia 377, 400, 407

F

Fickle Finger Of Fate 388
Five Foot Two 379, 381, 387, 390, 412
Flamin' Mamie 403
Floatin' Down To Cotton Town 384, 391, 401
Frankie And Johnny 373, 374

G

George Washington Abraham Lincoln Ulysses S. Robert E. Lee 372, 373
Getting Ready For Eddie 409
Gettin' My Boots 373, 379
Glad To Be Me 384, 409
Go Vote Nixon - Lodge 386

H

Hassan 372, 402, 409, 412
High Society 402
Hindustan 376, 377, 398
Home Again Blues 404
Honeysuckle Rose 386
Hot Time In The Old Town Tonight 396
How Come You Do Me Like You Do 400, 407
How's About Tomorrow Night 414
Huggin' And A Chalkin' 372, 373, 377, 385, 387, 391, 401, 402, 404, 412

I

I Ain't Gonna Give Nobody None Of My Jelly Roll 373, 377, 390, 398
I Ain't Got Nobody 388
I Ain't Working No More 404, 408
I Can't Get Started 382, 402
I Can't Give You Anything But Love 380
I Can't Remember To Forget 372

419

If He Comes In 403
If I Could Be With You 390, 411
If I Didn't Care 415
If I Love Again 415
I Give You My Word 414
I Had A Wonderful Time In
    Columbus 415
I Haven't Got A Ring 404
I Hear A Rhapsody 414
I Just Want To Live 372
I'll Introduce You To Those Southern
    Gals 408
I Love You Truly 415
I'm Comin' Virginia 388
I'm So Right Tonight 415
I'm Sorry I Made You Cry 381
I'm Waiting For Ships 414
In New Orleans 378, 381, 393, 409
Indiana 378, 409, 416
It Happened In Sun Valley 382, 409
I Thought I Heard Buddy Bolden Say
    409
It's All Forgotten Now 414
It Seems Like A Month Of Sundays
    Since I Saw You Saturday Night 372
It Seems To Be Spring 409
It's Never Too Late To Pray 414
I've Been A Fool About Love 410, 415
I've Been Floating Down That Old
    Green River 383
I've Been Working On The Railroad
    383, 408
I Want To Go Back To Michigan 378,
    402

J

Jada 378, 390, 397, 411, 413
Jealous 411
Jolene 409
Just A Cousin Of Mine 403
Just One Way To Say I Love You 416

K

Keeping Out Of Mischief Now 387,
    411, 413
Kentucky Babe 416

L

Laura 416
Lazy River 378, 385, 410, 412, 413
Let Me Call You Sweetheart 383
Let The Rest Of The World Go By
    383
Let's Dance The Ragtime Darlin' 382
Let's Dream This One Out 414
Lights Out Blues 378
Limehouse Blues 386, 402
Linda 382
Lonesome Road 347, 393, 410
Long Gone 377, 400, 403, 406, 411
Louisville Lou 403
Lovey Came Back 379
Lucky To Be Me 414
Lullaby Of Broadway 416
Lulu's Back In Town 382, 407

M

Mack The Knife 380
Make Me A Pallet On The Floor 409
Mama's Gone Goodbye 390
Mamie's Blues 373
Martha 414
Mecca Flat Blues 399
Melancholy 376, 392, 395, 398, 400,
    410
Memphis Blues 376, 377, 398, 399,
    402, 414
Michigan Water Blues 378, 387, 388,
    390, 409, 411, 412
Miss Annabelle Lee 382
Mississippi Mud 384
Mobile 372, 377

Moonglow 414
Mother To Me 390, 411
Mr. Joe (instrumental) 409
My Baby Just Cares For Me 416
My Bucket's Got A Hole In It 382, 399
My Dearest Darling 414
My Extraordinary Girl 373, 382
My Gal Sal 379
My Hat's On The Side Of My Head 414
My Heart Stood Still 417
My Home Is In A Southern Town 409, 410, 413
My Honey's Lovin' Arms 380
My Ideal 417
My Little Bimbo 373, 374, 388, 390, 391
My Romance 415
My Whole Day Is Spoiled 414

N

Nobody But You 373
Nobody Knows You When You're Down And Out 374, 385, 398, 417
Nobody's Sweetheart 388
Nothing's Gonna Stop Me Now 409
Now Is The Hour 373

O

Oceana Roll 372, 387, 403
Of All The Wrongs You've Done To Me 376, 377, 398, 409
Oh By Jingo! 372, 373, 374, 388, 396, 398, 413
Oh You Beautiful Doll 390
Old Folks At Home 409
Once and For Always 407
Original Dixieland One Step 385, 411
Otto's New Auto 372, 404, 405, 406

P

Paddlin' Madeline Home 387, 390, 411, 412
Paper Doll 417
Pardon My Southern Accent 414
Parsons Kansas Blues 377, 393, 400, 401, 402, 405, 406, 407, 412, 417
Peoria 374, 377, 390, 398, 400, 401, 402, 411
Poor Butterfly 393
Pretty Baby 390, 411
Put On Your Old Grey Bonnet 383, 391

R

Rain 410
River Stay 'Way From My Door 385, 402
Rockin' Chair 407
Roll Jordan Roll 373, 374, 396, 397
Rose Of Washington Square 372, 387, 388 - 390, 411, 412
Round And Round 287, 384
Royal Garden Blues 387, 395, 401

S

Sailing Down The Chesapeake Bay 374, 376, 391, 403, 412
Saloon 387
See See Rider (see C.C.Rider)
Sensation 403
Seven Or Eleven 403
Shake That Thing 399, 400, 404
She's A Good Gal (But 1000 Miles From Home) 405, 407, 411, 412
She's Just Perfect For Me 388, 391, 412
Shine On Harvest Moon 383
Sidewalk Blues 407
Silver Dollar 338, 374, 377, 390, 398, 401, 411

Singing The Blues 384
Sister Kate 375, 411
Sleepy Time Gal 410
Sob Sister Sadie 403
Somebody Loves Me 409
Somebody Stole My Gal 379
Somebody's Wrong 407
Someday Sweetheart 377, 400, 406
Some Enchanted Evening 416
Some Of These Days 397
Something's Always Happening On The River 279, 385, 412
South 375, 376, 396, 398, 401, 402, 415
Star of Me 416
Stardust 407
Stars Fell On Alabama 378
Stavin' Chain 403, 407, 413
St. James Infirmary 373, 374, 378, 395, 397, 401, 406, 407, 411, 413, 417
St. Louis Blues 374, 400, 410, 413
Strawberry Time 384
Street Of Regret 373
Struttin' With Some Barbecue 382
Stumbling 379
Sweet Georgia Brown 373, 377, 385, 393, 401, 412
Sweetie Pie 414
Sweet Sue 372
Swingin' Doors 376, 378, 399
Swinging on the Golden Gate 415

T

Ta Ra Ra Boom De Ay 416
Tea For Two 410
Tempo Train 415
Ten To One It's Tennessee 372, 378, 404, 405, 406, 407, 413
That's For Me 372, 416
The Curse Of An Aching Heart 417
The Duke Was Wont To Say 412
The Fat Girl 403, 404

The Five Piece Band 382
The Hermit Song 416
The One I Love Belongs To Somebody Else 410
The Storybook Ball 372
The Tattooed Lady 403
The Varsity Drag 378
The Whiffenpoof Song 383
Then I'll Be Happy 380
Theresa 415
There's A Long Long Trail 383
Three Little Words 407
Tin Roof Blues 388, 390, 393
Tishomingo Blues 390, 412
Tomorrow (I'll Be In My Dixie Home Again) 390, 415
Tonight At The Jazz Band Ball 410
Too Much Mustard 384
Travelin' Shoes 372, 378, 403
Trouble In Mind 379
True 415

U

Ugly Child 411
Unknown Blues 407
Unknown Cowboy Song 416

W

Wabash Cannonball 382
Waitin' For The Evening Mail 387, 392
Waiting For The Robert E. Lee 374, 382, 396, 397, 399, 416
Washboard Blues 385, 391, 409
Way Down Yonder In New Orleans 393
Weary Blues 397
Weddin' Day 404
Wedding Bells Are Breaking Up That Old Gang Of Mine 383
We'll Build A Bungalow 383

What A Life When Nobody Loves You 403
What Good's The Moon 414
When He's All Dolled Up 403
When The Midnight Choo Choo Leaves For Alabam 378, 411
When The One You Love Is Gone 378, 409
When The Saints Go Marching In 374, 397, 398, 402, 406
When You And I Were Young Maggie 386
Where Flamingos Fly 407
While You Are Far Away 384
Whispering 409
Why 409
Willie The Weeper 372, 385, 387, 390, 391, 395, 405, 407, 410, 412
Winin' Boy 409
Wise Guy 388
Witch Watch 409, 410, 411, 412
Wolverine Blues 372, 387, 392, 398, 406, 415
Wrap Your Troubles In Dreams 410
Wunderbar 416

Y

Yellow Dog Blues 384, 391
Yes Sir! That's My Baby 387, 390, 412
Yodel Blues 416
You Gotta See Your Mama 396
You Must Have Been A Beautiful Baby 382
You Tell Me Your Dream, I'll Tell You Mine 383
You Took Advantage Of Me 387, 407
You Were Meant For Me 417
Your Always Hanging 'Round My Man 404
Your Always Messin' 'Round My Gal 413
You're A Builder Upper 414

Z

Zizzy-Zizzy Zum Zum Zum 372

Index

Symbols

2.19 Blues 84
6200 North Kenmore xii, 143
7701 Biscayne Blvd. Miami 150

A

Abrahamson, Henry 72, 73
Abrams, Steve 404
Ace In The Hole xiv, 80, 84, 118, 128, 150, 163, 195, 239, 259, 262, 263, 336, 349
Ace records 94
A Cottage For Sale 296
Adinolfi, Dominic xxii, 55, 65, 256, 354, 364-6
Adinolfi, Sofia xxiv
African American Symphony 61
After You've Gone 223
A Good Man Is Hard To Find 90, 138
A Huggin' And A Chalkin' (See Huggin' And A Chalkin)
Ain't She Sweet 223
Albers Bros. ix, 31, 33, 307
Alcoholic Blues 345
Alexander's Jazz Band xi, xxv, 94, 96, 97, 98, 101, 102, 104, 106, 107, 119, 248
Alguire, Danny xvii, 243
Alioto, Joseph (Mayor) 212, 333, 334
All Dolled Up 295
All Shook Up 287
All Star Band 399
Alone Together 56
Ambassador Hotel, Los Angeles x, 37, 39, 40, 309

American Federation of Musicians xv, 185, 365
Arlt, Helen 163, 322
Armstrong, Louis 61, 70, 72, 115, 142, 147, 188, 200, 240, 285, 314, 337, 344
Arthur Fielder's Orchestra 149
Ashcraft, Squirrel 29, 271, 338
Aspen Jazz Party 170, 174, 222, 326
At Pierrot's Door 60
At The Angels' Ragtime Ball 93, 195, 244, 293
At The Devil's Ball 123
Auntie Skinner's Chicken Dinner xi, 88, 195, 244, 293
Aunt Jemima radio show ix, 27, 28
Austin, Claire 400
Austin, Gene 295
Avakian, George 107, 111
Avery, Ray 97

B

Baby It's Cold Outside 60
Bacin, Bill xiii, 188, 190, 191, 198, 219, 220, 221, 239, 337, 339, 369, 412
Back O' Town Blues 61
Badger Room 148
Baker, Clint xv, xxiv, xxxvii, 348, 368
Bales, Burt x, xxix, 56, 72, 77, 82, 83, 93, 98, 99, 101, 104, 113, 115, 119, 123, 128, 212, 223, 230, 238, 250, 348, 349, 370, 376, 395, 397-400, 404-8
Ball, Kenny xii, 156, 157, 346
Bannister, Anne xix
Bannister, Trevor xix, xx, xxiii
Bardin, Bill xxii, 77, 82, 83, 93, 230, 235, 250, 345, 348, 372, 395, 405, 415

Barnes, Mae 150
Barnhart, Jeff xvii
Bartha, Andy xii, 149, 150, 154, 184, 185, 237, 319, 347, 387
Bartlett, Tom 298
Basie, Count 68, 72
Bay City Boys 93, 147, 219
Bayside Jazz Society xi, xxv, xxvii, 103, 399
Beale, Bob x, 23, 38, 40, 102, 258, 370, 414
Beale Street Mama xi, 102, 105
Bean, Floyd xii, 137, 146, 339
Beattie, Marjorie x, 40, 41, 414
Beban, Walter 24, 25, 33, 34
Bechet, Sidney 100, 152
Beebe, Jim 115, 116, 136, 139, 140, 142, 146, 339, 345, 361, 384, 386, 403
Beeson, Tom 133, 362, 382, 383, 401
Beneke, Tex 185
Bennett, Russ 77, 82, 90, 227, 247, 373
Berg, George 385
Berghoffer, Chuck 390
Bigard, Barney 61, 188, 338
Big Bear x, xiii, 70, 71, 72, 251, 252
Big Bear Stomp 72
Bilk, Acker xvii
Bix Beiderbecke Jazz Festival xvii
Black And Blue 24
Black And White Rag x, 79
Black, Dave x, 24, 68, 69, 123, 133, 136, 139, 146, 362, 382 - 384, 401 - 403
Blackhawk 119
Blesh, Rudi 79, 82, 315
Blue Angel Jazz Club xii, xiii, 167, 192, 193, 194, 296, 348, 390, 391, 392
Blue Note 128, 129, 133, 134, 331, 401
Blues Alley xii, xiv, 185, 187, 251, 257, 293, 393
Blues Alley Cats 185, 293, 393
Blues My Naughty Sweetie Gives To Me 94, 95, 114, 191, 196
Blues Over Bodega 89

Bob Scobey's Frisco Band xi, xiv, xxxv, 110, 111, 115, 117 - 119, 130, 131, 133, 140, 141, 167, 251, 280, 281, 336, 362, 371, 376-8, 384, 398-403, 409
Bok, Fré 371, 404
Bonette, Charlene xxiv
Boogie Woogie on St. Louis Blues 61
Boswell Sisters ix, 30
Boulevard Room 146
Bourbon Street, Madison WI xii, 139, 142, 402
Bourbon Street, Chicago IL 144, 156, 157, 235
Bovero, Phil x, 54, 56, 58, 59, 416
Bow Legged Bill 280
Breakaway 24
Bridges, Harry 83
Broken Promises xxii, 267, 269, 277, 349
Brownbilt Footlights 31
Brown Palace Hotel 174
Brown, Pud 291, 384, 386,
Brubeck, Dave 119
Brunies, George 163, 325, 328
Buck, Jack xi, xiv, xxv, xxvi, xxxiv, 90, 98, 99, 101, 104, 106, 107, 110, 114, 115, 119, 127, 131, 133, 138, 280, 281, 360, 362, 373, 376, 376-84, 398-401
Bud McDonald and the Ranch boys 119
Burke, Raymond 195, 391
Burton, Tommy 241
Butterfield, Billy 149, 178, 179, 182, 185, 222, 337, 390, 391
Butzen, Jerry 331, 378

C
Cabin In The Cotton 34
Caen, Herb 201
Cafe Continental xii, 141
Cahill, Jack 60, 417
California Legislature Rules Committee 212, 334

425

California State Assembly xiii, 214
Campbell and Burr 349
Candy Matson Show 62
Caney, KA 1, 41
Cantor, Eddie 55
Capitol City 293
Care Free Carnival 51
Careless Love 338
Carey, Mutt 79
Carmichael, Hoagy 90, 212, 259, 264, 265, 274
Carolina Moon 49
Carroll, Julia xix, xxii, xxiii, 55, 65, 256, 354, 364-6
Carroll, Bill 389, 413
Carter, William (Bill) 235, 345, 348, 369, 376
Carter, Bob 385
Cary, Dick xxi, 188, 192, 390, 392
Castle Jazz Band 105
Castle Records xi
Cathcart, Dick 382
Catlett, Sidney 'Big Sid' 61, 152, 338
Cattolica, Vince 378
Chace, Frank 409
Charleston 11, 69, 134, 296, 350
Chee Chee Bonga 278
Cherie 25
Chicago vii, xii, xx, xxi, xxiv, 60, 100, 118, 128, 129, 130, 133, 134, 138-144, 146, 147, 148, 150, 152, 153, 154, 156, 157, 163, 166, 170, 184, 212, 225, 229, 318, 320, 323-6, 331, 338, 339, 346, 351
Chicago (song title) xi, 60, 108, 112, 113, 117, 243, 285, 302
Chicago Conservatory of Music 147
Chicago Tribune 118, 128, 129, 130, 139, 141, 144, 147, 148, 157, 225, 346
Christian, Charlie 200
Clancy Hayes Day xiii, xix, xxxviii, 208, 209, 211, 212, 213, 216, 299, 333, 334
Clancy's Corner 123, 127
Clancy's Dixieland Band 55

Clancy Hayes' Dixieland Band 291, 346, 385, 386
Clancy's Last Rag 282
Clancy's Piano Rag 282
Clark, Spencer 410
Clef Records 87, 374
Climbing The Stairs Into Your Heart 24
Cline, Hazel 7
Close Fit Blues 25
Club Hangover xi, 100
Club Zanzibar 90
Clute, Pete xxii, xxxv, xxxvii, xxxviii, 70, 75, 121-3, 152, 153, 171, 197, 227, 234, 235, 251, 296, 302, 327, 349, 351, 369, 389
Coffee Dan's 347
Coller, Derek xx, 146, 346, 347, 351
Colonna, Jerry 51
Condon, Eddie 200
Coney Island Washboard xi, 106, 117
Coon-Sanders Original Nighthawks xv, 11, 296, 366
Coon, Jack 192, 390
Coonley, Bill 82
Cooper, Johnny 171, 388
Copenhagen 72
Coquette 93
Corb, Morty 392
Cousineau, Cuz 378
Coy, Nathan xxii, 370
Crawford, Ham 12
Crawford, Paul 158, 163, 195, 322, 391
Cressey, Paul 69
Crook, Jack 90, 373, 389, 413
Crosby, Bing 59, 72, 182, 212, 234, 237, 241, 242, 249, 264, 277, 302
Crosby, Bob 301
Crump, Charlie 283
Crump, Jesse 'Tiny' xxiv, xxvi, 119, 281, 378, 379, 400, 401
Cusack, Kim 171, 388
Cutshall, Robert 'Cutty' 174, 259, 388, 389, 390, 391

D

Dance in Place Congo 61
Dancing with Clancy 53, 54
Daniels, Lyle 338, 385
Daniels, Ray 338
Dapogny, Jim 171, 388
Dapper Dan 29
Dark Dancers Of The Mardi Gras 61
Darnell Howard's Frisco Footwarmers 99
Dart, Bill xxvii, xxx, 71, 72, 73, 76, 77, 96, 101, 248, 249, 250, 373, 374, 395-9
Dawn Club x, xiv, xxvi, 54, 74-7, 81, 84, 212, 251, 253, 270, 302, 344, 345, 350, 373 - 375
Dawson, Clair 9
Deebach, Bob 387
Deep Elm Blues 296, 350
De Franco, Buddy 119
Delmark Records xii, 171, 172, 251, 292, 347, 388
Del Rio Woods, ix, 34
Denver Symphony Debutantes' Ball, 174
Dime Jigs 68, 69
Dinah 259
Dixie 60, 94, 170, 294, 316
Dixiecrats 146, 346
Dixieland Monterey xii, 189, 244, 412
Dixieland Rhythm Kings 168
Dobell, Doug 171
Docs of Dixieland xii, 168, 169, 347, 387
Donohue, Sam 385
Don't Forget 127th Street 292
Dorsey, Tommy 53, 174
Dotson, Ned 93, 250, 405
Dotson, Vince 93, 230, 250, 372, 404-6
Dovidio, Pete 133, 138, 362, 382, 383, 401
Down Home label xi, 84, 87, 88, 131, 243, 278, 279, 288, 290, 318, 349, 350, 374, 375, 378, 381

Down In Jungle Town 239, 243
Do You Know What It Means To Miss New Orleans 61, 114, 115, 163, 191, 336
Dragon, Carmen 60, 416
Dream House 138
Duda, Casey 146, 151
Dukes of Dixieland 168, 188
Duvivier, George 384
Dyer, Bill 7, 8, 129, 258, 259, 344, 345, 347, 417

E

Earthquake McGoon's xii, xxviii, xxxv, 152, 153, 156, 166, 173, 185, 190, 195, 198, 212, 216, 222, 230, 235, 242, 244, 262, 282, 292, 298, 300, 329, 330, 349 - 351, 389, 390, 411-4
East Of The Sun 56
Easy Street 291, 338
Edwards, Gordon 'Gramps' 72, 90, 98, 99, 104, 250, 373
Egloff, Z xvii
El Dorado Jazz Band xvii
Elitch Gardens 174, 176, 219, 260, 389-91
Elks ix, 9, 10, 129
Ellington, Duke xx, 68, 72
Elwood, Phil 190, 272, 348, 369, 412, 417
Embassy Room 139, 140-2, 144-6
Emmanuel Church of God in Christ 84
Erickson, 'Sugar' Willie 188
Ertegun, Nesuhi 99, 105
Erwin, Pee Wee 192, 390
Estes, Gene 192, 390
Ethiopian Baptist Church xiii, 231, 340
Eureka Brass Band 158
Evans, Doc 152
Evans, Elaine 144

427

Evans, Slim 93, 278, 405
Every Now And Then 24
Everything Is Peaches Down In
   Georgia 118, 123, 128
Ewell, Don 152, 195, 319, 391, 400, 410

F

Fack's II 140, 142
Feld, Morey 176, 178, 182, 338, 389-91,
   411, 413
Fickle Finger Of Fate 292
Finn, Mickey 188
Firehouse Five Plus Two xvii, 113, 188,
   243
Fischbacher, Myrtle 201, 202
Flamin' Mamie 235
Florida Musicians Union 150
Fontana, Carl 178, 179, 182
Foster, George 'Pops" xii, 188, 190,
   191, 244, 347, 412, 413
Francis, Panama 392
Fresk, Livio 385
Freeman, Bud 176, 178, 182, 222, 338,
   389, 390, 391
Frisco Jazz Band xi, xiv, 90, 91, 264,
   271, 272, 373
Frost, Robin 192, 390

G

Galbraith, Barry 385
Gallagher's Steak House 146
Gardner, Jack 146
Garland, Ed 79, 188
Garlinghouse, Esther and Bob xiii,
   204, 329, 330
Geary Theater 79, 83
George Probert Jazz Band 119
George Washington, Abraham
   Lincoln Ulysses S. Robert E. Lee
   xiv, 90, 269, 271, 272
Georgia Swing 248

Gettin' My Boots 90, 269, 271
Gibson, Dick xii, 170, 173, 174, 175,
   176, 177, 200, 222, 259, 280, 326
Gifford, Walt 149, 387
Gill, John xxii, xxiii, 241, 251, 255, 298
Gillham, Arthur 'Red' 90, 212, 373
Gin Bottle Seven 168, 387
Ginell, Cary 76, 345, 351
Girretto, Augie 212
Girsback, Eino William 'Squire' xxv,
   73, 93, 99-101, 107, 110, 196, 212, 230,
   237, 250, 292, 372, 376, 389, 390,
   399, 404-6, 415
Glad To Be Me 271, 269, 271, 287
Glaser, Joe 142, 147, 150, 346
Gleason, Ralph J. 115
Glow, Bernie 385
Goggin, Jim 227, 350, 351, 370
Goldstein, Sammy 382
Gonsoulin, Bertha 79
Goodman, Benny 53, 68, 129, 174
Good Time Jazz (GTJ) xviii, 84, 97,
   98, 113-5, 117-9, 121, 128, 131, 171, 223,
   243, 248, 262, 285, 286, 291, 297,
   301, 302, 318, 345, 346, 348, 371-3,
   376-8, 386
Go To Bed 25
Grant, Felix 185, 260, 346, 417
Granz, Norman 87, 130, 277, 290
Grauenhorst, Mart 29, 31
Great Jazz Revival xix, xxiii, xxxv,
   xxxvii, 52, 68, 72, 75, 302, 303, 348,
   351, 369, 370
Greats of Jazz xxxvii, 176, 183, 219,
   248, 260, 292, 389, 390, 391
Green, Freddie 249
Green, Lew 171, 388
Green, Urban 385
Greene, Bus 72
Grosz, Marty xvii, 410
Grover, John 60
Guarnieri, Johnny 385
Guerin, John 192, 390

Guidi Tri-Arts 114
Gurtler, Jack xiii, 174, 176, 199, 327
Gwaltney, Tommy xii, 185, 187, 280, 293, 393

H

Haggart, Bob xxxvii, 173, 174, 177, 178, 182, 222, 388-91, 411
Haggerty, Frank 389
Hall's Dancing School 12
Halstead. Jack 387
Hambone Kelly's xi, xxv, xxvii, 75, 84, 86, 88, 94, 97, 98, 107, 245, 251, 373-5, 395-8
Ham Crawford's Louisiana Blue Devils 12
Hanck, Bill 171, 385
Hanks, Clara 69
Harlem Globetrotters 144, 156
Harmony Aces 8, 9, 11, 258, 310
Hassan 230, 269, 281, 282
Havens, Bob 188, 392
Hayakawa, Samuel Ichiye xii, 137, 138, 238, 302, 400, 417
Hayes, Ann xiii, 64, 198, 201, 222, 232-4, 342, 365
Hayes, Ashton ix, xiii, xiv, xxi, 2, 5, 12, 18-20, 49, 210, 223, 300, 353
Hayes, Bill x, xiii, xxii, 64, 65, 210, 325
Hayes, Clancy (passim)
Hayes, Clara May (Mrs) ix, 1, 3, 17, 18
Hayes, Dean 2
Hayes, Della (aka Martha) 2, 18
Hayes, Glenn 2, 5
Hayes, Phil 2, 5
Hayes, Wallace ix, xiv, xv, 2, 5, 12, 18, 19, 353, 362
Hayes, William Kelly ix, 1, 3, 17
Hector The Garbage Collector 51
Heider, Wally 192

Helm, Bob xiv, xix, xxii, xxv, xxvii, xxx, 72 - 75, 77, 82, 208, 212, 248, 298, 345, 361, 373 - 376, 395 -399
Henley, Clarrie 369
Higuera, Fred xiii, xxv, xxvi, xxix, xxxii, 107, 110, 127, 131, 210, 212, 247, 250, 281, 348, 376, 378-82, 398-401
Hindustan 239
Hines, Earl 61, 100, 338, 344
Hirsch, Bob 149, 387
Hixson, Richard 385
Hodes, Art xix, 145, 146, 156, 315, 338, 385, 410
Holzfeind, Frank 128, 129
Honeysuckle Rose 291
Hoskins, Bob xxv, xxvii, 399
Hotaling, Bob 119
Hot Jazz Society of San Francisco x, 74, 83, 85, 200, 314, 315, 398
Howard, Darnell xxxiii, 24, 98-101, 107, 248, 376, 399, 409
How Come You Do Me Like You Do 345
Howe, Phil xiii, 188, 191, 210, 347, 410, 412, 413
How's About Tomorrow Night 40
Hubble, Eddie 149, 222
Hucko, Peanuts xiii, 174, 192, 207, 229, 326, 338, 389 - 391, 411, 413
Huggin' And A Chalkin, xi, xiv, xxxv, 59, 90, 92, 94, 118, 128, 212, 260, 264, 266, 267, 269, 274
Hulme, George xii, 135, 136, 137, 282, 345, 369, 374, 409
Hunt, Pee Wee 149, 150, 185
Hurlburt, Glen 53, 55, 372, 414
Hutchinson, Ralph 384

I

I Actually Am In Love 25
I Ain't Gonna Give Nobody None Of My Jellyroll 90
I Can't Remember To Forget 53

I Don't Want Your Kisses 25
If I Didn't Care 62
I Lift Up My Finger and I Say Tweet Tweet 25
I'll Close My Eyes 63
I Love You Truly 63
I'm Coming Virginia 172
I'm Gonna Charleston Back To Charleston 11, 296
I'm Hatin' This Waiting Around 49
I'm Only Making Believe 24
Indiana xxiv, 243, 254
Indiana University Library – Moving Image Archive xxiv, 254, 345, 417
In New Orleans 160, 269, 273, 278, 347, 349, 350
Iola, KA xxiv, xxxv, 1-3, 5, 7-9, 10-12, 203, 265, 329, 330, 344
I See By The Papers 28
Is I In Love, Is I? 34
It Seems To Be Spring 29
It's Never Too Late To Pray 58
I've Been A Fool About Love 269, 270
Ives, Burl 150, 225
I Want To Go Back To Michigan 123
I Want To Live 53

J

Jack of All Tunes xxxv, 60, 337, 417
Jack Webb Comedy Show 58, 416
Jack's Record Cellar 346
Jahnigen, Ray 90, 373
James, Harry 75
Janis, Johnny 150
Jazz in the Troc xii, xiv, 176, 183, 184, 259, 261, 262, 389 - 391
Jazz Ltd 150, 152, 153, 185, 346
Jazz Man (Records) x, xi, 75-79, 80, 90, 96, 98, 99, 101-3, 105, 113, 117, 345, 351
Jazz Record Mart 171
Jelly Roll Jazz Band 212, 244

Jenny Lind Hall xi, 106, 109, 118, 131, 279, 302, 378 - 381, 399, 400
Jerome Hotel, Aspen CO 174
Jingle-Town Gazette 49, 51
Johnson, Gus 222
Johnson, Lyle 61
Johnson, Willie 'Bunk' x, 79, 82, 83, 195, 249, 262, 314, 315, 339, 347, 372, 373, 387, 388, 391
Jolly Time Review 25, 29, 31
Jones, Casey 60
Jones, Isham 174
Jones, Spike 141, 144
Jones, Wayne 171, 172, 388
Jordan, Steve xiv, 185, 239, 257, 348, 351, 393
Juba Dance, 61
J Walter Thompson Co xi, 132

K

Kansas City Kitty 128
Kansas City Stomp 93, 248
Karloff, Boris 55
Kassel, Art 94
Kenkel's xii, 148, 149
Kenny Ball's Jazzmen 156
Kentucky Babe 60
Kettering Rotary Club 168
KGO, San Francisco xxxv, 23, 24, 34, 53, 57, 59, 75, 84, 106, 227, 306
Kinch, Don xxvii, 248, 399
King, Daphne June xxii, xxxviii, 94, 234, 235, 267, 269, 277-80, 349
King, Saunders, 51, 83
King Oliver's Creole Jazz Band 100, 147
King Tut Tooters 7, 8, 258
Klein, Emmanuel 'Mannie' 382
Klinginsmith, J.T. 8
Klinginsmith's Radio Trio, 8
Knox, Bertell 393
Koenig, Lester 113, 237

Koester, Bob 171
Kyser, Kay 55, 264

L

Ladowski, Mari xi, 123, 124, 225, 316, 317
Lamare, Joseph 'Nappy' 192
Lammi, Dick xiii, xiv, xxvii, xxxi, 72, 77, 110, 127, 245, 361, 373-7, 395-8, 400
Lamond, Don 385
Langham, Thomas 'Spats' iii, xvii, xxiii, 240, 241
Lanigan, Jim 410
Larkin, Duncan xxiv
Laura 60, 202
Lawson, Yank xxxvii, 173, 174, 178, 182, 191, 222, 292, 338, 339, 388-91, 411, 413
Lazy River 61, 212
Leach, Billie and Don xiii, 205, 330
Leatherwood, Ray 392
Leeman, Cliff 174, 176
LeGoullon, Martine 'Lom' 114
Lehman, Herm 387
Lehman, Joe 387
Leigh, Carol 298
Lenhart, J 401
Leonard, Will 1, 128, 129, 139, 150, 225, 346
Lesberg, Jack 413
Let's Dance The Ragtime Darlin' 287
Let's Have a Party 34
Levee Loiterers 390, 391
Levinsky, Walter 385
Lewis, Buddy 227
Lewis, Don 188
Lewis, Ernie x, 74 377
Limehouse Blues 291
Lincoln, Abe 192, 271, 329, 330, 382, 390-2
Linderman, Roy 72

Lingle, Paul 72, 73, 100, 239, 348, 417
Linschooten, Sam ix, xxiii, xxxvii, xxxix, xl, 17, 21, 25, 178, 189, 215, 267, 286, 287, 297, 369, 371, 395, 400, 406, 407, 409-11, 413, 414, 416, 417
Lionel Woods Brothers 158
Lippman, Sid 37
Little, Big Tiny 177
Livesy, Jay 414
Lofner, Carol 68, 72
Lonesome Road 347
Los Angeles Ostrich Farm ix, 31
Louisiana Bo-Bo 24
Lovey Came Back 123
Lowe, Mundell 385
Lucky To Be Me 58
Lu Watters' Yerba Buena Jazz Band x, xxvii, 54, 75-7, 94, 144, 243, 258, 371, 373-5, 384, 395-8

Mac, Mc

McConnell, Jack 384
McCormick, Hal xxvi, 281, 376, 378, 379, 380, 381, 400, 401
McCree, Johnson 'Fat Cat' 347, 391
McDonald, Janette 29
McDonald, Bud 119
McFall, Paul 387
McGarity, Lou 174, 178, 179, 182, 385, 389 - 391, 411, 413
McIntyre, Hal 77
McKenna, Dave 388
McKinley, Ellis 9
McPartland, Jimmy 410
MacPherson, Ann 198
MacPherson, William 'Bill' 192, 198, 222, 225

M

Mad Hatters 415
Mama's Gone Goodbye 167, 192

431

Mamie's Blues 90
Manassas Jazz Festival 195
Manne, Shelly 291, 386
Manone, Joseph 'Wingy' 12, 188
Maple Leaf Rag x, 78, 415
Marin County Community Festivals 90
Marshall, Charlie ix, 24, 25
Martha 58
Matlock, Julian 'Matty' 168, 192, 337, 382, 390, 392
Matteson, Rich 136, 139, 361, 384, 403
Maxted, Billy 149
Maxwell, James 385
Mayl, Gene 149, 250, 398, 399
Meakin, Jack 51
Melancholy vii, 108, 117, 193, 197, 243, 285, 301, 302
Melody Club xi, 96, 97, 398
Menuhin, Yehudi 55
Mercer, Johnny 90, 167, 264
Mercury (Label) xi, 87, 89, 91, 243, 373, 374
Merrick, Mahlon ix, 31, 32, 313
Michael Garrick Travelling Jazz Faculty xx
Michigan Water Blues 191, 287
Midnight In Moscow xii, 158
Mielke, Bob xix, 115, 208, 212, 244, 376
Miles, Lizzie 137, 138, 232-4, 318, 342, 400, 406
Miller, Glenn 68, 172
Miller, George 398
Miller, Julia 172
Minger, Jack 378
Mingie, Hank x, 42, 44, 310
Moldenhauer, Fred 229, 282, 412
Mole, Irving Milfred 'Miff' 152
Monterey Dixieland Jazz Festival 188, 189, 244, 261, 412
Moon, Bucklin 101
Moonrise On The Lowlands 49

Mordecai, Harry 75, 247, 251, 395, 396
Morgan, Freddie 144
Morning Chanticleer 38
Morton, Ferdinand 'Jelly Roll' 70, 79, 102, 238, 240, 248, 259, 295
Mortonia Seven xvii
Moten, Bennie 112
Mother's Cakes and Cookies 57, 62, 270, 415
Mount Whitney-Death Valley Highway 51
Mrs Robinson 182
Murphy, Melvin 'Turk' x, xiv, xxiii, xxv, xxvi, xxvii, xxxv, 70-3, 75-7, 84, 94-7, 100, 113, 115, 117, 121, 122, 152, 153, 188, 190, 195, 196, 197, 212, 216, 223, 226, 230, 235, 241-4, 248, 252, 253, 261, 285, 292, 303, 338, 346, 348, 351, 372, 389, 390, 395, 396, 399, 412-4
Musicians' Union Local Six 83
Music Map of America 60, 416
Muskrat Ramble 185
My Baby Just Cares For Me 59
My Bucket's Got A Hole In It 287
My Dearest Darling 58
My Dream Man 28
My Extraordinary Girl 91
My Gal Sal 123
My Ideal 138
My Little Bimbo xi, 84, 87, 172, 242, 293

N

Napier, Bill xi, xxvi, 119, 122, 127, 131, 146, 212, 248, 281, 291, 376-81, 382, 386, 400, 401

Nappy Trottier's Dixieland All Star Band xii, 148, 151
NBC Studio Orchestra 415
Neighbor, Bob xiii, 188, 208, 347,

389, 413
Nelson, Clara 69,
Nelson, Richard 146
Newman, Bill 101
New Orleans xii, xv, xvii, xviii, xx, xxiv, xxxv, xxxviii, 60, 61, 68, 79, 82, 83, 97, 102, 128, 135, 138, 144, 145, 157, 159-63, 166, 167, 188, 195, 247, 295, 298, 303, 351
New Orleans Jazz Club xii, xv, 135, 138, 145, 157, 159-63, 188, 239, 246, 320-3, 347, 351, 365
New Orleans Jazz Club of California 188
New Orleans Jazz Museum xxiv, 162, 320
New Orleans Trad Jazz Camp xvii
Newton, Don 200
Nicholas, Albert 102, 376, 399
Nichols, Keith 241
Nichols, Marshall 376
Nieuwkerk, Pim van xxiv, 371
Nine Greats of Jazz 260, 389
Noakes, Don 72, 373-5, 396-8
Noble, Ray 174
Nobody But You 91
Nobody Knows You When You're Down And Out 138
Now Is The Hour 91

O

Oakie, Jackie 29
Oakland Taxi Dance Hall 69
Oakley, Leon 298, 413
O'Casey, Pat 'Hots' 93, 98, 100, 101, 405-7
Oceana Roll 227, 242
Oceania Lounge xii, 184, 186
Of All The Wrongs You've Done To Me 114, 115
Offenberg, Charles Raymond 112
O'Flaherty, Terence 127

Oh By Jingo! xii, 84, 170, 171, 172, 173, 239, 240, 292, 293
Ole Buttermilk Sky 212
Oliver, Joseph 'King' 70, 73, 77, 79, 100, 102, 147, 240
Olsen, George 75
On The Midway 269, 279
Orchard Twin Dixieland Lane 148
Original Salty Dogs 129, 170, 171, 212, 243, 292, 388
Orth, Emile 115
Ory, Edward 'Kid' 79, 97, 100, 102
Ostrich Walk 94, 415
Otto's New Auto xiv, 93, 267, 269, 274, 275, 343
Oxo 51
Oxtot, Dick xiii, 97, 208

P

Pacific Vagabonds 25, 30, 31
Page, Stan 110
Palace Hotel ix, 23, 31, 32, 38, 40, 73, 174
Palace Hotel Vagabonds 31
Pancake Boy xxxv, 27, 42, 306
Parker, Patsy 75
Parry, Graham xxiv, xl
Parsons, KA xxiv, 5, 12, 280, 281
Parsons Kansas Blues 93, 129, 191, 195, 244, 267, 269, 280, 293, 336
Parsons Sun 2, 281,
Parsons Times 12
Pasadena Roof Orchestra xvii
Pasley, Frank 79
Pat Patton's Jazz Band 80
Patton, Pat xxvii, 90, 93, 223, 237, 247, 372, 373, 374, 396, 397, 398, 405-7
Paul, Les 91, 92, 258, 373, 408
Paul Crawford's Levee Stompers 158
Pearl Harbor 77, 149
Pearson, Mack 144

Peavey, Sister Lottie 84
Peck, Della (nee Hayes) ix, xxi, 3, 18
Peoria 114, 129, 293, 336
Perry, Van 195, 391
Persby, Archie x, 56
Petrillo, James 90, 91, 94
Pfeiffer, Bill 146, 151
Phil Bovero Orchestra 416
Phil Howe Festival All Stars 191
Philip, Jim xx
Philips, Dickie 146
Philips, John 393
Phillippe, Melissa iii, viii, xvii, xix, xxi, xxii, 299
Pistorius, Steve xxiv, xxxviii
Playboy 150, 157, 163, 166, 320, 346, 403
Plugged Nickel 170, 174
Pollack, Ben 174, 188
Pound, Clyde 133, 138, 362, 382, 383, 401
Powderpuff Review 34
Preview Lounge 134
Priestley, Bill 344, 350, 409, 410
Princecastle (YouTube) 344, 369, 370, 414
Probert, George xix, xxv, 106, 107, 110, 111, 114, 119, 188, 212, 237, 285, 376, 398-400
Purnell, Alton 188

Q

Quinn, Spencer 212

R

Radio Ramblings 31
Radlauer, Dave xxi, xxii, xxxviii, 70, 171, 197, 234, 235, 298, 345, 348, 349, 369, 370, 372
Ragged But Right 182
Ragtime Label xii, 101, 102, 105, 158, 345, 346, 380
Rancho Grande xi, 119, 120, 123

Ratsliff, Leon 378
Ray Charles Singers 112
Reagan, Ronald xiii, 56, 212, 215, 335
Reinhardt, Bill 152, 200
Retter, Jack 369
Reynolds, Fred 118, 130, 131, 142, 318
Rhodes, Robbie 298
Rhythm Vendors 33, 34
Rimington, Sammy xvii
Riverboard Shuffle xi, 108
Riverboat, The 176, 182, 195, 200
River Stay 'Way From My Door 287
Roosevelt Hotel 158, 320, 322
Rose, Wally xi, xiv, xix, xxv, 70, 71, 76, 77, 106, 107, 110, 114, 182, 188, 212, 244, 252, 260, 261, 285, 298, 359, 373-6, 378, 386, 388, 395-400
Rosenbaum, Dave 83
Rose Of Washington Square 182, 191, 248, 259, 260, 261, 338
Round And Round 287
Rush Street 134, 139, 144, 153, 156
Russell, Luis 102
Russell, Pee Wee xii, xiv, 187, 257, 388
Rusty Draper TV Show 106

S

Sailing Down The Chesapeake Bay 108, 111, 112, 117, 129, 191, 195, 243, 285, 293, 301, 302
Sailors with Saylors 49
Saloon 240
Salt City Six 168
San Diego Traditional Jazz Festival. xviii, 298
San Francisco, CA vii, ix, xv, xvii, xxiii, xxiv, xxxv, xxxvii, xxxviii, xl, 23, 32, 38, 40, 45, 53-5, 72, 74, 76, 79-84, 90, 94, 97, 100, 106, 111, 114-6, 118, 123, 128, 133, 134, 143, 148, 150, 152, 153, 156, 163, 167, 188, 198, 212, 222, 223, 225, 227, 231, 236, 241, 243,

251, 259, 261, 267, 277, 278, 280, 286, 298, 299, 303, 307, 309, 311, 314, 315, 317, 318, 327, 329, 330, 333, 334, 341, 344, 346, 347, 351, 364
San Francisco Chronicle x, 45, 115, 127, 311
San Francisco Examiner 188
San Francisco Jazz xxiii, xxxv, 52, 111, 157, 241, 277, 303, 371
San Francisco Jazz all stars xvii
San Francisco Museum of Modern Art 80
San Francisco Traditional Jazz Foundation (SFTJF) ii, xxiv, xxvi, xxxiv - xxxvii, 4, 6, 13-5, 17-22, 25-33, 35-41, 43-6, 48, 50, 52, 54, 56-58, 64, 66, 67, 71, 74, 76, 82, 83, 85, 86, 100, 101, 103, 104, 110, 111, 114, 121, 122, 124, 126, 127, 131, 132, 137, 151, 154, 159, 160, 161, 165, 175, 179 - 181, 187, 190, 199, 202-11, 213-15, 218-21, 228, 231-4, 245, 249-53, 257, 268, 275, 284, 285, 303, 344, 345, 347-51, 354-64, 369, 370, 372, 376, 394, 409, 412
San Francisco World's Fair 53
Santa Rosa xxi, 12, 49, 53, 59
Santa Rosa Memorial Park 223
Santa Rosa Republican 34
Santa Rosa Elk's Temple 49
Saunders, Al 328
Saunders King band 83
Schertzer, Hyman 385
Schlafman, Harry 387
Schneider, Elmer 382
Schroeder, Gene 384, 403
Schulz, Bob 170, 241, 298, 350
Scissors To Grind 28
Scobey, Bob ii, vii, ix-xii, xiv, xviii, xxiii, xxv, xxvi, xxxv, xxxvii, xxxviii, 71, 72, 76, 77, 84, 88, 94-102, 104-7, 110-19, 121-123, 127-31, 133, 134-42, 144-6, 148, 153, 156, 158, 167, 188, 193, 232, 238, 240, 243, 247-51, 253, 258, 262, 267, 271, 274, 278-81, 283-8, 291, 293, 297, 301-3, 317, 318, 335, 336, 338, 345, 346, 348-51, 355, 360-62, 371, 376-85, 394, 395, 397-404, 408, 409
Scott, Charles 7
Scott, Toni Lee 133, 135, 139, 140, 142, 146, 156, 271, 287, 384, 385, 401
Scott, Bud 240, 248
See See Rider 287
Selman, Frank iii, viii, xv, xviii, xxiii, xxxvii, xl, 38, 43, 56, 58, 85, 143, 151, 181, 257, 268, 297, 298, 364, 368, 369, 371
Severinsen, Carl 385
SFTJF *see* San Francisco Traditional Jazz Foundation
Shacter, James D. 176, 347, 351
Shafer, Ted 244
Shake That Thing 72
Shanley, Brian 135, 136, 139, 142, 146, 149, 339, 347, 361, 384, 386, 387, 403
Shavers, Charles 385
Shaw, Artie 53, 61, 68, 338
Shaw, Arvell 61, 338
Shaw, Sonia x, 56
Sheridan, Bob 57, 58, 62, 63, 230
Sherman, Don 150
She's A Good Gal (But 1000 Miles From Home) 94, 267, 269, 270,
She's Just Perfect For Me 230
Shirley, Charles 385
Short, Bob 248, 291, 376, 378-82, 384, 386, 400
Sievers, Red 68
Silver Dollar xiv, 118, 163, 176, 239, 248, 259, 262, 264, 320, 336, 338
Singleton, Zutty 195, 200, 391
Sinton Hotel, Cincinnati xi, 134, 135
Skinner, Doug xi, 133, 138, 362, 384, 401
Skjelbred, Ray xiii, xxiv, 208, 212, 213, 216, 217, 406
Smile 222
Smith, Billie 405, 406

Smith, Buddy 338, 385
Smith, Eddie 373
Smith, Hal iii, vii, xvii-xix, xxiii, xxv-xxxiii, xxxviii, 77, 89, 107, 166, 171, 184, 195, 216, 243, 247, 285, 291, 298, 302, 344, 348, 369, 370, 376, 395, 415
Smith, Kenneth 310
Smith, Stanley 269, 270
Smith, Stuff 315
Smith, Warren 374, 382
Smoot, Tom 146
Snow, Frank 378
Snyder, Denny 387
Snyder, Jim 388
Somebody Stole My Gal 123
Some Enchanted Evening 60
Some Of These Days xi, 102
Something's Always Happening On The River 279
Songer, Wayne 382
Song Of The Islands 24
Sonnanstine, Charlie xxvii, 298
Soper, Oro 'Tut' 140, 146, 410
Souchon, Edmond 'Doc' 157, 163, 239, 320, 321, 322
South 8, 108, 112, 117, 243, 285, 301, 302
South Frisco Jazz Band 349
South Market Street Jazz Band 188
Spanier, Francis 'Muggsy' 100, 147, 152
Sperling, Jack 192, 390, 392
Stacy, Jess xxi, 192, 223, 291, 386, 392
Standard Oil Schools' Broadcasts 416
Stanford Hospital 198, 212, 216
Stanford University Libraries ii, xxi, xxvi, xxxiv-xxxviii, xl, 4, 6, 13-15, 18 -20, 22, 26-33, 35-7, 39-41, 44-6, 48, 50, 52, 54, 57, 64, 66, 67, 69, 71, 74, 76, 82, 83, 86, 100, 101, 103, 104, 110, 111, 114, 121, 122, 124, 126, 127, 131, 132, 137, 154, 159, 160, 161, 165, 175, 179, 180, 183, 187, 190, 199, 202-11, 213, 214, 218-21, 228, 231-4, 245, 249, 250, 252, 253, 259, 275, 284, 285, 303, 329, 344, 345, 347-50, 354, 355-63, 369, 370, 394
Stanford University Pi Beta Phi 69
Stanislaus, Jimmie 212
Stanroy Music Centre 59
Starr Sisters 150
Stavin' Chain 295
Stavin' Change 294, 295
St. Cyr, Johnny 240, 247
Stegmyer, Bill 388
Stein, Lou 411, 413
Stephens, Phil 382
Stereoscopic Society xiii, 227, 228
Stiers, Rusty 68
Stinson Beach Surf Club 90
St. James Infirmary 138
St. Louis Blues xi, 61, 103, 294
Stoeltje, Rachael xxiv, 346
Stover, Robert 'Smokey' 328, 413
Street Of Regret 91
Strickler, Benny 77, 249, 262, 395
Stroup, Wilson 7
Struttin' With Some Barbecue 61
Stuart, Dave 76, 105
Stuhlmacher, Anna Marie 13
Sudmeier, Jack 378
Sudmeier, Will 378
Sundstrom, Bob 171
Sunnie's Rendezvous, Aspen, CO 174
Sunny 182
Sunset Café 147, 216, 244
Sutton, Ralph 142, 173, 174, 176, 178, 182, 222, 248, 288, 291, 338, 347, 351, 380 - 382, 386, 389 - 391, 401, 410
Sweet Georgia Brown xi, 191, 347
Sweetie Pie 40
Sweet's Ballroom 72, 73
Sweet Sue 230
Swingin' Doors 185, 269, 279
Swinging on the Golden Gate 57

T

Ta Ra Ra Boom De Ay 60
Taylor, Herb 23, 38, 258, 414
Taylor, Billy Jr 393
Teagarden, Jack 12, 61, 231, 319, 337, 344, 407, 408
Teagarden, Norma 212
Teddy Ludwig's Footwarmers 158
Tempo Train 94, 250, 292
Ten Cents A Dance 68, 140
Ten Cubes (Sugar Willie Erickson) 188
Ten Greats of Jazz 219, 248, 390, 391
Ten To One It's Tennessee xiv, 93, 269, 273, 274
The Buccaneers 33, 34
The Chanticleer, Madison WI 134
The Christmas Mouse 280
The Duke Was Wont To Say 230, 269, 282
The Five Piece Band 287
The Semantics of Popular Song xiv, 138, 254, 417
The Temperance Seven xvii
The Web of Love 24
The Yodel Blues 60
This Is Jazz 79, 82, 315
Thomas, Norman 201
Thomas, Porter 8, 9
Tilden, Ed 410
Tin Angel xi, xxviii, 123, 126, 127, 128, 225, 316, 317
Tin Roof Blues 163, 185
Tollinger, Ned 49
Tom King Detective Agency 72
Tomorrow (I'll Be In My Dixie Home Again) 40, 94, 196, 292
Tough, Davey 413
Towne Club, Madison WI 139, 142, 145
Travelin' Shoes 133, 237, 269, 278, 287
Treasure Island, San Francisco Bay 115
Triffon, Jim 387

Trilon label 96
Trip To Rio 293
Trocadero (Troc) xii, xiv, 173, 174, 176, 183, 184, 192, 260, 262, 291, 292, 338, 389-91
Trottier, Nappy xii, 146, 148, 151, 339, 386
Tumbling Tumbleweeds 49
Tune Termites 53, 167, 192, 277, 282, 372, 390, 391, 414
Turk Murphy Jazz Band xiv, xxiii, 113, 115, 121, 188, 195, 212, 223, 292, 361, 389, 390, 412, 413, 414
Tyler, George 192

U

University of Chicago 69
University of Pasadena Jazz Club 198
Up A Lazy River (see Lazy River)
Up Up And Away 182

V

Vandon, Thad 188, 261, 347, 389, 413
Van Eps, George 192
Van Ness, Clark 262
Vegaphone xii, xiv, 145, 251, 256
Victor's and Roxie's xi, 96, 99, 101, 104, 106, 113, 115, 119, 133, 399, 400

W

Waiting For The Evening Mail 12, 193
Waiting For The Robert E. Lee xi, 61, 89
Walbridge, Mike 298, 388, 413
Waldo, Terry 298
Waller, Thomas 'Fats' 195, 301
Walsh, Everett 79
Ward, Stan 115, 192, 390
Washboard Blues 176, 291, 338
Waterpik Co. 176
Watkins, Earl xiii, 206, 331, 377, 400

Watson, Clay 321
Watson, Ed xiii, 218, 219, 336
Watters, Lucius 'Lu' x, xviii, xxvi, xxvii, xxxv, xxxviii, 54, 68, 70-7, 82, 84, 88, 94-6, 98, 105, 113, 128, 144, 167, 190, 212, 216, 225, 240, 241, 243, 244, 247, 251, 253, 258, 262, 277, 285, 288, 293, 297, 302, 303, 314, 340, 345, 346, 348, 371, 373-5, 394, 395, 396-8, 408, 409
W.C. Handy's Orchestra 100
Webb, George 240
Weddin' Day xiv, 267, 269, 277
Weeks, Charlie 229, 411
Weems, Ted 75
We Just Couldn't Say Goodbye 34
Wells, Reverend Charles A 69
Westley, Ira 192, 390
Wetterau, Robin 298
Whaley, Wade 79
What A Life When Nobody Loves You 295
When He's All Dolled Up 295
When The One You Love Is Gone 136, 269, 278
When You And I Were Young Maggie 291
When Yuba Plays The Rhumba On The Tuba 34
Where Are You, Dream Girl? 25
Where Were You On The Night of June The 3rd 195, 244
Whiteman, Paul 53, 80, 296
Whitman, Russ xxiii, xxxviii, 228, 229, 270, 411
Whyatt, Bert xxi, 140, 146, 345, 346, 351
Wiggs, Johnny 195, 391
Wiggs-Burke Crescent City Stompers 391
Wilber, Bob 178, 182, 222, 391
Wilder, Joe 385
Wiley, Lee 243, 318, 409, 410

Willie The Weeper 195, 244, 291
Wilson, Russ 7, 79, 182, 190, 348
Winding, Kay 149
Winin' Boy 295
Wise Guy 150, 172
Witch Watch 136, 229, 267, 269, 281, 282
Wittwer, Johnny 395, 396, 406
Wolfe, John x, xiv, 49, 50, 52, 59, 60, 354
Wolverine Blues 93, 94, 117, 193, 223, 291
Wood, Jack xii, 184, 185, 186
World's Greatest Jazz Band xii, xxxvii, 173, 176, 177, 178, 182, 195, 222, 248, 411, 413
Wrightsman, Stan 192, 384, 390

Y

Yadon, George 94
Yankee, Pat 188, 212, 261
Yankee Clippers 292, 388
Yellow Dog Blues 287, 384, 391
Yerba Buena Jazz Band (YBJB) x, xiv, xxvi, xxvii, xxxv, 54, 73, 75 - 77, 82 - 84, 88, 90, 92 - 94, 96, 97, 113, 128, 144, 167, 238, 243, 249, 251, 253, 258, 262, 270, 277, 288, 290, 297, 298, 345, 371 - 375, 394 - 398
Yodel Blues 60
Young, Jim 198
You're A Builder Upper 40

Z

Zack, George xiii, 140, 146, 151, 203, 328
Zanzibar Club xi, 90, 91
Ziz-Zizzy-Zum-Zum 53
Zohn, Al 82, 405, 406, 415
Zohn, Joe 93, 404

www.ingramcontent.com/pod-product-compliance
Lightning Source LLC
Chambersburg PA
CBHW042042240426
43667CB00048B/2953